Ann Haley
7 mo 1854.

Engraved by P. Lightfoot,
from a Medallion done in Paris by David.

In loving fellowship,
farewel!
A Opie.
3d Mo 24th 1841

MEMORIALS

OF THE

LIFE OF AMELIA OPIE,

SELECTED AND ARRANGED

From her Letters, Diaries, and other Manuscripts,

BY

CECILIA LUCY BRIGHTWELL.

Second Edition.

NORWICH:
FLETCHER AND ALEXANDER;
LONDON: LONGMAN, BROWN, & Co.

MDCCCLIV.

PREFACE.

In the preparation of these Memoirs for publication, the principal part of the labour has been undertaken by my daughter; the pressure of other engagements having only permitted me to undertake the general direction and supervision of the whole.

As the Executor of Mrs. Opie, her papers and letters came into my hands; and it devolved on me to decide in what way to dispose of them. There had been, (I believe,) a general impression among her friends, that she would herself prepare an account of her Life; but although she seems to have made some efforts at commencing the task, and the subject was often affectionately recommended, and even urged upon her, she has left it a matter of regret to her friends, (and especially so to the compilers of these memoirs,) that no "Autobiography" was found among her papers. Nor did Mrs. Opie ever distinctly give any directions as to the publication of her MSS. or any Memoir of her Life; but we have, we think, strong presumptive evidence, that she anticipated, if not desired, that it should be done.

Not long before she died, she said, that her Executor would have no light task with her papers; and a few days before she breathed her last, when she could no longer hold a pen, she called her attendant to her, and dictated a most touching and affectionate farewell address, to me and my daughter, directing the delivery of various small articles as remembrances to a few most intimate friends, and requesting us to complete what she had left undone; adding, that she had confidence in our judgment, and believed that we should "do everything for the best."

It has been with an earnest desire to justify this trust, and to perfect, as far as in our power, that which she had, in fact commenced, but left incomplete, that these pages have been put to the press.

It will be seen, in the course of these Memoirs, that the materials from which they are compiled, are principally Papers, Letters, and Diaries, of Mrs. Opie's own writing; a few Letters preserved by her, and judged to be of general interest, and bearing upon her history, we have thought it well to give. It would have been no difficult task, to have greatly extended these Memoirs, had it been deemed expedient to make a free use of the Letters received by her, and of which a very large number were found among her papers; but we have not felt ourselves at liberty to adopt such a course, and we trust there will be found in this Volume few (may we say we hope *no*) violations of private and confidential communications.

My acquaintance with the subject of these Memoirs, commenced nearly forty years ago; and well do I remember the first impressions made on me by her frank and open manner, the charm of her fine and animated countenance, her artless cheerfulness and benevolence, and the extraordinary powers of her conversation. But it was not till the time of Dr. Alderson's last illness, that my acquaintance with Mrs. Opie ripened into confidential friendship. From that period to the time of her decease, I had the happiness to enjoy much of her society, and to hear her recollections of her earlier days, and her graphic descriptions of the scenes and characters, which had been subjects of interest to her during the course of her long life; and she subsequently often read me a large portion of the correspondence she continued to maintain.

Gifted with an extraordinary memory, a reverence for truth, extending even to the minutest details, a disposition to look at the best side of everything and everybody, and with almost dramatic power in the exhibition of character and manners; Mrs. Opie when she entered into any details of her former life, painted the whole scene with such truthfulness and power, as to make it live before her hearers, and fix it in their memory.

As an Author, her works have undergone the ordeal of public criticism, and some additional testimony is afforded by these Memoirs, to the favourable impression they made. It will be seen that Sir Walter Scott, Dr. Chalmers, Southey, and other men of note, alike agreed in paying their tribute of admiration to her power of touching the heart, and awakening the softer passions.

The great leading feature of Mrs. Opie's character was pure, christian benevolence; charity in its highest sense. None that knew her could fail to observe this. Unwearied in her efforts to relieve the distresses of others, and limited in her own means, she was almost ingenious in some of the methods she devised for doing so, and made it matter of duty to avail herself of her influence with her wealthier friends to induce them to assist her endeavours. Her patience in dealing with the incessant importunities of persons who applied for her aid, was almost *more* than exemplary: but she found a blessing in doing good; and, in her parting address, before alluded to, she has not failed to urge "the remembrance of the poor, so as to be blessed by them."

Of her religion, the latter part of this Memoir will best speak, and especially the short extracts from her private Journals. These, speaking from the depths of her own heart, shew how holily and humbly she walked before her God; how strictly she called herself to account day by day; and how firmly she relied on the atonement of the Lord Jesus Christ as her hope in life and support in death.

Mrs. Opie had no liking for religious controversy, and seemed to me always desirous of avoiding it. I believe she disliked dogmatic theology altogether. Her religion was the "shewing out of a good conversation her works, with meekness of wisdom."

She ever deemed her union with "the Friends" the happiest

event of her life; and she did honour to her profession of their principles, by shewing that they were not incompatible with good manners and refined taste. She met with some among them who have always appeared to me to come the nearest to the standard of christian perfection; *these* were her dearest friends on earth, and she is now, with them, numbered among the blessed dead who have died in the Lord, who have ceased from their labours, and whose works do follow them.

THOMAS BRIGHTWELL.

Norwich, May, 1854.

A Second Edition *of this work having been speedily called for, the Author has found but little opportunity for making additions to it, and the present is, therefore, excepting some trifling omissions, and the introduction of a few additional lines, simply a reprint of the former volume.*

C. L. BRIGHTWELL.

Norwich, July, 1854.

CONTENTS.

CHAPTER VI.

CHAPTER VII.

CHAPTER VIII.

CHAPTER IX.

CHAPTER X.

CHAPTER XI.

CHAPTER XII.

MEMORIALS

OF THE

LIFE OF AMELIA OPIE.

CHAPTER I.

BIRTH AND PARENTAGE; HER FATHER; HER MOTHER'S FAMILY; HER MOTHER; SONNET TO HER MOTHER'S MEMORY; EARLY REMINISCENCES; EARLY TERRORS AND THEIR CURE; THE BLACK MAN; CRAZY WOMEN; BEDLAM; VISITS TO THE INMATES; EARLY TRAINING; THE FEMALE SAILOR; ABRUPT CONCLUSION.

AMELIA OPIE, the only child of James Alderson, M.D., and of Amelia, his wife, was born the 12th of November, 1769, in the parish of St. George, Norwich; she was baptized by the Rev. Samuel Bourn, then the Presbyterian Minister of the Octagon chapel, in that city. Her father was one of a numerous family, the children of the Rev. Mr. Alderson, of Lowestoft, of whom some account is given in Gillingwater's History of that "ancient town." From this we gather that "Mr. Alderson was a very worthy, well-disposed man, of an exceeding affable and peaceable disposition, much esteemed by the whole circle of his acquaintance, and, as he lived much respected, so he died universally lamented." His death happened in 1760.

In a note the following account of his family is added: "Four sons and two daughters survive him; the sons are all distinguished for their industry and ability, and are eminent in their several professions; James, an eminent surgeon, at Norwich; John, a physician, at Hull; Thomas, a merchant, at Newcastle; and Robert, a barrister, at Norwich. Of the two daughters, Judith is married to Mr. Woodhouse, and Elizabeth unmarried."

This was written in 1790. Were the historian now to add a supplementary notice, with how much satisfaction would he record, that, in the third generation, this family numbered among its descendants, Amelia Opie and Sir E. H. Alderson; the former the child of the eldest brother, the latter the son of the youngest.

The tender attachment borne by Mrs. Opie to her father was perhaps her most prominent characteristic. They were companions and friends through life; and when, at length, in a good old age, he was taken from her, she wept with a sorrow which no time could obliterate, and for which there was no solace but in the hope of rejoining him in a better world. Deeply touching are the evidences of the love which prompted her pen in its most successful efforts, influenced her in all the steps she took throughout her career, and rendered her indefatigable in cheering and soothing him through the long years of his declining age. Best of all, she was enabled to direct his mind towards those great truths of the gospel, which she had learned to love, and in which she found her support, when the arm of her earthly friend was about to relax its hold, and leave her alone to pursue in solitude the remainder of her pilgrimage.

Probably the early loss of the wife and mother was one cause which drew more close the bond of union between the "Father and Daughter." It naturally followed that when, at the age of fifteen, she took the head of her father's table, and the management of his domestic arrangements, she should endeavour, as much as possible, to supply the place which had been left vacant, and that her young affections should cling more fondly around her remaining parent. There was also much in the father calculated to draw to him the love of his child. He was of fine person and attractive manners, and to these external advantages was joined something better and more enduring — a kind-hearted and generous sympathy for the sufferers whom his skill relieved, and a charity to the poor, which induced him freely to give them his valuable advice and assistance. His daughter says, "He prescribed for about four or five hundred persons at his house every week. The forms in our large hall in a morning were so full from half-past eight till eleven, that I could scarcely pass; and this he did till the end of the year 1820, or rather perhaps to the beginning of 1821, when, unable to go down-stairs, he received the people, at my earnest desire, in my little drawing-room, till he said he could receive no one again. Oh! it was the most bitter trial he or I ever experienced, when he was forced to give up this truly Christian duty; and I was obliged to tell the afflicted poor people that their kind physician was no longer well enough to open his house to receive them, and try to heal their diseases again. He wept, and so did I; and they were bitter tears, for I feared he would not long survive the loss of his usefulness." Those acts of kindness are not yet forgotten in his native city; an aged woman, being told the other day of the death of Mrs. Opie, recalled to mind the days of her father, "the doctor," and the time when he was "very good to the poor folks, that is, he gaw'n 'em his advice for nothing; and that was a true charity, lady."

Mrs. Opie's mother, Amelia, was the daughter of Joseph Briggs, of Cossambaza, up the Ganges, (eldest son of Dr. Henry Briggs, rector of Holt, Norfolk, and Grace, his wife,) and of Mary, daughter of Captain Worrell, of St. Helena. In an old pocket book, Mrs. Opie has entered the following memoranda concerning this branch of her maternal ancestors.

Account of my great, great, *great* grandfather, Augustine Briggs, M.P., for Norwich. (From the pedigree of the Briggs' in Blomefield's "History of Norfolk.") An ancient family of Salle, in Norfolk, who before the reign of Edward the First assumed the surname of De Ponte, or Pontibus, i.e. at Brigge or Brigges; as the ancient family of the Fountaines of the same place assumed theirs, of De Fonte or Fontibus, much about the same time, one we presume dwelling by the bridge or bridges, the other by the springs or fountains' heads. The eldest branch of both families continued in Salle till they united in one. William Atte Brigge, of Salle, called in some deeds W. de Fonte de Salle, was living at Salle in 1334. John Atte Brigge, his second son, was alive in 1385. Thomas Brigge, of Holt, the fourth brother, was alive in 1400; and, in 1392, went to the Holy Sepulchre of our Lord, an account of which pilgrimage written by himself is still extant, in a manuscript in Caius

College Library. Augustine Briggs, mayor, alderman, and member for Norwich in four Parliaments, was turned out of the Corporation by the *rebels,* and restored at the king's restoration. He joined the Earl of Newcastle's forces at the siege of Lynn, in 1643. There is a long sword in the family, with a label in Augustine Briggs' own hand writing tied to it. "This I wore at the siege of Linn, in the servis of the royal martyr, K. Charles ye First, A. Briggs." He lies buried in a vault in the church of St. Peter's Mancroft, built by himself, but he alone of the family lies there. It has been since appropriated by the Dean and Chapter to another family, as it was supposed no one was alive to claim it; but I, A. Opie, am the lineal descendant and representative of this excellent man, and the vault was my property. The following is a translation of part of the Latin inscription on his mural monument in St. Peter's church:—"He was indeed highly loyal to his king, and yet a studious preserver of the ancient privileges of his country; was also firm and resolute for upholding the Church of England, and assiduous and punctual in all the important trusts committed to him, whether in the august assembly of Parliament, his honourable commands in the militia, or his justiciary affairs on the bench: gaining the affections of the people by his hospitality and repeated acts of kindness, which he continued beyond his death, leaving the following charities by his will, as a more certain remembrance to posterity, than this perishing monument erected by his friends, which his posterity endeavours by this plate to continue to further ages." He died in 1684, aged 67. He lived in the Briggs' Lane, called after him, which lane is now (1839) widening, and is to be called D'Oyley Street, a proper tribute of respect to the public spirited individual who subscribed £1600 to further this improvement.*

Augustine Briggs was also a public benefactor to this, his native city, for he left "estates and monies to increase the

* For all that it is Briggs' Street still!—Ed.

revenue of the Boys' and Girls' Hospital, and for putting out two poor boys to trades every year, as can read and write, and have neither father nor mother to put them forth to such trades." My cousin, Henry Perronet Briggs, R.A.,* his male representative, has a very fine picture of him, a half-length, in his military dress, painted, he believes, by a pupil of Vandyke. I have a tolerably good three-quarter picture of him,†—Amelia Opie. I have also a portrait of his daughter-in-law, Hannah Hobart, heiress of Edmund Hobart, son of the Lord Chief Justice Hobart, afterwards ennobled, and wife of Dr. W. Briggs, M.D., of the University of Cambridge, a man of great science and learning, and an eminent physician.

* * * * * *

Of the mother of Mrs. Opie but few memorials remain. She was of a delicate constitution, and appears to have cherished the habits of retirement, so naturally preferred by an invalid. Her early death bereaved her daughter of a mother's care and guidance at the most critical period of woman's life; and we may perhaps trace some features of Mrs. Opie's character to this event. From the occasional glimpses we catch of the mother in her daughter's short record of her own early days, it is evident that she was possessed of firm purpose and high principle; a true-hearted woman, and somewhat of a disciplinarian. Her steady hand would have curbed the high spirit of her child, and softened those ebullitions of youthful glee, which made the young Amelia such an impetuous, mirthful creature: she would have

* Since deceased.

† This portrait is the first of those which she apostrophizes in her "Lays for the Dead," and begins—

"There hangs a Soldier in a distant age,
Call'd to his doom—my honour'd ancestor."

been more demure and decorous had her mother lived, but perhaps less charming and attractive. Speedily as the mother's influence was withdrawn, it left, notwithstanding, some indelible traces in the memory of her daughter, who frequently referred to her, even in her latter days, and usually with reference to some bad habit from which she had warned her, or some good one which she had inculcated. Mrs. Alderson died on the 31st of December, 1784, in the 39th year of her age.

A series of Letters referring to the death of Mr. Joseph Briggs and his wife, and the transfer of their little orphan daughter to England, still exist. They are principally written by Mr. William Briggs, the second son of Dr. Henry Briggs, who having died in 1748, (just about the time of his eldest son's decease in India,) the family affairs were committed to the care of his next surviving son. He writes thus:—

Several years ago my elder brother, Joseph Briggs, went over to Bengal as a writer in the Company's service; he married Miss Mary Worrell; he died in May, 1747, and his widow in the December following; leaving behind one child, Amelia. Captain James Irwin, out of friendship to my brother, took care of his little daughter after the death of her mamma. The latter end of May, 1749, the child arrived here in England, and is now in perfect health.

To this kind friend of the orphan, Captain Irwin, the grateful uncle writes:—

London, August 23rd, 1749.

Worthy sir, your letter of December 24th, 1748, and my very dear niece, Amelia Briggs, came safe to England the latter end of May last, praised be God! My honoured father dying in May 1748, yours to him came to me with one directed for myself, in both which you give very uncommon proofs of real friendship. Friendship in prosperity is common; but in adversity none are true friends but the pious.

Your great care of my niece has given very sensible pleasure to all her relations, and all unite with me to return you sincere and hearty thanks; at present we can only express our gratitude in words, but should you ever be pleased to give us an opportunity, I doubt not but you will find us ready to testify our thanks by useful deeds. I believe you will meet with a reward more substantial and durable from our gracious God.

My very great affection for my dear brother Joseph naturally leads me to love and care for the little orphan as if it was my own. She will never want whilst I have it in my power to assist her. She will be a burden to none of her relations; for, before she will have any occasion for it, she will be in possession of a very handsome annuity. At present she is with my mother in Norfolk, one hundred miles from London. She is a charming child, and the country agrees very well with her. The black girl, her nurse, is not reconciled to England; and, thinking she never shall be so, she is determined to return to Bengal by the Christmas ships. As my mother will give her entire liberty to be at her own disposal, I believe her design is to enter into service, as other free women do. If it be in your power, you are very much desired by all my niece's friends to prevent Savannah's being bought or sold as a negro.

May the God of all grace and consolation keep and bless you, dear sir, and all your family, with everything necessary to make your short passage easy and agreeable through time into a happy eternity, is the sincere wish and prayer of,

Dear Sir,

Your most obliged humble servant,

W. B.

Seven years after her mother's death, (1791,) she addressed to her memory the following sonnet.

ON VISITING CROMER FOR THE FIRST TIME SINCE THE DEATH OF MY MOTHER, WITH WHOM I USED FREQUENTLY TO VISIT IT.

Scenes of my childhood, where, to grief unknown,
And, led by Gaiety, I joy'd to rove,
'Ere in my breast Care fix'd her ebon throne,
And her pale rue, with Fancy's roses wove.
No more, alas! your wonted charms I view,
Ye speak of comforts I can know no more;
The faded tints of Memory ye renew,
And wake of fond regret the tearful power.
But would ye bid me still the beauties prize
That on your cliff-crowned shores in state abide,
Bid, aim'd in awful pomp, yon billows rise
And seek the realms where Night and Death reside;
Unusual empire bid them there assume,
And force departed goodness from the tomb!

Many years after, among her "Lays for the Dead," appeared some further lines dedicated to her mother, and, as they have several references to the recollections she retained of her, and are in themselves very sweet and full of earnest tenderness of regret, they are reprinted here:—

IN MEMORY OF MY MOTHER.

An orphan'd babe, from India's plain
She came, a faithful slave her guide!
Then, after years of patient pain,
That tender wife and mother *died.*
Where gothic windows dimly throw
O'er the long aisles a dubious day,
Within the time-worn vaults below
Her relics join their kindred clay—

And I, in long departed days,
Those dear though solemn precincts sought,
When evening shed her parting rays,
And twilight lengthening shadows brought—
There long I knelt beside the stone
Which veils thy clay, lamented shade!
While memory, years for ever gone,
And all the distant past pourtray'd!
I saw thy glance of tender love!
Thy cheek of suffering's sickly hue!
Thine eye, where gentle sweetness strove
To look the ease it rarely knew.
I heard thee speak in accents kind,
And promptly praise, or firmly chide;
Again admir'd that vigorous mind
Of power to charm, reprove, and guide.
Hark! clearer still thy voice I hear!
Again reproof, in accents mild,
Seems whispering in my conscious ear,
And pains, yet soothes, thy kneeling child!
Then, while my eyes I weeping raise,
Again thy shadowy form appears;
I see the smile of other days,
The frown that melted soon in tears!
Again I'm exiled from thy sight,
Alone my rebel will to mourn;
Again I feel the dear delight
When told I may to thee return!
But oh! too soon the vision fled,
With all of grief and joy it brought;
And as I slowly left the dead,
And gayer scenes, still musing sought,
Oh! how I mourn'd my heedless youth
Thy watchful care repaid so ill,
Yet joy'd to think some words of truth
Sunk in my soul, and teach me still;
Like lamps along life's fearful way
To me, at times, those truths have shone,
And oft, when snares around me lay,
That light has made the danger known.

Then, how thy grateful child has blest
Each wise reproof thy accents bore!
And now she longs, in worlds of rest,
To dwell with thee for evermore!

* * * * * * *

Mrs. Opie evidently designed, at one time, to write a record of the most interesting events of her life; she commenced the task, but abruptly broke off when she reached the age of early youth. This interesting fragment was clearly written at a late period of her life, it commences thus:—

"*Ce n'est que le premier pas qui coûte,*" says the proverb, and when I have once begun to put down my recollections of days that are gone, with a view to their meeting other eyes besides my own, the difficulty of the task will, I trust, gradually disappear.

But I should be afraid that my garrulities, as I may call them, would not be so interesting to others as I have thought they might be, had I not observed such a hunger and thirst in the world in general for anecdotes, whether biographical or otherwise, and had I not experienced, and seen others evince, such interest and amusement while reading of persons and things; and I am thus encouraged to record my recollections of those distinguished persons with whom I have had the privilege of associating, from my youth upwards, to the present day. Therefore, without further delay or apology, I mean to relate a few "passages" in my very early days, in order to make my readers acquainted with the preparation for my future life and occupations, which these days so evidently afforded.

One of my earliest recollections is of gazing on the bright blue sky as I lay in my little bed, before my hour of rising came, and listening with delighted attention to the ringing of a peal of bells. I had heard that heaven was beyond those blue skies, and I had been taught that *there* was the home of the good, and I fancied that those sweet bells were ringing in heaven. What a happy error! Neither illusion nor reality, at any subsequent period of my life, ever gave me such a sensation of pure, heartfelt delight, as I experienced when morning after morning I looked on that blue sky, and listened to those bells, and fancied that I heard the music of the home of the blest, pealing from the dwelling of the most high. Well do I remember the excessive mortification I felt when I was told the truth, and had the nature of bells explained to me; and, though I have since had to awake often from illusions that were dear to my heart, I am sure that I never woke from one with more pain than I experienced when forced to forego this sweet illusion of my imaginative childhood.

I believe I was naturally a fearful child, perhaps more so than other children; but I was not allowed to remain so. Well do I remember the fears, which I used to indulge and prove by tears and screams, whenever I saw the objects that called forth my alarm. The first was terror of black beetles, the second of frogs, the third of skeletons, the fourth of a black man, and the fifth of madmen.

My mother, who was as firm from principle, as she was gentle in disposition, in order to cure me of my first fear, made me take a beetle in my hand, and so convince myself it would not hurt me. As her word was law, I obeyed her, though with a shrinking frame; but the point was carried, and when, as frequently happened, I was told to take up a beetle and put it out of the way of being trodden upon, I learnt to forget even my former fear.

She pursued the same course in order to cure me of screaming at sight of a frog; I was forced to hold one in my hand, and thence I became, perhaps, proud of my courage to handle what my playfellows dared not touch.

The skeleton of which I was afraid was that of a girl, black, probably, from the preparation it had undergone; be that as it may, I was induced to take it on my lap and examine it, and at last, calling it my black doll, I used to exhibit it to my wondering and alarmed companions. Here was vanity again perhaps.

The African of whom I was so terribly afraid was the footman of a rich merchant from Rotterdam, who lived opposite our house; and, as he was fond of children, Aboar (as he was called) used to come up to speak to little missey as I stood at the door in my nurse's arms, a civility which I received with screams, and tears, and kicks. But as soon as my parents heard of this ill behaviour, they resolved to put a stop to it, and missey was forced to shake hands with the black the next time he approached her, and thenceforward we were very good friends. Nor did they fail to make me acquainted with negro history; as soon as I was able to understand, I was shewn on the map where their native country was situated; I was told the sad tale of negro wrongs and negro slavery; and I believe that my early and ever-increasing zeal in the cause of emancipation was founded and fostered by the kindly emotions which I was encouraged to feel for my friend Aboar and all his race.

The fifth terror was excited by two poor women who lived near us, and were both deranged though *in different degree.* The one was called Cousin Betty, a common name for female lunatics; the other, who had been dismissed from bedlam as incurable, called herself "Old Happiness," and went by that name. These poor women lived near us, and passed by our door every day; consequently I often saw them when I went out with my nurse, and whether it was that I had been told by her, when naughty, that the mad woman should get me, I know not; but certain it is, that these poor visited creatures were to me objects of such terror, that when I saw them coming (followed usually by hooting boys) I used to run away to hide myself. But as soon as my mother was aware of this terror she resolved to conquer it, and I was led by her to the door the next time one of these women was in sight; nor was I allowed to stir till I had heard her kindly converse with the poor afflicted one, and then I was commissioned to put a piece of money into her hand. I had to undergo the same process with the other woman; but she tried my nerves more than the preceding one, for she insisted on shaking hands with me, a contact not very pleasing to me: however, the fear was in a measure conquered, and a feeling of deep interest, not unmixed with awe, was excited in my mind, not only towards these women, but towards insane persons in general; a feeling that has never left me, and which, in very early life, I gratified in the following manner:—

When able to walk in the street with my beloved parents, they sometimes passed the city asylum for lunatics, called the bedlam, and we used to stop before the iron gates, and see the inmates very often at the windows, who would occasionally ask us to throw halfpence over the wall to buy snuff. Not long after I had discovered the existence of this interesting receptacle, I found my way to it alone, and took care to shew a penny in my fingers, that I might be asked for it, and told where to throw it. A customer soon appeared at one of the windows, in the person of a man named Goodings, and he begged me to throw it over the door of the wall of the ground in which they walked, and he would come to catch it. Eagerly did I run to that door, but never can I forget the terror and the trembling which seized my whole frame, when, as I stood listening for my mad friend at the door, I heard the clanking of his chain! nay, such was my alarm, that, though a strong door was between us, I felt inclined to run away; but better feelings got the mastery, and I threw the money over the door, scarcely staying to hear him say he had found the penny, and that he blessed the giver. I fully believe that I felt myself raised in the scale of existence by this action, and some of my happiest moments were those when I visited the gates of bedlam; and so often did I go, that I became well known to its inmates, and I have heard them say, "Oh! there is the little girl from St. George's" (the parish in which I then lived.) At this time my mother used to send me to shops to purchase trifling articles, and chiefly at a shop at some distance from the bedlam, which was as far again from my home. But, when my mother used to ask me where I had been, that I had been gone so long, the reply was, "I only went round by bedlam, mamma."

But I did not confine my gifts to pence. Much of my weekly allowance was spent in buying pinks and other flowers for my friend Goodings, who happened to admire a nosegay which he saw me wear; and as my parents were not inclined to rebuke me for spending my money on others, rather than on myself, I was allowed for some time to indulge in this way the interests which early circumstances, those circumstances which always give the bias to the character through life, had led me to feel in beings whom it had pleased the Almighty to deprive of their reason. At this period, and when my attachment to this species of human woe was at its height, a friend of ours hired a house which looked into the ground named before, and my father asked the gentleman to allow me to stand at one of the windows, and see the lunatics walk. Leave was granted and I hastened to my post, and as the window was open I could talk with Goodings and the others; but my feelings were soon more forcibly interested by an unseen lunatic, who had, they told me, been crossed in love, and who, in the cell opposite my window, sang song after song in a voice which I thought very charming.

But I do not remember to have been allowed the indulgence of standing at this window more than twice. I believe my parents thought the excitement was an unsafe one, as I was constantly talking of what I had said to the mad folks, and they to me; and it was so evident that I was proud of their acquaintance, and of my own attachment to them, that I was admonished not to go so often to the gates of the bedlam; and dancing and French school soon gave another turn to my thoughts, and excited in me other views and feelings. Still, the sight of a lunatic gave me a fearful pleasure, which nothing else excited; and when, as youth advanced, I knew that loss of reason accompanied distressed circumstances, I know that I was doubly eager to administer to the pecuniary wants of those who were awaiting their appointed time in madness as well as poverty. Yet, notwithstanding, I could not divest myself entirely of fear of these objects of my pity; and it was with a beating heart that, after some hesitation, I consented to accompany two gentlemen, dear friends of mine, on a visit to the *interior* of the bedlam. One of my companions was a man of warm feelings and lively fancy, and he had pictured to himself the unfortunate beings, whom we were going to visit, as victims of their sensibility, and as likely to express by their countenances and words the fatal sorrows of their hearts; and I was young enough to share in his anticipations, having, as yet, considered madness not as occasioned by some physical derangement, but as the result, in most cases, of moral causes. But our romance was sadly disappointed, for we beheld no "eye in a fine phrensy rolling," no interesting expression of sentimental woe, sufficient to raise its victims above the lowly walk of life in which they had always moved; and I, though I knew that the servant of a friend of mine was in the bedlam who had been "crazed by hopeless love," yet could not find out, amongst the many figures that glided by me, or bent over the winter fire, a single woman who looked like the victim of the tender passion.

The only woman, who had aught interesting about her, was a poor girl, just arrived, whose hair was not yet cut off, and who, seated on the bed in her new cell, had torn off her cap, and had let the dark tresses fall over her shoulders in picturesque confusion! This pleased me; and I was still more convinced I had found what I sought, when, on being told to lie down and sleep, she put her hand to her evidently aching head, as she exclaimed, in a mournful voice, "Sleep! oh, I cannot sleep!" The wish to question this poor sufferer being repressed by respectful pity, we hastened away to other cells, in which were patients confined in their beds; with one of these women I conversed a little while, and then continued our mournful visits. "But where (said I to the keeper) is the servant of a friend of mine (naming the patient) who is here because she was deserted by her lover?" "You have just left her," said the man. "Indeed," replied I, and hastened eagerly back to the cell I had quitted. I immediately began to talk to her of her mistress and the children, and called her by her name, but she would not reply. I then asked her if she would like money to buy snuff? "Thank you," she replied. "Then give me your hand." "No, you must lay the money on my pillow." Accordingly I drew near, when, just as I reached her, she uttered a screaming laugh, so loud, so horrible, so unearthly, that I dropped the pence, and rushing from the cell, never stopped till I found myself with my friends, who had themselves been startled by the noise, and were coming in search of me. I was now eager to leave the place; but I had seen, and lingered behind still, to gaze upon a man whom I had observed from the open door at which I stood, pacing up and down the wintry walk, but who at length saw me earnestly beholding him! He started, fixed his eyes on me with a look full of mournful expression, and never removed them till I, reluctantly I own, had followed my companions. What a world of woe was, as I fancied, in that look! Perhaps I resembled some one dear to him! Perhaps—but it were idle to give all the perhapses of romantic sixteen—resolved to find in bedlam what she thought *ought* to be there of the sentimental, if it were not. However, that poor man and his expression never left my memory; and I thought of him when, at a later period, I attempted to paint the feelings I imputed to him in the "Father and Daughter."

On the whole, we came away disappointed, from having formed false ideas of the nature of the infliction which we had gone to contemplate. I have since then seen madness in many different asylums, but I was *never disappointed* again.

Faithful to the views with which I began this little sketch of my childhood and my early youth, I will here relate a circumstance which was romantic enough to add fresh fuel to whatever I had already of romance in my composition; and therefore is another proof that, from the earliest circumstances with which human beings are surrounded, the character takes its colouring through life. Phrenologists watch certain bumps on the head, indicative, they say, of certain propensities, and assert that parents have a power to counteract, by cultivation, the bad propensities, and to increase the good. This may be a surer way of going to work; but, as yet, the truth of their theory is not generally acknowledged. In the meanwhile, I would impress on others what I am fully sensible of myself; namely, that the attention of parents and instructors should be incessantly directed to watching over the very earliest dispositions and tastes of their children or pupils, because, as far as depends on mere human teaching, whatever they are in disposition and pursuit in the earliest dawn of existence, they will probably be in its meridian and its decline.

When I was scarcely yet in my teens, a highly respected friend of mine, a member of the Society of Friends, informed me that she had a curious story to relate to me and her niece, my favourite friend and companion; she told us that her husband had received a letter from a friend at Lynn, recommending to his kindness a young man, named William Henry Renny, who was a sailor, just come on shore from a distant part, and wanted some assistance on his way (I think) to London. My friend, who was ever ready to lend his aid when needed, and was sure his correspondent would not have required it for one unworthy, received the young man kindly, and ordered him refreshments in the servants' hall; and, as I believe, prepared for him a bed in his own house. But before the evening came, my friend had observed something in the young man's manner which he did not like; he was too familiar towards the servants, and certainly did not seem a proper inmate for the family of a Friend. At length, in consequence of hints given him by some one in the family, he called the stranger into his study, and expressed his vexation at learning that his conduct had not been quite correct. The young man listened respectfully to the deserved rebuke, but with great agitation and considerable excitement, occasioned perhaps, as my candid friend thought, by better meals than he had been used to, and which was therefore a sort of excuse for his behaviour; but little was my friend prepared for the disclosure that awaited him. Falling on his knees, the young man, with clasped hands, conjured his hearer to forgive him the imposition he had practised. "Oh, sir," cried he, "I am an impostor, my name is not William Henry R. but Anna Maria Real, I am not a man, but a woman!" Such a confession would have astounded any one; judge then how it must have affected the correct man whom she addressed! who certainly did not let the woman remain in her abject position, but desired immediately to hear a true account of who and what she was. She said, that her lover, when very young, had left her to go to sea, and that she resolved to follow him to Russia, whither he was bound; that she did follow him, disguised as a sailor, and had worked out her passage undetected. She found her lover dead, but she liked a sailor's life so well, that she had continued in the service up to that time, when (for some reason which I have forgotten) she left the ship, and came ashore at Lynn, not meaning to return to it, but to resume the garb of her sex. On this latter condition, my friend and his wife were willing to assist her, and endeavour to effect a reformation in her. The first step was to procure her a lodging that evening, and to prevent her being seen, as much as they could, before she had put on woman's clothes. Accordingly, she was sent to lodgings, and inquiries into the truth of her story were instituted at Lynn and elsewhere.

But what an interesting tale was this for me, a Miss just entered into her teens! Of a female soldier's adventures I had some years previously heard, and once had seen Hannah Snelling, a native of Norfolk, who had followed her lover to the wars. Here was a female sailor added to my experience. Every opportunity of hearing any subsequent detail was eagerly seized. What a romantic incident! The romance of real life too! How I wanted to see the heroine; and I was rather mortified that my sober-minded friend would not describe her features to me. Might I (I asked) be at last allowed to see her? and as my parents gave leave, I, accompanied by a young friend, called at the adventurer's lodgings, who was at home! Yes,—she was at home, and to our great consternation we found her in men's clothes still, and working at a trade which she had acquired on board ship, the trade of a tailor! Nor did she leave off though we were her guests, but went on stitching and pulling with most ugly diligence, though ever and anon casting her large, dark, and really beautiful, though fierce eyes, over our disturbed and wondering countenances, silently awaiting to hear why we came. We found it difficult to give a reason, as her appearance and employment so totally extinguished any thing like sentiment in our young hearts, upon this occasion. However, we broke the ice at last, and she told us something of her story; which, however touching in the beginning, as that of a disguise and an enterprize prompted by youthful love, became utterly offensive when persisted in after the original motives for it had ceased. Her manner too was not pleasant: I wore a gold watch in my girdle, with a smart chain and seals, and the coveting eye with which she gazed, and at length clapped her hand upon them, begging to see them near, gave me a feeling of distaste; and, as I watched her almost terrible eyes, I fancied that they indicated a deranged mind; therefore, hastening to give her the money which I had brought for her, I took my leave, with my friend, resolving not to visit her again. Out of respect to our friends, she went to the Friends' meeting with them, and they were pleased to see her there in her woman's attire; but when she walked away, with the long strides and bold seeming of a man, it was anything rather than satisfactory, to observe her.

I once saw her walk, and though this romance of real life occupied the minds of my young friend and myself, and was afterwards discussed by us, still the actress in it was becoming, justly, an object with whom we should have loathed any intercourse.

I do not recollect how long she remained under the care

of my excellent friends, but I think much of her story was authenticated by the answers to the inquiries made. All that I know with certainty is, that a collection of wild beasts came to town, the showman of which turned out to be Maria Real's husband, and with him she left Norwich!

* * * * * *

Thus abruptly does Mrs. Opie's narrative of her early days break off. Had she turned the next leaf in that history it must have been to record her first sorrow.

CHAPTER II.

FIRST SORROW; THE ASSIZES; SIR HENRY GOULD; THE USURY CAUSE; "CHRISTIAN;" MR. BRUCKNER; GIRLISH DAYS; HER FRIÉNDSHIP WITH MRS. TAYLOR; MRS. T.'S MEMOIR OF HER.

In one of his letters to a friend, Southey remarks:—

"Few autobiographies proceed much beyond the stage of boyhood. So far all our recollections of childhood and adolescence, though they call up tender thoughts, excite none of the deeper feeling with which we look back upon the time of life when wounds heal slowly, and losses are irreparable. This is, no doubt, the reason why so many persons who have begun to write their own lives have stopped short when they got through the chapter of their youth."

The poet elsewhere observes, that the wounded spirit, which shrinks from such a record of past griefs, finds solace in breathing out its regret in the tender strains of verse. And so it was in the present instance. The loss of her mother was deplored in pathetic numbers; and no other record of this event is given.

Another passage in the history of her earlier days is found in her note book, a few pages after the former, shewing how early she manifested a predilection, in the gratification of which she found so much enjoyment in after life. It should be mentioned before we proceed further, that the house in which

Mrs. Opie was born was situated in Calvert Street, immediately opposite a handsome mansion, once the residence of an individual of note in his day, and after whom the street was named. This house Dr. Alderson afterwards inhabited for some years; but in the interim, he removed from the one in which his daughter was born, to another, opposite St. George's church, and in which they were living at the time referred to in the following pages:—

To a girl fond of excitement it will easily be believed that the time of Assizes was one of great interest. As soon as I was old enough to enjoy a procession, I was taken to see the judges come in; and, as youthful pages in pretty dresses ran, at that time of day, by the side of the high sheriff's carriage in which the judges sat, while the coaches drove slowly, and with a solemnity becoming the high and awful office of those whom they contained, it was a sight which I, the older I grew, delighted more and more to witness: with reverence ever did I behold the judges' wigs, the scarlet robes they wore, and even the white wand of the sheriff had an imposing effect on me.

As years advanced, I began to wish to enter the assize court; and as soon as I found that ladies were allowed to attend trials, or causes, I was not satisfied till I had obtained leave to enjoy this indulgence. Accordingly some one kindly undertook to go with me, and I set off for court: it was to the *nisi prius* court that I bent my way, for I could not bear the thoughts of hearing prisoners tried, as the punishment of death was then in all its force; but I was glad to find myself hearing counsel plead and judges speak where I had no reason to apprehend any fearful consequences to the defendants. By some lucky chance I also soon found myself on the bench, by the side of the judge. Although I could not divest myself of a degree of awful respect when I had reached such a vicinity, it was so advantageous a position for hearing and seeing, that I was soon reconciled to it, especially as the good old man, who sat then as judge, seemed to regard my fixed attention to what was going forward with some complacency.

Sir Henry Gould was the judge then presiding, and he was already on the verge of eighty; but the fire of his fine eye was not quenched by age, nor had his intellect as yet bowed before it; on the contrary, he is said while in Norwich to have delivered a charge to the jury, after a trial that had lasted far into the night, in a manner that would have done credit to the youngest judge on the bench.

This handsome and venerable old man, surprised probably at seeing so young a listener by his side, was so kind at last as to enter into conversation with me. Never, I think, had my vanity been so gratified, and when, on my being forced to leave the court, by the arrival of my dinner hour, he said he hoped I was sufficiently pleased to come again, I went home much raised in my own estimation, and fully resolved to go into court again next day. As I was obliged to go alone, I took care to wear the same dress as I wore the preceding day, in hopes that if the judge saw me he would cause way to be made for me. But being obliged to go in at a door where the crowd was very great, I had little hopes of being seen, though the door fronted the judge; at last I was pushed forward by the crowd, and gradually got nearer to the table. While thus struggling with obstacles, a man, not quite in the grade of a gentleman, pushed me back rather rudely, and said, "there miss, go home—you had better go away, what business have you here? this is no place for you; be advised—there go, I tell you!" But miss was obstinate and stood her ground, turning as she did so towards the judge, who now perceived and recognized her, and instantly ordered one of the servants of the court to make way for that young lady; accordingly way was made, and at his desire I took my place again by the judge's side. It was not in nature, at least not in my weak nature, to resist casting a triumphant glance on my impertinent reprover, and I had the satisfaction of seeing that he looked rather foolish. I do not remember that on either of these days I heard any very interesting causes tried, but I had acquaintances amongst the barristers, and I liked to hear them plead, and I also liked to hear the judge sum up: in short, all was new, exciting, and interesting. But I disliked to hear the witnesses sworn. I was shocked at the very irreverent manner in which the oath was administered and repeated; and evidently the Great Name was spoken with as much levity as if it had been merely that of a brother mortal, not the name of the great King of kings. This was the drawback to my pleasure, but not a sufficient one to keep me from my now accustomed post, and a third time, but early enough to have my choice of places, I repaired to court, and seated myself near the extremity of the bench, hoping to be called to my accustomed seat when my venerable friend arrived. It was expected that the court would be that day crowded to excess, for the cause coming on was one of the deepest interest. One of our richest and oldest aldermen was going to be proceeded against for usury, and the principal witness against him was a gentleman who owed him considerable obligation. The prosecutor was unknown to me; the witness named above I knew sufficiently to bow to him as he passed our house, which he did every day; and he was reckoned a worthy and honourable man. These circumstances gave me an eager desire to be a witness of the proceedings, and I was gratified at being able to answer some questions which the judge asked me when, as before, he had beckoned me to sit by him.

The cause at length began, and it was so interesting that I listened with almost breathless attention, feeling, for the first time, what deep and agitating interest a court of justice can sometimes excite, and what a fearful picture it can hold up to the young of human depravity; for, as this cause went on, the witness for the accused, and the witness for the accuser, both swore in direct opposition to each other! One of them therefore was undoubtedly perjured! and I had witnessed the commission of this awful crime!

Never shall I forget that moment; as it seemed very soon to be the general conclusion, that my acquaintance was the person perjured. I felt a pain wholly unknown before, and though I rejoiced that my friend, the accused, was declared wholly innocent of the charge brought against him, I was indeed sorry that I should never be able to salute my old acquaintance with such cordiality in future, when he passed my window, as this stain rested on his reputation; but that window he was never to pass again!

The next morning before I was up, (for beginning influenza confined me to my bed,) the servant ran into the room to inform me that poor ——— had been found dead in his bed, with strong suspicions of suicide by poison!

Instantly I dressed myself, forgetting my illness, and went in search of more information. Well do I remember the ghastly expression of the wretched man's countenance as he left the court. I saw his bright grey eye lifted up in a sort of agony to heaven, with, as I supposed, the conviction that he was retiring in disgrace, and I had been told what his lips uttered, while his eyes so spoke. "What! are you going," said a friend to him. "Yes; why not? What should I stay for now?" and his tone and manner bore such strong evidence of a desponding mind, that these words were repeated as confirming the belief that he had destroyed himself.

I never can forget with what painful feelings I went back to my chamber, the sensation of illness forgotten, by the sufferings of my mind!

What would I not have given to hear that the poor man who had thus rushed unbidden into the presence of his heavenly judge, urged by the convictions of having been condemned in the presence of an earthly one, was innocent of this second crime! It had been terrible to believe him guilty of the first.

My mind was so painfully full of this subject, that it was always uppermost with me; and, to increase my suffering, the unhappy man's grave was dug immediately opposite our windows; and although I drew down the blinds all day long, I heard the murmuring voices of the people talking over the event, some saying he was an injured man, and venting curses on the heads of those who had brought him to that pass. The verdict having been that "he was found dead in his bed," the interment took place in the usual manner; and it did so early in the morning. I took care to avoid the front of the house till all was over; and when the hour in the following morning arrived, at which I used to go to the window, and receive the bow and smile of our neighbour, I remembered with bitter regret that I should see him no more, as he lay beneath the wall before me.

Even while I am writing, the whole scene in the court, and the frightful results, live before me with all the vividness of early impressions; and I can scarcely assert, that, at any future stage of life, I ever experienced emotions more keen or more enduring.

Judge Gould came to Norwich again the next year, and as I heard he had inquired for me, I was not long in going to court. One of his first questions was concerning the result of the Usury cause, which he had found so interesting, and he heard with much feeling what I had to impart. I thought my kind friend seemed full a year older; and when I took leave of him I did not expect to see him again. Perhaps the invitation which he gave me, was a proof of a decay of faculties; for he said that if ever I came to London, he lived in such a square, (I forget the place,) and should be pleased to introduce me to his daughter Lady Cavan. I did go to London before he died, but I had not courage enough to call on Sir Henry Gould; I felt it was likely that he had forgotten me, and that he was unlikely to exclaim, like my friends at the bedlam, "Oh! here's the young girl from St. George's!"

It may be remembered that in the short memorial of her earlier days, given in the preceding chapter, Mrs. Opie says that her attention was drawn away from an interest that was becoming too absorbing in the unhappy inmates of the bedlam, by new sources of occupation and interest. "Dancing and French school," she says, "soon gave another turn to my thoughts, and excited in me other views and feelings." The master who first instructed her to thread the gay mazes of the dance was one, "Christian," a man well skilled in his art, and who attained such celebrity in it, that the room in which he taught is still called after him, "Christian's room." Here the young Amelia received her first lessons in dancing; and in after years she was wont to refer to those days, and would close her recollections of the worthy Christian, by telling how on one occasion, when she and her husband were in Norwich, they accompanied a friend to see the Dutch Church. "The two gentlemen were engaged in looking around and making their observations; and I, finding myself somewhat cold, began to hop and dance upon the spot where I stood. Suddenly, my eyes chanced to fall upon the pavement below, and I started at beholding the well-known name of 'Christian,' graved upon the slab; I stopped in dismay, shocked to find that I had actually been dancing upon the grave of my old master—he who first taught me to dance!"

The gentleman who gave her instruction in the French language was a remarkable man, and one for whom she entertained an affectionate respect which continued during the remainder of his life. As he is frequently referred to in her letters and elsewhere, it may not be irrelevant here to give some particulars respecting him, which are principally gathered from an article in "the Monthly Magazine," written by the late Mr. Wm. Taylor. It appears that in 1752, Mr. Colombine, one of a French refugee family, then residing in Norwich, was entrusted by the members of the Walloon church, in that city, on occasion of his going over to Holland, to seek out for them a suitable pastor. In the execution of this commission, he applied to Mr. Bruckner, then holding a pastorship at Leyden. This gentleman, who had been educated for the theological profession, was of eminent literary acquirements; he read the Hebrew and the Greek, composed correctly, and was able to preach in four languages: Latin, Dutch, French, and English. He listened favourably to the invitation of the Norwich church; and in 1753 settled amongst them, and continued to officiate during 51 years with increasing satisfaction: about the year 1766, Mr. B. also undertook the charge of the Dutch church, of which the duties had become almost nominal, in consequence of the diminished numbers of Dutch families, and the gradual disuse of that language.

The French was Mr. Bruckner's favourite tongue; and in it he gave lessons, both public and private, to the young people of his adopted city, for many years: he also cultivated music, and delighted in practising upon the organ. He was, besides, an author, and published a work entitled "Théorie du Systême Animal," and, under an assumed name, a pamphlet entitled "Criticisms on the Diversions of Purley." His death took place in the month of May, 1804; at his house in St. Benedict's street. Mr. Opie painted an admirable likeness of him, which appeared in the London Exhibition of 1800. This picture was in the possession of Mrs. Opie at the time of her death, and is the subject of one of her "Lays." There was a very singular expression in the eyes, and on one occasion a visitor who was calling upon her, gazing on the picture, remarked, that he was painfully affected by this look, as he remembered to have seen the same strange appearance in the countenance of a person who committed suicide. This remark forcibly struck Mrs. Opie, and no wonder, as it was the fact that her poor master died by his own hands! A gradual failure of spirits overtook him in his old age; sleep forsook his eyelids, and the fatal stroke terminated his existence, to the regret of all who had known him; for he was much beloved for his kindliness and affability, and his society was courted to the last, as his conversation shewed good sense, humour, and information. A small piece of paper, written in her delicate and minute characters, and found among her letters, proves that his friend and pupil continued to think of him after the lapse of more than half a century.

Lines, addressed to me by my dear friend and French master, John Bruckner, a Flemish Clergyman, on my requesting him to let my husband paint a portrait of him for me.

Pourquoi me demander, aimable Amélie
De ce front tout ridé, le lugubre portrait?
Pour être contemplé jamais il ne fut fait,
Assez il a déplu—Permettez qu' on l'oublie!

John Bruckner, 1800.

Translation in prose:—

Why do you ask of me, amiable Amelia, the gloomy portrait of this wrinkled brow? It was never meant to be contemplated. It has enough displeased—Let it now be forgotten.—*A. O.* 1852.

To this amiable man and accomplished scholar Mrs. Opie was indebted, not only for instruction in French, but for much general information, which he was well qualified to impart.

The premature death of Mrs. Alderson occasioned (as we have seen) the introduction of her daughter into society at a very early age. Her father delighted to make her his constant companion, and introduced her to the company of the friends with whom he visited, and whom he welcomed to his house. Hence, at a time when girls are usually confined to the school room, she was presiding as mistress of his household, and mingling in the very gay society of the Norwich circles of that day. The period of which we write was shortly before the breaking out of the French revolution, and was one of great commercial prosperity, in which the merchant-manufacturers of the old town shared, in an extraordinary degree. This state of things lasted until the troubles consequent upon that event disturbed the commercial relations of the continent; when the trade declined, and a season of unparelleled depression ensued. But at the time of which we speak, it was a thriving and prosperous city, and abounded in gaiety and amusements of various sorts.

A young girl placed in such circumstances must have greatly needed the counsel and friendship of a wise female friend; and such an one Miss Alderson happily found in Mrs. John Taylor, a lady distinguished for her extensive knowledge and many excellencies. She was living at that time in Norwich, not far from Mr. Alderson's, and an intimacy was early formed between the two ladies, which appears to have lasted uninterruptedly through life. After Mrs. Opie's marriage, she continued to correspond with this friend of her early days, and happily many of her letters to Mrs. T. have been preserved.

Frequent mention is made of Mrs. Taylor in Sir James Mackintosh's life, and she is spoken of as one of the principal attractions amid the circle of friends whose society he sought, when carried by his professional duties to Norwich. Mr. Montague, his companion on some of these occasions, says:—

"N. was always a haven of rest to us, from the literary society with which that city abounded. Dr. Sayers we used to visit, and the high-minded and intelligent Wm. Taylor; but our chief delight was in the society of Mrs. John Taylor, a most intelligent and excellent woman, mild and unassuming, quiet and meek, sitting amidst her large family, occupied with her needle and domestic occupations, but always assisting, by her great knowledge, the advancement of kind and dignified sentiment and conduct.

Manly wisdom and feminine gentleness were in her united with such attractive manners, that she was universally loved and respected. In 'high thoughts and gentle deeds' she greatly resembled the admirable Lucy Hutchinson, and in troubled times would have been equally distinguished for firmness in what she thought right. In her society we passed every moment we could rescue from the court."*

How dear must such a friend have been to one whom she so tenderly loved! When some years later a portrait of Mrs. Opie was brought out in "The Cabinet," a periodical of the day, Mrs. Taylor drew up a short notice of her friend, to accompany this likeness. This paper was written about the time of Mr. Opie's death, but it principally refers to the early part of Mrs. Opie's life. After speaking of the circumstances of her birth, of the early death of her mother, and of the proofs she

* See Life of Sir James Mackintosh.

gave, even in childhood, of poetical genius and taste, the writer continues:—

"Mrs. Opie's musical talents were early cultivated. Her first master was Mr. Michael Sharp, of Norwich, who possessed a degree of love for his profession which comparatively few, employed in the drudgery of teaching, evince. Mrs. O. never arrived at superiority as a player, but she may be said to have been unrivalled in that kind of singing in which she more particularly delighted. Those only who have heard her can conceive the effect she produced in the performance of her own ballads; of these, 'The poor Hindoo' was one of her chief favourites, and the expression of plaintive misery and affectionate supplication which she threw into it, we may safely say has very seldom been equalled. She may fairly be said to have created a style of singing of her own, which, though polished and improved by art and cultivation, was founded in that power, which she appears so pre-eminently to possess, of awakening the tender sympathies and pathetic feelings of the mind."

After enumerating some further accomplishments possessed by her friend, Mrs. Taylor closes her tribute of affectionate regard, by speaking of the excellencies of a heart and mind "distinguished by frankness, probity, and the most diffusive kindness;" and appeals to the many who could bear witness from experience, to those sympathies which "made the happiness of her friends her own, and to the unremitting ardour with which she laboured to remove the miseries that came within her knowledge and influence."

CHAPTER III.

NORFOLK AND NORWICH, AND THEIR INHABITANTS; YOUNG LOVE; THE DRAMA; SONG WRITING AND CROMER; POLITICS; VISIT TO LONDON; LETTERS FROM THENCE; THE OLD BAILEY TRIALS.

Mr. Holcroft, in his Autobiography, writes thus of East Anglia:—

"I have seen more of the county of Norfolk than of its inhabitants; of which county I remark, that, to the best of my recollection, it contains more churches, more flints, more turkeys, more turnips, more wheat, more cultivation, more commons, more cross roads, and from that token probably more inhabitants, than any county I ever visited. It has another distinguishing and paradoxical feature, if what I hear be true; it is said to be more illiterate than any other part of England, and yet, I doubt, if any county of like extent have produced an equal number of famous men."

The praises of Norwich were written thus, in old monkish rhymes in days of yore;

"Urbs speciosa situ, nitidis pulcherrima tectis,
Grata peregrinis, deliciosa suis."

If common fame speak true, the Inhabitants of the old City have been noted for three peculiarities—the resolute purpose and strongly marked character of her men; the fair looks of her women; and the deep-rooted attachment which is entertained for her by those born and bred within her walls. The subject of this memoir certainly shared largely in this love for the city of her birth. During the eight and twenty years of her life which preceded her marriage, with the exception of occasional visits to London and elsewhere, she remained in her native town and in her father's house; and when, at the expiration of nine years, she became a widow, she returned to live under her father's roof again; nor at his death did she manifest a desire to quit the place endeared to her by the recollections of so many long and happy years.

At the period to which we have arrived in her history, she possessed the advantages of a pleasing personal appearance. Her friend, Mrs. Taylor, delicately alludes to the graces of "person, mind, and manner," so happily united in her; and Mr. Opie's portraits fully bear testimony to the truth of these friendly representations. Her countenance was animated, bright, and beaming; her eyes soft and expressive, yet full of ardour; her hair was abundant and beautiful, of auburn hue, and waving in long tresses; her figure was well formed; her carriage fine; her hands, arms, and feet, well shaped;—and all around and about her was the spirit of youth, and joy, and love. What wonder if she early loved, and was beloved! She used to own that she had been guilty of the "girlish imprudence" of love at sixteen. From the following lines in one of her poems, it should seem that this fancy of her youth was but a day-dream destined to pass away like the rest!

I've gazed on the handsome, have talked with the wise,
  With the witty have laugh'd, untouched by love's power,
And tho' long assailed by young Corydon's eyes,
  They charmed for a day, and were thought of no more!

But once, I confess, (t'was at tender sixteen,)
  Love's agents were busy indeed round my heart,
And nought but good fortune's assistance I ween,
  Could ere from my bosom have warded the dart.

Numerous admirers, indeed, seem to have paid her homage, and courted her favour in those days. Some perhaps enjoyed a short season of hope, and there were two or three, whose rapturous effusions were committed to some secret receptacle, there to await a season of leisure when their claims might be considered. But alas! none such came; they lay forgotten; and only came to light when she, whose bright young charms they told of, had closed a long life.

High spirits, uninterrupted health, a lively fancy, and poetic talent, were hers; and she fully enjoyed and exercised these natural advantages.

One of her earliest tastes was a love of the drama, and Mr. Capel Lofft, writing to her in 1808, observes, "Your uncle, the barrister, was saying yesterday evening, how struck he was, almost in your childhood, with your power of dramatic diction and recitation, and that he had never thought it equalled by any one." This taste she cultivated; and, when not more than eighteen years of age, wrote a tragedy, entitled "Adelaide," which is still extant. It was acted for the amusement of her friends; she herself performing the heroine's part, while Mr. Robert Harvey played the rôle of "the old father."

It should seem from an expression in one of her

letters, that this was not a solitary effort in theatrical composition, and that she even aspired to see some of her plays performed in public. It was probably this taste which early introduced her to an acquaintance with the Kemble family; as she says, in a very early letter to her father, signing herself 'Euridice,' "My claim to this name was revived in my mind the other day, by Mr. Kemble coming up to me, saying, 'Euridice, the woods, Euridice, the floods,' &c." She ever entertained an ardent admiration for the illustrious Mrs. Siddons; an admiration mingled with a warm sentiment of personal regard. This was manifested in a touching and natural manner after the death of that lady, when, as she was one day visiting the Soanian museum, (in company with the friend who now records the fact,) happening unexpectedly to see a cast of Mrs. Siddons' face, taken after death, and unable to control her emotion, she burst into a passionate flood of tears!

Mrs. Taylor was probably right in her judgment when she said to Mrs. Opie, "You ought to rest your fame upon song writing." Many of the most popular songs she published after her marriage had been early productions of her pen; and were, perhaps, not excelled by any efforts of that kind in her later years. Some of them first appeared separately in newspapers and magazines, and a few in a periodical miscellany called "The Cabinet."

The Lay to the memory of her mother was written (as we have said) at Cromer, in the year 1791; and is the first in an old manuscript book containing her earlier poems, many of which she afterwards published. They were produced in this and the following year, and are inscribed "Verses written at Cromer." This place seems to have been, throughout life, very dear to her; owing no doubt, in part, to the fact that she had frequently spent the summer season there with her mother in her childhood; hence it became associated in her mind with these earliest recollections.

There she indulged in fond memories and fancies, spending the long summer days roving along the shore, and weaving her thoughts into verse, grave or gay. She deplores her fate when compelled to leave

> These scenes belov'd upon whose tranquil shores,
> Thoughtless of ill, I breathed my earliest songs,
> While childish sports and hopes—a joyous throng—
> In soft enchantment bound the guiltless hours.

And concludes,

> Here I would wander, from day's earliest dawn,
> Till o'er the western summit steals dark night;
> And from the rugged cliff or dewy lawn,
> Reluctant fades the last pale gleam of light.

Visits among her numerous friends, and excursions on business and pleasure, in which she not unfrequently accompanied her father, occasionally afforded themes for her pen, and her wanderings may often be tracked by the titles she gave to these effusions. "A sonnet written in Cumberland," bears date 1790. Another "in a bower in Wroxham Churchyard," August, 1792. A serio-comic poem written at Windermere, in a letter to her father, gives an account of the merry antics played by herself and a gay party of young folks with whom she made the trip, and one, which we give to the reader, was

"WRITTEN ON SEEING A BUST OF MINERVA AT FELBRIGG HALL, THROWN INTO A CORNER AMONGST RUBBISH."

Who should have thought in Windham's breast
  Ingratitude to find!
Who should have thought that *he* could prove
  To his best friend unkind!

Yet sure I am, my eyes beheld
  In Felbrigg hall this morn,
Unmeaning heads exalted high,
  And Wisdom left forlorn!

* * * * * *

From these tranquil scenes we must make a somewhat abrupt transition, and carry the reader to the busy world of London, where we find her in 1794, and writing to her friend, Mrs. T., from thence. The allusions to political events, contained in these letters, render it necessary to say a few words respecting the opinions entertained by Dr. Alderson, and the friends with whom he associated on these subjects; as his daughter's views were naturally to a great degree formed after those of her father and his companions.

During the later years of the last century, at the time when this country was so vehemently excited by the great changes then occurring in France, and which were regarded by many as the commencement of a new and happier era for the nations of Europe generally; party strife ran to a fearful height, and scarcely any, even of the weaker sex, remained passive spectators of the struggle.

Dr. Alderson was among those who hailed the dawn of the French revolution with pleasure; and, though he afterwards saw cause to moderate his expectations as to the results of that movement, he seems (in common with many sincere patriots) to have held his allegiance true to the original revolutionary cause. It is well known that at this time various societies were organized, in different parts of the kingdom, for the purpose of discussing the political questions then agitating the public mind, and Norwich was among the foremost in these associations. A local society was instituted, in which were canvassed reforms and changes, many of which, advocated by the most influential statesmen of our day, have since been safely yielded to the irresistible force of public opinion. Three of the leading measures contended for were the Abolition of Negro Slavery, the repeal of the Corporation and Test Acts, and the reform of the House of Commons.

The policy of the government was, however, (not without reason,) hostile to associations such as these, and severe measures were adopted to put them down, and to bring their leaders under the fearful ban of high treason.

During Miss Alderson's stay in London, in 1794, she attended the famous trials of Horne Tooke, Holcroft, and others, for treason, at the Old Bailey; and in her letters home she gave her father a lively account of the events which transpired. It is known that Dr. Alderson, after reading these letters to his confidential friends, thought it prudent to destroy them. A few letters, to Mrs. Taylor, written previous to her marriage, have been preserved; but as that lady was in the habit of reading those addressed to Dr. Alderson by his daughter, they contain no account of the events which she described to him. The three which follow were written in 1794, during her visit to some friends who lived near London, but her letters being mostly without date, cannot always be arranged with certainty. It is evident that a fellowship in political opinions was the only bond which united her to many with whom, at this time, she associated. Her own good sense and firm rectitude of principle, happily preserved her from the follies and errors into which not a few around her were led, by their extravagant zeal for a liberty which speedily degenerated into license. She too, was enthusiastic, ardent, perhaps imprudent, at least so she seems to have judged in cooler moments; but there was too much of the pure womanly character in her, to suffer her ever to sympathize with the assertors of "woman's rights," (so called;) and she was not to be spoiled even though exposed to the influence of Horace Walpole's "philosophising serpents, the Paines, the Tookes, and the Wollstonecrofts."

Tuesday, 1794.

MY DEAR MRS. T.

At length I have found an opportunity of writing to you at my leisure, but now, though I have begun with the resolution of being very grave and very sentimental, I feel such an inclination to run into plain matters of fact and narration, that I shall beg leave to content myself with a recital of the events of my journey to town yesterday, requesting at the same time a recital of the events of your life, since I saw you, in return. We will leave gravity and sentiment to be the order of the evening when we resume our Wednesday *tête a têtes*, and rejoice in the absence of husband and father.

Mr. J. Boddington and I set off for town yesterday by way of Islington, that we might pay our first visit to Godwin, at Somers' Town. After a most delightful ride through some of the richest country I ever beheld, we arrived at about one o'clock at the philosopher's house, whom we found with his hair *bien poudré*, and in a pair of new, sharp-toed, red morocco slippers, not to mention his green coat and crimson under-waistcoat. He received me very kindly, but wondered I should think of being out of London;—could I be either amused or *instructed* at Southgate? How did I pass my time? What were my pursuits? and a great deal more, which frightened my protector, and tired me, till at last I told him I had not yet outlived my affections, and that they bound me to the family at Southgate. But was I to acknowledge any other dominion than that of reason?—"but are you sure that my affections in this case are not the result of reason?" He shrugged disbelief, and after debating some time, he told me I was more of the *woman* than when he saw me last. Rarely did we agree, and little did he gain on me by his mode of attack; but he seemed alarmed lest he should have offended me, and apologised several times, with much feeling, for the harshness of his expressions. In short, he convinced me that his theory has not yet gotten entire ascendancy over his practice. He has promised to come over to spend a day at Southgate, when I shall pit rational belief in Mr. M., against atheism in Mr. Godwin. Mr. B. was disgusted with his manner; though charmed with that of Barry, whom we called on last week. Godwin told me he had talked of me to Mrs. Inchbald, that she recollected me, and wished to see me; so I determined to call on her after I had paid my visit to Mrs. Siddons. From Godwin's, we went to Ives Hurry's in the City, where we left our chair and horses, and proceeded in a coach to Mrs. Betham's, to have my profile taken, and thence we drove to Marlborough Street. I found Mrs. Siddons engaged in nursing her little baby, and as handsome and charming as ever. She played last Wednesday before her month was up, and is now confined to her room with the cold she caught behind the scenes. There too, I saw Charles Kemble, as I passed through his sister's dressing room, and thought him so like

Kemble, Mrs. Twiss, and Mrs. Siddons, that it was some time before I could recollect myself enough to know whether he was a man or a woman. Sally and Maria, tell my father, are quite well, and inquired much concerning him. The baby is all a baby can be, but Mrs. S. laughs, and says it is a wit and a beauty already in her eyes; she leaves town to-day, or she would have invited me for a longer visit. From Marlborough Street, we drove to Mrs. Inchbald's, who is as pretty as ever, and much more easy and unreserved in her manner, than when I last saw her. With her we passed an hour, and when I took my leave, she begged I would call on her again. She is in charming lodgings, and has just received two hundred pounds from Sheridan, for a farce containing sixty pages only. From her house we drove into the city. You will wonder, perhaps, where we dined. Be it known unto you, that we never dine when we visit London. Ives Hurry, as soon as we arrive at his house, always treats us with as much ice and biscuits as we can eat; we then sally forth, and eat ice again when we want it; so we did yesterday, and Mrs. Siddons' roast beef had no temptations for us. As we returned to I. H.'s, we went to Daniel Isaac Eaton's shop; we had scarcely entered it, when a very genteel-looking young man came in. He examined us, and we him; and suspicion being the order of the day, I dared not talk to Mrs. Eaton till the stranger was engaged in conversation with Boddington. I then told her that curiosity led me to her shop, and that I came from that city of sedition, Norwich. Her eyes sparkled, and she asked me if I knew Charles Marsh? "You come from Norwich, (cried the stranger,) allow me to ask you some questions," &c., &c. He put questions, I answered them, and in a short time Mr. J. B. and myself were both so charmed with his manners and conversation, that we almost fancied we had known him before. We saw that he was intimate with Mrs. E. and her sweet girl, and seemed to be as much at home in the shop as the counter itself. So we had no fears of him; at last we became so fraternized, that Mrs. E. shut the shop door and gave us chairs. I will not relate the information I heard, but I could have talked with him all night. "Well, but who was he?" Have patience and you shall hear. Finding that he was just returned from Scotland, and was *au fait* of all the proceedings there, and that his connexions were those of high life; I asked where Lord Daer was, and lamented that he was not one of the *arrested members.* He smiled, and said that Lord D. wanted nerve then, and fortitude to resist the anxieties of his mother, and sisters, the most accomplished women in England; that the very day of the arrest he had received a letter from Lord Daer, promising to be with them if possible; and in the evening another note to say Lady Selkirk was ill, and that he could not leave her. "Indeed! I thought he *bailed* you," said Mrs. Eaton. "Oh! no," replied the other. Mr. B. and I looked at each other, wondering who "you," was; but I began to suspect, and went on questioning him. He said they dared not hurt Lord D; that they dared not attack any man of connexions and estate in Scotland: that had he himself been condemned, or sent to Botany Bay, his connexions would have *risen to a man.* I ventured to say, that however amiable Lord D's family might be, he ought to have disregarded their influence. He replied that I was quite right, and that he himself had disregarded them;—that democratic women were rare, and that he heartily wished he could introduce me to two charming patriots at Edinburgh, who were, though women, up to circumstances—and a great deal more, that raised my curiosity to a most painful height; at last, having said that he had laid it down as a rule for his conduct, that a patriot should be without the *hope of living,* or the *fear of dying,* he took his leave, leaving our minds elevated and delighted. Mrs. E. told us it was Mr. Sinclair, Sir John's nephew, he who was tried, and acquitted. He says Lord D. is supposed to be dying, and he himself looks in bad health, but his countenance is fine, and his manners elegant.—"What think you of Mr. Windham?" said I, "Oh! the poor creature is out of his element; he might have done very well for a college disputant or a Greek professor, perhaps, but that's all. "Why do the Norwich patriots espouse Mingay? what can they expect? (said he,) he might be a very good implement of resentment against Windham, but, though the friend of their necessity, not of their choice." Is he not right? * * * *

The following letter begins quite abruptly, and is without date.

* * * How strange it is, my dear friend, that I should have suffered your kind letter to remain so long unanswered, but, as I am certain that you will not impute my silence to any diminution of affection towards you, I will not fret about my oddity, but endeavour to make amends for it, by writing as good a letter as I *can*, and that will be, alas! very stupid; for the state of the times and other things press upon my mind continually, and unfit me for everything but conversation. My father will have told you a great deal; he will have told you too how much we are interested and agitated by the probable event of the approaching trials. Would to God, you and your husband were equally so, for then would one of my cares be removed; as you would, like us, perhaps turn a longing eye towards America as a place of refuge; and one of the strongest ties that binds me to Norwich would be converted into an attraction to lure me to the new world. On this, at least, I hope we are at all events resolved; to emigrate, if the event of the trial be fatal; that is, provided the Morgans do not give up their present resolution, and that we can carry a little society along with us, in which we can be happy, should Philadelphia disappoint our expectations. I write to you on this subject in confidence; as we do not wish our intention to be much known at present. How changed I am! How I sicken at the recollection of past follies and past connexions, and wish from the bottom of my soul, that I had never associated but with you and others like you. But it is folly to dwell on the past; it only incapacitates one for enjoying the present; it shall now be

my care to anchor on the future, and I trust in God that it will not disappoint me.

You see I am not in high spirits; but then I am the more natural; and my flighty hours are long gone by, and my time for serious exertion is, I hope, arrived; but why should I write thus? I shall perhaps infect you with this *seeming* gloom; for, after all, if I carefully examine my heart, it will tell me, that I am happy. My usual spirits have been lowered this morning, by hearing Mr. Boddington and Mr. Morgan mark the printed list of the jury. Every one almost is marked by them as unfit to be trusted; for almost every man is a rascal, and a contractor, and in the pay of government some way or another.

What hope is there then for these objects of ministerial rancour? Mr. B. objects even to his own uncle, whom he thinks *honest*, because he is so prejudiced an aristocrat, that he looks upon rigour, in such cases, to be justice only. What a pass are things come to, when even dissenters lick the hand that oppresses them! Hang these politics! how they haunt me. Would it not be better, think you, to hang the *framers* of them?

What is a woman made of, think you, that can *sue* a man for inconstancy? Truly of very coarse materials; yet I really believe Miss Mann's trial would have attracted me more than that for sedition. It would have given me so many new ideas. * * * * I wish my father could have remained with us, but he was very good to stay so long as he did; and I have the satisfaction of knowing he was happy while he did stay. He will tell you enough about Mrs. Inchbald, for he is quite smitten with her. Nay, I rather suspect he paid her a farewell visit. Pray tell him to write to me soon.

What a pity it is that The Cabinet is dangerous. I should have enjoyed it else so much. I admire what is already written. We are going to-night, as usual, to W. Morgan's, where I shall sing as usual, your husband's song. How I wish he was here to sing it instead of me. Farewell. Pray write to me soon.

A. A.

Although, as we have said, the letters describing what she saw at the Old Bailey were destroyed, she has fortunately preserved an anecdote of much interest relative to them, which was recalled to her recollection many years subsequently, on occasion of a visit she paid to Madame de Stael; she says:—

With this woman of excelling genius and winning manners, I had the pleasure of being acquainted in the year 1813; when, with her daughter, then of the age of sixteen, who afterwards became Duchess de Broglie, and Mr. Rocca, to whom she was then privately married, she was residing for some months in London, when exiled by Napoleon from France. One morning I went to call on her by appointment, accompanied by a friend of mine whom she wished to see, on some particular business. Scarcely had that business been concluded, when the servant announced Lord Erskine, who came in with books in his hands, and when he saw me he cried, "I am glad to see you here, for I want you to read something for me." He then gracefully bowed to Madame de Stael and presented the two books to her, containing, he said, his most celebrated speeches; and opening the first volume he turned to the first page, on which he had written a dedication to la Baronne de Stael in English, which he begged me to read to her. "No, no, not so," she exclaimed eagerly, taking the book from me, "I can read it myself." Accordingly she began; while I, myself an author, soon felt painful sympathy with poor Lord E.'s feelings; for the writing was, I dare say, difficult for her, a foreigner, to read; and the poor writer's smooth and elegant periods were, in a great measure, deprived of their charm, by their meaning being sometimes stammered out, and, possibly, not entirely understood. However, the lady was flattered with what she did understand, and Lord E. soon recovered the steadiness of his nerves: and taking up the second volume, which contained his speeches at the Old Bailey trials in the year 1794, he read some favourite passages to her, and finished by alluding to the evident dislike which the Lord Chief Baron Eyre, who presided at them, entertained for him, and how strongly he proved it during the trial of Horne Tooke, who was the second person tried for his life, and was (like the first person, Thomas Hardy) entirely acquitted. He then related what had passed between himself and the Chief Justice, after the trial was over and the crowd dispersed, and which I, who was present, well remembered having, by accident, overheard. Liking to be near the eloquent man and to hear him speak, I had contrived to get so near as to overhear what passed, and which I thought was too loud, not to be intended to be heard. The judge had, I saw, to repeat what he said; but at length he was answered in a manner which he little expected; for the indignant speaker replied, "My lord, I am willing to give your lordship such an answer as an aggrieved man of honour like myself is willing to give to the man who has repeatedly insulted him, and I am willing and ready to meet your lordship, at any time and place that you may choose to appoint." At this point of his story our hostess cried, "What! my lord, that was a challenge, *n'est ce pas?*" "Yes, ma'am." "Well, what did he say?" "Oh! nothing to the purpose; but I assure you I was irritated into saying what I did." "Yes, indeed,—I was behind you, Lord E. (said I,) and heard all that passed; and though such things were quite new to me, I felt sure what was said by you amounted to a challenge; but when I told the friends with whom I went home what had passed, they said I was a silly girl and that I was mistaken." He looked at me with some surprise, and, I fear, with a doubt of my veracity; but I could affirm to the truth of my assertion. I do not wonder, however, as he did not then know me personally, and was not conscious of my proximity, or that of any one else perhaps, that he was inclined to distrust my truthfulness; but it was a fact, that the circumstance and the words he related, were, I believe, witnessed and overheard by me alone; and a curious fact or coincidence it was, that this conversation, overheard by me in the year 1794, I should be present to hear related to the

Baronne de Stael by Lord E. himself in the year 1813. The circumstance and the words he has published at the end of the trial of Horne Tooke; and I could, with a safe conscience, *underwrite* all that he there relates. I fear that he really believed I was romancing, or he would have named this odd corroboration of his conduct, which no doubt he thought the noble daring of a man of worldly honour.

Among Mrs. Opie's loose papers was one written within a short time of her death, containing some introductory remarks to a reminiscence she purposed to write of this eventful period. It begins—

> "'Tis pleasant from the loophole of retreat
> To look on such a world,"

wrote Cowper: but these words do not exactly express my present feelings; for from my loophole of retreat I am looking with pleasure, *not* on the world as it is, but on the world as it was.

The occurrences of the year 1794 have lately been pressing with such power on my remembrance, demanding from me a decided confession that it was the most interesting period of my long life, (or nearly such,) that I am inclined to give an account of what made it so, and acknowledge that it was the opportunity unexpectedly afforded me of attending the trials of Hardy, Horne Tooke, and Thelwall, at the Old Bailey, for High Treason. What a prospect of entertainment was opening before me when (while on a visit at Southgate, near London) I heard that at these approaching trials, to which I hoped to obtain admission, I should not only hear the first pleaders at the bar, but behold, and probably hear examined, the first magnates of the land; and on the event depended, not a *nisi prius* cause, or one of petty larceny, but interests of a public nature, and most nearly affecting the safety and prosperity of the nation; aye, and much personally interesting to myself; as I knew, in the secret of my heart, that my own prospects for life might probably be changed and darkened by the result. To such a height had party-spirit reached on both sides, in my native city and elsewhere, that even innocent men were accused of treasonable intentions and practices, who *talked*, when excited by contradiction, the fearful things they would never have thought of acting; and I had reason to believe that if the "felons" about to be tried should not be "acquitted felons," certain friends of mine would have emigrated to America, and my beloved father would have been induced to accompany them!

This was, indeed, an alarming idea to me, who was only beginning to taste the pleasures of London society, and who could still say, in spite of the excitement of party feeling, and my unity of opinion with the liberals of that day, "England! with all thy faults I love thee still;" and when, on the 28th of the 10th mo., the trial of Thomas Hardy began at the Sessions-house in the Old Bailey, existence acquired, in my eyes, a new but painful interest; and, with the pleasing anticipations of the unexpected enjoyment awaiting me, were mingled some apparently well-founded fears of evil to come. How vividly do I often now, in my lone and lonely portion, live over the excitements of those far distant days, in the many, many evening hours, which I pass not unwillingly alone.

"Alone! if 'tis to be alone, when mem'ry's spells are cast
To summon phantoms from the dead, and voices from the past,
Long woven in the tangled web of the mysterious brain,
Till time and space are things of naught, and all is ours again." *

Yes! how often (as I said) do I recall with all these alternate emotions of pain and pleasure, of disappointment and fruition, the last days of October, and the first five days of November, 1794! * * *

Here the manuscript breaks off.

* From a charming Poem called the Desert Dream, written by Anna Savage, and published in the Monthly Magazine for April, 1847.—A. O.

CHAPTER IV.

FRENCH EMIGRANTS; LETTER TO MRS. TAYLOR; LETTER OF THE DUKE D'AIGUILLON; VISIT TO LONDON, AND LETTER FROM THENCE; LONDON AGAIN; LETTER FROM MRS. WOLLSTONECROFT; FIRST INTRODUCTION TO MR. OPIE; MR. OPIE'S EARLY HISTORY; RETURN TO NORWICH; PREPARATIONS FOR MARRIAGE.

The sufferings endured by the upper and proscribed classes in France during the time of the French Revolution, obliged (as is well known) multitudes of them to take refuge in this country; and, in the year 1797, London and its suburbs alone were found, by an official return, to contain seven thousand and forty-one *Aliens.* Many of these were subjected to the extremes of want and misery; their condition exciting the compassion, as well as the indignation, of the humane. Amongst them were not a few men of high standing and repute, who were received into society, and found friends among the wealthier classes of the community. It was just at this period, that the celebrated Count de Lally Tolendal, published his "Defence of the French Emigrants;" a work well known all over Europe, as soon as it was published. To this gentleman Mrs. Opie addressed a "Quatrain," on reading his "Defence of his Father," which subsequently appeared among her published poems. This favour he acknowledged, in a letter dated from Cossey, (near Norwich,) accompanied by a

French poem of one hundred lines, which she preserved among her papers. It was very natural that she, whose sympathies were ever so keenly alive to the sorrows of others, should become warmly interested on behalf of these unhappy exiles; and she appears to have formed many acquaintances among them, during the time she spent in London. The following letter to Mrs. Taylor gives a lively narrative of one of the *soirées*, at which she met a party of the emigrants, among whom was the Duc d'Aiguillon; and we have added a letter from him, received by her the following year, on the cover of which she has written, "From the Duke d'Aiguillon, the ex-minister; one of the second importation of emigrants."

TO MRS. TAYLOR.

Sunday Morning, 1795.

It is so long, my dear friend, since I conversed with you, even through the imperfect medium of a letter, that I joyfully take advantage of the first favourable opportunity for writing you a long epistle, in hopes that I may rouse you to pay me in coin. Besides you are in a state of widowhood and require all the attention possible to console you for so forlorn a condition! What shall I tell you by way of anecdote? My father has read you, perhaps, my account of Charles Lameth; take some more particulars respecting that extraordinary man. You may suppose that I felt a new and pleasing sensation while contemplating him, as I knew him to be one of the actors in the first revolution; and as soon as my silence yielded to my curiosity, I began questioning him concerning some of the patriotic leaders. Amongst others I inquired what he thought of Legendre? He says Legendre, though misled, has some good points in his character, and is not a bad man; he then gave us the following instance of his determined spirit and resolution; "I was, at the time I mention," said Lameth, "president of the National Convention, and had been supping at your house, (turning to the Duc d'Aiguillon,) when, at midnight, my servant came to me, and said, 'A man muffled up is in a hackney coach at the door, and wants to see you.' 'Tell him to come in.' 'He refuses.' 'Go and ask his name,' He did so, and returned saying, 'His name is Legendre.' Hearing this, I went into the coach to him, and demanded his business. 'I come to you,' replied he, 'as president of the National Convention; I hear that an accusation is bringing forward against me, and as I shrink not from the charge, I came to surrender myself, and save you the trouble—here I am, guillotine me, if you will, I am firm and steady.' I endeavoured to convince him the decree of accusation might be repealed, and that all that was necessary was his concealment till the danger was gone by. 'Conceal me then in your house, my own is not safe,' cried he; but I convinced him that mine was too public. However, I sent to a friend in whom I could confide, who concealed Legendre in his, till the decree was annulled."

"Oh!" said Sam. Rogers to me, some time after, "I do not like the fellow's looks, I would not have gone muffled up to his house, at midnight, and have given him leave to kill me, for fear he should have taken me at my word!" This led Mr. Rogers to give his opinion of the three *émigrés* then with us, and of Duport, another of considerable talents, who was prevented coming; and he defined them thus:—"Though I have often entertained Lameth at my house, I should expect he would treat me insolently, and make me feel the distance between us, even if he admitted me to his table. The Marquis would grin at me, and pass on; the Duc would be glad to see me, and do me immediately all the service and civility in his power; but Duport would open his arms to me!" Lameth entertained the *gentlemen* very much, by his account of the fascinating Madame de Condorcet, and of her method of acquiring votes for the members whom she wished returned. These favoured men were called "the majority of Madame de Condorcet;" and, on my innocently asking what it meant, I saw enough, from the laugh I excited, and L's mysterious manner of answering, to know that the majority of Madame de Condorcet meant no good. "Does she live still?" said I; "Oh, yes," cried the Duc, "she is in no danger; all parties will be her friend; she is so pretty and so accommodating; and I'm sure she 'll be the *friend of all parties.*" The Marquis, who was the intimate friend of the Duc de Rouchefoucault, says, though he brought Condorcet forward, fed him, lodged him, and married him, Condorcet was *justly* suspected of being privy to his assassination. When Lameth was forced to fly, as he was denounced in the Jacobin Club, and orders given for his detention, he sent to desire such a portmanteau to be forwarded directly to him; having received it, and wanting some of the money and papers which it contained, he opened it as soon as he was out of France, and found, to his utter surprise and dismay, that the wrong portmanteau had been sent, and instead of money, that it contained his wife's child-bed linen! "Et les voilà encore, mesdames! (continua-t-il) car, en vérité, je n'ai pas eu *encore* occasion d'en faire usage." * *

à Hambourg, chez Mr. Fortune de la Vigne,
Negociant, ce 6 février, 1796.

TO MISS AMELIA ALDERSON, MR. ALDERSON'S, NORWICH.

MADEMOISELLE,

Daignez agréer l'assurance bien sincère, de la vive reconnaissance que m'inspire le marque aimable, de souvenir et d'intérêt, que vous avez bien voulu me donner. Je vous dois mille remerciemens, et de la lettre donc vous avez chargé Mr. le Chevalier de Bercley, et de m'avoir procuré le plaisir de le connaitre. Je l'ai vu assez pour que le peu de séjour qu'il a fait ici, m'ai laissé beaucoup de regrets. J'ai mille excuses à vous faire d'avoir autant tardé à vous répondre; mais j'ai été, pendant plus de quinze jours, tellement malade d'un rhume mêlé de fievre, et de goutte (ma constante ennemie) que j'étois dans l'impossibilité absolue d'ecrire un seul mot. Croyez, je vous prie, Mademoiselle, qu'il a fallu une raison aussi forte, pour m'empêcher de vous exprimer plutot toute ma gratitude, et le plaisir que j'ai, d'être assuré par vous, que je ne partage pas le sort ordinaire aux absens.

Recevez mes remerciemens des jolis airs que vous m'avez envoyés. Je les conserverai avec soin, et ne les donnerai quoique vous en disiez, à personne. Ils ont renouvellé mes regrets, en me rappellant ces tendres et jolies romances que vous chantiez avec l'expression de la musique et toute celle du sentiment, ce qui vaut bien mieux.

Je vous rends graces, Mademoiselle, des souhaits, vraiment pleins de bonté que vous faites en ma faveur. Je crains qu'ils ne soyent encore longtems à s'accomplir; cependant, je n'en suis pas moins sensible à votre obligeance. Mais vous! que desirer pour votre bonheur? La nature n'a-t-elle pas pourvu à tout, en vous donnant les qualités du cœur, celles de l'esprit, des graces, des talents? Je me bornerai donc à souhaiter que vous soyez toujours aussi heureuse que vous meritez de l'être, et c'est tout dire.

Il me paroit que vous avez à Norwich une Societé de Français assez agréable. Je ne connois point ceux que vous me nommez; mais j'envie leur sort, d'être aupres de vous, et de vous plaire,—à propos!—que peut fonder ce reproche d'aristocratie fait à mon ami, M. de L? Voilà, vraisemblablement, la première fois qu'il en est accusé. Cela est assez plaisant, et le singularité du fait, l'empêche, en verité, d'être aussi affligé qu'il le seroit, d'être jugé par vous aussi sévèrement.

Adieu, Mademoiselle. Adieu! Croyez que je regarderois comme un vrai bonheur d'être instruit quelquefois de ce qui peut vous intéresser. Veuillez bien agréer l'hommage du tendre respect et de l'attachement sincère, que je vous ai voué.

D'AIGUILLON.

Miss Alderson's visit in London seems to have been protracted to a period of some months; a season full of constant occupation and variety, passed amidst a gay round of visits and amusements, which, however, did not merely serve the end of the fleeting hour's enjoyment, but in which she studied human nature, and became acquainted with the world and its ways, to good practical purpose. There are two other letters to her friend, of this period, from which we make the following extracts:—

* * * Yesterday morning I had the unexpected pleasure of a visit from Mr. Wrangham. He did not stay long, but he has promised to call again, and is as gentle, elegant, and interesting as ever; he gained the Seatonian prize for a poem this year, which is published, and he has promised to send me one. I am much pleased with Mr. W. Taylor's Ode to the ship that conveys Gerald. Though he would not favour me with a copy of the elegant sonnet he sent me on the morning of my departure, my memory retains every word of it; and I catch myself repeating the first and last line, whenever home and its varied associations crowd on my mind. Month follows month in this *wilderness* of pleasure, if I may call it so, where fruits and flowers dispute pre-eminence with weeds; and yet I cannot say, "I'll stay here no longer," till, as I said before, my natal soil and its comforts press on my mind, and I exclaim, "Ah! not for ever quaff at pleasure's distant fount!" To-morrow I am going to enjoy "the feast of reason and the flow of soul," with Mrs. Barbauld and Dr. Geddes, at Mrs. Howard's. I wish I could *wish* you there. Godwin drank tea and supt here last night; a leave-taking visit, as he goes to-morrow to spend a fortnight at Dr. Parr's. It would have entertained you highly to have seen him bid me farewell. He wished to salute me, but his courage failed him. "While oft he looked back, and was loth to depart." "Will you give

me nothing to keep for your sake, and console me during my absence," murmured out the philosopher, "not even your slipper? I had it in my possession once, and need not have returned it!" This was true; my shoe had come off, and he had put it in his pocket for some time. You have no idea how gallant he is become; but indeed he is much more amiable than ever he was. Mrs. Inchbald says, the report of the world is, that Mr. Holcroft is in love with her, *she* with Mr. Godwin, Mr. Godwin with *me*, and I am in love with Mr. Holcroft! A pretty story indeed! This report Godwin brings to me, and he says Mrs. I. always tells him that when she praises *him*, I praise Holcroft. This is not fair in Mrs. I. She appears to me jealous of G.'s attention to me, so she makes him believe I prefer H. to him. She often says to me, "Now you are come, Mr. Godwin does not come near me." Is not this very womanish? We had a most delightful conversation last night. A dispute on the merits of different poets,—Mr. G. abusing Collins, I defending him,—G. setting Gray above him, and I putting him below him; but we agreed about Churchill, who was one of my *flames*. How idle I am! I cannot write, and I read but little, but I shall mend. Farewell! Mr. Batty and I both wear you "in our heart's core," and so would Mrs. B, if she knew you. I love and admire them more every day. Love to the Barnards; my love to the Smiths. Dear love and good wishes to the boys and girls.

Yours, ———

Thursday.

My dear Mrs. Taylor,

* * * * I flatter myself with the idea that you hear most of my letters to my father; consequently that you know my movements, and can judge of the probable quantity of enjoyment I experience. I am now about to enjoy pleasant society in a pleasant country, one of the first luxuries at this season of the year; but still I sigh for home, that is, I sigh for a day or two of confidential intercourse

with you and others, and to wash off the dirt of London in the sea of Cromer; to write poetry on the shore, to live over again every scene there that memory loves (and never did she love them so dearly as now;) and, having rioted in all that my awakened fancy can give, return to Norwich, and endeavour to make one of my plays, at least, fit to be offered to one of the managers of the winter theatres. Such is my plan; and in it I live, move, and have my being.

Bless me! what a busy place Norwich has been, and I not in it! but then I heard H. Tooke and Fox speak, and that's something. To be sure I had rather have heard Buonaparte address his soldiers; but as pleasure *delayed* is not pleasure *lost*, I may still hope to hear *him* when the *bonnet rouge* has taken place of the tiara, and a switch from the tree of liberty dangles from that hand which formerly wielded the crozier. But alas! this is no laughing matter,—or rather let us laugh while we can, for I believe an hour to be approaching when *salut et fraternité* will be the watchwords for civil slaughter throughout Europe; and the meridian glory of the sun of Liberty, in France, will light us to courting the past dangers and horrors of the republic, in hopes of obtaining her present power and greatness. It will be an awful time; may I meet it with fortitude! But I shrink, and shrink *only*, from the idea of ties dear to my heart, which it will for ever break; of the friendships I must forego; of the dangers of those I love; and of friends equally dear to me, meeting in the field of strife opposed in mortal combat! I feel heart-sick at such possibilities; yet which amongst us dare assert that such possibilities may not, ere long, be probable?

Mrs. Imlay tells me, no words can describe the feelings which the scenes she witnessed in France gave birth to continually—it was a sort of indefinite terror. She was sitting alone, when Imlay came in and said, "I suppose you have not heard the sad news of to-day?" "What is it? is Brissot guillotined?" "Not only Brissot, but the *one-and-twenty* are." Amongst them she immediately could conjure up the faces of some lately endeared acquaintances, and before she was conscious of the effect of the picture, she sunk lifeless on the floor: and Mrs. Imlay is not a fine lady—if any mind could be unmoved at such things hers would; but a series of horrors must have a very weakening tendency. When we meet I shall have much to tell you. Yesterday I had a letter from Catherine; she is well and happy, she says; but we'll read her letter together.

Farewell! Mrs. Barbauld is more charming than ever; both he and she speak of you as you deserve. Love to Mrs. Beecroft, and Fanny Smith, and all the circle of home. * * *

In the spring of 1797 we find her again in town, accompanying her friend Mrs. Inchbald on the 17th April, to Westminster, to hear a sermon from Bishop Horsley. Again she extended her visit to several months; and a most eventful time it proved to be in her history, as will be gathered from her communications to Mrs. Taylor. Some unexpected changes too had occurred amongst her acquaintances, since she left them, twelve or fourteen months before. The philosophic Godwin had justified her opinion of him, and proved that his heart was not so wise as his head; he had married Mrs. Wollstonecroft, a strange incomprehensible woman, whose unhappy existence terminated shortly after this marriage. A letter from her to Miss Alderson, seems to have been written at this time, and as it is of painful interest, and curious in more respects than one, we subjoin it:—

MY DEAR GIRL,

Endeavouring, through embarrassment, to turn the conversation from myself last night, I insensibly became too severe in my strictures on the vanity of a certain lady, and my heart smote me when I raised a laugh at her expense. Pray forget it. I have now to tell you that I am very sorry I prevented you from engaging a box for Mrs. Inchbald, whose conduct, I think, has been very rude. She wrote to Mr. Godwin to-day, saying, that, taking it for granted he had forgotten it, she had spoken to another person. "She would not do so the next time he was married." Nonsense! I have now to request you to set the matter right. Mrs. Inchbald may still get a box; I beg her pardon for misunderstanding the business, but Mr. G. led me into the error, or I will go to the pit. To have done with disagreeable subjects at once, let me allude to another. I shall be sorry to resign the acquaintance of Mrs. and Mr. F. Twiss, because I respect their characters, and feel grateful for their attention; but my conduct in life must be directed by my own judgment and moral principles: it is my wish that Mr. Godwin should visit and dine out as formerly, and I shall do the same; in short, I still mean to be independent, even to the cultivating sentiments and principles in my children's minds, (should I have more,) which he disavows. The wound my unsuspecting heart formerly received is not healed. I found my evenings solitary; and I wished, while fulfilling the duty of a mother, to have some person with similar pursuits, bound to me by affection; and beside, I earnestly desired to resign a name which seemed to disgrace me. Since I have been unfortunately the object of observation, I have had it in my power, more than once, to marry very advantageously; and of course, should have been courted by those, who at least cannot accuse me of acting an interested part, though I have not, by dazzling their eyes, rendered them blind to my faults. I am proud perhaps, conscious of my own purity and integrity; and many circumstances in my life have contributed to excite in my bosom an indignant contempt for the forms of a world I should have bade a long good night to, had I not been a mother. Condemned then, to toil my hour out, I wish to live as rationally as I can; had fortune or splendor been my aim in life, they have been within my reach, would I have paid the price. Well, enough of the subject; I do not wish to resume it. Good night! God bless you.

MARY WOLLSTONECROFT,
femme GODWIN.

Tuesday Night.

From this letter, it is cheering to turn to the bright joyous spirit, evinced in the following, which contains the first announcement of the important event to which we alluded just now.

TO MRS. TAYLOR.

Tuesday, 1797.

Why have I not written to you? it is a question I cannot answer; you must answer it yourself, but attribute my silence, *not* to any diminution of affection for you * * * * Believe me, I still hear the kind fears you expressed for me when we parted, and still see the flattering tears that you shed when you bade me adieu. Indeed, I shall never forget them. I had resolved to write to you as soon as ever I had seen Richard, but it was a resolution made to be broken; like many others in this busy scene. Had I written to you as soon as I left, of all those whom I have heard talk of and praise you as you deserve, I should have ruined you in postage. Poor Mr. C. is desperately in love with you, by his own confession, and his wife admires his taste. Mr. Godwin was much gratified by your letter, and he avowed that it made him love you better than he did before, and Mrs. Godwin was not surprised at it; by the bye, he never told me whether you congratulated him on his marriage or not; but now I remember, it was written before that wonder-creating event was known. Heigho! what charming things would sublime theories be, if one could make one's practice keep up with them; but I am convinced it is impossible, and am resolved to make the best of every-day nature.

I shall have much to tell you in a *tête à tête*, of the Godwins, &c.—so much that a letter could not contain or do it justice; but this will be *entre nous;* I love to make observations on extraordinary characters; but not to mention those observations if they be not favourable.

"Well! a whole page, and not a word yet of the state of her heart; the subject most interesting to me"—methinks I hear you exclaim; patience, friend, it will come soon, but not go away soon, were I to analyze it, and give it you in detail. Suffice, that it is in the most comical state possible; but I am not unhappy, on the contrary, I enjoy everything; and if my head be not turned by the large draughts which my vanity is daily quaffing, I shall return to Norwich much happier than I left it. Mr. Opie, has (but *mum*) been my declared lover, almost ever since I came. I was ingenuous with him upon principle, and I told him my situation, and the state of my heart. He said he should still persist, and would risk all consequences to his own peace, and so he did and does; and I have not resolution to forbid his visits. Is not this abominable? Nay more, were I not certain my father would disapprove such, or indeed *any* connexion for me, there are moments, when, ambitious of being a wife and mother, and of securing to myself a companion for life, capable of entering into all my pursuits, and of amusing me by his,—I could almost resolve to break all fetters, and relinquish too, the wide, and often aristocratic circle, in which I now move, and become the wife of a man, whose genius has raised him from obscurity, into fame and comparative affluence; but indeed my mind is on the pinnacle of its health when I thus feel; and on a pinnacle one can't remain long! But I had forgotten to tell you the attraction Mr. O. held out, that staggered me beyond anything else; it was that, if I were averse to leaving my father, he would joyfully consent to his living with us. What a temptation to me, who am every moment sensible, that the claims of my father will always be, with me, superior to any charms that a lover can hold out! Often do I rationally and soberly state to

Opie the reasons that might urge me to marry him, in time, and the reasons why I never could be happy with him, nor he with me; but it always ends in his persisting in his suit, and protesting his willingness to wait for my decision; even while I am seriously rejecting him, and telling him I *have* decided. * * * Mr. Holcroft too, has had a mind to me, but he has no chance. May I trouble you to tell my father that, while I was out yesterday, Hamilton called, and left a note, simply saying, "Richardson says he means to *call* on you, I have seen him this morning." Before I seal this letter I hope to receive my farce from him; I will put my letter by till the boy returns from R. I have been capering about the room for joy, at having gotten my farce back! now idleness adieu, when Dicky and I have held sweet converse together! * * *

The first time Mr. Opie saw his future wife, was at an evening party, at the house of one of her early friends; among the guests assembled, were Mr. Opie, and a family, personally known to the writer of these Memoirs. Some of those present were rather eagerly expecting the arrival of Miss Alderson; but the evening was wearing away, and still she did not appear; at length the door was flung open, and she entered, bright and smiling, dressed in a robe of blue, her neck and arms bare; and on her head a small bonnet, placed in somewhat coquettish style, sideways, and surmounted by a plume of three white feathers. Her beautiful hair hung in rich waving tresses over her shoulders; her face was kindling with pleasure at sight of her old friends; and her whole appearance was animated and glowing. At the time she came in, Opie was sitting on a sofa, beside Mr. F., who had been saying, from time to time, "Amelia is coming;

Amelia will surely come: why is she not here?" and whose eyes were turned in her direction. He was interrupted by his companion eagerly exclaiming "Who is that? Who is that?" and hastily rising, he pressed forward, to be introduced to the fair object whose sudden appearance had so impressed him. He was evidently smitten; charmed, at first sight, and, as she says, "almost from my first arrival Mr. Opie became my avowed lover."

It will not be necessary for us to give more than a short reference to Mr. Opie's career before he became acquainted with Amelia Alderson. He was born of poor and respectable parents, and early showed a remarkable strength of understanding and indomitable perseverance. His father would fain have brought him up to his own business, (that of a carpenter,) but to this the boy evinced a most decided disinclination, and even so early as his 10th year the bent of his talents was determined. In vain his father endeavoured to discourage his attempts at drawing; he persisted in covering the walls of their house with pictures of his family, his companions, and favourite animals. Accident brought him to the knowledge of Dr. Walcot, (the Peter Pindar of well-known celebrity;) who assisted and recommended him, and eventually introduced him, in his 20th year, to the notice of the artistic world in London; there he was hailed as a wonder and a genius, and immediately surrounded and employed by amateurs and many of the nobility. The street in which he lived was so crowded with carriages that, as he jokingly observed, he thought he should have to plant a cannon at his door to keep the multitude off! This popularity, however, did not last long; although he was really improving by diligent practice, and advancing towards excellence, the world began to cool upon him when he ceased to be a novelty; and soon neglected one it had perhaps at first somewhat overvalued. By a wise economy he had, even at this time, secured a considerable sum of money; and with praiseworthy diligence cultivated his mind, and in some degree supplied his early want of education.

About this time, he unhappily married a woman, wholly unworthy of him, who is reported to have possessed some property. Before long he found himself compelled to procure a divorce from her. Probably this domestic trouble had a serious effect upon his temper and manners. His address was naturally somewhat rugged and unpolished, especially before his second marriage; but those who knew him well, found that his disposition was the very reverse of unfeeling or vindictive. Mrs. Inchbald says, "the total absence of artificial manners was the most remarkable characteristic, and at the same time the adornment and the deformity of Mr. Opie." At the time when he paid his addresses to Miss Alderson he was in his 36th year. Mr. Allen Cunningham, in the pleasing biography he has given of him in his "Lives of the Painters," says, "in person Opie looked like an inspired peasant."

We have no further record, reporting how he fared in his courtship; she vowed that his chances of success were but one to a thousand! But the indomitable one persevered. He knew *his* mind, and persuaded her at length, that he had read her heart. So she went home again to Norwich, to think of the future, and prepare for it; one last short note heralded her approach; probably the last she ever addressed to her friend, bearing the signature, "A. Alderson." *

Englefield Green,
Friday, August 12th, 1797.

MY VERY DEAR FRIEND,

I cannot meet even the kindest glance of your eye, without having written a few lines, before our reunion. I must tell you, that of all the letters I have received from my friends, yours gave me the most pleasure, though I had not the grace to say so till now: when we meet I will tell you *why;* indeed I must put off a great many communications till that time. Suffice, that whatever you hear about me, you must disbelieve!

Here I am, on a high hill, wishing most fervently, though not warmly, for a fire, and in the middle of August too! Shall we, (I fear not,) have some hot evening walks? I shall want them by way of relaxation from my studies, (do not laugh.) Positively, I must set hard to work, as the theatre opens in September. Farewell! I must conclude, I

* For the benefit of our fair readers we subjoin a list found among her old letters, of what probably formed a part of the contents of her Trousseau.

Blue satin bonnet russe with eight blue feathers; nine small feathers and a feather edge; three blue round feathers and two blue Scotch caps; one striped gold gauze bonnet russe; four scollop'd edged caps, à la Marie Stuart; one bead cap; one tiara; two spencers, one white, one black.

2nd Box, No. 1. Two yards broad figured lace, for neck and wrists; buff satin slip; buff net gown; three muslin gowns and one skirt; three frilled handkerchiefs; one lace cap and two bands; a set of scarlet ribbon for the gown lined with blue; three lace frills; worked cambric gown and flounces; seven flat feathers and three curled ones, &c., &c., &c.

have been writing a long time; with love to your spouse and children, believe me most affectionately yours,

A. ALDERSON.

The time was approaching when she was to leave her father's house, and the home and friends of her youth, to become the wife of Mr. Opie. An ardent love letter, still in existence, tells with what intense desire he was awaiting her arrival; for it was arranged that she should go, accompanied by her father, to the house of one of their friends in London, and be married from thence; towards the close of this epistle he enters into some details respecting the preparations he was making, in his domestic arrangements, for the reception of his bride; and concludes:—

I am puzzled, dearest, to know whether you expect to hear from me to-morrow. If I think of anything particular I'll write; else not. To love thee much better than I did, is, I think, impossible; but my heart springs forward at the thought of thy near approach. God bless thee ever, my dearest love, and guard thee up safe to thy fond, anxious, devoted,

J. O.

CHAPTER V.

MARRIAGE; EARLY MÉNAGE; AUTHORSHIP; LAY ON PORTRAIT OF MRS. TWISS; LETTER TO MRS. TAYLOR; VISIT TO NORWICH; LETTER FROM MR. OPIE; MRS. OPIE TO MRS. TAYLOR; MR. OPIE'S MOTHER.

MR. AND MRS. OPIE were married in Marylebone church on the 8th of May, 1798.

In the Memoir prefixed to her husband's life she speaks with touching naiveté and feeling of the earlier years of their married life; "great economy and self denial were necessary," she says, "and were strictly observed by us at that time." The habits and tastes of Mr. Opie were, happily, very inexpensive, and so domestic in their nature, that he preferred spending his evenings at home to joining in society abroad; and liked nothing better, by way of relaxation after the labours of the day, than to spend the evening hours in converse with his wife, in reading with her books of amusement or instruction, in studying prints from the best ancient and modern masters, or in sketching designs for his pictures. His love of his profession was intense, and his unremitting industry in the pursuance of it drew from Mr. Northcote the observation, that while other artists painted to live, *he* lived to paint. He was incessantly engaged in his painting-room during the hours of day-light, and no society, however pleasant, could long detain him from it. It was indeed a passion to which the whole energies of his being were devoted. In one branch of his art he appears to have been much indebted to his wife, and in what way this was shewn will be best told in her own words:—

When Mr. Opie became again a husband, (she says,) he found it necessary, in order to procure indulgences for a wife whom he loved, to make himself popular as a portrait-painter, and in that productive and difficult branch of the art, female portraiture. He therefore turned his attention to those points he had long been in the habit of neglecting, and his pictures soon acquired a degree of grace and softness to which they had of late years been strangers. At the second exhibition after our marriage one of his fellow artists came up to him and complimented him on his female portraits, adding, "we never saw any thing like this in you before, Opie; this must be owing to your wife."

Her husband related with evident delight this pleasing compliment to her who had inspired his efforts. Her modesty did not permit her to speak of another mode in which she assisted to promote his interests; but her friend Mrs. Taylor has mentioned that "in her own house, where Mr. Opie's talents drew a constant succession of the learned, the gay, and the fashionable, she delighted all by the sweetness of her manners, and the unstudied and benevolent politeness with which she adapted herself to the taste of each individual."

Happy it was for them both, that Mr. Opie was disposed to aid and encourage his wife in her favourite tastes, and the exercise of her literary talent. She observes:—

Knowing at the time of our marriage that my most favourite amusement was writing, he did not check my ambition to become an author; on the contrary he encouraged it, and our only quarrel on the subject was not that I wrote so much, but that I did not write more and better. Idleness was the fault that he was most violent against in both sexes; and I shall ever regret those habits of indolence which made me neglect to write while it was in my power to profit by his criticisms and advice, and when, by employing myself more regularly in that manner, I should have been sure to receive the proudest and dearest reward of woman, the approbation of a husband, at once the object of her respect and of her love.

Mr. Opie entertained a partiality for works of fiction, and not unfrequently indulged himself in reading a novel, even if it were not of the first class; and his wife remarks in defence of this taste:—

He was above the petty, yet common affectation of considering that sort of reading as beneath any persons but fools and women; and if his fondness for works of that description was a weakness, it was one which he had in common with Mr. Burke and Mr. Porson.

Encouraged by the sympathy and approval of the man to whom she had united her fortunes, she soon began to exert her powers with diligence, and ere long became (as she expresses it) "a candidate for the pleasures, the pangs, the rewards, and the penalties, of authorship."

In one respect, indeed, they were not congenial in

their tastes; she ardently loved society, to which she had been so much accustomed, and in which her talents so peculiarly fitted her to appear to advantage. On the contrary, it was with difficulty that Mr. Opie could be induced to join a numerous and mixed assemblage. He preferred to spend an evening occasionally at the theatre, or rather at the opera; for he loved music, and had so quick an ear that he would remember accurately a tune that pleased him, after having heard it once. When he sought society, he preferred select dinner parties, where he could meet persons whose friendship he valued, and from whom he might hope to learn. With honourable pride his wife observes:—

> He was conscious that he aimed at no competition with the learned; while, with a manly simplicity, which neither feared contempt nor scorned applause, he has often, even in such company, made observations, originating in the native treasures of his own mind, which learning could not teach, and which learning alone could not enable the possessor to appreciate.

In the year after her marriage Mrs. Opie wrote a Lay "addressed to Mr. Opie on his having painted for me the picture of Mrs. Twiss;" it was published the same year, in the 1st volume of "The Annual Anthology," and was (she tells us) one of her earliest; the concluding lines contain a pleasing tribute of affection to her husband:—

> Within my breast contending feelings rise,
> While this lov'd semblance fascinates my eyes;
> Now pleas'd, I mark the painter's skilful line,
> Now joy, because the skill I mark, was thine;

And while I prize the gift by thee bestow'd,
My heart proclaims I'm of the giver proud,
Thus pride and friendship war with equal strife,
And now the friend exults, and now the wife.

A. O. 1799.

This picture was in her possession at the time of her death; it is "Portrait the Second" in her "Lays for the Dead," which commences:—

The gift of love
That speaking picture was—of bridal love,
Now both the painter and his subject are
Where pictures come not. * * *

Mr. Opie's ardour in the pursuit of his profession made him also unwilling to leave his home, even for a short change of scene and relaxation. In the frequent visits paid to Norwich by his wife, it was with difficulty she could prevail on him to accompany her; and whenever he was induced to do so, she says she had no chance of detaining him there, unless he found business awaiting him. In the autumn after their marriage, she turned her steps towards her early home, and rejoiced in greeting once more her father and the friends of her youth. After her return to London, we find her again resuming her pen to write to Mrs. Taylor: this letter bears date—

27th of January, 1800.

My dear Friend,

* * * * John, I suppose, informed you he called on us; he promised to come and dine with us, but has not been since; and as I have been tied by the foot ever since the day after Christmas day, from having worn a tight bound shoe, which made a hole in my heel, I do not regret

his false-heartedness, as when he does come we are to go church and meeting hunting. * * * * * *Apropôs*, I was very sorry to hear of your husband's severe return of gout, but as he had a long respite before, I hope he will again. Severe illness has (I often think) on the frame, the same effect that a severe storm has on the atmosphere. I myself am much better in every respect, since my late indisposition, than I was before; and the mind is never perhaps so serene and tranquil, as when one is recovering from sickness. I enjoyed my confinement, as I was not, like your good man, in pain. My husband was so kind as to sit with me every evening, and even to introduce his company to my bedside. No less than three beaux had the honour of a *sitting* in my chamber. Quite Parisian you see, but I dare not own this to some women. I have led a most happy and delightful life since my return, and in the whole two months have not been out more than four times; so spouse and I had no squabbles about visiting, and that is the only thing we ever quarrel about. If I would stay at home for ever, I believe he would be merry from morning to night; and be a lover more than a husband! He had a mind to accompany me to an assembly in Nottingham place, but Mrs. Sharpe (a most amiable woman) frightened him, by declaring he should dance with her, if he did.

What the friendships of dissipated women are, Mrs. ——— going to a ball, while poor H. T. was dying, sufficiently proves. I remember with satisfaction that I saw her, and shook hands with her at the November ball. Indeed she had a *heart;* and I can't help recollecting that when I had the scarlet fever she called on me every day, regardless of danger, and sat at the foot of my bed. Besides, she was the friend of twenty years, and the companion of my childhood, and I feel the older I grow, the more tenderly I cling to the scenes, and recollections, and companions, of my early hours. When I now look at Mr. Bruckner's black cap, my memory gets astride on the tassel of it, and off she gallops at a very pleasant rate; wooden desks, green bags, blotted books, inked hands, faces, and gowns, rise in array before me. I see Mrs. Beecroft (Miss Dixon I should say) with her plump good-humoured face, laughing till she loses her eyes, and shakes the whole form; but I must own, the most welcome objects that the hoofs of memory's hobby-horse kick up, are the great B.'s, or bons, on my exercises! I do not choose to remember how often I was marked for being *idle.* * * So you have had riots. I am glad they are over. Mrs. Adair called on me this morning, and she tells me that Charles Harvey was terribly alarmed after he had committed Col. Montgomery. A fine idea this gives one of the state of a town, where a man is alarmed at having done his duty!

I am very much afraid my spouse will not live long; he has gotten a fit of tidyness on him; and yesterday evening and this evening, he has employed himself in putting his painting-room to rights. This confirms what I said to him the other day; that almost every man was *beau* and sloven, at some time of his life. Charles Fox once wore *pink heels;* now he has an unpowdered crop. And I expect that as my husband has been a sloven hitherto, he will be a *beau* in future; for he is so pleased with his handyworks, and capers about, and says, "look there! how neat! and how prettily I have disposed the things! Did you ever see the like?" Certainly I never did, where he was, before. Oh! he will certainly be a *beau* in time. Past ten o'clock! I must now say farewell; but let me own that I missed you terribly when I was ill. I have no *female* friend and neighbour; and men are not the thing on such occasions. Besides, you, on *all* occasions, would be the female neighbour I should choose. Love to your spouse. Write soon, and God bless you.

In the autumn of 1800 she again visited Norwich, accompanied by her husband; and on this occasion Mr. Opie painted the portrait of Dr. Sayers, an engraving from which is prefixed to the Life of that gentleman by Mr. W. Taylor; who says, "Dr. Sayers conversed much with Mr. O. on art, and listened to his native strength of talent and originality of judgment, and has happily applied to him a Greek distich in his Essay on Beauty."

Mr. Opie seems to have returned to London after completing this picture, leaving his wife to spend some longer period with her father. His patience, however, became exhausted before she felt disposed to return to him, and he remonstrated with her in a half lover-like strain of complaint.

My dearest life, (he writes,) I cannot be sorry that you do not stay longer; though, as I said, on your father's account, I would consent to it. Pray love forgive me, and make yourself easy, for I did not suspect, till my last letter was gone, that it might be too strong; I had been counting almost the hours till your arrival for some time, and have been unwell and unable to sleep these last three weeks, so that I could not make up my mind to the disappointment. As to coming down again, I cannot think of it; for though I could, perhaps, better spare the time at present from painting, than I could at any part of last month, I find I must now go hard to work to finish my lectures, as the law says they must be delivered the second year after the election, and though they have never acted on this law, yet there are many, perhaps, who would be glad to put it in force in the present instance. I had almost given way to the suggestions of idleness, and determined to put them off till another year; but since I have been acquainted with the above-mentioned regulation, I have shut myself up in the evenings, and, I doubt not, shall be ready with three or four of them at least. We had a thin general meeting on Monday last, and elected Calcot an associate of the R.A. Lawrence and Hoppner attended. Thompson was also there, and we were very sociable; but he has not called, nor was there any notice taken, on either side, of our long separation. Pray, love, be easy, and as (I suppose) you will not stay; come up as soon as possible, for I long to see you as much as ever I did in my life.

A very short time elapsed after her return before we find her writing again to Mrs. Taylor.

12th December, 1800.

* * * * Are you not very much obliged to me, my dear friend? I am good for nothing to-day, so I am going to write to you! But one ventures to show one's person in *dishabille* at a friend's fireside, and why not one's mind? and so I'm resolved, though my mind is not just now smart enough for Parnassus, to exhibit it at St. George's. Here's weather! But you Norwich people can't, even from recollection, I think, conceive half the horror of a London fog. At present my husband's mind is more affected by it than my health (for it is a terrible time for a painter). I hope I shall not suffer this winter as I did last; on the contrary, I continue to grow fat, and have an excellent appetite for everything but breakfast; and alas! I still "sigh and lament me in vain" for Mrs. Lessy's hot half-baked cakes. Fye upon her! she has made me so dainty. My visit to Harleston was a very satisfactory one; it seemed the burial of unpleasant feelings, and the resurrection of amiable ones. I left Eliza Merrick a *plump* image of health and content, and I found Betsey Fry yester-evening at her own house a *lean* image of the same. How women vary! I am surprised to see the leanness of the one, and the fatness of the other; formerly the lean one was fat, and now the fat one is lean; but now she is so very comfortably settled, no doubt she will soon grow fat again. In all Quaker houses there is a most comfortable appearance of neatness, comfort, and affluence. Betsey Fry is settled down with everything requisite to domestic happiness. Mr. Fry pleases me very much.

Richard and I have frequent meetings now. On Sunday he is to breakfast with me, squire me to the Catholic chapel in King Street, where French Bishops (and sometimes the Archbishop of Narbonne) officiate, and then eat his beef with us.

To-morrow, if Anne Plumptre returns, I shall go with her into the pit of Drury lane to see a new tragedy, the author nameless to me, (though known to others I find,) and so I wish him to continue; for I should like to form of the piece, for the first time in my life, an unprejudiced judgment. Mrs. Siddons, indeed, told me not to go, because the play was stupid; but I have since recollected, to counteract her influence, that Kemble says she knows nothing about a play. So I flatter myself I am still unprejudiced.

I shall have left Norwich a month only next Sunday, and it seems to me three, at least, so much have I done and seen since my return. Mr. Opie, too, has been constantly employed. The T.s will be here in a month; that is a great joy to me. I purposely avoid saying anything of my evening at Mrs. Siddons' on Tuesday evening last, as I expect to fill my letter to my father with it to-morrow.

I am uneasy about Mr. Opie's mother. She has again taken to her bed; and I fear the long struggle she had with death last winter, though she overcame him, will have weakened her too much to make it possible for her to endure another—and I did so ardently wish to see her! A committee of Academicians is to meet every Saturday till means are found to execute Mr. Opie's plan for a Naval Pantheon; and this looks well. Just room for love to your circle, and my name,

A. Opie.

The fear expressed in this letter was, happily, not realized; Mr. Opie's mother survived till the spring of 1805, when she died at the advanced age of ninety-two. To this parent he was most tenderly attached, and neither time nor the pressure of business, diminished his filial devotion to her. He delighted to dwell upon her early tenderness, her careful attention to his childish wants, and the encouragement which she afforded to his first attempts in the art he loved; his eye would glisten and his face kindle with affection when he spoke of her; and no sooner was it in his power to assist her, than he rejoiced in affording her the means of comfort and independence.

How cordially could his wife sympathize with him in this fervent attachment; she, who was, throughout life, so sensitively alive to the claims of relationship, even in the remotest degrees, and whose whole being was devoted with tenderest love to her parents while living, and to their memory when dead! She appears to have been permitted the gratification of her wish to see her husband's mother, and "I believe (she says) that scarcely any one who knew her would have thought this description of her an exaggerated one."

CHAPTER VI.

"THE FATHER AND DAUGHTER;" CRITIQUE IN THE EDINBURGH; THREE LETTERS TO MRS. TAYLOR; VOLUME OF "POEMS;" "GO, YOUTH BELOVED;" LETTER FROM SIR J. MACKINTOSH; S. SMITH'S LECTURE.

In the year 1801, Mrs. Opie gave to the world the "Father and Daughter;" her first acknowledged publication. She had, before her marriage, published an anonymous novel, entitled "the Dangers of Coquetry," which does not appear to have attracted any attention. It will presently be seen that she refers to it in a letter to Mrs. Taylor, and it is included in the list of her works given in Watt's Bibliotheca Britannica, although without date, and placed in order after her earlier publications. The "Father and Daughter," in the first edition, was accompanied by a poem called "The Maid of Corinth," and some smaller pieces. It is unnecessary to do more than remind the reader of the warmth of approval with which this tale was received by the public.* In the preface to it Mrs. Opie modestly confesses her diffidence in appearing as an *avowed* author at the bar of public opinion, and disclaiming for her little book the ambitious title of a novel, says, "Its highest pretensions are to be a simple moral tale."

* It was afterwards taken as the groundwork for one of the most popular Italian operas of the time, the "Agnese" of Paer.

In the first volume of "The Edinburgh," there is a review of her poems,* in which the writer thus criticises the "Father and Daughter."

* * * "Mrs. Opie's mind is evidently more adapted to seize situation than to combine incidents. It can represent, with powerful expression, the solitary portrait, in every attitude of gentler grief; but it cannot bring together a connected assemblage of figures, and represent each in its most striking situation, so as to give, as it were, to the glance of a moment, the feelings and events of many years. When a series of reflections is to be brought by her to our view, they must all be of that immediate relation which allows them to be introduced at any part of the poem; or we shall probably see before us a multitude, rather than a group. * * * * She has, indeed, written a novel; and it is one which excites a very high interest: but the merit of that novel does not consist in its action, nor in any varied exhibition of character. Agnes, in all the sad changes of fortune, is still the same; and the action, if we except a very few *situations* of the highest excitement, is the common history of every seduction in romance. Indeed, we are almost tempted to believe that the scene in the wood occurred first to the casual conception of the author; and that, in the design of fully displaying it, all the other events of the novel were afterwards imagined."

The three following letters to Mrs. Taylor admit us behind the scenes, and allow us to see the palpitations of her heart.

Sunday Evening, 1801.

MY DEAR FRIEND,

The only paper I can find consists of two half sheets, *comme vous voyez*. But no matter. I will not, for appearance' sake, baulk my inclination to write to you.

* Written by Dr. Brown.

* * * I am very sorry that Mrs. Jordan and the Duke of Clarence have hitherto managed their matters so ill, as always to disappoint you; but the lady is now about again, though, from pecuniary disputes with the manager, probably, she is, as yet, invisible to the public. However, by the time you come, I hope she will be on the boards again. I believe you were very right in what you said to me, about the good arising from my having delayed publishing my juvenile pieces; but some of those things which have now gained me reputation *are* juvenile pieces, written years ago; however, I am contented that I have, till now, lived unconscious of the anxieties of an author. I wish I were launched! As usual, all the *good* I saw in my work, before it was printed, is now vanished from my sight, and I remember only its faults. All the authors, of both sexes, and artists too, that are not too ignorant or full of conceit to be capable of alarm, tell me they have had the same feeling when about to receive judgment from the public. Besides, whatever I read appears to me so superior to my own productions, that I am in a state of most unenviable humility. Mr. Opie has no patience with me; but he consoles me by averring that fear makes me overrate others, and underrate myself. Be so good as to tell my father that, as a subscriber to Dyer's book, he has half a guinea to pay for the volume I have received for him, and when the other two volumes are done, he will have to pay half a guinea more! Poor man; but tell him, as some little consolation, that there are three pretty stanzas addressed to me in the first volume, the old verses lengthened and improved, but they are "To a Lady," not to Mrs. Opie. Viganoni was with me from twelve to three to-day, alternately singing with me and talking; he has, with all his genius, a great deal of what the French call *bonhommie*, which makes him talkative and confiding, when he is with those he thinks his friends. I was pleased, for his sake, to hear him say he should sing only two or three years longer, as he had saved money enough to live quite at his ease in his native country. He says music is now so cultivated and

courted in England, that it is at its height, and must soon fall "*en décadence;*" but he thinks the present taste a vicious one. "*Le monde Anglais,*" he says, "like nothing equal to bravura singing," which he thinks no singing at all, and which never goes to the heart like simple sentimental singing. Indeed he never puts in a grace, but what tends to illustrate the sentiment of the words, and the style of the air; his singing is conversation, put into sweet sounds. My plaudit is of no weight, perhaps; but Viganoni has, unrivalled, that of all the oldest, most experienced, and able professors of music—men who unite theory with practice, and are the *only good* judges, from having, from their situations, an opportunity of comparing singers and styles—men who have *learnt* to *hear,* an art, nothing but hearing constantly the first music and performers, can teach. I long to hear Mara again. V. says she sings better than ever, though her voice is on the wane. How strange it is that Bante retains her *unequalled* voice, though she gets drunk every day. This extraordinary creature can't even write her name, and knows not a note of music. V. is sometimes forced to pinch her to keep her in time, and make her leave off her vile shake, or rather no shake, at the proper point. A gentleman declared to me he saw this; but I did not believe it, till I asked V., who told me it was true. Adieu! Love to all.

1801.

My dear Friend,

I began a letter to you full a fortnight ago, but I know not what is become of the precious scrawl; it is "wasting its sweetness on the desert air," somewhere or other, so I must begin a new one. All I remember of it is, that it began with very sensible reproaches for your having thought it necessary and becoming in you to *thank* me for what you were pleased to call kindnesses, from me, to you and yours; as if such words and such ceremonies were proper between you and me, and as if, in showing attention to you and Richard, I did not do myself honour by proving the sense I entertain of superior merit. Tol de rol lol!

So you are coming to the great city! but let me advise you to come in mourning, for there seems to be a rot amongst royalty, and one court mourning succeeds to another; the present one will scarcely be over before you arrive. One of our great grandmothers is dead, but which I do not know. I shall have a great deal to tell you about new people and new characters when I see you, which a letter could neither contain nor do justice to. It is a world to see! I dearly love to get a peep at it now and then; and what I do see of it only serves to endear the safety and quiet of my own home. You will be up just time enough for one of my pleasantest parties, and I expect you and I shall be two merry wives when we get together again. You will see the exhibition too; and I hope *que vous y verrez briller mon Mari.*

I am glad on reperusing "The Dangers of Coquetry," that you think so highly of it. I read it at Seething soon after I married, and felt a great respect for it; and if I ever write a collection of tales, I shall correct and re-publish that, as *I originally wrote it*, not as it now is, in the shape of a novel, in chapters. I believe I told you that Mr. Hoare was so struck with it, as to intend writing a play from it. I wish he would. Heigho, I am very stupid to-night, so my ideas do not come *coulamment;* so for want of something better to say, I will tell you a characteristic anecdote of Mr. Northcote. Mr. Opie, and he, and Sir Francis Bourgeois (the landscape painter) dined at Sir William Elford's the other day, and met there a Colonel Elford. After dinner some disputatious conversation took place, in which my husband and Mr. N. took a principal part; after some time, the Colonel said, in a low voice to Sir Francis, "Painters are queer fellows; how oddly they converse. One knows not what to make of them; how oddly these men run on!" Sir Francis assented, and consoled himself as well as he could, for being so little eminent as not to be known to be a painter himself. After tea, he took an opportunity of telling this story to Northcote; who, starting back with a face of horror, exclaimed, "Gude G—! then he took *you* for a gentleman!" I dare say he did not sleep that night. My husband says very truly and admirably of this queer little being, that his mind resembles an old family mansion, in which some of the apartments are furnished and in good repair, while the major part are empty or full of rubbish. * * * (Enter Mr. Northcote!) (Sunday.) I have nothing to tell you in consequence of the little man's visit, except a fresh proof of the care he takes of his little health. I had some cheese toasted and brought up. "Gude G—! how unwholesome, one piece if you please, and no more." Presently after, he says, "Bless me, Mrs. Opie! eating still? how much have you ventured to eat?" "Two pieces." "Oh, then so will I, I'll venture to eat two pieces too." As a proof of his *politeness*, I will tell you that on my saying Sir Roger L'Estrange was a Norfolk man, he exclaimed, "A Norfolk man! could anything good or great come out of Norfolk?"

I am told my father certainly means to visit us this spring, but I am resolved not to expect him, as I was so disappointed last year. I am sorry you will come up too late for the Oratorios. I am going to day to carry Mrs. Inchbald my book to read. She has promised me her opinion of it; and I long to receive it. She is a judge of the tale only; poetry is to her an undiscovered country. The ballads she already admires very highly. As this letter will not go till to-morrow, I shall leave it open.—(Sunday eve.)—I had written thus far, when your kind letter came. I repeat my advice to you to come in a black muslin; a white gown and black ribbons, or even a coloured gown, will do occasionally in a morning, to spare the other, and then you will always be either dressed or undressed; for black suits all companies; black stockings and a black petticoat you would find so useful too. All black continues fashionable, and is economical too. I am very glad you like my tale. The Hoares called to-day, and expressed themselves much pleased and affected by it, Mr. H. could not sleep all night after it, it made him so wretched. You will undoubtedly see both Coome and Mrs. Jordan. Adieu, just room to send kind love. Yours, &c.,

A. O.

Monday, 1801.

* * * I did not expect, my dear friend, that my asking one favour of you should procure me *two*; viz., fowls for Viganoni, and a letter for myself; but I like to take all heaven sends—and the more the better. Your question to me "what is this indescribable charm which attends the overflowings of one mind into another when it finds itself understood?"—I can't answer; though, as you observe, the enjoyment is known to me. But this pleasure is not confined to the contemplation of well assorted minds; in everything we delight to see things *fit*, as we call it; even a scissors-sheath delights us when, on buying it, we find it sits *flush*—as the phrase is. No wonder then that, when mind fits mind, the pleasure should be so great. Yes!—as you say, July is coming; and I am coming, but late in July I doubt. I have not made out the author of the anonymous letter—I wish I had; yet, there I lie; mountains look largest and most sublime when they are shrouded partly in mist. The "British Critic" is something *awful;* but what is Parson Beloe? Pray tell my father that 750 are to be printed of the *Tale;* it will be time enough to settle the number of the other volume when it is ready for the press. At present I am so incapable of writing!

I have been giving myself a great deal of trouble to-day, and I doubt at last I shall be disappointed. Viganoni, with great readiness and great humility, granted my request that he would set the little song I wrote the other day; but to enable him to do this, I have just written it out, leaving a space between each line wide enough for him to write the cadence of the words, as if they were Italian, underneath; then at the bottom, in French prose, I have translated the song, that he may comprehend the sentiment; and I have also written it again with a literal translation of each word by a *French* one under it, regardless of French construction, that he may catch the proper emphasis; thus:—

New friends, new hopes, new joys, to find—
De nouveaux amis, de nouvelles espérances, de nouveaux plaisirs, à trouver.

And, after all, if he should not do it well! he says he will do *son possible*, but I have my fears; if he succeeds I shall be so pleased! * * What a labour it is to laugh for a continuance! I am quite sore to-day with immoderate laughter yesterday! I was irritable, and then anything sets me off. Not but what my uncle and aunt, at whose house I dined, and Mr. Biggs who dined there also, were very agreeable; but had I been quite well, and my husband not gone to Chatham, I should not have been so noisy. Yet I declare I laugh now at some of the fun. I expect my husband home in half an hour. He went to please me, and after he was gone I repented of my persuading him to go, but I thought the air and exercise would do him good. Do not laugh, but though only two days absent, the house seems so strange without its master, that I have learned to excuse, nay to commend, women for marrying again! How dreadfully forlorn must be the situation of a widow! I think I shall write an essay recommending second marriages, and dedicate it to Mrs. Merrick. Well, God bless you! I think I have written nonsense enough. Love to your spouse and bairns; and believe me, ever yours,

A. Opie.

"The other Volume" was the "Poems," which appeared early in 1802, and for a critique upon which we must again refer the reader to the article in the Edinburgh Review for October, 1802. After some rather severe criticism of her deficiencies and faults, the writer observes, "It is in the smaller verse of eight syllables, which requires no pomp of sound, and in the simple tenderness, or simple grief, to which the artlessness of such numbers is best suited, the power of Mrs. O.'s poetry consists. * * * The verses of feeling, on which she must rely for the establishment of her fame, are certainly among the best in our opuscular poetry. As a specimen we select the following song, which is scarcely surpassed by any in our language:—

Go, youth beloved, in distant glades,
New friends, new hopes, new joys to find!
Yet sometimes deign, 'midst fairer maids,
To think on her thou leav'st behind.
Thy love, thy fate, dear youth, to share,
Must never be my happy lot;
But thou may'st grant this humble prayer
Forget me not! forget me not!

Yet should the thought of my distress
Too painful to thy feelings be,
Heed not the wish I now express,
Nor ever deign to think of me!
But oh! if grief thy steps attend,
If want, if sickness be thy lot,
And thou require a soothing friend,
Forget me not! forget me not!

Sir James Mackintosh, in a letter written to Mr. Sharpe, from India, refers to these lines in the following manner: "Tell the fair Opie that if she would address such pretty verses to me as she did to Ashburner, I think she might almost bring me back from Bombay, though she could not prevent his going thither. I beg that she will have the goodness to convey Lady M.'s kindest compliments and mine, to her friend Madame Roland, of Norwich." (By this playful epithet Mrs. Taylor was designated, in consequence of a fancied resemblance to her portrait.) It was probably, the delivery of this message which produced the impromptu by Mrs. Opie, on being asked if she had written verses on the absence of Sir James Mackintosh, in India:—

No! think not in verse
I his absence deplore:
Who a sorrow can sing
Till that sorrow is o'er?
And when shall his loss
With such sorrow be classed?
Oh! when shall his absence
Be *pain that is past?*

Sir James acknowledged the compliment thus paid him by the following letter, dated,

Bombay, 30th September, 1805.

My dear Mrs. Opie,

Many thanks for all your late presents, your good cousin, your most affecting novel, and your elegant verses. Your cousin will do well, and return to you, I hope, in a few years, with a reasonable fortune, and an unbroken constitution. At present I think he looks fresher than I ever saw him in Norfolk. Of Adeline, I cannot speak with quite so much unmixed complacency; she has occasioned many painful moments, and even cost us some tears. The verses I am sure I should admire, even if they had not bribed me to do so. The first four lines in particular are so ingenious and so natural, so lively and so easy, that they resemble the light poetry of the French, in which they so much surpass all nations. Standing by themselves, they would make an admirable *impromptu* answer to the question which is the subject. Perhaps you will allow me to prove the sincerity of this praise, by adding that the remaining lines though excellent, are not perhaps of quite so high a cast as the first four. I have some thought of publishing these four in our Bombay Paper, in the form of which I have spoken; if I do, I bespeak pardon by anticipation.

The character of the Hindu is, in your songs, and in most European descriptions, beautiful and poetical; but on near approach it is base and odious enough. Their fine forms and graceful attitudes might indeed furnish subjects for Mr. Opie's pencil, but their minds will seldom be worthy of your verse or your prose. I agree with you about the commencement of the third volume of Godwin's novel. It is most masterly. There are other admirable parts; but, taken throughout, I think it the worst of his three; though far indeed above the limits of a vulgar fate. So unlettered and incurious is this place, that the copy of Fleetwood which came here, was suffered to lie on the shop counter with all the common trash of the Minerva press, undistinguished by our novel readers, to whom Godwin has no name; and might have so remained till it was devoured by the white ants, if I had not heard of it by chance, and eagerly snatched it from these animals, or from others of nobler shape, but not much nobler nature. I need scarcely say that no hostility was mixed with my eagerness; on the contrary, I expected, and I found great pleasure. I hope you are in love with Walter Scott's "Lay of the Last Minstrel." Nowhere else, but in "Warwick Castle," are antique character and dignity reconciled with modern elegance and regularity. It has many charming passages, and the narrative is full of warlike and Homeric spirit; if the poem be sometimes tedious, so is Homer himself, the prince of ballad-makers, and of border minstrels. I presume that you have read Madame de Genlis' "Duchesse de la Valière;" which, though not precisely a novel, is surely a most fascinating work. Have you ventured on the Abbé Delille's translation of "Paradise Lost?" I presume it is a capital crime to praise it in England; and perhaps the importation of it may be prohibited; I see it is most profusely panegyrized in the *Moniteur*, and the only fault in the opinion of the French critics, is that the Translator has *not altered Milton sufficiently*. How would this sound on the banks of my beloved Thames? It would be blasphemy in England, and would be very bad taste anywhere, not to mention its glaring inconsistency with the first idea of *translation*. The bearer of this letter is Mrs. Stewart, a very amiable, and rather unfortunate woman, who brought here beauty and understanding fit for happier spots, and who is now going to England in search of long-lost health; any attention that you may have the goodness to show her, Lady M. and I shall consider as a great favour to us. I am confident, that when your own ingenious delicacy has gently dispelled the clouds that dejection and retirement have spread around her, you will see in herself sufficient motives for kindness to her.

I am, my Dear Madam,
Truly and faithfully yours,
JAMES MACKINTOSH.

A triple crown was to be awarded to this song "Go, youth beloved." It was selected by the Rev. Sydney Smith, in one of his "Lectures on Moral Philosophy," delivered at the Royal Institution in 1804-5, as possessing peculiar excellence in its style; he says, "If any man were to discover the true language of nature and feeling in this little poem of Mrs. Opie's, he would gain no credit for his metaphorical taste, because the beauties of it are *too* striking for a moment's hesitation."

The authoress was present at the time when Mr. Smith pronounced this eulogium upon her verses; and she used laughingly to tell how unexpectedly the compliment came upon her, and how she shrunk down upon her seat, in order to screen herself from the observation of those around her.

CHAPTER VII.

THE TRIALS OF GENIUS; DOMESTIC TROUBLES; LETTERS TO MRS. TAYLOR; JOURNEY TO FRANCE; ARRIVAL AT PARIS; THE LOUVRE; THE FIRST CONSUL; CHARLES JAMES FOX; THE SOIRÉE; KOSCIUSKO.

We have seen how diligently Mrs. Opie laboured during the year 1801, and with what success her efforts had been crowned. Yet this was the severest season of domestic anxiety and trouble, she was, as a wife, destined to experience. She tells us, in her Memoir of her husband, that although he had a picture in the Exhibition of 1801, which was universally admired, and purchased as soon as beheld, yet "he saw himself at the end of that year, and the beginning of the next, almost wholly without employment; and even my sanguine temper yielding to the trial, I began to fear that, small as our expenditure was, it must become still smaller. Not that I allowed myself to own that I desponded; on the contrary, I was forced to talk to him of hopes, and to bid him look forward to brighter prospects, as his temper, naturally desponding, required all the support possible. But gloomy and painful indeed were those three alarming months, and I consider them as the severest trial that I experienced during my married life. However, this despondency did not make him indolent;

he continued to paint regularly as usual; and no doubt by that means increased his ability to do justice to the torrent of business which soon after set in towards him, and never ceased to flow till the day of his death."

There is something very touching in these few and simple words. The earnest hopeful nature of the wife supporting the desponding spirits of her gifted husband. Like all men of true genius, he was subject to dark shadows and melancholy broodings. He aspired high, studied much, laboured hard, and was too painfully alive to his deficiencies, ever to rest satisfied with the point to which he had attained; the voice within cried ever, "higher!" and he must run until he fell. "During the nine years that I was his wife, (she continues,) I never saw him satisfied with any one of his productions, and often, very often, have I seen him enter my sitting room, and throwing himself in an agony of despondence on the sofa, exclaim, 'I never, never shall be a painter, as long as I live!'"

Happily for women they have, in the little domestic cares of every day life, a source of employment and interest, which, compelling their attention, diverts their thoughts into wholesome channels, and saves them from uselessly brooding over evils they cannot avert. The domestic *ménage* of the painter's household had to be governed, its mistress tells us, with a strict and watchful economy, and an observant eye must be kept upon all that went on there. But this was not all; as a mistress, the conduct of her servants appears to have occasioned her no small trouble, and to her faithful *confidante* she reveals her anxieties on more than one occasion; from two of these letters we find that she learned by experience, what she afterwards described with her pen; the first letter seems almost a comment upon one of her tales on "Lying," or rather to have furnished the text for it. Both must have been written early in the year 1802, as in the month of August following, the journey to Paris took place.

MY DEAR FRIEND,

Your most kind and gratifying letter, so wholly undeserved on my part, and (considering your many avocations) so generous on yours, demanded an earlier acknowledgment; but it is one of the charms of our intimacy that it is proof against neglects like mine. I know you will not cease to love me, nor think that I have ceased to love you, though even months pass without my assuring you of my unaltered regard. But at last I sit down to write to you, and you might suppose I take up my pen *conscience-urged;* no such matter; I write to crave your advice on a subject that weighs heavy on my mind, and one on which at present I cannot consult my husband; a difficult affair to act properly in, as I want to reconcile pity and justice. You must know, that, after having for some time past had some reason to suspect the strict honesty, in trifles, of my maid Anne, I had, last Friday, the mournful certainty of detecting her in a course of most flagrant iniquity; and what is worse, when I brought my charge against her, she was most firm in denial, and accused me of the grossest cruelty and injustice in accusing her; while a series of ready *lies,* abounding in contradictions, which left no doubt of her guilt on my mind, sunk her still lower in my opinion. I was easily prevailed on to keep the affair a secret from my husband for a short time, in order to avoid an *éclat,* which would blast the poor wretch's character for ever; yet how, my dear friend, can I any way act as I ought, without doing this? Her cry is, "give me a character for God's sake!" but how can I? Even if I keep her till August, can I then, however correct her future conduct, say "yes" to an enquiry concerning her honesty? If she had a *heart,* (but I am certain she has not,) I would keep her and conceal her fault, (for while reputation is safe, there is hope of amendment,) but of her I have no hope. Now, my dear friend, tell me how I can stand between her and the punishment of her guilt, with honour and justice to myself? A young maid-servant turned out, without the chance of a character, is in so exposed and desperate a situation, that I shudder to think of the consequences, and, as my too great confidence and my carelessness *may* have laid temptation in her way, I feel a degree of responsibility for her faults, which distresses me exceedingly.

I really should feel it incumbent on me to make an apology for worrying your brains with my domestic concerns, did I not know it is the honest pride of your life to be useful, and that you are always glad of an opportunity of serving me.

The string that pulls me towards Norwich begins to grow tight. To Cornwall, or even to France, we cannot afford to go; at least so Mr. Opie thinks; and that is the same thing.

My next letter (and I shall certainly *answer* your answer) shall contain more amusing stuff. At present I have only time to say, Kemble was arrested for a debt, kindness had made him incur, (for £200,) as he came out of the theatre on Saturday last. He is not yet in limbo, but to jail he is resolved to go on Wednesday, unless Mr. Sheridan pays the money; and never will he play again, till it is paid. Sheridan swears and protests that he will pay the debt, and that he knew not of the transaction; whereas, it is certain Sheridan went to the bailiff, and for fear of a riot, prevailed on him to put off the arrest till the play was over. We think Sheridan dares not let him go to jail, and go he will. Adieu! anxiously hoping to hear from you,

I remain,

Yours most affectionately,

A. Opie.

How well this letter illustrates some of her most strongly marked characteristics! that earnest desire "to reconcile pity with justice;" that readiness to take to herself any blame she might possibly have incurred, as an extenuation of the fault of another, and the lingering hope that the delinquent might be reclaimed. These are traits which those who knew her well will recognize as her very own.

Here is her promised answer to Mrs. T.—

Tuesday, 1802.

MY DEAR FRIEND,

As opening and detaining letters to and from active partizans is the order of the day, and as the enclosed contains *numbers,* I write to you instead of my father, and shall get my letter directed for me. Franks are now of no use, as even *Peers* can't frank, being no longer Lords of parliament; therefore, were they sacred to these *licensed* rogues, the one I have for to-morrow is good for nothing. *Indefatigable,* alias your cousin Peter, whom I saw just now at Mr. Smith's, desired me to send Lord C.'s letter; so I obey. Be so good also, as to tell my father that his letter, franked by Mr. Smith, did not reach till Saturday; and tell him I wrote to him yesterday, enclosing the peer's first letter.

Your kind answer to my statement of vexation gave me the greatest satisfaction, and I hope by your excellent advice and assistance to be able, with a very little trouble, to put such a degree of order in my subsequent *ménage* as shall prevent, in future, any gross imposition. Anne's conduct since the detection, and what I have heard of it previously to it, takes from me all idea of my carelessness having led her into temptation. I believe her to be thoroughly bad.

Yesterday evening, at half-past five, we saw the balloon, from the painting-room window, distinctly. Suddenly it was lost in a cloud, and the feeling it gave me was a very strange one. Soon after it emerged again, considerably higher than it was before; then it entered another cloud and disappeared. It is past two, and Mr. Garnerin is not returned, but I have been to the Pantheon to inquire concerning him, and I find he landed at Colchester in an hour and forty minutes!

Of election matters what can I say? Till I read the squibs, &c. I could not, *con amore*, say, I wished Mr. Windham to be ousted; but now indignation has assisted principle to conquer feeling, and I will *not* say of the agreeable delinquent,

> "If to his share some manly errors fall
> Hear him converse, and you'll forget them all,"
> or, "Look in his eyes, and you'll forget them all,"

(which you please, Mrs. Taylor.)—I was to have gone to Mr. Hiliar's on Sunday or Monday; but, if the election is to be on *Monday*, I can't leave town to be out of the way of the news on Tuesday, especially as I should not meet with sympathy in my feelings there. Adieu! I must go to see again whether Garnerin is returned. I wonder when your travellers come back.

Believe me, ever most affectionately yours,

A. O.

P. S. I want to come down to the election ball. What a shock poor Garnham's death was to me!

In the autumn of this year her long cherished desire to visit France, and more especially Paris, was gratified.* Her husband needed relaxation after the

* Mrs. Opie published an account of this journey in Tait's Magazine, vol. iv., 1831. From this account we have extracted several of the most interesting passages. She says, in a few prefatory remarks, that it had originally been her intention to give an account of her visit to Paris in 1829, but that, while endeavouring to do this, so many recollections of her first journey recurred to her mind, that she was induced to alter her purpose, and prefer relating the events of the earlier visit. Probably in doing this she made use of the original letters which she is known to have written home to Dr. Alderson at the time; and having done so, no longer preserved them.

anxiety and labour of the last few months, and there was now an unexpected opportunity afforded to the painter to study those glorious *chefs d'œuvre* of art which the conquering arms of Napoleon had assembled at the Louvre.

They were joined in this excursion by a party of friends, of whom Mrs. Opie mentions Samuel Favell, Esq. and Mrs. Favell, and her early acquaintance, Miss Anne Plumptre. On the 14th of August, 1802, they reached Calais, and for the first time she experienced " the strangely interesting moment when one's foot first touches a foreign land, and when one hears on every side a foreign language spoken by men, women, and children." The first impression seems to have been one of bewilderment, for which she was not at all prepared, occasioned by the confusion of voices that greeted them. Having recovered from this perplexing sensation, she was agreeably surprised to see a well known face, that of Le Texier; he who for many years delighted the English public by his admirable French readings. The recognition was mutual, and she was welcomed by him to the land of his birth.

An amusing adventure befell our inexperienced traveller, as she seated herself at the Hotel de Grandsire, to enjoy the delicious fare of the excellent *table d'hôte*, and be initiated at once into the mode of a French dinner, " so contrary to our own;"—

Opposite to me (she says) sat a gentleman, wearing what I conceived to be a foreign order; and as he was very alert in rendering me the customary table-attentions, I ventured to address him in French, but he did not reply. I therefore concluded that he was of some nation in which French was not very generally spoken; and so far I was not very wrong in my conjecture, as my opposite neighbour turned out to be an English messenger, just arrived with dispatches from our government! and the order which gave him such distinction, in my curious eyes, was nothing more than a silver greyhound, which messengers then wore! My mistake exposed me to some good humoured banter; but, perhaps, it was well for me that I made it, as it put me a little on my guard against one of my infirmities, that of forming hasty conclusions. * *

The next morning the travellers started for Paris, going a very long stage before breakfast,

The tediousness of which, (she says,) as the country had no charms to boast, was in a degree relieved to me by the occasional beauty and picturesqueness of the costume of the peasants, both men and women; but the whiteness of the caps and full sleeves, of even the young women, sometimes formed an unpleasing contrast with their dark, sunburnt, and almost parchment-looking complexions.

After many tedious delays on the road, occasioned by the voiturier's "unreasonable care of his horses, as he would not allow them to move after seven o'clock," and various little events of small interest, they reached Paris, and she thus describes her feelings on the occasion:—

At length we entered the suburbs of the metropolis, and saw written in chalk on the walls on both sides, and in giant letters, "*L'Indivisibilité de la Republique;*" but all traces of republicanism were so rapidly disappearing, that the word without the second syllable would have described it better; namely, "invisibility." But to me every other consciousness was soon absorbed in the joyful one of being at last in Paris, that city which I had so long desired to see.

Being advised to go to the Hotel of the Rue des Etrangers, they repaired thither, and were soon installed in commodious apartments; the street, then the best in Paris, opening at one end, on the Place de la Concorde, where "the perpetual guillotine" stood, while at the other end was the Church de la Madeleine.

By this time my restless curiosity was at its height, and I was anticipating some days of great enjoyment, when my husband, who had run off to the Louvre long before the rest of us were ready, returned with a countenance of such vexation and suffering, that I could not help asking him what calamity had occurred? "Calamity indeed!" he replied, "the Louvre is shut to-day, but then it will be open to-morrow, so that it would not much signify; but I cannot stay here—the whiteness of everything—the houses—the ground we walk upon— all dazzle and blind me; and if I stay, I shall lose my eyesight, and then I shall be a lost man." This was uttered in such evident suffering, that for a few minutes I was overwhelmed with consternation and disappointment. I knew that go we must, if staying endangered my husband's sight; and I still recall, with exquisite pain, the trial of that hour.

Happily they succeeded, by some means, in procuring admittance to the Louvre immediately, and she says:—

As the painter, while contemplating the wonders of the museum, ceased to feel the inconvenience which the man had thought unbearable, I had the joy of finding that we should not quit Paris that day. * * * * *

Why should I dwell on emotions which every one probably has felt on entering the Louvre gallery? My own pleasure, my ignorant pleasure, was nothing to the more scientific delight of my husband; and I recall with melancholy satisfaction, the enjoyment which he derived from this visit to the French metropolis; an enjoyment purchased and deserved by many years of the most assiduous labours in his difficult profession; and which, with the single exception of a week spent in a visit to Flanders, a few years previously, was the only relaxation to his well principled industry, in which he ever allowed himself to indulge.

On the second day after her arrival in Paris, she thus records an event which greatly delighted her.

I was in the Louvre gallery and standing alone before the picture of the Deluge, by N. Poussin, (my favourite station,) when I heard some one say that the First Consul was just going to enter his carriage, on his way to the Conservative Senate. "Oh that I could but see him!" exclaimed I aloud, and in French; on which, one of the guardians of the gallery said, "*Eh bien! mademoiselle, suivez moi et vous le verrez.*" Without daring to lose a moment in order to seek for my companions, I followed rapidly whither he led. He took me through a door at the extreme end of the gallery, opening into a room on the floor, and against the wall of which were several unframed pictures. Another door led us into an apartment, which looked immediately on the Place du Carousel. Ladies were sitting at the window, who, at my guide's request that they would make room for an English stranger, kindly allowed me a seat beside them.

I arrived just in time to see the procession form. The carriage of Buonaparte, drawn by eight bays, was already at the palace gate, and was soon followed by that of the other consuls, Cambaceres and Le Brun, drawn by six black horses. Soon after, the *corps d'élite*, the body guard, and the troop of Mamelucs, made their appearance; and Rustan, the favourite Mameluc of Napoleon, was also at his post, awaiting his master. At length an increased noise at the door announced that he was coming, and I gazed to an almost painful degree of intensity, in order to catch one glimpse of this extraordinary man; but he sprang into his carriage with such rapidity that not one of us could see him! Rustan quickly jumped up behind, and the procession went forward. It was, I own, a striking sight; but I did not think equal in beauty and grandeur to the procession of our king to the House of Lords, when he goes to open or prorogue the Parliament.

Who knows what views of royal splendour to come, were, even then, floating before the mind of Napoleon! He was going that morning to realize and enjoy the highest present object of his "vaulting ambition." He was going, for the first time, to open the Conservative Senate, as First Consul for life. He had taken the first step on the path to despotic power; he had ascertained the extent of his own influence; he had succeeded in his endeavours to be voted a sort of Dictator for life; and he had proved that the self-denying and noble example of Washington had been thrown away on him. But even then, at this seeming height of his proud career, I do not remember to have heard him greeted by a single shout; the evidences of a people's love did not hail his presence; and no eager and exulting crowd hung on his carriage wheels; and when I turned from the window, as the *cortège* disappeared, I felt disappointed, not only because I had not seen Buonaparte, but because there was no expression heard of animating popular feeling.

Returning to join her party in the picture gallery after this adventure, Mrs. Opie found there an object of nearly equal interest to her; the "loved and distinguished patriot" of her own country, Charles James Fox, who, with his wife and party, had arrived in Paris the day before, from the Netherlands. Being introduced by a mutual acquaintance, Mr. Opie took the opportunity of presenting a letter of introduction from Mr. Coke, of Holkham, and they were presently engaged in conversation together. At this moment an officer of the court came to announce to Mr. Fox that he would be admitted, at all times, into the Louvre, adding that a room as yet closed to the public and containing some first-rate works of art, should be immediately opened to him and his party. Availing themselves of the courteous invitation given them to accompany him, the party gladly followed in his train;

But my husband, (says the proud delighted wife,) walked by his side; and as they walked along, the Jerome of Domenichino drew their attention, and they stopped before it. On some part of this celebrated picture they differed in opinion. Mr. Fox, however, instead of replying to the artist's remarks, with proud superciliousness, as if he wondered that he should presume to disagree with him, said, "Well, to be sure, you must be a better judge of such points than I am." And I saw by my husband's pleased and animated countenance, as they proceeded, (though I did not hear their subsequent remarks,) that he felt conscious he was conversing with one, who was capable of appreciating the soundness of his opinions, and generous enough to respect his judgment.

Having reached the promised room, I found to my surprise, that it was the one into which I had already been, and I was rather ashamed to see that I had passed, without noticing it, the *chef d'œuvre* of Raphael, the far famed Transfiguration! When, however, raised up as it was by the attendants, and placed to advantage, sideways to the light of the window on the left, I, as well as the rest of the party, stood before it, lost in admiration! Some of its admirers had seen it before, but to the painter—to him who was the most capable of appreciating all its various beauties, it imparted a new and intense delight, beyond the power of words to express. How he rejoiced that we had arrived before it was hung up, as its present situation enabled him to view it to perfection! While we were still gazing on this wonder of art, some one said the First Consul was returning in state from the Conservative Senate, and that the procession could be seen from the window near us. Accordingly, all the company, myself excepted, crowded to the window; but our greatest man, I own, turned away, and resumed his station before the picture, while his wife observed to me that, considering Buonaparte was a republican, he seemed very fond of state and show. Again her distinguished husband went to the window, and again turned away. It was the first time he had ever seen aught appertaining to the consular government, and it was natural that his curiosity should be excited; but there was evidently a feeling uppermost in his mind, which struggled with his wish to indulge in it, and before the procession was out of sight, it had ceased to appear an object of interest to him.

The day after the events just mentioned, Mr. and Mrs. Opie called at the Rue Richlieu, to pay their respects to Mr. Fox, and accepted his invitation to dine with him there on an early day. The company they met on that occasion, was too numerous to admit of general conversation, and she only records one fact mentioned by their host, as illustrating the strange changes in times of revolution.—He said, "that nine-and-twenty years before, he had supped in the room in which they were then dining, with the celebrated and witty Maréchal Richlieu, whose residence the hotel then was."

Mrs. Opie mentions, *en passant*, that this was the only time they saw Mr. Fox, until he came to sit to her husband, for the whole length picture which Opie painted of him, for Mr. Coke. This far-famed picture cost the painter much anxiety; and, during the progress of the work, he was greatly distracted by the conflicting opinions of friends, who crowded to watch the work; and interrupted by the impatience of the sitter, who was eager to be released from the annoyance of sitting. Mr. Fox perceived and felt for the uneasiness of Opie, and kindly whispered him, "Don't mind what these people say, you must know better than they do."

The picture, when completed, gave general satisfaction, and Mrs. Opie says, "I think I may without partiality say, it is worthy of the artist, the owner, and the original."*

The last time she ever saw Mr. Fox was when he was chaired on his return to Parliament, after he had accepted office, and alarming was the change in his appearance:—

> With a heavy heart (she says) I plucked a laurel leaf from that car of triumph, which I feared that he filled for the last time; and I, indeed, saw him no more; but on his decease, I went to the house of Nollekens, to see the cast taken from his face immediately after death. It was lying on the table, by the side of that of his dear friend Georgiana Duchess of Devonshire, and of William Pitt, his powerful opponent. The two latter masks I could look at, and did look at with painful interest and serious meditation: but when I took up the other, I laid it down, and ran out of the room; I could not bear to survey the ravages which disease and death had made in that benevolent countenance; indeed the features were not recognizable, and though I often returned to gaze on the others, on *that* I could never look again.

Mrs. Opie next gives some pleasant recollections of the evenings she spent in the society of the most distinguished persons then in Paris, and especially in the house of Helen Maria Williams, and a beautiful

* This picture is now at Holkham.

Irish Countess, the friend of that lady. We select the account of her interview with Kosciusko.

One evening, at Lady —'s, we met a party, consisting chiefly of ambassadors from different nations, and other strangers. I had not long entered the room, when our hostess led me up to the Turkish ambassador, and desired me to "make the agreeable to him." "Can he speak French?" said I. "No, but here is a gentleman who will interpret between you." At the same time she introduced to me a gentleman in Asiatic costume, and I readily seated myself by the Turk. He was a little elderly man, splendidly attired in the dress of his country; and I prepared to answer his questions. One of them was, "how long I had been in Paris?" and when my reply, "a few days only," was repeated to him, he said, not very gallantly, "that he concluded so, from my complexion," which, I was very conscious, was tanned, by the broiling heat of the sun on the recent journey, to a red brown. At last we ceased to converse through our interpreter, and substituted signs for words. For instance, he took my fan, and made me understand that he wanted to know what I called it; and I tried to make him comprehend that it was fan in English, and *éventail* in French. He then pronounced its name in Turkish; and I was learning to speak it after him, when I was interrupted by my husband, who, with a glowing cheek and sparkling eye, exclaimed, "Come hither, look, there is General Kosciusko!" Yes, we did see Kosciusko; "Warsaw's last Champion!" he who had been wounded almost to death in defending his country against her merciless invaders; while (to borrow the strong expressive figure of the poet)—

"While Freedom shriek'd as Kosciusko fell!"

Instantly forgetting the ambassador, and, I fear, the proper restraints of politeness, I took my husband's arm, and accompanied him to get a nearer view of the Polish patriot, so long the object to me of interest and admiration. I had so often contemplated a print of him in his Polish dress, which hung in my own room, that I thought I should have known him again anywhere; but whether it was owing to the difference of dress, I know not, but I saw little or no resemblance in him to the picture. He was not much above the middle height, had high cheek bones, and his features were not of a distinguished cast; with the exception of his eyes, which were fine and expressive, and he had a high healthy colour. His forehead was covered by a curled auburn wig, much to my vexation, as I should have liked to have seen its honourable scar. But his appearance was pleasing, his countenance intellectual, his carriage dignified; and we were very glad, when our obliging hostess, by introducing us, gave us an opportunity of entering into conversation with him. He spoke English as well as we did, and with an English accent. On our expressing our surprise at this unusual circumstance, he said he had learned English in America. The tone of his voice was peculiar, and not pleasing; however, it was Kosciusko who spoke, and we listened with interest and pleasure; though, at this distance of time, I am unable to say on what subject we conversed. What I am going to relate, however, it was not likely that I should forget—

During the course of the evening, while I was standing at some distance, but looking earnestly at him, and speaking to some one in his praise, contrasting, as I believe, his unspotted patriotism with the then suspected integrity of Buonaparte, he suddenly crossed the room, and coming up to me, said, "I am sure you were speaking of me, and I wish to know what you were saying." "I dare not tell you," replied I. "Was it so severe then?" I bade him ask my companion. And on hearing her answer he thanked me, in a tone of deep feeling. "I have a favour to beg of you," said he, "I am told that you are a writer, pray do write some verses on me; a quatrain will be sufficient, will you oblige me?" I told him I could rarely write extempore verses, and certainly not on such a subject, as I should wish to do it all the justice possible. "Well then," said he, "I will await your pleasure."

I saw him again only once before I returned to England; but the next time that his birthday was commemorated at Paris, I wrote some verses on the occasion, and sent them to him by a private hand.

During the rest of that memorable evening, when we had the gratification of seeing the Polish patriot and of conversing with him, I did not venture to resume the seat next the Turkish ambassador which I had so unceremoniously quitted; but I contrived to enter into conversation with the interpreter, whose handsome figure and features, added to the gracefulness of his costume, made him, next to our hostess, the most striking looking person in the assembly. He spoke French fluently, and his manner was particularly pleasing.

CHAPTER VIII.

THE REVIEW AND BUONAPARTE; "FESCH;" GENERAL MASSENA; RETURN TO ENGLAND; LETTER TO MRS. COLOMBINE; VISIT TO NORWICH; "ADELINE MOWBRAY;" LETTER TO MRS. TAYLOR; MR. ERSKINE.

At length the long desired object (a sight of Buonaparte) was attained; she thus relates her impressions of the scene:—

We had now been several days in Paris, and yet we had not seen the First Consul! I own that my impatience to see him had been abated, by the growing conviction which I felt of the possible hollowness of the idol so long exalted.

But still we were desirous of beholding him; and I was glad when we received a letter from our obliging acquaintance, Count de Lasteyrie, informing us that Buonaparte would review the troops on such a day, on the Place du Carousel, and that he had procured a window for us, whence we should be able to see it to advantage. But, on account of my short-sightedness, I was still more glad when our friend De Masquerier, (a very successful young English painter,) informed us that he had the promise of a window for my husband and myself, in an apartment on the ground-floor of the Tuilleries, whence we should be able to have a near view of Buonaparte:—our friends, therefore, profited by M. de Lasteyrie's kindness, and we went to the palace.

As the time of seeing the First Consul drew nigh, I was pleased to feel all my original impressions in his favour return. This might be a weakness in me, but it was, I hope, excuseable; and our sense of his greatness and importance was, as my husband observed, heightened by seeing the great man of our own country,—he who was there a sight himself to many, —cross the Place du Carousel, with his wife on his arm, going, as we believed, to gaze like us, on, at least, a more fortunate man than himself—for, at that time, Charles James Fox had not seen Napoleon Buonaparte.

The door which opened into the hall of the palace was shut, but, after some persuasion, I prevailed on the attendant to open it; and he said he would keep it open till the First Consul had mounted his horse, if I would engage that we would all of us stand upon the threshold, and not once venture beyond it.

With these conditions we promised to comply; and, full of eager expectation, I stationed myself where I could command the white marble stairs of the palace; those steps once stained with the blood of the faithful Swiss guards, and on which I now expected to behold the "Pacificator," as he was called by the people and his friends—the hero of Lodi.

Just before the review was expected to begin, we saw several officers in gorgeous uniforms ascend the stairs, one of whom, whose helmet seemed entirely of gold, was, as I was told, Eugène de Beauharnois. A few minutes afterwards there was a rush of officers down the stairs, and amongst them I saw a short pale man, with his hat in his hand, who, as I thought, resembled Lord Erskine in profile; but, though my friend said in a whisper, "*C'est lui,*" I did not comprehend that I beheld Buonaparte, till I saw him stand alone at the gate. In another moment he was on his horse, and rode slowly past the window; while I, with every nerve trembling with strong emotion, gazed on him intently; endeavouring to commit each expressive, sharply chiselled feature to memory; contrasting also with admiring observation, his small simple hat, adorned with nothing but a little tri-coloured cockade, and his blue coat, guiltless of gold embroidery, with the splendid head adornings and dresses of the officers who followed him.

A second time he slowly passed the window; then, setting spurs to his horse, he rode amongst the ranks, where some faint huzzas greeted him from the crowd on the opposite side of the Place du Carousel.

At length he took his station before the palace, and as we looked at him out of the window, we had a very perfect view of him for nearly three quarters of an hour. I thought, but perhaps it was fancy, that the countenance of Buonaparte was lighted up with peculiar pleasure as the *corps d'élite*, wearing some mark of distinction, defiled before him, bringing up the rear—that fine gallant corps, which, as we are told, he had so often led on to victory; but this might be my fancy. Once we saw him speak, as he took off his hat to remove the hair from his heated forehead, and this gave us an opportunlty of seeing his front face, and his features in action. Soon after, we saw him give a sword of honour to one of the soldiers; and he received a petition which an old woman presented to him; but he gave it, unread, to some one near him. At length the review ended; too soon for me. The Consul sprang from his horse—we threw open our door again, and, as he slowly re-ascended the stairs, we saw him very near us, and in full face again, while his bright, restless, expressive, and, as we fancied, dark blue eyes, beaming from under long black eyelashes, glanced over us with a scrutinising but complacent look; and thus ended, and was completed, the pleasure of the spectacle.

I could not speak; I had worked myself up to all my former enthusiasm for Buonaparte; and my frame still shook with the excitement I had undergone.

The next day sobered me again, however, but not much, as will be soon seen.

The day after the review, our accomplished countrywoman Maria Cosway, took the president of the Royal Academy, Benjamin West, and ourselves, on a round of picture-seeing;

and at length we proceeded to the residence of a gentleman, who was, I concluded, only a picture dealer, or one of the many *nouveaux riches*, who had fine collections; because, whenever she spoke of him, Maria Cosway called him nothing but "Fesch." We stopped at the door of a very splendid hotel in the Chaussée d'Antin, and were met at the top of a magnificent flight of stairs, by a gentleman in the garb of an ecclesiastic. His hair was powdered, and he wore it in a full round curl behind, after the fashion of an *abbé;* his coat was black, but his stockings were of a bright purple; his shoe and knee buckles were of gold; round his neck he wore a glossy white silk handkerchief, from under which peeped forth a costly gold crucifix. His countenance was pleasing; his complexion uncommonly blooming; his manners courteous; and his age (as I afterwards learned) was thirty-nine.

This gentleman was the "Fesch" we came to visit, but I soon discovered that though he lived in the house, it was not his own; for Maria Cosway was summoned into an adjoining room, where I overheard her conversing with a female; and when she returned, she told us that Madame Buonaparte Mère, (as she was called to distinguish her from her daughter-in-law,) the mistress of the hotel, was very sorry that she could not see us, but that she was so unwell, she was obliged to keep her bed, and could not receive strangers. So then! we were in the house of Letitia Buonaparte, and the mother of Napoleon! and in the next room to her, but could not see her! how unfortunate! however, I was sure I had heard her voice. I now supposed that "Fesch" was her spiritual director, and believed his well studied dress, *si bien soignée,* was a necessary distinction, as he belonged to the mother of the First Consul.

He seemed a merry, as well as a courteous man; and once he took Maria Cosway aside, and showed her a letter that he had only just received, which, to judge from the hearty laugh of "Fesch," and the answering smiles of the lady, gave them excessive pleasure.

By and by, however, I heard and observed many things which made me think that "Fesch" was more than I apprehended him to be. I therefore watched for an opportunity to ask the President who this obliging person was.—"What!" cried he, "do you not know that he is the Archbishop of Lyons, the uncle of Buonaparte?" I was astonished! What the person so familiarly spoken of as "Fesch," could he be indeed "*du sang*" of the Buonapartes, and the First Consul's uncle! How my respect for him increased when I heard this! How interesting became his every look and word; and how grateful I felt for his obliging attention to us!

While we were looking at the pictures, his niece, the wife of Murat, drove to the door; and I saw the top of her cap as she alighted, but no more, as she went immediately to her mother's bedside.

After devoting to us at least two hours, the Archbishop conducted us down the noble staircase, to the beautiful hall of entrance, and courteously dismissed us. My companions instantly went away, but I lingered behind; for I had caught a view of a colossal bust of Buonaparte in a helmet, which stood on a table, and I remained gazing on it, forgetful of all but itself. Yes! there were those finely cut features, that "*coupe de menton à l'Apollon!*" and, though I thought the likeness a flattered one, I contemplated it with great pleasure, and was passing my hand admiringly over the salient chin, when I heard a sort of suppressed laugh, and, turning round, saw the Archbishop observing me, and instantly, covered with confusion, I ran out of the house. I found Maria Cosway explaining what the letter was which had given "Fesch" and her such evident satisfaction. It was nothing less than a letter from Rome, informing him that he would probably be put in nomination for the next cardinal's hat.

How soon he was nominated I cannot remember, but it is now many years since the blooming ecclesiastic of 1802, exchanged his purple for scarlet stockings, his mitre for a red hat, and his title of Archbishop of Lyons, for that of Cardinal Fesch.

As the time drew near when she must bid farewell to Paris, Mrs. Opie evidently longed for an extension of a season so full of enjoyment to her; but since her wish could not be gratified, she determined to make the most of every hour that remained; and she relates several anecdotes, relative to what she saw at the places she visited; among others the *atelier* of David, whither she accompanied her husband, and where she was forcibly struck with one of that artist's pictures, "Brutus returning from the tribunal after adjudging his sons to death." The emotion of compassion awakened in her mind by this picture was so strong, that she was unable to gaze on it without pain, so real was the illusion. Another visit the party made was to the Hotel of Murat, which, being furnished in the most elegant style of French luxury, was thought worth seeing: and splendid indeed it was.

The bed of the lady of the house was too elegant, and then, too uncommon, to be forgotten; it stood in a recess which was lined with looking-glass, and at the foot of the bed were, as I think, two finely chiselled marble cupids. The draperies were of the clearest muslin, lined with rose-coloured satin; and the counterpane as well as the valance was flounced with deep point lace. The panels of the room were painted in drab and rose colour; and all the decorations of the apartment were in the most costly but tasteful style. But what pleased me most in this hotel, was a picture of General Moreau, which, unframed, stood against one of the walls. It was a whole-length, as large as life, from the pencil of Gérard, and was one of those real portraits, which resemble life so much, that we are apt to fancy, when we recall the features, that we have seen, not the portrait, but the original.

Just as they were leaving the hotel, their attention

was directed to a gentleman who was talking energetically to the porter, and whom their guide informed them was General Massena. Pleased indeed, to see one of whom she had read and heard so much, she scanned him attentively, and thus describes his appearance :—

His head was one of the largest I had ever seen, his hair long and thick and curled, *à la Brutus*, and his features large and not fine. His eyes, however, were bright; in his ears he wore gold rings of large dimensions, (then commonly worn by French officers,) and his person was large, his height apparently nearly six feet. On the whole, however, his appearance was not prepossessing, and there was a look of coarse brutal daring, which contrasted unfavourably with the pleasing expression in the countenance of his rival in military fame, General Moreau.

Sorry as our enthusiastic traveller felt, when the hour of departure from Paris arrived, she yet greeted (she tells us) with heartfelt delight the white cliffs of her own dear native land. On the homeward journey she mentions a somewhat amusing incident; a little dog, purchased by Mr. Opie, was entrusted to her care, and made so many claims upon her time and attention, that she owns it was no matter of regret to her, that the poor brute shortly died, "which saved me (she adds) from the danger I seemed likely to incur, of becoming the slave of a pet animal."

Some of those who accompanied Mr. and Mrs. Opie on this tour used afterwards to relate, what ardour and intense delight she manifested in all the objects of interest she beheld; and how she sat on the Boulevards and sang, with heart and voice, "Fall, tyrants fall!" At the theatre they heard Talma, as "Cain," in the "Death of Abel;" and so deep an impression did this wonderful actor produce on her memory, that within a few years, she has been heard to refer to that occasion, dwelling on his look and manner, and the preternatural tone with which he answered the voice, "*Où es tu Cain?*"—"*Ici, Seigneur;*" the sounds, deep and sepulchral, appearing to issue from the ground beneath him.

Of the ensuing winter, and spring of the year following, we have no record from her hand; one letter alone remains, dated 25th February, 1803, addressed to her old and esteemed friend Mrs. Colombine. It is too long to be inserted entire, although of much interest, illustrating as it does her benevolence, and that kindliness of heart which was throughout life one of her most distinguishing characteristics. After expressing her friendly sympathy in the troubles that had befallen those to whom in early life she had been attached, she says:—

* * I assure you I cannot enough express how much I admire and honour the fortitude you have throughout displayed. Not to feel would be downright insensibility; but to feel so acutely as I know you do, and still to bear up so well, is a proof of strength of mind which I am *proud* to see in one whom I so sincerely love and esteem. But you would not, I know, exchange your feelings, for the insensibility of some mothers; for instance, of Mrs. B—, whom I almost hated for your sake, for daring so to intrude on the sacredness of recent sorrow. Do not scold me for speaking thus of her, because she is dead. I think "speak only good of the dead," is a silly and pernicious maxim; I had rather speak ill of the dead than of the living. * * * Give my kind love to Mr. C. and tell him that he must, and ought to be, cheerful, because

he has reason to be proud. Respect and esteem attend him into retirement and misfortune, and though he may be allowed to blush for others, he must respect himself. I think we Norwich people have reason to be proud of our native city! such liberality, and so well directed, makes it an honour to belong to it.* It gives me great pleasure to see, both in you and Mrs. B. that ardent piety which can *alone* fortify and cheer the afflicted mind; and when I hear virtuous infidels (for there *are* such) declare that they do not regret either the hopes or consolations of religion, I hear with surprise and pity, and end by believing that they do not know or do not own, their *real* feelings.

Farewell, and believe me,

Most affectionately yours,

A. OPIE.

During the summer of this year Mrs. Opie paid her usual visit to Norwich, and again her lengthened stay called forth the remonstrances of her husband. He writes, "my affection for you is even increased in point of general feeling and interest, so that if I do not admire you more, I feel you more a part of myself than I ever did at first," and urging her speedy return, for that he "longs so very much to see her."

In this letter he mentions that as soon as he has an opportunity he means to send her—

A letter, with a volume of poems, by Henry Kirke White, a "visionary boy," of seventeen, who, with all becoming diffidence, presumes to lay his youthful productions at the

* We find in Matchett's "Norfolk and Norwich Remembrancer," p. 63, under date, October 13th, 1802, this entry; "Alderman Francis Colombine resigned his gown as Alderman, to whom and his daughter the Corporation of Norwich granted an annuity of £100."

feet of one, "who so eminently enjoys the holy impulse" as yourself. He was "struck with the resemblance of one of his poems to one of yours, though to compare the former to the latter, is like comparing O'Keefe to Shakespeare"—there! I hope this will give you pleasure. Let me hear on Wednesday how you are. The cat and parrot are both well, and the kitten* beautiful and merry. The guns have been firing to-day, but on what account I am ignorant yet.

Adieu, my only love.

Again, probably shortly after this, her husband writes to her, enclosing a letter containing some complimentary verses on her "Elegy to the memory of the late Earl of Bedford," and adding, by way of postscript,

This came to me in a cover on Monday, so I thought it too delicious not to be sent immediately; who is the author? Your letter is arrived; and I am very sorry to find this cursed election lasting so long, and I wish you would not appear so prominent in it. I asked Mrs. N. about the box, and she says it was not to go till I went; however, I shall now have it sent as soon as possible. I have seen nothing of Erskine or Reynolds for some time. The cloak I am afraid is lost, for Mr. Bunn wrote me that he had made every inquiry in vain. Dr. Haweis has been sitting two or three times, and makes a good head. I shall write to you to-morrow or next day, so, God bless you, yours ever. J. O.

Let me hear again, Friday or Saturday at furthest; I feel

* This creature became a great pet. Mrs. Opie taught it some pretty tricks, and it was so fondly attached to Mr. O. that during his illness it used to sit and watch at the door of his chamber like a dog. Mrs. O. often talked of it. It came to an untimely end, and she was so much distressed about it, that this probably was the reason she never would again have any pets; for, in later years she evinced no disposition to fondle animals. No favourite dog, cat, or bird, was permitted to domicile with her.

desirous enough of seeing you, but I have not much more to say at present, unless I begin scolding you about the election. What business had you to get mounted up somewhere so conspicuously? But there is no more room; I am going now to dine with Thomson, to meet little J. A Mr. Best called on Saturday, and said he meant to be or to have somebody painted, but I have heard no more.

In 1804, Mrs. O. published "Adeline Mowbray," or "Mother and Daughter," a Tale, in three volumes, the object of this work is to pourtray the lamentable consequences which would result from the adoption of lax principles on the subject of matrimony. "The second volume of this beautiful story is perhaps the most pathetic and the most natural in its pathos, of any fictitious narrative in the language," says the writer of the 19th Art. in "The Edinburgh Review" of 1806.

The following letter to Mrs. Taylor was probably written about this time:—

(without date.)

MY DEAR FRIEND,

* * * I am just returned from Deptford, where I have been ever since Thursday; a sad loss of time, and nothing would have made me patient under it, but the extreme pity I feel for Miss M.'s forlorn situation. But perhaps, as my company gives her comfort, I ought not to call my visit to her a loss of time. I was lamenting to Mrs Barbauld, to whom I related this poor orphan's story, that Miss M. did not seem to have any taste for reading. "So much the better," was her answer, "I do not think such a taste desirable. Reading is an indolent way of passing the time"—and so she went on. I was extremely surprised, as

you may think, and began to combat her assertions; but I recollected that I had heard it said that Mrs. B., like W. Taylor, often contradicted for the sake of argument, and when I feel this, as it is a proceeding which I thoroughly disapprove, I am too angry to keep up the ball.

I find that Mrs. B. admires Cowper's letters very much. In my opinion they have been much overrated. The letters to Lady Hesketh are beautiful; but those to Hayley and J. Johnson, abounding as they do in "dearests" and "fondnesses" and "dearest of all dear Johnnies," make me sick *à la mort!*

* * * * You have not ridden much in stage coaches I believe, at least not round town. O! what a pleasure I should lose were I to ride in my own carriage and forsake stages! I find egotism the prevailing characteristic of my fellow-travellers. This morning I found, when I entered the stage, one passenger only in it, and that was a little girl. "Are you going to town?" said I. "Yes, I know the gentleman, and so I came." "What gentleman?" "The coachman, he lives by us; and so, as I wanted to go for my shoes, he said he would take me; he promised me my shoes to wear to-day, and I am going to see arter'em; I ha' known Mr. Wheeler a long time," &c.—and so she ran on, till I was tired of listening; and convinced me egotism is of all ages. As I went down, a fine, jolly, florid young countrywoman, a great deal fatter than I am, was complaining to a gentleman (who informed us he was just recovered from a fit of illness) that she was very unwell too; and as she had not seen her friends at Deptford for two years, she was sure they would be quite *shocked* at the change in her, for when she left them she was quite jolly and healthy looking. I could hardly keep in my laughter at this. Her Deptford friends must be droll persons, and great amateurs in fat indeed, to be dissatisfied with her magnitude, and regret what she had lost; I protest she might have played the goddess of health at Dr. Graham's.

I shall see you now soon, and I hope to see you nearly well. Farewell! With kind love to Mr. Taylor and all the family, I remain, *toute à vous*,

A. Opie.

In 1805 she was again in Norwich, and during that visit she enjoyed the unexpected pleasure of hearing Mr. Erskine plead; happily she has given an account of this event, which is preserved among her MSS. As usual when about to relate anything connected in her mind with an earlier period, she goes back, on the present occasion, to the time when she first saw Mr. Erskine. This was in the Nisi Prius court in Norwich, whither he had come down on a special retainer in a Right-of-Way cause, which for some reason was not heard at that assizes. She says:—

Well do I remember him, as I first saw him, entering for a few minutes, and taking a hasty survey of the court. I was immediately struck with the look of intelligent inquiry which he cast over the eager, but disappointed crowd, assembled to hear him; that eye reminded me of the description of Ledyard, the eastern traveller's eye, for it seemed "bright and restless," and its rapid glance appeared to observe, in its brief survey, as much as other eyes in a more lengthened one; and I much regretted that the interest which his appearance excited in me was not to be increased by the well known melody of his voice.*

Soon after, I had the privilege of becoming acquainted with him, when I was staying at the house of a dear friend

* I observed the same expression in the eye of Buonaparte, when, standing near the marble stairs of the Tuilleries, I saw him as he ascended them and looked on a group of English assembled to gaze at him.—A. O.

near London, and in the course of conversation he informed us that he was going down special to Huntingdon, on a most interesting occasion. A young man, lately come into possession of a large fortune, had been proceeded against by the next heir as being a supposititious child; and he told us that he was counsel for the defence, and that the cause was likely to be very long and very interesting, as the defendant was universally beloved; kindly adding, that as he saw I was interested in such things, when he met me at dinner again, on his return to London, he would then give myself and my friends an account of the trial. Consequently, great was my impatience till the day of the dinner came, and the great orator arrived; but though he again talked most pleasantly, and on law subjects too, not one single allusion did he make to the Huntingdon cause. In vain did I try to take courage, and remind him of his promise; I was not then a married woman, and fancied it would be presuming to do so; but, when I heard his carriage announced, and saw him about to depart, made valiant by despair, I exclaimed "Oh! Mr. Erskine, you have not fulfilled your promise! you have not told us the particulars of the Huntingdon cause!" "True!" he replied, starting and turning back, "but you shall not be disappointed," and leading me to the sofa, he seated himself beside me, and went through the whole of the proceedings. He gave us the evidence on both sides, told us what his opponent had said for the plaintiff, and he for the defendant; and, warming as he proceeded, he soon grew as much interested in the details as we were; and when he came to the verdict of the jury which was in favour of his client, his countenance beamed with animation, while he described the general plaudit with which the verdict was received in the court, and the shouts which were heard outside the walls from the assembled multitude!

He then hastily jumped into his carriage, leaving me exulting in having drawn from him a gratification so unusual and so complete.

But I experienced a still greater and much longer enjoyment of his eloquence in the year 1805, when he went down to Norwich, on the same Right-of-Way cause before alluded to; and I, being then on a visit to my father, had the pleasure of hearing him speak when he appeared on the side of the plaintiff.

As I was very early in court, I obtained a seat by the side of the judge, Sir Alexander Macdonald, and saw and heard everything to the greatest advantage. In that place I remained the whole day, except when, on being assured that my seat should be kept for me, I went home to tea, but soon returned to the scene of action, where I staid all night; as I could not bear to go away without hearing the great orator's reply to the defendant's counsel. As I was desirous that the plaintiff should gain her cause, I had been alarmed to find by the speech of the eloquent advocate for the defendant, how much could be said on both sides, and was therefore anxious to hear by what means his arguments could be rendered powerless; therefore, though listening with delighted attention and wonder to the powerful cross-examination, I wished it over: but witness, on the defendant's side, succeeded to witness; the audience became gradually smaller and smaller, and although Lord Brougham with his usual eloquence and felicity of expression has said, "that juries declared they found it impossible to remove their looks from Mr. Erskine when he had, as it were, rivetted and fascinated them by his first glance," I am obliged to confess that some of this Norfolk jury began visibly to nod, and it seemed likely, that, except the judge, the high sheriff, the barristers, the officers of the court, and myself, there would soon be no hearers left awake, and the beams of rising day were forcing themselves through the windows!

The observant Erskine took the hint, so palpably given, and coming up to me, he kindly said, "go home! go home! I shall not reply to night; but you had better be here by eight in the morning," and soon after the court adjourned to that hour.

When I reached the terrace of the castle* my steps were arrested, and even the necessity of sleep forgotten, by the sight of the most splendid sunrise I had ever beheld! I did not pause to gaze on it alone, and I should not have paused in my narrative, in order to mention so irrelevant a circumstance, had not my companion been one whom I never again beheld; one whom I have pleasure in recalling to my memory, and of whom I have lately been agreeably reminded by Dr. Bowring's amusing memoir of Jeremy Bentham. I allude to the late George Wilson, who for many years went the Norwich Circuit, and to whom I was made known at an early age, and by whom my love of attending courts was good humouredly encouraged. When impaired health (rather than age) obliged this amiable and intellectual man to quit the bar, he retired into Scotland, his native country, and I think he took up his abode in the delightful city of Edinburgh, where he died a few years ago, lamented and regretted by all who had the privilege of his acquaintance. It is a satisfaction to me to have had the oportunity of paying even this little tribute to his memory.

I was in court again by half-past seven, but too late to obtain a seat, and I stood many hours, in a painful position, but I was soon made unconscious of it by the eloquence of Erskine; for during those hours he spoke, and hushed a court, crowded even to suffocation, into the most perfect stillness. Never was the power of an orator over his audience more evident or more complete.

The plaintiff gained her cause, and her advocate new laurels; for I know that those best qualified to form a correct judgment on the subject, namely, his brother lawyers, who were present, declared that they had "never before heard Mr. E. so great in reply."

Fortunate, therefore, were those who heard him that day, as never again was he heard to equal advantage. A few

* The Assizes were held at this time in a building at the top of the Castle Hill adjoining the Castle.

months afterwards he was made Lord Chancellor, and when, while talking to him at a party in London, I told him I was every day intending to go into the Court of Chancery, in hope of hearing him speak in his new capacity—his reply was, "Pray do not come! you will not hear anything worth the trouble. I am nothing now; you heard the last and best of me at Norwich last year!"

This was indeed too true; and those powers of forensic eloquence for which he was so celebrated, he could exercise no longer. His audiences, in future life, were almost wholly different from his former ones, and those attractions so peculiarly his own, were not necessary on the judgment-seat, in the Court of Chancery, and would have been in a measure thrown away in the House of Lords.

Fortunate, therefore, I repeat it, were those who heard him in the Right-of-Way cause at Norwich, and when he forcibly reminded me of the portrait of Garrick so admirably drawn by the pen of Sheridan in his unequalled monody—a portrait which might have been supposed to be that of the Honorable Thomas Erskine, for his indeed were

> "The grace of action, the adapted mien,
> Faithful as nature to the varied scene;
> The expressive glance, whose subtle comment draws
> Entranc'd attention and a mute applause;
> Gesture that marks, with sense of feeling fraught,
> A sense in silence, and a will in thought.
> Harmonious speech, whose pure and liquid tone
> Gives verse a music scarce confess'd its own:
> As light from gems assumes a brighter ray,
> And cloth'd with orient hues transcends the day.
> Passion's wild break, and frowns that awe the sense
> And every charm of gentler eloquence."

CHAPTER IX.

PROSPERITY; "SIMPLE TALES;" VISIT TO SOUTHILL; LADY ROSLYN; MR. OPIE'S "LECTURES;" HIS ILLNESS; HIS DEATH.

The year 1806 was, to the subject of these memoirs, prosperous, and full of joyful anticipation for the future, beyond any that had preceded it. The time so long desired seemed now at hand; Mr. Opie saw himself justly rewarded, for all his labour and perseverance amid difficulties and disappointments, by success and fame; "he was conscious (his wife says) that our circumstances were now such as would enable us to have more of the comforts and elegancies of life, and to receive our friends in a manner more suited to the esteem which we entertained for them; I was allowed to make the long projected alterations and improvements in my own apartments; and he had resolved to indulge himself in the luxury (as he called it) of keeping a horse." But alas! when the time did come, it came too late!

Not, however, to anticipate—in the spring of this year, Mrs. Opie published her "Simple Tales," in four volumes; tales which are characterized by the same merits, as well as defects, as are found in her other works of this description. For a critique upon them, and on Mrs. Opie's merits as an author, we must refer the reader to the article, before alluded to, in the July number of "The Edinburgh Review," for 1806, from which we may be allowed to quote a short extract. After alluding to the deficiencies of her style, and observing that few of her personages can be said to be original, or even uncommon, the writer says:—

"They have, however, a merit in our eyes incomparably superior; they are strictly true to general nature, and are rarely exhibited except in interesting situations; * * * there is something delightfully feminine in all Mrs. O.'s writings; an apparent artlessness in the composition of her narrative; and something which looks like want of skill or practice in writing for the public, that gives a powerful effect to the occasional beauties and successes of her genius; there is nothing like an ambitious, or even a sustained tone in her stories; we often think she is going to be tedious or silly; and immediately,. without effort or apparent consciousness of improvement, she slides into some graceful and interesting dialogue, or charms us with some fine and delicate analysis of the subtler feelings, which would have done honour to the genius of Marivaux. She does not reason well; but she has, like most accomplished women, the talent of perceiving truth, without the process of reasoning, and of bringing it out with the facility and the effect of an obvious and natural sentiment. Her language is often inaccurate, but it is almost always graceful and harmonious. She can do nothing well that requires to be done with formality; and, therefore, has not succeeded in copying either the concentrated force of weighty and deliberate reason, or the severe and solemn dignity of majestic virtue. To make amends, however, she represents admirably everything that is amiable, generous, and gentle."

The following note by Mr. Sydney Smith, was

written soon after this time, when she was preparing to publish one of her subsequent works:—

DEAR MRS. OPIE,

I have read your manuscripts, upon the whole, with great satisfaction; two or three I have advised you to suppress; two or three to correct and polish; and upon many I have bestowed a praise, which I hope, for your sake, is as enlightened, as it is warm and sincere. Tenderness is your forte, and carelessness your fault.

Direct me how to dispose of your MS., and believe me,

Ever yours most truly,

S. SMITH.

Mrs. S. begs her kind compliments to you. You will find my remarks scrawled in pencil under each page. I have left emendations to you, merely marking where they are wanted.

In the summer of this memorable year, (when, as the phrase is, "all the talents were in," so soon to be driven out by the death of Fox,) Mr. and Mrs. Opie went, accompanied by Mr. Wilkie, on a visit to Southill, the seat of Mr. Whitbread; "and never," says Mrs. Opie, "did I see my husband so happy, when absent from London, as he was there; for he felt towards the host and hostess every sentiment of respect and admiration which it is pleasant to feel, and honourable to inspire. But though he was the object of the kindest and most flattering attention, he sighed to return to London and his pursuits; and when he had been at Southill only eight days, he said to me, on my expressing my unwillingness to go away, 'Though I shall be even anxious to come hither again, remember that I have been idle *eight days!*' "

In a letter to her father, during this visit, she gives a pleasing account of some of the events that transpired:—

1806

My dear Father,

I received the parcel safe, and beg you to thank Mr. Taylor for his letter, and tell him I am quite convinced of his sobriety, but not the less of my neglect. Your letter is just arrived. I had already asked about the boroughs and borough-mongers; but Mr. W. knows not where to find the latter, and nothing certainly about the price of the former; but he fancies it is £4000 for a single seat, and five, or more, for two seats. * * * *

We arrived here after a pleasant journey of forty-two miles, (not sixty, as we were told it was,) at three o'clock on Saturday. Part of the country through which we passed was pleasant, but for some miles before we approached Southill, we went through such bleak barrenness, as was scarcely cheered by the sight of a large white house seen at a distance, which we took to be Mr. Whitbread's. In two miles more we entered the park, "and paradise seemed opened in the wild." The entrance is near the house, which is, however, perfectly concealed by a thick shrubbery aud high trees, skirting a winding gravel walk up to the house, which bursts upon you very beautifully indeed. The country is flat; but in the front of the house there is a slight inequality of ground, and the lawn is so beautiful, and the trees so fine, and the shrubs so richly diversified; in short, it is so truly a smiling scene, and at the same time so comfortably sequestered, that, for a dwelling, I would not change it for one commanding views of bolder country. On entering the house, the true use and enjoyment of unbounded opulence force themselves at once on one's conviction. Everything is rich, but at the same time tasteful and comfortable; and the more you see, and the longer you inhabit Southill, the more you feel assured that, used as it is there, opulence is a blessing. The family, not expecting us till near six, were out when we arrived; so the groom of the chambers led us to our apartments, consisting of a large dressing-room and bed-room; and we had the pleasure to find that our room commanded the pretty view at the front of the house, of which a pond, prettily shaded, is an agreeable feature. As soon as we had had sandwiches, &c., the barouche and the family arrived, and we had the sorrow to find Lady Elizabeth very unwell, and so she had been all the time on her journey. She immediately went to lie down. Mr. Opie accompanied Mr. Whitbread, &c., in the barouche, in a drive which he was going to take, four-in-hand; and Mr. Wilkie and I took a walk. At six we all met at dinner.

Wednesday. I began this yesterday before breakfast, but had no opportunity of resuming my pen till to-day, nine o'clock. Nobody down but my husband and myself. He is standing under a colonnade, going from the open window at which I am now sitting, enjoying the rolling of the thunder and the forked lightning, which, untired with its tremendous violence last night, has renewed the elemental strife to-day. It reminds me of the storm some twenty years ago, which made a tour through the whole country. Hark! it comes nearer and nearer, and the lightning flashes across my face. I doubt there has been mischief done somewhere.—But to resume my narrative.—I need not tell you our dinner was excellent, and French enough to delight me. The dessert consisted of ice, pine apple, and every variety of fruit and wine. The only guests here are Reynolds, Wilkie, ourselves, and Lady Roslyn and her children. After a pleasant evening, Lady Elizabeth being much recovered, we retired at eleven, and were summoned to meet the next morning at the breakfast table at nine, that we might get off for Woburn Abbey in good time. We got away a little before eleven, Tom Adkin and Wilkie in a gig, Lady E. W., Lady Roslyn, Miss Whitbread, her brother, Reynolds, and ourselves in the barouche and four greys, driven by Mr. Whitbread. The day was only too fine, as its extreme brightness almost made it impossible for us to gaze on the really pretty country which we passed. * * * Interrupted by the tempest, and for the first time in my life *terrified* and awed almost to fainting by the nearness and overpowering brilliancy of the lightning, and the loudness of the thunder; it is quite over the house, and one feels as if the vast building was rived in twain. It was quite mournful to hear the cattle lowing and the sheep bleating their fears last night. Another and another louder yet! the rain falling in torrents. The poor green parrot by me, its powers sharpened by fear, is trying to imitate the thunder; the other parrot, a grey one, seems too much alarmed to speak. I never felt so nervous before at a storm, but it quite oppresses me! * * I think it abates. How I pity those who are always afraid at such times, during the awful continuance of such a tempest as this! At eleven Lady Roslyn was to leave us; she can't go now certainly, and I wish her departure may be delayed till to-morrow. On the stairs I met three lovely children the first day I came, and the nursemaid said, "this is Lady Janet Sinclair." And who is that lovely boy in petticoats? "That is Lord Loughborough." I thought I should have laughed in the child's face, for my associations with that name are a great wig and a parrot face! The child himself, an uncommonly grand and handsome boy, of four years old, says, "my *real* name is *James*, that is what my friends call me, but my nickname is Lord Loughborough." "And who calls you by your nickname?" "The maids in the nursery."

The storm is greatly subsided, at least it is further off, or I could not have told you this trifling story. If I have time after breakfast, before the post goes off, I will describe our delightful day at Woburn, and our drive yesterday. To-day Lady St. John is to dine here, and with her come Mr. Peakwell and his mother. Mrs. Bouverie writes to Lady R. (her daughter) every day, the most delightful accounts of Mr. Fox's health!

The envelope of this letter is missing.

Mrs. Opie has recorded, in her note book, some further particulars of this delightful visit; and especially in reference to Lady Roslyn, whom she had long wished to see and know.

At first (she says) I was rather disappointed in her beauty, but there was a charm in her manner and conversation which soon won upon me, and we shortly became mutually interested in each other, and visited Bedford Jail together, and two or three country houses, at one of which, belonging to our host, we remained for some time with the old dame who took care of it. Lady R. begged her to fetch us a draught of new milk, and the good woman, who was basting a leg of mutton, hastily laid down her basting-spoon and departed to fulfil her wishes. "It were a pity the good soul should suffer for her kindness," said the lady, and immediately seizing the ladle, the graceful countess commenced operations; while I, admiring her benevolence, pleased myself with observing her, and thought that among the interesting sights of the morning, that of seeing Harriet, Countess of Roslyn, basting a leg of mutton, was not the least.

The last paragraph in the preceding letter speaks of "delightful accounts of Mr. Fox's health;" soon to be exchanged for tidings of his lamented death, which happened on the 13th of September following.

On his return from this short period of relaxation, Mr. Opie betook himself with increasing diligence to the duties of his profession. "To the toils of the artist, during the day, (says his wife,) succeeded those of the writer, every evening; and from the month of September, 1806, to February, 1807, he allowed his mind no rest, and scarcely indulged in the relaxation of a walk, or the society of his friends." He was engaged in completing his Lectures on Painting, to be delivered as Professor of Painting, at the Royal Academy. Each of them, as he finished it, he read to his wife, and, after the delivery of the first lecture in the Academy, "he was complimented by his brethren, escorted home by Sir William Beechey, and appeared to his wife in a flush of joy. Next morning he said he had passed a restless night, for he was so elated that he could not sleep!"* The first of the lectures was delivered on the 16th February, 1807; the fourth and last, on the 9th of March following.

To the completion of these Lectures his life perhaps fell a sacrifice, at least so thought Mrs. Opie, and, in the bitterness of her regret, she wished they had never been thought of. When they were completed, his friend, Mr. Prince Hoare, requested of him an article for his periodical paper, called "The Artist." "I am tired, (he replied,) tired of writing; and I mean to be a gentleman in the spring months, keep a horse, and ride out every morning."

But it was otherwise determined. He shortly after sickened; a slow and consuming illness attacked him, and wasted his vital energies, baffling the skill of the most experienced physicians, who hastened to his bedside, and attended him during the few remaining weeks of his life, with unremitting attention. His poor wife said she had, at least, the soothing conviction, that no human means had been left untried to ward off the inevitable stroke. Her memoir concludes with a few details respecting the closing scenes, which are best given in her own words.

* A. Cunningham's Lives of British Artists.

I cannot dwell minutely on these painful hours. Great as my misery must have been at such a moment, under any circumstances, it was, if possible, aggravated by my being deprived of the consolation and benefit of my father's presence and advice, at this most trying period of my life; for he was attending the sick bed of his, apparently, dying mother. Yet she recovered, at the age of 85, to the perfect enjoyment of life and happiness, while Mr. Opie was cut off in the prime of his days! But let me dwell on the brighter side of the picture. Let me be thankful for the blessing I experienced in the presence of that sister, so dear to my husband, who, by sharing with me the painful, yet precious tasks of affection, enabled me to keep from his bed all hired nurses,—all attendants, but our deeply interested selves; that was indeed a consolation.

Of this sister Mrs. Opie speaks frequently with affectionate regard; and many years after, when she visited her husband's relations in Cornwall, expressed her tender regret that she was no longer living to welcome her, and to go over with her the memories of the past.

After paying a tribute of thanks to the numerous friends who evinced their sympathy and respect, and shared, with affectionate solicitude, her anxieties, she says:—

The most soothing consciousness which I now have to look back upon, when I revert to the painful scenes of his illness, is the certainty that my husband's last perceptions in this world were of a pleasurable nature. By the kindness of his friend and former pupil, Mr. Thompson, R. A., he was gratified in his desire to see his picture of the Duke of Gloucester, which he was most anxious should appear in the exhibition, completed, and when it was brought to the foot of his bed, he looked at it with the greatest satisfaction, and said, with a smile, "Take it away, it will do now." This incident seemed to give the turn to the delirium which followed, for he was painting in imagination upon it, until the last hour of his existence.

When Sir Joshua was buried in St. Paul's, Mr. Opie exclaimed to his sister, with the proud consciousness of innate power, "Aye girl! and I too shall be buried in St. Paul's." His prophecy was accomplished. On the 9th of April, 1807, in the 46th year of his age, he expired; and on the 20th, the remains of John Opie were interred close beside those of Sir Joshua Reynolds!

It was said of him, by one of the first painters of his day, "Others get forward by steps, but this man by strides;" and so Goethe said of his great rival Schiller, "Er hatte ein furchtbares Fortschreiten; und so ging er immer vorwärts, bis sechs und vierzig Jahre; dann war er denn, freilich, weit genug!"*

* "His strides were astounding: and so he continued ever onwards, for forty and six years; then indeed, he had gone far enough!"

CHAPTER X.

RETURN TO NORWICH; "POEMS;" MEMOIR OF HER HUSBAND; LETTER FROM LADY CHARLEVILLE; FROM MRS. INCHBALD; VISIT TO LONDON; PARTY AT LADY E. WHITBREAD'S; VISIT TO CROMER; "TEMPER;" "TALES OF REAL LIFE;" SOIRÉE AT MADAME DE STAEL'S.

On the death of her husband Mrs. Opie returned to the home of her youth, and to her father, for whom she now felt the more concentrated and entire affection, as he was the only object united to her by the dearest ties of nature. For, unhappily, her marriage was a childless one; the desire she cherished had been denied her, and no son was given her, to inherit the talents of his father, and be the joy of his mother's heart.

Providence, however, had preserved to her the parent whom she had left with regret, and whose love she still so dearly prized. It was now her duty and delight to devote herself to render him happy, and she left her sad abode, where all reminded her of the loss she had sustained, and came back to her father, and like a sunbeam her presence gladdened his home; and as a guardian angel she blessed him, the delight and the ornament of his declining years.

Of the seven years that followed the death of Mr. Opie not many traces remain among her papers; some there are, and we proceed to record them. That she left London very shortly after that event, is evident from a letter written by one of her friends dated July the 11th, 1807, and addressed to her at Norwich; as well as from a note, short enough to be given at length, signed Comtesse d'Oyenhausen.*

"Parmi les noms qui vous marquent autant d'estime que d'attachement, veuillez bien Mme. ajouter le mien, comme une preuve de n'être point oubliée. Vôtre départ trop prompt, laisse ici un vuide que tout le monde aperçoit, et très particulièrement vôtre," &c., &c.

In 1808 she published a second volume of poetry, entitled "The Warrior's Return, and other Poems;" in the preface to which she says, "The poems which compose this little volume were written, with two or three exceptions, several years ago, and to arrange and fit them for publication has been the amusement of many hours of retirement."

In the spring of 1809 were published her husband's "Lectures on Painting," to which was prefixed the "Memoir," from which we have so frequently quoted. This book was published by subscription, and some of her friends interested themselves in procuring names; one or two letters on the subject were found among her papers, and among them one from Lady Charleville, from which, as it contains some allusions to Mrs. Opie's writings, and shews the impression her manners produced upon those with whom she associated, we venture to select a few passages.

* This lady's name is among the subscribers to the "Lectures."

Charleville Forest, August 23rd, 1809.

MY DEAR MADAM,

I did not expect that you could find leisure to write to me before your return to Norwich, and I feel more obliged by your not delaying it long after, than I can easily express. Your amiable, modest manners, joined to talents far beyond the pretensions of most women, attracted me immediately; and all I have seen of you, permit me to say, has so confirmed this first bias, that I do feel a sincere wish to continue to cultivate the acquaintance I have so happily begun. * * * I believe you enjoy gay scenes, and what is called pleasure, with somewhat yet of pristine vivacity. May it fulfil your hopes or wishes whatever they are! * *

Poor dear Lady Cork's activity in pursuit of amusement is a pleasant proof of vivacity and spirit surviving youth. I think, however, small plays seldom succeed with an English audience; "*la vache qui trotte*," is Rousseau's simile for French music, and may be applied to John Bull's facetious and playful humours quite as well; but he does very well at a concert, where some must be quiet, and I envied you that evening you described so well. * * *

Our best bookseller here has fallen into a state of epilepsy; his shop is closed, and we shall await the arrival of your last publication with impatience, through the common channel; but I think you should not have awaited Lady C.'s interference to mention its being published by subscription; as I should be happy to be considered as your friend. Neglect me so no more, I request, in this way; begin a good, long, Clarissa-like novel; you have principles and fancy to compose an elevating and interesting work, and a knowledge of the manners of the world, which Richardson wanted. Write now all the summer, and let there be no episodes, no under plot, but give me a character, acting and developing itself under a variety of circumstances, to interest my feelings and exert my understanding; and set her feet on English ground, and let us not have mystic notions, or Asiatic refinements, to perplex our intellects, too well braced by this northern temperature to sympathize with mysteries, embroideries, and odours, or start at every creaking hinge in an old castle. Miss Owenson, whom I saw in Dublin, tells me she is writing a Hindostan tale. Let's keep plain English for yours; and believe me, in its full sincerity, your faithful servant,

C. L. CHARLEVILLE.

The following letter from Mrs. Inchbald appears to have been written in the winter of this year (1809.) Its only date is Wednesday, 7th December.

MY DEAR MRS. OPIE,

I thank you much for your letter, and especially for your consideration in telling me the secret of Mr. Barbauld's death; for contemplation is my great source of entertainment, and the events of the day kindly afford me almost as much as I require.

I certainly think Buonaparte has acted, in the affairs of Spain, with less honour to his name than upon all former occasions; yet he was compelled to protect his firm ally, Charles IV., and to punish the criminal Prince who drove his parents from their throne, and imprisoned them. Still, you will say, why did he not replace Charles? The people of Spain would not have suffered his return; and, no doubt, many of the first importance invited Buonaparte to take the government. That he did so by artifice, I can only excuse, upon the supposition that he meant thus to spare the people all that calamity, which open violence must now draw upon them. No doubt his reign would have been a blessing to them, would they at first have submitted. But now the avenger is the character he must take, and we shall have to lament another nation, added to the number of those, on whom we have forced him to draw his sword.

I have not been from London yet, and I purposely did not date my letter, because I wished to have no presents this year, and had not time to explain why. My sister has been very ill again, and is in that kind of weak state, that she now never comes to see me, and I fear much that the winter may prove fatal to her. She always partook of your presents, and I had rather not be reminded of the loss I feel from the want of her occasional visits, by having any feasts during her absence.

Poor Godwin is a terrific example for all conjugal biography; but he has marked that path which may be avoided, and so is himself a sacrifice for the good of others. His name I now see added to his library advertisements. The title of Miss Owenson's new work has something very charming in it. "Ida of Athens."—I have not yet been able to read any of her novels. I am now reading Leo the X., by Roscoe. War, religion, laws, and elevated mankind are my delight, for among them I increase my love for politics of the present day, and find that our great enemy is less wicked than most heroes and politicians have been; at the same time a vast deal wiser than them all.

With my best respects to Dr. Alderson,

Dear Madam,

E. INCHBALD.

In the spring of the following year Mrs. Opie was in London, and it seems to have been from this time her established custom to pay an annual visit to the metropolis. The spring of 1810 was a stirring one, and she, who so dearly loved (as she says) to have a peep at the busy world, has given in one of her reminiscences of this period, a short account of a dinner party at Lady Elizabeth Whitbread's, the day after the removal of Sir F. Burdett to the Tower. The Government had been obliged to have recourse to the Speaker's warrant, to obtain legal entrance into Sir F.'s house, which he had purposely barricaded, being determined to resist what he thought an unjust sentence.

I went (she says) to the dinner in Dover Street, full of hope that I should hear at that table some interesting conversation relative to these peculiar circumstances, for it was a time of no common excitement, as great fears of a popular tumult had gone forth, and I had myself seen, with a sensation difficult to describe, cannon planted in Hanover Square at this period, as I returned late from a party to my lodgings in Prince's Street; and soldiers were watching by their guns. (I think I am correct in speaking in the plural number.) My expectation of hearing the subject of Sir F. B.'s arrest discussed, was increased, when I saw of whom the party assembled round the dinner table consisted; there were no ladies present but our hostess, the Countess G., her venerable mother, and myself; the gentlemen were Lord King, and I think two whig M.P.'s, members of the Lower House, and also some gentlemen not in public life.

I was, however, disappointed, and learned to believe that Members of Parliament hear too much of state matters when there, to wish to discuss them in their hours of relaxation, as the only allusion made to the event of the preceding day, was this. The master of the house found it a difficult, and, for some time, an impossible task, to open the hard rind of an immense shaddock which stood before him, and said he must give it up in despair. "He had better send for the Speaker's warrant," said one of the guests; but this observation was not heard, therefore it led to nothing. Amongst the evening guests came Lady Roslyn; and soon, engaged in the bloodless, but not pointless, strife of tongues, were lady R., J. W. Ward, the late Lord Dudley, W. Lyttleton, Sheridan, and the ever welcome Sydney Smith.

Sheridan did not arrive till late, and when some of the company, who yet remained, were seated at the supper tables, to which he immediately repaired. Soon after, my attention was forcibly arrested by his deep sonorous voice, exerted in questioning, as if with a view to cross-examination, a very handsome youth in a Greek dress, and who was by birth also a Greek, according to his own shewing. This young man was much in request in certain circles; and his right to be there, and to be acknowledged as what he declared himself to be, would probably not have been questioned, had he not chosen to wear this very peculiar and becoming dress. As soon as I found what was going on, I went and stood by Sheridan's elbow, and was amused by the extraordinary questions by which he sought to discover the reality of the youth's pretensions. I could not but feel for a youthful foreigner, exposed to such an ordeal, inflicted by such a man, but he seemed to bear it unmoved. At last Sheridan turned round to us who stood behind him, and said, "A quack, nothing but a quack."

Two years afterwards, I saw a young Greek of the same name at another party, with whom I overheard Lord Byron talking with great fluency, in what I was told was modern Greek. The tones of Lord B.'s voice were always so fascinating, that I could not help attending to them; and when I turned round to see with whom he was conversing, I thought I saw the same face and person in an English garb, whom I had seen in 1810, set off by a beautiful turban and a crimson robe; but I was told this was a brother of that youth, and I never afterwards had an opportunity of ascertaining, with accuracy, whether it was the same person or not; yet I wished to do so, in order to establish the truth or falsehood of the charge of quackery which I had heard. If these youths were brothers, it was very unlikely that either of them was a quack; and surely the harmless vanity of wishing to appear in his own native costume, was not sufficient to authorize so severe an appellation.

Be that as it may, of all the merry combatants in the strife of tongues at the party to which I allude, Sydney Smith is the sole survivor! he is merry still, and the provoker of mirth in others; but perhaps, like me, when he feels his memory crowded with the names of departed friends and associates, an involuntary sadness comes over his mind, as it does over mine, and I weep as I remember the exquisite and incomparable lines of Moore—

> "When I remember all
> Once linked in love together," &c.

Lady Roslyn expressed a wish that when I visited Edinburgh I would go to Roslyn, and that she might have the opportunity of shewing me its beauties. Alas! when I went there in 1816, she was in her grave, and I stood within the chapel on the stone which covered her remains!

The autumn of this year found Mrs. Opie once more at her favourite Cromer; and her stay appears to have been prolonged to an unusual extent; so that one of her friends, writing to her in the month of December, speaks of sending a second Ulysses in search of the truant. There is an allusion in this letter which seems to intimate that it was not *faute de solicitations* that she remained a widow; and it is evident that at subsequent periods she received similar addresses. Turning, however, a deaf ear to such proposals, she continued diligently to use her pen; and in the spring of 1812 published "Temper," a tale, in which she diverged from the pathetic style of writing she had hitherto most affected, and evidently aimed more, in the character of a moralist, at practical usefulness; and happily with pleasing evidence of success. In the third volume of this work, Mrs. Opie carries her heroine to Paris, and introduces the very scenes which she records in her journal of her own Parisian trip—the visit to the Louvre—her own words on being told the First Consul was expected to pass—the scene that followed, &c.

The following extract from a letter she received after the publication of this work, affords a pleasing evidence of its beneficial influence.

November 14th, 1812.

You have, my dear Mrs. Opie, shown such clear discernment of what is good and virtuous, and exhibited reason and conscience, as triumphant over the passions, with so masterly a pen, in your late publication, that it has carried with it the suffrage of many a young and amiable mind.

My daughter may perhaps have told you what effect your book had, upon a young married lady whom she chanced to meet. "I have read," said she, "Mrs. Opie's 'Temper,' I hope to my lasting improvement; certain I am that it has shewn me many of my faults, and, I trust, has taught me to overcome them." By the pleasure this gave me, I can judge, in some degree, my dear Madam, of the pleasure it must afford you; for I think there cannot be a greater, than to fortify the young in habits of virtue; and when you consider these volumes, you may exclaim, with more propriety than Sheridan did, "that on the review of his publications, nothing gave him such great, such inexpressible pleasure, as the thought that he had never written one word derogatory to the cause of virtue." * * *

In the following year (1813) appeared the "Tales of Real Life;" they were published (unlike her former works) without a paragraph, introductory or dedicatory. There is, as usual, much inequality in the merits of the various stories composing the series; "Lady Anne and Lady Jane" occupies the whole of the first volume, and is, perhaps, on the whole, equal, or superior, to any tale she wrote. The one entitled, "Love and Duty," was a favourite with herself.

In a former chapter, reference has been made to an interview Mrs. Opie had with Lord Erskine, at the house of Madame de Staël during this year; she has given another short account of an evening visit to that celebrated woman, which we subjoin:—

I had been spending the evening at a soirée, given by Madame de Staël, during the year 1813, which was particularly interesting, from its having been composed chiefly of the *élite* of London society. That admirable man, W. Wilberforce, had been among the dinner guests, but was gone before I arrived; there were, however, many still left, some of whom threw over the circle the spell of beauty, and others that of their high talents. Lady Crewe, Lord Dudley, William Spencer, the Mackintoshes, the Romillys, were among the brilliant group, who, witty themselves, were the cause of wit in others; and, while they grouped around her, called forth the ever-ready repartees, and almost unrivalled eloquence, of our hostess. She had recently left the court of Bernadotte, and from time to time indulged herself in descanting in his praise. At length she produced a portrait in miniature of her favourite, painted in profile; and, when it had gone round the greater part of the circle, she put it into the hand of Sir Henry Englefield, well known as a man of virtu, science, and taste for the fine arts; and, while she stood by the side of the chair on which he was indolently lounging, she evidently awaited, with much anxiety, the result of his examination. Carefully and long did he examine the painting, and then, holding it up to the light which hung near him, he observed with a slow distinct utterance, and in rather loud voice, "he is like a ferocious sheep!" on which, uttering an exclamation of justly indignant surprise, Madame de Staël snatched the miniature from him, and turned hastily away. I turned away also, for I could not help smiling because, though displeased at Sir Henry's want of courtesy I felt the truth of the remark; for *I* had examined the picture, and seen, with no admiring eye, the long projecting nose, and the receding chin, so truly the profile of a sheep; the eye, too, was black, but it did not, like a sheep's eye, resemble a blockhead when seen sideways; on the contrary, it was bright and *piercing*, as a friend would have said, but it was easy for an enemy of the Swedish Prince (and such I concluded Sir H. was) to have called the expression *ferocious*. But the incident and its effects were soon forgotten; and the circle had not lost its charm, when, reminded by a pendule of the lateness of the hour, I had placed myself near the door, and was watching an opportunity to retire unseen, as the door opened; and unannounced, and unattended, a shortish, middle-sized, and middle-aged man entered the room, and, finding himself unobserved, did not advance further than where I was. I was struck by the plainness of his dress and his unpretending appearance, altogether, yet his manner was dignified rather than otherwise; and I was wondering who he could be, when our hostess saw him, and ran up to him with a degree of delighted yet respectful welcome, which instantly proclaimed him to be somebody. In a short time he was seen by others, and he had soon a little court around him; but who he was I could not yet discover; however, I delayed my departure, and joining the circle, heard him converse with a simplicity consonant to his manner and appearance.

At length I heard him addressed "votre Majesté," and I could not forbear to ask who this royal stranger was, and learned that it was the king of the Netherlands, who was awaiting, in our country, a change of things in his favour in his own. Little, probably, did he, or any of those present, imagine that change was so near; but, before the year came round, Buonaparte was at Elba! His changes of fortune, however, were not yet over: when I saw him he was King of the Netherlands; and, soon after, became their *restored* king; but had I seen him again in the year 1835, I should have beheld him deprived of half his dominions, and only King of Holland!

CHAPTER XI.

LETTERS OF MRS. OPIE TO DR. ALDERSON, WRITTEN DURING HER VISIT IN LONDON IN THE YEAR 1814.

"IN 1814, the Emperor of Russia, the King of Prussia, and other royal and distinguished foreigners were, as everybody knows, in London," says Mrs. Opie, in one of her reminiscences of the scenes she witnessed at that stirring time; for she was there, in the very midst of all the gaiety and whirl. Many of the letters she wrote home to her father, during her three months' stay in London at this time, have been preserved, and we give them almost entire.

11, Orchard Street, Portman Square,
21st May, 1814.

MY DEAR FATHER,

You would be sure that, so tempted, I should go to Hudson Gurney's, and I did. The company consisted of Lady Nelson, Mrs. Forbes, her daughter, Lady James Hay, Armine and Edmund Wodehouse, M. Bland, Mr. Maltby, his wife's nephew, just returned from the army, Mr. Hume, of the India House, Dr. Southey, and Frank Morse: I was so fortunate as to sit between the two Wodehouses. I must tell you a *bon mot* of Dudley North's which was told me. "Sheridan, (said Dudley N.) I hear you are coming forward for Westminster again." "Pho! replied he, if I were, I am sure I must be *wound up* again." "And if you were wound up (returned D. N.) you would go on as usual, tick-tick-tick."

The Prince has sunk himself in the mud, with all parties, by his endeavour to get to himself the exclusive privilege of inviting all the royalties, that he might exclude his wife, the Princess of Gloucester, and the Dukes of Sussex, Kent, and Gloucester. Lord Seyton had sent to give tickets to the Princess, and on being pressed by Lord Yarmouth to recall them, he replied, "Yarmouth, go and tell the Prince Regent that I am no dancer, but that if the Princess of Wales will do me the honour of dancing with me, I will open the ball with her." This, Lord Montford told me, as a fact, on Thursday evening. At Boodle's, on the Prince's applying for the same privilege as at White's, they voted three to one against him. Lord M. added, that if, as she is likely to do, goaded as she is, (silly woman!) she goes to White's, and is refused admission, it is probable that the populace may take her part, and endanger the house. For my part, I see no necessary difference between the conduct proper for a royal wife and a wife in a private station; and as a public brawl between an angry wife and a brutal husband would excite just indignation in private life, I cannot do otherwise than consider the Princess as violating her duty, however great her wrongs, by exposing herself to insult, and her husband also, by persisting to do what is disagreeable to him; let her take care to fulfil her *own* duties, and she will meet what she deserves, the respect and pity of every one. But I believe her to be a weak vixen, or at least that she loves to teaze the Prince.

Next day, in the evening, the L. M.s came and took me to the Hamiltons' ball. We went late, and found the rooms so crowded, that we took our station on the stairs, where Lady Montford joined us, and talking occasionally to Edward, Tom, Lord M., and two or three other men, we made ourselves amusement, till we thought Mrs. H. thought us acting fine, so then we entered the hot room, where we staid till the carriage got up, and then came away, though the H.s said they would not forgive us if we did not stay to supper; but I was more fit to be in bed, having then, and *now*, a crying cold, that is most trying, and makes me look like an owl. Yesterday I went out with Mrs. Gurney and left some cards. In the evening I went to Miss White's, (having dined at home on eggs and coffee) where I found some rank, talent, and odd looking notoriety and ability. Lady Mackintosh asked me to dine there on Monday, and Mrs. Philips, to a party, on Wednesday; but business and duty take me to Mitcham on Monday for two or three days. Just as Lady M. turned away from me, a young man who had been talking to her said to me, "that odd looking man yonder is a distinguished character; that is Mr. Gallatin, the American commissioner." "So Lady Mackintosh told me." "I told you," he replied, "because we all like to have lions pointed out; I shall do *him* the same kindness, for I shall point you out to him." "You are very obliging," said I, making him a low curtsey, and thinking I had never seen anything so impudent since the days of Mr. Hirst, and wondering who he could be. "For my own part," continued he, "I am remarkable for being, what you may think is not very remarkable in this great city, namely, a very impudent fellow, in thus introducing myself to you." I laughed, but would not ask his name of himself. I asked it of Lady M., and found him to be a Mr. Cullen, son of Dr. Cullen. Farewell! till Wednesday, and pray write and let me know all about you.

A. Opie.

Mitcham, 25th May, 1814.

My dear Father,

I wonder much I have not yet heard from you; it is now ten days since I heard of or from home!

On Sunday C. breakfasted with me, and we went to Bedford Chapel to hear S. Smith preach; Mrs. H. C. saw us in the aisle, and took us into her pew. We had an excellent sermon, but, *entre nous*, I saw C. nearly asleep several times. She said she liked the sermon exceedingly, but I am sure she did not hear some fine parts. (There's Ella Roberts taking off a little dog howling or barking, so like *nature* that I have been calling her a little howling puppy; the noise a dog makes when his toe is trodden upon is most admirable. * * * * She has now exhausted herself so much with the fatigues of her canine madness, as she calls it, that she is quiet, and I stand a chance of finishing my letter in peace.)

My *levée* on Sunday was rather splendid, consisting of twenty-seven persons, who (men excepted) chiefly came in carriages. These carriages succeeded each other so quickly, that the servants asked my servant what was to be *seen* at No. 11; and when he said "a lady," they answered, "what, is she ill?" My cousin came first, and told me his brother had been in town, and had often talked of visiting me, and when he returns I am to see him.

The next day I took a coach, and came to Mitcham! a sad arrival! But, as you may suppose, the freshness of grief was all mine, and it became my duty to conquer the expression of it as soon as possible; but I am only now in my usual spirits. * * * We are very comfortable together; there is too, here, the *nicest* set of children; we had them all in last night, and we played at magical music, and I made myself hoarse with singing through a comb.

Upon my word I shall be very savage if I don't hear from you, and of the romans, alias romances or novels, in Pottergate Street and St. Helen's. * * * Of all things in the world, truth and ingenuousness, the foundation of all virtue, are the rarest. Farewell! till Saturday.

A. Opie.

Tuesday, 31st of May, 1814.

I begin my letter to day, my dear father, as I shall probably be hurried to-morrow. * * * On Sunday Tom went with me to hear S. Smith at Baker Street chapel; and luckily a friend of Tom's, hearing him say I was coming, secured a place for me with a friend of his. This gentleman went home with us, and I was amused by his account of Spurzheim, the lecturer on Craniology, whom I am going to meet at Dr. Busk's. * * * * I had a very pleasant morning, for my court, as L. M. calls it, was full and agreeable. Rollis, Busks, Mr. Blair, Hamiltons, a new acquaintance they brought, a Mr. Bainbridge, Mr. Kingston, Mrs. C. Hanbury and her daughter, &c. At dinner I met Lady Cork, Professor Spurzheim, Tenant, Dr. Rogier, or Roget, (I forget which it is) and a young surgeon who is craniology mad. Tenant talked all dinner, and in no way was the philosopher called out. I thought this very rude and English, and so did Lady Cork; therefore when the gentlemen joined us, she seated herself by Mr. Spurzheim, and began to talk to him of his art. I joined them; and he was explaining to me his ideas of the brain, when *my* ideas were distracted, and my brain rendered wool-gathering, by the arrival, not of a very large importation of clever men and women, but of Dr. Brown, *the* Dr. Brown, professor and lecturer on moral philosophy, the successor of Dugald Stuart, the Edinburgh Reviewer, and the recondite reviewer of Mrs. Opie, in the first number of that celebrated work. He came with the L. M.s, and was soon presented to me. I recollected L. M.'s character of him, that he liked *faire le galant, vis-a-vis des dames,* better than to converse in society, therefore I expected what I found, a flattering Scotchman, and I could have broken my silly head, because I felt fluttered while talking to him; however, I recovered myself at last, and, as I told Mr. Blair I would do, I contrived to be civil in my turn, though he (Mr. Blair) assured me he thought the philosopher quite conceited enough already. I must leave off, I am grie * * * *Wednesday,* 1st June. *Grieved* for Henry Burrell I meant to say, but if I had, I should have mourned foolishly, he being yesterday alive and better: this is to me incomprehensible, unless, which I hope cannot be the case, W. Burrell himself is ill. * *

To resume my Journal. I did contrive to say civil things

to Dr. Brown; but the wonder of the crowd, and the persons who sucked us all in turn into their vortex, were Professor Spurzheim and Lady M. Shepherd. Her ladyship fairly threw down the gauntlet, and was as luminous, as deep, as clever in her observations and questions, and her display of previous knowledge of Gall's theory and Hartley's, as any professor could have been, and convinced *me*, at least, that when Mr. Tierney said, of Lady Mary, she was almost the best metaphysician he ever knew, and the most logical woman, *by far*, he ever met with, he was probably *right*. The professor looked alarmed, and put on his pins; and Lady Mary began her dialogue at ten, and it was not over at a little past twelve.

Dr. Brown listened occasionally, and with an *anatomizing* eye, for he does not like literary women; therefore a woman, entering his own arena, must have called forth all his reviewer bitterness. L. M. had assured Dr. B. our parties were mixed ones, and nothing like science or learning displayed; and on his first introduction he meets with a scene like this!

On the 11th I dine at L. M.'s to meet Dr. Brown and Lord Erskine, &c. When S. Smith breakfasts with me I mean to ask Dr. B. also. Farewell! I must conclude.

Dr. Brown has just called on me, uninvited and self-introduced. He is gone again. Adieu!

4th June, 1814.

My dear Father,

I expect a frank from Mr. Heathcote every minute. Last Tuesday was a miserable day, for it rained hard; my sense of duty made me keep my engagement, and accompany Mrs. Parry to the speeches, at Harrow. Her other friends left her in the lurch, and Mr. P. was too unwell to go; we dined at Harrow, at the Inn; and I returned too tired, unfortunately, to dress and go to Mrs. S.'s assembly, which was, I hear, very pleasant. Friday (yesterday) evening, Lord Tamworth called on me; he arrived the day before, and is come for a month to lodgings in the next street (Somerset Street.) Mr. Rolls met Lord T. in the street and asked him to an evening party of music, &c., at his house yesterday evening; and when Lord T. arrived, we were a complete Leamington party. Lord T. called on Lady Cork yesterday to announce himself, and be ready for the dinner she promised us. But alas! she has fixed it for to-morrow, and Lord T., Lord Erskine, and I, are engaged, and cannot go! I dine to-day at Mr. Philips', and go to Lady C's misses and muffins in the evening; however, I must say, to Lord T.'s credit, that he is our only L. beau who looks here, even better than he did there; indeed, better, for he threw more dignity into his air last night, and all the other men looked comparatively vulgar. How I honour Lady N. Dr. O. had the officious brutality to write her a letter of four sides, disapproving Lord N.'s goings on, and telling tales of him; that is, repeating scandal concerning him; on which Lady N. said to her lord, "I dare say N. you deserve all this and much more, but it is an insult to a wife, for a man to dare abuse her husband to her, and I shall write as follows," and she wrote thus:—"Sir, I conclude the time will come when you will repent having written such a letter to me; I return it to you, that you may have the satisfaction of burning it with your own hands!" There's a wife for you! I brought tears into her husband's eyes, by my praises of her.

On Monday, Doly and I walk over to dine at four, at cousin Briggs', and I am not yet engaged in the evening. I went yesterday to pay visits; I found Lady Shepherd at home, and as friendly as ever; but she sees less of her charming husband than before, even. I found Lady Mary also at home, and she wanted me to go thither in the evening, but I was engaged. She was nervous about her display on Sunday last; but I assured her she was thought to talk well, though I could have added, but not by Dr. Brown. By the bye, I had only just sealed my letter to you when Dr. Brown came in uninvited; he apologised for his impudence in coming, we shook hands, and I found myself *tête à tête* with an Edinburgh reviewer, and a lecturer on moral philosophy! However, I did not *die* of it, as I offered to take him to Lady C.'s *pink* party to-night, and her *blue* one on the 11th, and to the latter he will probably go. Lady Mary Shepherd told me she had inquired, and the foundation of my mysterious stranger, did really happen to her father's eldest brother, Lord Dunmany, my Lord D.; with this addition, that when Lady D.'s coffin arrived at Deal or Dover, the first husband, in a sort of frenzy, stabbed the coffin, that he might get a sight of his lost wife's face. I find Joseph Gurney was gentleman-usher at the Meeting to the Duchess of Oldenburg. I shall like to hear his account of her. I will not seal this till the last moment. I now recollect I might have sent my letter to be franked, but then I must trust other people's servants.

11, Orchard Street, June 14th, 1814.

MY DEAR FATHER,

* * * Margaret came, just before Doly and I set off, and was glad to go to the concert, so I was easy. She eats nothing but pudding or tart, and potatoes, and drinks only water. She is a very fine creature, and has the most graceful dignified carriage possible, and I assure you I like much to have to *shew* her. Yesterday a party of us went to Franklin's, the fruiterer's, in Pall Mall, to see the Emperor, &c., arrive, and there we waited fruitlessly till near six, and to this hour we know not when the royals arrived, but sure it is we were all disappointed, high and low. While we were there, B. was called out of the room by Mr. Franklin, who went backwards and forwards into Carlton House, and he told him first that the Prince was so afraid of an attack on his palace, that he had, under a pretence of its being a guard of honour, gotten a party of *blues* into the palace, and next he said, that the Prince was so low and so nervous that they could not get him downstairs, and that he would not go to meet the kings, and declared he would not stir at all, or shew himself. Last Saturday he was going out at the left-hand gate, but seeing a crowd at it, he drew the string, ordered the gate to be closed, and drove to the other; but by that time the mob was

there also, on which he ordered that to be closed, and went out a backway. This shews how shattered his nerves are. It seems strange that he should not have gone to meet the kings now come, in the same way as he met the king of France; and as, whatever he may be, he has at least been doing the honours of the country and of a sovereign *well*, I am sorry that he is deprived of the only opportunity he has or *values*, of appearing to advantage. Still, he has only himself to blame in the first instance; but I disapprove and dislike as much the woman and the wife, who stirs up the nation against her husband; she violates *her* duties, I think, *et l'un vaut bien l'autre.* Foolish vixen as she is! if she stirs up a flame to consume her husband, the same flame in the end must consume her; let her look to that, and for that "even-handed justice, which returns the poisoned chalice to one's own lips." I enjoyed my day at H. Briggs' much; Doly and I walked thither, and back again, at night. A night dark as Erebus; and the effect of the bright city, when we reached the bridge, and St. Margaret's bells ringing a peal of expectation of the Emperor, and the crowds of persons still gathering in hopes of his arrival, had a most striking and novel effect.

Thursday, 9th. I resolved not to finish this letter, but get a frank at Mr. W. Smith's, as I was going to attend Mrs. S.'s *levée*, and I am now expecting it by the morning post. One knows not whom or what to believe; but I now find that it was the mob's breaking in to see old Blucher that so alarmed the Prince that he sent for a guard; and an aid-de-camp to the Prince of Wurtemberg, a handsome young Prussian, told me yesterday, that the Prince *did* go to meet them, and that it was he that took them to London by the road, and a way by which they were not expected. "Ah!" said I, "*c'est qu'il avoit peur.*" "*Mais oui, (repondit-il,) c'est bien vrai; c'est qu'il avoit peur.*" But really of public things and people you must know more than I can tell you, by the papers. Yesterday, however, on our return from Mrs. Smith's, we walked home by the Pulteney Hotel, and just in time to get in amongst the crowd, and on a step, whence, in due time, we saw the Emperor and his sister pass, in the Prince's state coach. I only saw, however, his back, left arm, and curl. But the king of Prussia, who followed, I saw perfectly; and he is a most interesting looking man. But we are all Emperor mad, and from morn till eve the streets are thronged with people and carriages, waiting patiently for hours, to see him pass. Yesterday morning by ten, he was, with his sister, *tête à tête*, at the British Museum; and a gentleman we know saw him very near, and said he was like J. Smith.

We dined at Westmacott's and I sent Meg home, and went to Lady Charleville's, where I found a large circle listening to music, by Naldi, Chiodi, &c.; to my glad surprise I was kindly greeted by my old friend Lord Carysfort, whom indisposition, of a severe kind indeed, has kept out of company four years. There too I saw J. Smith, who repeated to me a poem on H. Twiss's parodies, called "the mocking-bird," which is admirable; he says Mr. Poole wrote the "who wants me." When most of the company was gone, Lady C. took the seat vacated by Lady Mornington, that mother of great men, and it was next a venerable-looking blind woman, whom Lord C. had previously pointed out to me as the once celebrated beauty, Lady Sarah Lennox. She is now grey, blind, and seems both by her voice and manner to be bowed by various cares; but perhaps I fancied this.—No frank yet! Just room and time to say I have seen, from head to foot, and *touched* the Emperor. Other ladies touched his hand, I squeezed his wrist only. I bribed the porter and got into his hotel!!! To-morrow, from a balcony, we shall have a chance of seeing him again, and in safety. Adieu.

11th June, 1814.

MY DEAR FATHER,

Lest you should have thought me *mad* by the conclusion of my last, I shall begin by giving you a full explanation of it. The other morning Mrs. L. M. took me and Margaret out in her carriage, and I persuaded her to drive opposite the Pulteney Hotel; but other and heavier carriages obstructed our view; so I borrowed the servant, and said, "I will try and get on the steps, and if I succeed, I will send back for you." Accordingly, off I set, and was told by the constables I must not stand on the steps; however, the men's hearts relenting, they told me, if I ran up and made friends with the porter, perhaps I should get into the hall. I took the hint, and opening the door, I accosted Cerberus, who told me admission was impossible, but, *tout en me grondant, il avoit la bonté d'accepter une pièce de trois chelins, que je lui mis dans la main, et il me permit d'entrer.* There I found about ten ladies, one of whom, whose face I know as well as my own, came up to me and said, "I'm sure Mrs. Opie you would be welcome to be here," and seating herself by me, proceeded to discuss divers important matters, *en attendant* the return of the Emperor from Carlton House. At length he arrived, and we formed a line for him to pass through. He was dressed in a scarlet uniform, (ours,) and wore our blue ribband. His head is bald, his hair light, his complexion is blond and beautiful, his eyes blue, his nose flattish, with a funny little button end to it; his mouth very small, and his lips thin. His chest and shoulders are broad, and finely formed, his manner graceful and dignified, and his countenance pleasing; and he is the Emperor of all the Russias, therefore, he is handsome, delightful, and so forth. I said that we formed a *line*, and I, simple soul, meant to *keep* it, but not so my companions; for they all closed round him, and one took one hand, one the other, and really I did not know how far they meant to presume; for my part, I dared not, for some time, even think of touching him, but "evil communications corrupt good manners," and at last, when he was nearly past, I grasped his wrist, but the grasp would not have crushed a fly. The lady who knew me, said to me, when he was past, "what a soft hand he has." Lord Yarmouth, who was with him, came afterwards, and talked with that lady. What a fright *he* is!

Now to go back to Lady Sarah, who, as I said before, is blind. * * * Lord Tullamore came to me, and said, "Now almost all the company is gone, you will sing a little ballad." I rose, and went to Lady Charleville. "This," said she, "is Lady S. Napier, will you sing her a ballad?" and, recollecting how ill I once used Lady C. in not answering a letter of hers for three years, and eager to make amends, I said I could not sing anything worth hearing, but I would try. "Surely," said Lady Sarah, "that was injudicious; Mrs Opie would rather not have had the attention of the company so loudly solicited." "Very true," replied Lady C., "but your ladyship is always the best-bred woman in the world, and I the worst, and I never see you without taking a lesson in manners." * * * Well, after having beguiled my fear a little, by inquiring of Lady S. after her sister, Lady Louisa Conolly, I begun, and sung, "Nay, take it, Patty,"* and *decently,* considering. By Lady Sarah, was one of her sons, who, with his brothers, was wounded in every engagement abroad, and one of them taken up for dead. I never saw a handsomer man! I could not help looking at him! He is very black, with black moustachios, that make him look like a picture of some young Venetian by Titian, and his manner was so pleasing! He has his mother's outline, enlarged into manly beauty, and he has such fine dark eyes! Thursday I dined at the Maxwells', and liked my day. Sir James Saumarez dined there; a Mr. Lamb, M.P., and his wife and son. Dr. Young, a Miss Caldwell, and Sir Nathaniel Conant, the magistrate. I sat at dinner between Sir Nathaniel and Mr. Lamb, and liked my companions much. I went home at eleven, undressed, and robed myself to walk to see the illuminations, with Margaret, Tom, and Mr. Barber. We did not get home till three in the morning, and were not in bed till four. Yesterday we staid at home; I had refused a dinner-party, and we kept quiet, and were in bed by half-past ten.

This morning, by a little past eight, we were at the

* This ballad was called "The Soldier's Farewell," and was composed by Mrs. R. Cumberland.

Pulteney Hotel, and in the hall. By ten the hall was very full, so I placed my young companion on a table, and we had a good view of the Emperor and his sister, who came in arm-in-arm, and extended their hands graciously on either side; neither Margaret, however, nor I, had resolution enough to take them; but two young women pressed forward, one *on her knee,* and *kissed his hand,* which he drew back as if shocked or ashamed, and I am sure I was, for I did not recognise my country-women in such forwardness. M. touched his arm, and I tried to touch the Duchess's hand, but had no chance of success. She is very like him, but plain; her nose plainer than his, and though as fair, she has not his colour, but a beauty would have been disguised by such dress; an immense Leghorn gipsy hat, with white feathers; but they say her manners are most captivating. Ask Joseph J. Gurney what *he* thinks. To-day I dine at Lady Cork's in the evening. Adieu!

The next letter in this series formed the material for a paper which Mrs. Opie published in "Tait's Magazine," February, 1844; at the close of that article, she makes a few reflections, which will be of interest to the reader, as shewing the feelings with which she looked back upon those scenes of earlier days:—

I had dined (she says) that day in company with Lord Erskine, and the lamented Dr. Brown, of Edinburgh, the professor of moral philosophy, at the house of my dear and highly valued friend J. G. Lemaistre, (*now,* alas! no more,) and I had finished the evening in a party, more than usually marked by interesting incidents and conversation. Yet I fear I have not said much in favour of those gay and busy scenes in which I once moved, by confessing myself so highly gratified by what I have been describing; still I cannot retract my words; pleased and grateful I was—it might perhaps be a weakness in me to feel so; but I cannot be so disingenuous as not to own it to its full extent.

The original Letter bears date the 16th.

MY DEAR FATHER,

I really could not write yesterday, so I got a frank, that to-day I might write a great deal; but I have seen so much, and seem to have so much to say, that I know not where to begin. On Saturday last I met at dinner Lord Erskine, Sir John Sinclair, Dr. Brown, his brother, the mayor, &c. I sat between Dr. B. and Lord E.; but the peer, by his very agreeable though incessant egotism, and tales of himself, intermingled with interesting anecdotes of the Emperor Alexander, rather seduced my attention away from the philosopher. Rarely have I seen Lord E. more amusing, but Sir J. Sinclair was new to me, and I wanted to hear him. So it was really "*l'embarras de richesses,*" for any one of these three lions would have been enough at once. In the evening came an addition to the company, but Lord E. and I went away to Lady Cork's; the professor was tired and would not go, though I got Lord E. to offer to take him. Had it not been for my sacred vow never to break an engagement, I should have gone to the opera to see the royalties, which was, I hear, the finest sight of the sort ever seen. At Lady C.'s I found Mrs. Harvey, (the author of many novels, and latterly of the excellent one of Amable,) James Smith, the Boddingtons, Professor Spurzheim, Monk Lewis, Horace Twiss, Lord and Lady Carysfort, Lord Limerick, Miss White, Lord Cumbermere and his betrothed, Miss Greville and her sister, Lady Caroline Lamb, just as ever, and doing her possibles to amuse this very small party, in three large rooms, thrown open for Blucher, who was expected; but the opera had spoiled the party, for Greys, Lansdownes, and Whitbreads, had intended being there. Past midnight, however, some came in from the opera, and broke up our conversation, which had been pleasant; for Lady Carysfort had been very entertaining with accounts of Berlin, and Lord Limerick very eloquent in describing the preparations for White's ball, so vast and so elegant as to make me very curious, because I shall not see them. However, perhaps I shall escape being *burnt alive,* for the same decorations exposed Prince Schwartzenberg's palace to that fire in which his wife was burnt; as the pillars are all made of fluted muslin, to represent alabaster; and the capitals of rose-coloured ditto.

But, to return—on the entrance of Miss Fox, (Lord Holland's sister,) and Miss Vernon, a new subject of interest was started; for they brought the astonishing intelligence, that the emperor, and the king, and lastly the regent, had bowed to the princess! No, I am wrong—Some one else asserted the fact, and they said it was *equivocal,* or that he might be said to have bowed either to the pit or the princess. Oh! the glorious uncertainty of reports, even from eye-witnesses! Well, there we were, all on the *qui vive* —first one came in, then another, and the first question was—"Well what do *you* say? Did the prince bow to the pit, or the princess?" and, as you may suppose, no two persons gave the same statement. "See," said I, to Lady C. Lamb, "how difficult it is to ascertain the truth!" "Aye, indeed," she replied, "it teaches us to receive all reports doubtingly;" she added, "still the historian will describe this as it really was, and *he* will be overruled by the majority of voices on the subject." "If that be the way of judging," thought I, "then the prince *did* bow to the princess, for the majority were in favour of it," but I shall insert here, though not in its turn, that the princess herself told S. Smith, who told me, that he did *not* bow to her, nor was there any strong ground for fancying it. To resume my narration—the company had begun to disperse, and no Blucher came, when, to keep up Lady Cork's spirits, Lady C. L. prepared to act a proverb, but it ended in their acting a word; and she, Lady Cork, and Miss White, went out of the room, and came back digging with poker and tongs. To be brief, the word was *orage:* they dug for *or*, and they acted a passion for *rage,* and then they acted a storm, for the whole word, *orage.*

Still, the old general came not, and Lady Caroline disappeared; but, previously, Mrs. Wellesley Pole and her daughter had arrived, bringing a beautiful Prince—Prince Leopold, of Saxe Coburg; but saying she feared Blucher would not come. However, we now heard a distant, then a near, hurrah; and a violent knocking at the door. The hurrahs increased, and we all jumped up, exclaiming, "There's Blucher at last!" and the door opened, the servant calling out, "General Blucher;" on which in strutted Lady Caroline Lamb, in a cocked hat and a great coat! In the meanwhile, Lord Hardwick had arrived from the British Gallery, where he had been in attendance on the Princess Charlotte, the Grand Duchess, &c., and to him Lady Caroline went, with clasped hands and lifted eyes, saying she was come to ask the greatest favour—it was that he would give her some money. "What for?" "Oh! to pay the servants for that *pretty hurrah*, they did it so well!" So poor Lord H. gave her a dollar; looking, I thought, rather silly at having his pocket so gracefully picked; and Lady C. ran downstairs delighted. So end the adventures of yesterday. Sunday I heard Mr. Moore preach, and admirably. Mrs. L. M. took me to the crowded drive; and though we did not see the kings, we saw Blucher very near. We dined with the L. M.s, and in the evening went to Miss White's, where, after talking some time to a gentleman who knew me, though I did not know him, I found it was Sir William Dunbar, that interesting Captain Dunbar I have seen at Norwich. He is very odd, but clever. I forgot to say that I had a very crowded *levée*, where, again, every one told me a new story of the Prince's bow, and all were equally positive! * * * * *

(Rest of letter lost.)

22nd of June, 1814.

MY DEAR FATHER,

I have not time to write much, but I will write as it is my day; and I have to acknowledge the receipt of the parcel. Pray let me have two pairs of black boots made as soon as possible; mine are quite worn out, and the filthy weather does not allow of my wearing light ones. I can't wait. * * *Thursday*, eleven o'clock. Thus far I had gotten yesterday at half past four o'clock, when Lord Tamworth, and Mrs. L. M. after him, came in and interrupted me, and I was forced to turn the latter out, that I might dress to go to Mackintosh's to dinner, at six o'clock; but I consoled myself by the certainty of getting a frank. I will now go on to that of which my mind is most full, namely, my yesterday's dinner; which it was almost worth coming up to town on purpose to be at. I got to M.'s at six, the hour appointed; found no fire, alas! and no one to receive me; happily soon after arrived Mr. Wishawe, horror struck at no fire, and saying in all civilized houses there must be one in such weather; but he warmed himself and me by inveighing against poor Lord Cochrane's pillory, which all the lawyers, and all London, I hope, disapprove. How unwise too! for it leads us to forget his fault in his punishment—but this is by the by. Next arrived Dr. Brown, whom I presented to Wishawe. Then came Lady M., and then Sir James, and I found three different hours for dining had been named to the different guests; and Mr. W. and I anticipated hunger being added to cold. Next came Playfair, then Richard Payne Knight, then John William Ward, just come from Paris, and lastly, at about half past seven, the great traveller, and so forth—Baron de Humboldt; he was not presented to me, therefore I could not ask whether he, or his brother, brought my letter from Helen Williams; and to dinner we went, Ward handing me, so I sat by him, and on my other hand was Mr. Knight. I certainly never saw so many first-rate men together; but again it would have been *l'embarras de richesses* with me, had not each person been a whetting-stone to the wit and information of the other.

Politics, science, literature, Greek, morals, church government, infidelity, sects, philosophy, characters of the Emperor of Russia, King of Prussia, of Blucher, of Platoff, given in a clear and simple manner by the Baron, and commented on by others, formed the never flagging discourse, throughout the dinner. I did not talk much, as you may guess, for I had scarcely ears enough to listen with. Ward was more charming and more maliciously witty, more Puck-like than I had seen him for years; and what he did not choose to venture aloud, he whispered in my ear—more agreeable than polite; but once I caught myself in an argument with Mr. Knight, and I trembled at my own temerity. Talk across the table, I could not have done; but Mr. K. was my neighbour, and none but he heard my daring. I will give you one of Ward's sarcasms; but an unusually good natured one, as it would flatter, not wound, the persons at whom it was aimed. "I hear (said I) you returned from Paris with a Cardinal." "Yes, the Cardinal Gonsalva, and I had the great satisfaction of putting him at length under the protection of a Silesian Jew." "Not being able (said Sir James) to find any Scotch philosophers at hand to take his place." "But had there been any Scotch philosophers at hand to consign him to, I should still have preferred the Jew, because I know there would be some chance of his converting *the Jew.*" The philosophers present laughed; and this introduced a curious discussion on infidelity. * * (Enter the Baron de Humboldt to breakfast with me, and then I take him to Mrs. Siddons.) Alas! it was no Baron—so I may go on. Ward saw Lafayette at Paris; almost the only man of a revolution who has survived one, and lived to enjoy life. He owned to me he did not care to see him; for in his opinions on such a subject, he was too much of a Burkite, to relish seeing Lafayette. De Humboldt spoke highly of him, and mentioned with pleasure, as a proof of tolerance of opinion, that Lafayette has always been beloved and associated with, by persons of totally opposite opinions to his own; and has been enriched by them at their death: lately, he has acquired much by the death of Monsieur de Lusignan, whom I once knew very well. * * Here is the Baron indeed! He is very charming! So full of information, and so simple in his manner of giving it. * * *

Two o'clock. I have lived more in two or three hours to-day than I usually live in a month. I have been to Peru, to Mexico, climbing the Table Mountain, besides hearing much on all subjects, amusing, instructive, and interesting. This charming Chamberlain of Frederick William (I mean the King of Prussia) goes to-day; but I am to see his brother, who is now appointed ambassador from Prussia to France, on Sunday certainly, if not before. * * *

(Rest of letter lost.)

Thursday, July 1st, 1814.

My dear Father,

I would not write yesterday, that I might acknowledge the receipt of the parcel to-day. I had no idea they could all come together, *meat* and *clothes*. Gregory is *not* a Catholic. We may go in fancy dresses, but *all* must wear a *mask;* though no one is forced to assume a character. The verses I sent you were tame enough; but those I have since written, if I had not been forced to introduce the name of Wellington, with my own approbation, and at the suggestion of a very good critic, (Col. Barry,) are tolerably good, I think. Mrs. B. S. has undertaken to sing them, and, if she can't adapt, to set them herself. Lady Cork has given me a most beautiful trimming for the bottom of a dress which I am to wear on the 4th. It is really handsome; a wreath of white satin flowers worked upon net.

Our day on Tuesday was delightful, the scene enchanting. My favourite companion there was Sir William Dunbar, more odd, but more amusing and original, than ever. Still, however pleasant the people at Fulham, M. and I enjoyed the drive to and fro, more than the day itself. James Smith went with us, and he sang funny songs, and repeated epigrams and *bon mots* all the way there. While waiting in the hall for the carriage, (for we wisely came away at eleven,) he gave us an extempore comedy; and, when in the carriage, on my telling him that Sir W. Dunbar had told me he was *blasé* with everything, and that he was a disappointed man;

he said; "It is evident that *he* is so; I dare say there is something interesting and particular in his story; suppose I *invent* one for him." So off he set, and gave us three letters of a novel in letters, and, without pausing a moment, beginning, "Sir W. Dunbar to General Evelyn.—When we last parted, my dear General, I was in the prime of life; every hope full of vigour," &c., &c., and during the last mile or two, he relieved the monotony which was stealing over all this, by quotations from Young and Swift, well remembered and well repeated. Certainly, never did a man so completely pay, by his brains, for a seat in a carriage. I persuaded Edward to dance with Miss M., having vainly tried to persuade Sir W. D., though he owned her to be very pretty, as did Edward. We left them dancing. The baron, William de Humboldt, was forced to attend Lord Castlereagh in a conference of nine hours, yesterday; therefore he wrote me an elegant note of excuse for not going to see Mrs. Siddons with me, calling me "Mademoiselle Opie;"—no doubt from my juvenile appearance. So we walked over to tell Mrs. Siddons this, and she was somewhat mortified; but recovered herself, and was most delightful. We staid two hours and more, and we none of us knew how late it was. She said she had passed a most happy two hours, and had no regrets. M. came home raving all the way, saying she was the most beautiful, delightful, agreeable, and, I believe, even the *youngest* woman she ever saw; and she has put up in paper, the bud of a rose she gave her, to keep for ever. Yesterday we dined at H. G.'s, and went to the Maxwells' in the evening. Old Albinia, of Buckinghamshire, has made me promise to go to her masquerade breakfast, and *en masque.* I owe her this, for her kindness to me, when I sang to the Prince. On Sunday we were to dine at the Solicitor-General's, in Bloomsbury Square; but it is now put off to Sunday se'nnight, at Wimbledon. As I was offered a ticket for the ball to the Duke of Wellington for £4 7s., I accepted the offer, and wrote my last commands to Lord Tamworth; so I hope I did not write too late to prevent the exchange.

I go full dressed, but no train, and high feathers; with a pink domino of calico, made high and long, to give me height and disguise me, thrown over all, that I may be *incog.*, and be masked till I am tired, and then appear as myself. Mrs. P. goes with us. I have had the kindest letter from Mr. Coke! promising to do all he can for Mr. D., and entreating me to visit him in the winter, whenever I choose.*—I have just room to insert the lines.

Why sons of Britain rush ye forth
Like torrents from the mountain's height,
To shout, untired, for foreign worth
And glad with foreign chiefs, your sight?
Can Britain boast no chiefs renown'd,
Whose arm can crush, whose heart can *spare!*
No Leader who, with conquest crown'd,
Can *wisely plan*, and *greatly dare?*

Yes, Britains, yes! and now again
In shouts your myriad voices raise!
But louder, longer, be the strain
That speaks a grateful nation's praise.
For Wellington now glads our sight,
Whose valour guards his Sovereign's throne,
He, in untarnish'd glory bright;
And Wellington is all OUR OWN!

I allude in the sixth line to the mercy he showed at Toulouse. The Baron, Alexander de Humboldt, said to me, "This certainly was the first man in Europe!" and no doubt, when party feeling is forgotten, he will be done *justice* to. Farewell!

* Mrs. Opie visited Holkham in January, 1816, and wrote some lines to Lady Anson on her birthday, while there.

CHAPTER XII.

FRIENDSHIP WITH THE GURNEY FAMILY; TWO LETTERS FROM MR. J. J. GURNEY; DEATH OF HIS BROTHER; MRS. OPIE'S RETURN FROM LONDON; EARLY RELIGIOUS OPINIONS; MRS. ROBERTS; RECOLLECTIONS OF SIR W. SCOTT; VISIT TO EDINBURGH; "VALENTINE'S EVE;" VISIT TO MR. HAYLEY; "TALES OF THE HEART;" LETTER TO MR. HAYLEY; LETTER FROM MRS. INCHBALD; HER DEATH.

From the gay and brilliant scenes depicted in the preceding letters, Mrs. Opie was suddenly and painfully called away, by an event which excited deep feeling in her heart, and which must have been rendered more peculiarly distressing, by the contrast in which it stood with all that had been occupying her thoughts, during the months of her absence from home.

Preserved with her letters of this date, there were found two, of a very different character from her own, addressed to her by a friend who was destined, in after years, to exercise great influence over her opinions and subsequent course; we speak of Mr. J. J. Gurney, that highly honoured and admirable man, whose friendship, thus early commenced, she retained, with ever-growing satisfaction, until his deeply-lamented death.

It may be remembered that Mrs. Opie, in one of her early letters, speaks of "Elizabeth Fry," to whom she had been paying a visit on occasion of her marriage. They had been acquaintances in youth; and, in the life of Mrs. Fry, there are occasional allusions to visits paid by Dr. Alderson to Earlham, the home of the Gurney family, when Elizabeth was a gay and lively girl.* Shortly after Mrs. Opie's marriage, Miss E. Gurney visited London, and in her diary she records a day spent with "Amelia Opie," and says: "I had a pleasant time of it; I called on Mrs. Siddons, and on Dr. Batty, then on Mrs. Twiss; and, in the evening, Mr. Opie, Amelia, and I, went to the concert," &c.

After Mrs. Fry's marriage she was brought into the society, almost exclusively, of strict "Friends," and there does not appear to have been much intercourse between her and her early friend; but when Mrs. Opie returned to Norwich, on the death of her husband, she resumed her former habits of intimacy with the family at Earlham; and found, among the large and happy circle there, friends whose influence had a beneficial effect upon her. The youngest sister, Priscilla, who was a most lovely creature, and who died in 1821, seems to have been especially endeared to her; and Mr. J. J. Gurney

* The friendship between Dr. Alderson and the Gurney family was indeed of very early date; for when Mr. John Gurney, senior, first hired Earlham, he invited Mr. and Miss Alderson to go and see the place, which they did; Mr. A. on horseback, and Miss, on her little pony, by his side. They drank tea with Mr. G. in a room afterwards known as the ante-room, the only place where there was a seat to be had.

said, that her friendship with this sister and himself, appeared to be the principal means of producing that gradual change of sentiment, which eventually led to her joining the Society of Friends.

We are, however, anticipating the progress of events.—To return to the letters of which we have spoken; we find, in the first of them, allusions to the illness of Mr. Gurney's brother, whose death, which followed a few weeks subsequently, was the cause of Mrs. Opie's hasty return.

Norwich, 6th mo., 4th, 1814.

I have a mind, my dear friend, to write thee a letter; this is all the apology I offer for the intrusion. There are two or three things I wish to say to thee; the first is, that I remember, with true pleasure, thy affectionate conduct to us all, during the last few months of affliction. It has been like that of a sister, and has been prized by us, I trust, as it ought to be; however thou mayest be engaged in the gay whirlpool of London life, rest assured, therefore, thou art not forgotten by thy retired friends at Earlham. I thank thee for thy last note, which is an instructive inmate of my pocket-book, since it bespeaks a *tender conscience.* Wilt thou pardon thy friend if he tell thee, that he greatly admires this tenderness of conscience with regard to all thou sayest of others? It appears to him that thy mind is particularly alive to the duties of Christian charity; and he now wishes to express his desire that the same fear, (shall he call it "godly fear?") may attend thee in all thy communications with the world.

To leave the third person; I will refer to two texts, "Pure religion and undefiled before God and the Father is this—to keep one's self *unspotted from the world,*" and again, "Be ye not conformed to this world, but be ye transformed by the renewing of your minds, that he may know what is the good, acceptable, and perfect will of God." Now, what wilt thou say to me? perhaps thou wilt say that thy countrified, drab-coated, methodistical friend, knows nothing of the "world," misinterprets the meaning of the apostle, and is frightened by the bugbear of a name, as a child is by a ghost.

There may be some truth in these observations of thine, and I must allow that the world is not idolatrous *now*, as it was *then;* and again, that we all alike are citizens of the world, and there is no department of it which is not tinctured with evil; but I refer particularly to the "fashionable world," of which I am apt to entertain two notions—the first, that there is much in it of *real evil;* the second, that there is much also in it, which, though not evil in itself, yet has a decided tendency to produce forgetfulness of God, and thus to generate evil indirectly. On the other hand, there is little in it, perhaps, which is *positively good.*

With regard to the apostolic precepts; perhaps they intimate that there are two spirits or dispositions, moving amongst mankind; the one celestial, leading to good; the other terrestrial, tending to evil; perhaps they are meant to warn us, not literally against the world, but against *a worldly spirit.* Now I will close my grave remarks, by saying, that it is my earnest desire, both for thee and myself, that we may be redeemed from a *worldly spirit*, and that in our communications with the world, whether fashionable, commercial, or common-place, we may be enabled simply to follow an unerring guide within us, which will assuredly inform us, if we will but *wait for direction*, what to touch and what to shrink from—what to follow, and what to eschew.

I returned home with Pris, last fourth day, and found my dear brother considerably more feeble than when I left him; I think this may be owing, principally, to his having fallen and hurt his knee, and to the confinement which the accident has rendered necessary. Upon the whole we are much at ease about him, and *ought* to be thankful whether we *are* so or no.

Do not be angry with me; write me a letter; and farewell, in every sense of the word.

I remain, thy affectionate friend,

J. J. Gurney.

The second letter (dated Earlham, 7th mo., 22nd, 1814) is much longer, and as a large part of it will be found inserted in the Life of Mr. Gurney, we shall content ourselves with a few extracts taken from it. After apologizing for "addressing something in the shape of advice, to one so much older and more experienced than himself," he says: —

My chief desire is, that thou mayst be willing to give up everything which the light of truth may point out as inconsistent with the holy will of God. True happiness, here or hereafter, can consist in nothing, but in conformity to that will. The world has, undoubtedly, many pleasures to bestow, perhaps none so great as that of being universally *liked, admired, and flattered;* but it is not in the world we are to find that "peace which passeth understanding." It is striking to observe the *essential* difference which exists between the pleasures of the world, and the religious happiness of the soul. The *temporality* of the former seems to be proved, by their all being conveyed to us through our *natural senses;* but "eye hath not seen, nor ear heard, nor hath it entered into the heart of man to conceive the things which God hath prepared for those who love Him." How clearly one sees, all the way through, that the one belongs to our mortal, the other to our immortal part.

Thou wilt observe, my dear friend, that I have underscored the words, "liked, flattered, and admired." It is because I know thou art so; and, unless thou art of a very different composition to thy friend, I am satisfied it must afford no small temptations to thee, and require, on thy part, the utmost stretch of watchfulness. I really should like to know how thy mind was affected by Lady B.'s day-masquerade. Because, I am sure, that if I could sing and converse in that way, and procured all manner of favour and applause, from innumerable lords and ladies, I should be vain as a peacock thereupon. Now, I confess, if thou art vain, thy vanity* does not show itself; but it may be there is some lurking particle of it in the bottom of thy heart, which may put thee to some trouble. But mind, I do not want to draw thee to confession.

My dear brother has been a good deal weaker, especially in mind, during the last fortnight; but he continues full of peace, and, I think I may add, of Christian love. Again and again farewell, saith thy sincere and affectionate friend

J. J. GURNEY.

This brother, Mr. John Gurney, declined rapidly, and early in September his death took place. In the Life of Mrs. Fry this event is recorded; and she mentions in a letter dated from Earlham, whither she had gone to take her leave of him, that on the last morning of his life, Dr. Alderson had called and seen him, and that he desired his love to Amelia Opie.

The second of her Lays for the Dead is addressed to this "departed friend," and was written (as the title to it informs us) after attending his funeral, in the Friend's burying-ground at Norwich, having travelled all night, in order to arrive in time.

It commences thus:—

"Friend, long beloved! on thy untimely bier
I came to drop the sympathizing tear;
I came to join the long funereal train,
And heave the bitter sigh which mourns in vain."

From this period Mrs. Opie attended the religious services of the Friends, and continued to do so until she united herself to their communion, eleven years after; and in a note written the year of Mr. Gurney's

* Mrs. Opie has marked a large (!) against these words.

death, to the writer of these memoirs, she says, "in 1814 I left the Unitarians."

It does not, indeed, appear, from any record of her early days, nor from the recollections of her friends is it ascertainable, that she, at any time, was in actual communion with the Unitarian body. She was, in her youth, in the habit of attending at the Octagon chapel, where, during the ministry of Mr. Pendlebury Houghton, Dr. Sayers, and Mr. William Taylor, and others of similar opinions, attended, and highly eulogised the sermons of that eloquent, though by no means evangelical, preacher. When in London, it is evident, from her letters, that Mrs. Opie went to church, and did not act as a conscientious Unitarian would, under the circumstances, have done; and we can hardly avoid the inference, that she had no very fixed opinions on religious subjects, and that the mere circumstances of her birth and education had occasioned her connexion with the Unitarians. From the time, however, at which we have now arrived, she ceased to attend the Octagon chapel; and although she did not at once embrace the religious opinions of the Friends, nor sever herself from her former associates and pursuits, she gradually, but surely, yielded to an influence to which she had hitherto been a stranger, and experienced a progressive change in her religious views.

Mrs. Opie, shortly after this time, edited a little book, entitled "Duty," written by her friend Mrs. Roberts, to which she prefixed a sketch of the character of the authoress. This sketch was published separately in the "Gentlemen's Magazine," for 1815. It is a pleasing tribute of affectionate regret, to the memory of one whose friendship, she said, would always be among the most pleasing recollections of her life, and to have lost her so soon, one of her most lasting regrets.

In the spring of the year 1816, Mrs. Opie paid her usual annual visit to London; and in her note book has recorded her "recollections of Sir W. Scott," whom she then, for the first time, saw, or rather heard. She had *seen* him on two or three previous occasions—first, shortly after the publication of the "Lay of the Last Minstrel," at the assembly of a widow lady, in London; but the crowd was so great that she caught a very imperfect glimpse of him, merely sufficient to tell her that "he wore powder and his hair tied behind." The next time she saw the great man was at a picture gallery, somewhere in London, when, as he passed near and was pointed out to her, she observed that he was lame, but there was a freshness in his complexion and an air of robust health about his whole contour. At length, in 1816, she met him, and she says,

It was the *last* time I ever saw him, and I might say the *first*, according to the idea of him, who said on the introduction of a stranger, "speak, that I may see thee!" for certainly the face of W. Scott, when speaking and animated, and the same face in a quiescent state, were two different things. And what a seeing that was! It was at breakfast, at the house of Sir George Phillips, in Mount Street; I had been invited to meet Sir Walter, and I went with the anticipation of no common pleasure, arriving precisely at the time specified. Sir W., however, was there before me; and for some time, to my great satisfaction, we, with the master and mistress of the house, continued uninterrupted by other guests. I know not what led to the subject; but he gave us a most animated description of a cockney's hunting in the Highlands; I think the person was a militia officer, and his terror, when he found himself going full gallop up and down crags, steeps, and declivities of which he had before no idea, was pictured with a living spirit which I cannot do justice to. This narrative was interrupted by the arrival of other guests, and Sir W., to my great joy, was desired to hand me downstairs; consequently I sat beside him; the company was too large for much general conversation, though there was also present another whose conversational powers were first-rate—Wordsworth, who came late, being one of the party. I did not, however, regret this, as I was enabled to keep the conversation of my right-hand neighbour to myself. One subject succeeded another, and the gifted man condescended to speak to me of my "Father and Daughter," and told me he had cried over it more than he ever cried over such things. I felt emboldened to speak of his own writings, and ventured to ask him why, with such dramatic power, he had never tried the drama? he said many reasons had prevented him; amongst others, he was, he said, a proud man, and his pride would never have allowed him to dance attendance on the managers, and consult the varied tastes of actors and others—or words to that effect. But he owned that he had once serious thoughts of writing a tragedy, on the same subject as had been so ably treated by his friend, Joanna Baillie; meaning the "Family Legend"—founded, as I need not say, on a true story. Sir W. said, had he gone on with his tragedy, (I think he had begun it,) he should have had *no love in it.* His hero should have been the uncle of the heroine, a sort of misanthrope, with only one affection in his heart, love for his niece, like a solitary gleam of sunshine, gilding the dark tower of some ruined and lonely dwelling! Never shall I—never *can* I, forget the fine expression of his lifted eye, as he uttered this! The whole face became elevated in its character, and even the features acquired a dignity and grace from the power of genius! How fortunate did I consider myself in having that morning been favoured with a specimen of his *two* manners, if I may so express myself.

In the autumn of this year Mrs. Opie went to Edinburgh; and she has given a short account of this visit, in connexion with her reminiscences of Sir Walter Scott.

From my earliest days (she says) I was such an admirer of Scotch literature and Scotch music, and I was so prepossessed in favour of Scotland, that I have often run eagerly to the window of my own house, only to see a Scotch drover pass by, in his blue bonnet and plaid; and it was with gladness of heart that in the autumn of the year I had met Sir Walter, I found myself at liberty to visit Edinburgh! "Tell me, (said I to the postillion,) when we reach the Tweed," and as soon as I saw its silver waters sparkling in the summer sun, I hailed it with delight, and warmly congratulated myself on being, at last, in Scotland. That day we went to Dryburgh; I had seen the Earl of Buchan at my own house, in London, when he was in England; and, having promised to return his call at the first opportunity, I went, at the end of sixteen years, to perform my promise, and was most kindly received. Before dinner was served, we went to see the grounds and the beautiful ruins of the abbey, where was pointed out to us the part of the ruin apportioned off for the place of interment of Sir W. Scott and his descendants.

During the nine days I remained in Edinburgh, Sir W. did not come thither, so that I had no opportunity of seeing him; but I had the pleasure of sitting opposite Raeburn's picture of him every day, at the house of my kind host Constable, whose guest I was. Eagerly did I tell every body who would listen to me, of my meeting him in London, and of the impression which he made on me: but I was mortified when, on my praising the beauty of his countenance, under strong excitement, and the fire of his blue grey eye, Dr. Brown, the celebrated professor, interrupted me with, "Nay, nay, Mrs. Opie, do not go on with these flights of fancy; the face is nothing but a roast-beef and plum-pudding face, say what you will!" Whatever that face was, would I had had the happiness of seeing it again! However, the remembrance of the enjoyment which that morning at Mount street gave me, I treasure as one of the greatest which was ever afforded me, by worldly intercourse.

This year was published " Valentine's Eve," a tale in three volumes, interesting as shewing the state of her religious feelings at the time it was written. The lesson it inculcates is the superiority of religious principle as a rule of action, and as a support under affliction and unmerited calumny. The heroine of the story, pronouncing her conviction that " moral virtues are only durable and precious as they are derived from religious belief and the consequence of it," says,

Some suppose that morality can stand alone without the aid of religion, and even fancy that republican firmness will enable us to bear affliction; but *I* feel that the only refuge in sorrow and in trial, is the Rock of Ages, and the promises of the gospel.

In 1817 Mrs. Opie made an excursion into Sussex, and among other friends, visited Mr. Hayley. In consequence, she says, of this gentleman's flattering mention of her in the twelfth edition of his "Triumphs of Temper," she went on a visit to his house, in the year 1814; and in his " Life," by Dr. Johnson, there is a short sketch, from her pen, of the manner in which they passed their time, during that and subsequent visits she paid him. " In 1816," (writes Mrs. O.) " I went to Scotland, and did not see Eartham till 1817. I then found Mr. Hayley was become fond of seeing occasional visitors; but, for the most part, our life was as unvaried as it had been in my former visits to him."

She corresponded with him after leaving him, and fulfilled the promise she had made, to send him her portrait. He acknowledged the receipt of this picture, in a letter, from which we give an extract.

* * * * I rejoice that a petty incident prevented my letter from beginning its travels yesterday; for, in the evening, the eagerly expected portrait arrived: a fine head nobly painted in the *gusto grande!*

After assigning to it, this early morn, its proper station, in an excellent light, your paternal hermit burst into the following extempore benedictions, in contemplating his *carissima figlia.*

Thy portrait, dear Amelia, in my sight,
  My eyes are charmed with beauty's blooming flower;
But when thy books my sympathy excite,
  I feel thy genius, the sublimer power;
Pleased, of thy various charms to bless the whole,
  I praise thy form, and idolize thy soul;
Such worship's thine, from "threescore and eleven,"
  Whose higher adoration mounts to heaven.

I can devise no better mode of expressing my gratitude to you for this delightful proof of your filial regard, than by putting into the case, which conveyed you to my cell, that sweet picture* of Virgil's Tomb, by my friend of Derby, which I had long intended as a legacy for you; yet some time must elapse before the picture can arrive at Norwich, because it is to halt on its transit through London, at the house of a very amiable young artist, who is to execute for me a *diminutive* copy of it, as a companion to another

* This picture Mrs. Opie in her will bequeathed to "her friend Thos. Brightwell." It is by Wright, of Derby, and is curious, as attempting to give the three effects of moonlight, fire-light, and twilight, in the same piece.

small picture. And now I must hastily say *addio carissima!* not to lose the post of to-day. *Addio.*

In October of this year Mr. Hayley wrote:—*

"I have much enjoyed a social visit of several weeks, from our admirable Amelia Opie, who, after having kindly devoted some pleasant months to various friends, in her excursion, is just settling herself at home again, with a mind well prepared to exert its powers in several projected works, that will, I trust, in due time, afford a copious supply of pleasure and instruction to the literary world."

In 1818 Mrs Opie published her "Tales of the Heart," probably one of the works alluded to in this letter. In the first volume of this series there are two, entitled, "The Odd Tempered Man," and "White Lies." The former of these, is an original picture of an eccentric phase of the infirmities of temper; to the latter Mrs. O. evidently refers in the following letter to Mr. Hayley:—

Norwich, 24th Jan., 1819.

My dear Friend,

You are too just to expect that the author of "White Lies," the *tale*, should be guilty of "White Lies," the *fault*—therefore though I can, *en toute sureté de conscience* say, that I was very glad to hear from you again, yet I must own that I did not feel your excuses for not having written *at all* satisfactory. * * * I am going to send you (perhaps to-morrow) some dried apples, apples being once more plentiful here; and the box will also contain an etching of my dear father, from a drawing by my husband: it is like, but *too full* about the *jawbone*, and my father's hair must have been by accident rough, when my husband drew him; *now*

* See Memoirs of Wm. Hayley, vol. 2, p. 191.

it is close to his head, and his head is well shaped. However, on the whole, it is very like, and the etching does credit to the artist, a lady, the wife of Dawson Turner, and a most admirable person she is. * * * My father is now, blessed be God! quite well, in all respects; but soon after my return home in July he sprained his ancle, and was lame, unwell, dispirited, and broken down in mind and body *for weeks, nay months*, and I suffered *much*, but he now *walks* well, and *is* well, and enjoys himself. Farewell!

Believe me ever affectionately yours,

A. Opie.

William Hayley, Esq., near Chichester.

Shortly after the date of this letter, Mrs. Opie was alarmed by tidings of the severe illness of her aged friend; she says, (in the sketch given in Hayley's life before referred to,) "I went down to Bognor, not certain that I should not arrive too late to see him; but I found him out of danger, and had the happiness of returning to London at the end of the week, leaving him recovering. But I saw him no more. He died in November of the following year."

Another of her old friends (Mrs. Inchbald) wrote to her this year, under the pressure of a malady beneath which she speedily succumbed. She wrote again, for the last time, at the Christmas of the following year, thus:—

Kensington House, 19th Dec., 1820.

My dear Mrs. Opie,

Your kind Christmas-box arrived safe, and temptingly beautiful, yesterday evening; many thanks.

We are, even in these dark and short days, as brilliant on the high road, and in open air, as during the long and bright days of summer and autumn. I think I never saw a more gaudy, yet numerous and sober procession, (processions, I should say, for they lasted from morning till night,) than passed the house yesterday. I think myself particularly fortunate in the place of my abode, on this account. The present world is such a fine subject to excite intense reflection.

Mr. Kemble called on me, during the short time he was in England; he looked remarkably well in the face, but as he walked through the court-yard, to step into his carriage, I was astonished to perceive him bend down his person, like a man of eighty. How, I wonder, does she support her banishment from England? He has sense and taste to find "books in the running brooks, and good in everything."

By the bye, your books are lying on the table of our drawing room most days, and I hear great praise of them; and yet I do not feel the slightest curiosity to open one of them. The reason is, there are also a hundred of Sir Walter Scott's in the same place, and as it is impossible to read *all*, I have no wish to read *any;* for to read without judging, is to read without amusement; and how can I judge without comparing, detecting likenesses, or admiring originality? Besides, I have so many reflections concerning a *future* world, as well as concerning the *present*, and there are, on that awful subject, so many books still unread, that I think every moment lost, which impedes my gaining information from holy and learned authors.

It rains, and I fear I cannot send my letter to the post by a safe hand, till fine weather. My best compliments to Dr. Alderson, and believe me,

Yours most sincerely,

E. INCHBALD.

She died in 1821. Mrs. Opie had not been aware of her illness, and wrote on the 9th of August to Mr. Phillips, thus:—

DEAR SIR,

The paper of to-day contains an account of the *funeral* of Mrs. Inchbald, and I had heard neither of her illness, nor her death! I need not say how shocked and sorry I am; and I take the liberty of requesting that you will be so kind as to give me some account of her illness, last moments, &c.

I have not seen her this year, because I *now never leave my father*, and have been in Norwich almost ever since I saw her last, which was last September. Pray excuse, &c.

Yours respectfully,

A. Opie.

G. Phillips, Esq.,

Surgeon to his Majesty, Carlton Palace.

CHAPTER XIII.

ILLNESS OF DR. ALDERSON; HIS DAUGHTER'S ANXIETY; PRISCILLA GURNEY; BIBLE AND ANTI-SLAVERY MEETINGS; "MADELINE;" LETTER FROM SOUTHEY; "LYING;" LETTERS TO MRS. FRY; MRS. OPIE JOINS THE SOCIETY OF FRIENDS; DR. ALDERSON'S DECLINE AND DEATH.

Dr. Alderson became seriously ill in December, 1820, and his daughter accompanied him to London, for medical advice, on the 23rd January, 1821. On the 26th, they went to stay at the house of Mr. Hudson Gurney, by whom the following particulars were communicated to the writer;—"Davies Gilbert and a few friends dined with us; and Dr. Alderson was, apparently cheerful and pretty comfortable; but, in a day or two, he was seized with extreme depression of spirits, and went back to Norwich on the 2nd of February. He never, I believe, or hardly ever, left his house afterwards, till the time of his death. During the whole time of his illness, Mrs. Opie most assiduously attended him; she had latterly joined the Quakers; and read to him much in the Bible and other religious books, and his views, on religious subjects, appear to have undergone an entire change. Mr. J. J. Gurney was very frequently with them both."

On their journey home from town, after this visit, an alarming accident occurred. The horses took fright, the coachman and passengers were thrown off the coach, and the leaders broke the traces; by some means the vehicle was stopped, but their lives had been endangered; and when Dr. Alderson, who was not at first aware of the peril they had incurred, was told, by his daughter, the particulars of the accident, he exclaimed, as he thanked God that they had reached Norwich in safety, "I have been mercifully spared, my dear child, and I wonder *why?*" His daughter, speaking of the event, said—"afterwards, when his serious impressions daily deepened, he said, 'Oh! my dear child! I know *now* why I was spared.'"

From this time the continued and increasing illness of her father occupied her time, and engaged her constant thought, while numerous friends gathered around them, desirous to cheer and soothe the invalid, and to aid his daughter in her task of love. "I suffered much!" she wrote, when the first symptoms of this "sickness unto death" appeared; *how much* we learn, in some degree, to estimate, by the grief of after years, when the blow, she was then dreading, had fallen. But, if it be true (and every Christian will set his seal to it) that "since the day Jesus redeemed us on the cross, all that is great, powerful, and salutary, partakes of a serious nature, and that all the seeds of life and regeneration, are sown in sorrow and in death," then we may recognise, in this afflictive visitation, the "blessing in disguise," which was sent by her heavenly Father to wean her from the world and call her to himself.

Two prayers, written at this time, were preserved among her papers, and remain affecting testimonials of the "thoughts of her heart" within her.

A PRAYER.—25TH OF APRIL, 1821.

O gracious and long suffering God! now that those trials and infirmities are come upon me, from which I have hitherto been mercifully exempted, let me not, I beseech Thee, forget Thy past mercies, in Thy present chastisements; but rather let me consider those chastisements as *greater mercies still*, and as designed to draw me, in humble supplication and heartfelt thankfulness, to the foot of Thy throne, there to confess my sins and my long forgetfulness of Thee; and to acknowledge, that I have no hope of salvation, but through the merits of Jesus Christ, my Lord and my Redeemer, who died the death of a sinner, that I, and sinners like myself, might be forgiven and *live*.

A PRAYER.—26TH OF APRIL, 1821.

O Thou! "the God that hearest prayer," and even amidst innumerable choirs of angels for ever glorifying Thee and hymning Thy praise, canst hearken to the softest breathings of a supplicating and contrited heart, deign Lord to let the prayers of a child, for a beloved parent, come up before Thee. In grateful return for that life which he gave me here, and which, under Thy good providence, he has tenderly watched over, and tried to render happy, enable me, O Lord! to be the humble means of leading him to Thee. O let us "thirst," and come together "to the waters, and buy the wine and milk without money and without price;" and grant, O Lord! that before we go hence, and are no more seen of men, our united voices may ascend to Thee in praises and in blessings! grant that we may together call upon the name of Him who has redeemed us by His most precious blood, that in that blood our manifold sins may be washed away.

This year died her lovely friend, Priscilla Gurney. In the Memoirs of Mrs. Fry (vol. 1, pp. 391, 399,) a most touching account is given, of the closing scenes of her life. She must have been singularly pleasing, for, notwithstanding her early death, her memory still remains sweet to many, and she is yet spoken of with affectionate regret. Some lines (not among her "Lays") were written by Mrs. Opie in remembrance of this dear friend; they are headed

"PRISCILLA'S GRAVE."

There is a spot in Life's vain scene,
  Which oft, with willing feet, I tread;
It is yon still, sequester'd *green*,*
  Where lowly sleep the nameless dead.

There, underneath that elm's soft shade,
  Now waving in the zephyr's breath,
Belov'd Priscilla, thou art laid,
  Within thy grassy home of Death!

I would not call thee back again
  To this dark world, unworthy thee,
Faith bids my heart that wish restrain,
  Yet oh; how vast thy loss to me!

I miss thy soothing *smile* of love,
  Thy *voice*, that could my fears control,
Thy *words* that bade my doubts remove,
  And breath'd conviction o'er my soul.

I miss thee, while with pilgrim feet
  I now my course to Zion bend;
For *thou*, upon her way wouldst greet,
  And fondly hail, thy fainting friend.

But thou art where each promise given
  Is now fulfill'd, (thine, endless day,)
Then, full of gratitude to Heaven,
  I'll breathe a prayer, and turn away.

* The Friends have no tombstones, and the field for the graves is usually green.—A. O.

There was much passing in the religious world at this period, calculated to engage the attention, and attract the warm sympathies, of Mrs. Opie. The spirits of many highly gifted and eminent men were aroused to do great things in the cause of religion and philanthropy. In 1811 the first Meeting of the Norwich Bible Society was held in St. Andrew's Hall, and was noted as "a day indeed; one that might be called a mark of the times." Then were seen, for the first time, united for one great object, in the spirit of christian union, Churchmen and Dissenters; Bishop Bathurst presided, and Clergymen and Dissenting Ministers, Lutheran, Independent, Baptist, Quaker, and Methodist, joined hand in hand. On this occasion, the Hall at Earlham was made the head-quarters of the deputation; and a numerous circle of friends gathered around, to share in the pleasures of holy intercourse and christian fellowship. These meetings were annually renewed, and year by year the honoured host at Earlham opened his mansion, and greeted his friends and fellow-workers, and cheered them with his generous hospitality. They who were wont to meet on these occasions, have often felt their hearts burn within them, as they "talked one with another" on the great things of the heavenly kingdom, whose interests had gathered them together, and united them as the heart of one man.

In 1820 the Anti-slavery Society was formed, and was brought before the friends of the cause in Norwich, at a meeting, superintended by Mr. Gurney, and largely attended. In both these Societies Mrs. Opie took a deep interest, which (to use a favourite and constantly repeated expression of her own) "grew with her growth and strengthened with her strength."

The pressure of domestic affliction did not interrupt Mrs. Opie's literary occupations, and perhaps she found (as many others have done) a relief in such absorbing engagements. In 1822 she published "Madeline," the last of her Novels, (for though she commenced writing another, it was never completed.) In the following year, she contributed to the European Magazine, a series of poetical "Epistles from Mary Queen of Scots to her Uncles," prefacing them by saying, "Ever since I have been able to compare the strength of opposing evidence, and to enter into the probable motives of human actions, I have believed Mary Queen of Scotland to be entirely innocent of the atrocious guilt of which she has been accused—adultery and murder." There are also some Tales and a short memoir of Bishop Bathurst, from her pen, in the same volume.

She appears to have made some application to Mr. Southey, with reference to a Review of her "Madeline," which drew from him the following letter:—

Keswick, 11th April, 1822.

My dear Madam,

Your Madeline is a great favourite here, and well deserves to be so. The tale is beautifully told, and everywhere true to nature; if there be a little of that ideal colouring, which belongs to this species of composition, as much as to poetry, it is in your *hero* rather than your heroine. The tragic catastrophe would, as you say, have made the story more perfect, but it would have made the book painful, instead of pleasing, in recollection. I am sure that I should not have looked at it a second time, compared one part with another, and dwelt upon particular scenes, if there had been death at the end; and this, I think, is not so much the weakness of my individual temper, as it is a natural feeling. The theatres shew it to be so, by the preference which is given to comedy; they who have borne a part in the tragedies of real life (who is there that can go through the world without?) shrink, even from the sorrow which is produced by fiction.

The Quarterly Review will be much better employed in recommending Madeline to notice, than in pointing out in the Pirate, beauties which everybody must have seen, and defects which nobody can have overlooked. The part which I bear in that journal is greatly overrated, and the influence which I possess there, quite as much so. For two years I have been vainly endeavouring to get a book by Sir Howard Douglas reviewed there, though the subject is of great importance, and national interest, as well as national credit, concerned in it. I could not do it myself, because it required scientific knowledge, which I do not possess.

To convince you, however, that your tale has really interested me, I will write to Mr. Gifford, and ask him to admit an article upon it; most likely he will consent; I cannot be quite sure of this, nor can I promise anything farther for the paper, than that it will be written in right good will. As for my prose—anybody's prose is mistaken for mine; and what is far more strange, anybody's opinions! The guessing at anonymous writings is almost as much a matter of hap-hazard, as the attempt to discover any person, by his walk and figure, at a masquerade.

Mrs. S. desires me to present her compliments. Remember me to William Taylor, when you happen to see him.

Farewell, my dear Madam,

And believe me yours truly,

ROBERT SOUTHEY.

Her next work was one of a widely different character; on "Lying, in all its branches," a subject affording ample scope for the moralist, and handled in a manner at once novel and ingenious. It received the best of all sanctions, that of *success;* and she had the exquisite satisfaction of knowing that she attained the object at which she aimed. Some few years afterwards, when Mrs. Opie was at Paris, she was introduced to several American friends, who cordially greeted her, thanking her for this book, which they assured her was universally acknowledged to have done good in their country; and that it had found its way into the cottages in *the interior*, and might be seen there, well thumbed by frequent use. Shortly after the publication of this work, Mrs. Opie wrote thus to Mrs. Fry:—

Norwich, 12th mo., 6th, 1823.

MY VERY DEAR FRIEND,

As it is possible that thou mayst have been told that a new novel from my pen, called "*The Painter and his Wife*," is in the press, I wish to tell thee this is a falsehood: that my publishers advertised this only *begun* work, unknown to me, and that I have written to say the said work is not written, *nor ever will be.* I must own to thee, however, that as several hundreds of it are already ordered by the trade, I have *felt* the sacrifice, but I do not *repent* of it.*

Joseph and Catherine are highly pleased with my new work, on "Lying, in all its branches," (each sort of lie illustrated by a simple anecdote, or tale,) and they think it must do good. We go on as usual; my dear father I think better on the whole, in body, and, I hope, not gone back in mind. I am at times very low, but there is safety in lowness for some people, and I am one of them. I know a tortoise pace is a safe pace, but still I am dissatisfied with my slow progress. Farewell! dearest Betsy! I remember thy visit

* The unfinished MS. was found among her papers.

with true and grateful pleasure; with kind love to all thy circle,

I am, thy affectionate Friend,

A. Opie.

To Elizabeth Fry, Plashet, Essex.

Dr. Alderson attained the age of four-score, in the spring of this year; and his daughter thus greeted him on the return of his birthday.

TO MY FATHER.

7th April, 1823.

And thou art eighty; 'tis thy natal day!
Then oh! forgive me that I dare to pray
(Since from so dear a tie 'tis hard to part,
A tie, sole treasure of this lonely heart)
That many a year thou yet may'st with me stay,
Resign'd in pain, and cheerful in decay!
While the bright hopes redeeming love has taught,
Prompting each pious, purifying thought,
Live in thy soul, to tell of sins forgiven,
And plume its pinions for its flight to heaven.

Some years had now passed since Mrs. Opie first attended the religious services of the Friends; and it will have been apparent to the reader, that she had, during that time, been approaching more and more nearly, in her religious sentiments, to their principles. Another letter which she wrote to Mrs. Fry shortly after the above, speaks of the difficulties she felt on some points; and mentions that "many of her relations, on the mother's side, had been united for generations past to the Wesleyan Methodists," which consideration had sometimes disposed her to incline towards "a union with that sect of worshippers."

It was not without considerable anxiety, and after long deliberation, that the decisive step was taken, and she applied for membership with the Society of Friends. On looking back to that period, she always rejoiced in that decision, and expressed, on her bed of death, her satisfaction in it.

Of the perplexities and anxieties of her mind at this time, her letters to Mrs. Fry give sufficient proof. In January, 1824, she again wrote to her, and, after stating the great difficulty which she experienced in adopting "the plain language," and her earnest desire to be guided aright in this matter, she proceeds:—

* * * It is indeed true that I never feel so comforted, as when I feel humbled, and experience a deep sense of my own sinfulness; when I rise from my knees, or leave meeting with an arrow striking in my heart, as it were, I feel a sort of pleasure, which I now would not exchange for aught the world can give. I hope this will not seem to thee unreal or fantastical: but no, I think thou wilt understand it. * * * * To say the truth, much as I should like to belong to a religious society, and much as I see, or think I see, the hand of my gracious Lord in leading *me*, to whom have been given so many ties to a worldly life, in the various gifts bestowed on me, (I mean *accomplishments*, as they are called,) to communion with a sect which requires the sacrifice of them almost *in toto*, thereby trying my faith to the uttermost, still I feel no necessity for haste in doing so. It is by no means clear to me, that, though generally strong, I am not locally infirm. I have lately had severe colds, and coughs, and have queer feelings in my heart, which may be merely nervous, and may be not so. Be this as it may, I am never without the consciousness now, that this may be for me "no continuing city." In the next place, should I survive my father, and be in a condition of

body and mind favourable to travelling, it has long been the desire of my heart to visit foreign countries; my wishes, I own, extending even to Palestine; and it might be far better for me to travel, unfettered by any ties. * * * Meantime, I feel my reliance on my Saviour grow stronger every day, and a sort of loathing of worldly society, which I must strive against. But no one, but that wise and merciful and *just* Being who has tried, and is now trying me, knows, or ever will know, what I have to endure from the many unseen peculiarities of my situation. However, I take comfort and encouragement from my difficulties; I know that I am most vile, and that I ought to be for ever striving to show my gratitude to my blessed Redeemer, by devoting myself entirely to his service; and I feel a repose and peace, in spite of my conscious sins, which the world cannot give nor take away, and which I humbly hope will continue to bear me up unto the end. Above all, I am conscious of a daily increasing spirit of prayer, and a desire of constant communion with the Bestower of it. What a letter of egotism! But I know thy mind will be interested in the "dealings" with mine, and I wish thee, dearest Betsy, always to know whereabouts I am. Dear Joseph is come back well, and looking well. With kind love to you all,

I am, thy affectionate Friend,

A. Opie.

To Elizabeth Fry,
Plashet, East Ham, Essex.

In another letter, dated Norwich, 3rd mo., 2nd, 1824, addressed to Mrs. Fry, after thanking her for her reply to the former letter, she tells her that on the 14th of the preceding month, she had, after much anxious consideration and indecision, decided to act without delay, according to the dictates of her conscience; and that a gentleman, a stranger, chancing to come and call on her that morning, she spoke the "plain language" to him, and had continued to do so ever since; and she says, "Nor have I had a misgiving, but feel so calm and satisfied, that I am convinced *I have done right;* and I feel now utterly cast for comfort, support, and guidance, on the Searcher of hearts, and the great Shepherd, the merciful Redeemer.

In the following year Mrs. Opie addressed this letter to the Friends of the Monthly Meeting.

RESPECTED FRIENDS,

Having attended your place of worship for more than eleven years, and being now fully convinced of the truth of Friends' principles, I can no longer be easy without expressing my earnest desire to be admitted into membership with your Society. My former opinions and habits, were, I own, at variance with yours; but having, through Divine mercy, been convinced of the error of my early belief, and of the emptiness of worldly pleasures, I trust that the same mercy has led me to desire to "walk in the narrow way" that seems to lie before me, and to promise me "that peace which the world cannot give."

I am, yours, with respect and esteem,

A. O.

As the result of this application, she was received into membership on the 11th of August, 1825.

Dr. Alderson expressed his warm approval of the step his daughter had taken. He had, during the lengthened period of his gradual decline, been much comforted and assisted by the attentions and religious counsels of Mr. J. J. Gurney, and had become attached to those friends whose society she so much esteemed. He wished also to be permitted to find his last resting-place in the Friends' burial ground; and it was evident that he was destined soon to occupy the "abode appointed for all living."

There exists an affecting record of the last two years of his life, in a ledger-like book, into which he entered all his medical cases, day by day. The first entry is dated January 25th, 1824, and the last, September 7th, 1825, little more than a month before his death! In this book, he has, every now and then, in the midst of his professional notes, made an entry of some personal feeling or event. Thus, under date 27th January, 1824, he writes, "Southey came—his portrait taken—his hair grey." 4th March, 1825, "*Miserere mei, Domine, precor;*" and again, August 16th, "Never felt so like dying, as I have just now done; the sensation was indescribably bad." At length, on the closing page of the book, he writes:—"I never thought I should live to finish this book. If I live till to-morrow, I shall begin a new one. My pain, at this moment, is bad, my intellects clear, and I look forward to my being saved for happiness hereafter. How much I long for my last end! but in this I act wrongly; for a man ought to wait patiently till his end comes; for I can live no longer than God pleases, let a man talk to me ever so long about curing my legs."

On the cover of this book Dr. A. has written the following verse of Dr. Watts:—

"Let all the heathen writers join,
To form one perfect book,
Great God! when once compared with Thine,
How mean their writings look."

During his illness, Mrs. Opie used to play on the piano, and sing the hymns and psalms of Dr. Watts to her father, at his request; he appeared to find great consolation in listening as she sung, and often called to have the hymn repeated; and that music was like a medicine that soothed him to rest, when any other might have been administered in vain.

Shortly before his death, he was visited by Mr. Gurney, and, in reply to an observation made by him, expressed, with great feeling, his humble confidence in the atoning work of the Lord Jesus Christ.

So died the father of Amelia Opie. As she gazed upon his lifeless countenance, she was able to entertain a hope that supported her soul, and preserved her from sinking under the blow. How deeply and enduringly she lamented him, and how tenderly she cherished his memory, was evident in every day of her after life. Dr. Alderson's record was written upon his daughter's heart. And is not Carlyle right when he says, "Oh! great, or little one, according as thou art loveable, those thou livest with will love thee?"

CHAPTER XIV.

CONSOLATION IN SORROW; LETTER TO A FRIEND; JOURNAL FOR THE YEAR 1827.

* * * * * *

In the months that followed her father's death, Mrs. Opie, though suffering deeply, was sustained by her faith in the promises of Him whose voice she had heard and obeyed, and for whose service she had renounced the approval and the pleasures of the world. In the kindness and sympathy of her friends she found comfort, and thankfully acknowledged that there is "good in friendship, and delight in holy love," and, in her turn, she sought to "bind up the heart that was broken," and to minister to the consolation of others—one of the surest and best means of obtaining relief under the pressure of sorrow. It is impossible to read her journals and letters of this time, without recognizing in them a depth of piety, that could only spring from a Divine source. Her tender compassion for the afflicted, and her labours of love, in visiting the sick, the prisoner, and the necessitous, remind one of Horace Walpole's words to Hannah More, "Your heart is always aching for others, and your head for yourself."

The following letter is almost the only record of the year that followed Dr. Alderson's death; it was addressed to a lady to whom she was much attached, and who afterwards came to live in Norwich. When she died, Mrs. Opie's letters to her were returned, and some of them will be found occasionally in these pages.

Norwich, 3rd mo., 26th, 1826.

My beloved Friend,

* * * I had thought that I could never feel anything again, but thy news really affected me! I am, I own, uneasy at the idea of thy suffering; but thy present sweet, spiritual, and submitted state of mind, will, I doubt not, strew thy path with those unfading flowers, which, blown here, will blossom to all eternity, and sooth and cheer thy passage to the tomb.

For a year at least, my place of abode must be unfixed; it may be London; in that case, I should be near thee: but when we meet we will speculate on the earthly future, which is equally uncertain to us both.

What a mercy it is, dear friend, that thou wast enabled, through faith, to bear thy apparent sentence, so abruptly pronounced. In nothing are the Lord's dealings with us so wonderful and gracious, as when he enables us to bear trials, which we should once have expected to shrink from and to sink under. How I have been permitted to experience this!

My health is quite restored, my recent journey having, I trust, been beneficial. On my way home I was alone from Scole to Norwich, with a young man apparently dying of decline, and I felt it a duty to talk on serious subjects; and found him, I trust, teachable, and I promised to send him J. J. Gurney's Letters and others. He was so delighted! but, poor thing, he was full of hopes of recovery. I have been tolerably tranquil for some days; and to-day I visited my dear father's grave! he hoped I would sometimes do so! I felt *peace* both for him and myself, while I looked on it, and looked forward with cheerfulness to sleeping beside him! H. Girdlestone comforted me much, the other day, by reminding me how often in *mercy* the child was summoned away soon after the parent! The idea brought closer the prospects of eternity, and the necessity, therefore, of preparation, as more urgent, that the day's work may be done in the day. May my attention be fixed on present duty, that my remaining time may be usefully and well spent, and that I may be ready when the summons shall come to call me hence.

J. J. Gurney is on a long and distant journey; when he returns, and when we meet, which may not be for two months, if I can say ought to him for thee, command me.

Farewell, write soon, thine affectionately,

A. OPIE.

In the autumn of this year, Mrs. Opie went on a visit to some friends residing near the Lakes. The change of scene, and friendly intercourse, were beneficial to her; and she returned refreshed to her now solitary home.

From this time she kept an occasional diary, in which she noted the events of each day; from these records we select some portions, commencing with one headed,

1827, *My Journal, New Year's Day.*—Too unwell to venture to the Sick Poor Committee to-day. Sorry to begin the year with the omission of a duty. My aunt and other friends called; also the dear Earlham children—welcome visitants! Day calm, on the whole, but was not quite satisfied with myself; nay, was far otherwise. Read the 46th psalm to the servants; felt the force of "Peace, be still, and know that I am God," and also the comfort of "God is our refuge," &c.

(2nd of 1st mo.) Rose better in health, after a peaceful night, and felt calm and thankful. Walked to Bracondale and made calls there, and attended the Infant School

Committee. Was, in the evening, at a party; the conversation not general, but rather pleasant. I could have wished not to have left the vicinity of ———, who always talks well, but was obliged, through courtesy, to change my seat. I believe things and public persons, not private individuals, were talked of; this is always desirable, but rare. Had only time to read a psalm to the servants, being so late, which I regret. On looking over the day, I am not sure it was better spent; in one respect, I had, indeed, more self-blame to undergo. Night peaceful and favoured, when I awoke, which was not often; but my morning thoughts full of painful recollections of little slights and trials. Oh! my pride of heart! not subdued yet: "Oh! for a broken contrite heart."

(4th.) Had a sweet, sleepful, and favoured night; but have passed a self-indulgent day. Read F. Hemans' poetry; it is unique and exquisite, and breathing always of salvation and heaven. How have I thrown away my time to day; done nothing of my book, except writing the introduction to a fable for it; but have written two necessary letters. Felt comfort while reading A. L. Barbauld's beautiful hymn on charity, "Behold where breathing love divine!" I hoped I was not slow to kind offices; but other convictions kept me full of counteracting humility. Sent dear S. M. B. some pomegranates. How pleased I am when I can shew her and dear A. G. any attention. How much were they to me in my darkest hours; how true and tender their sympathy! never to be forgotten. How can I help feeling for them who felt so much for me?

(4th day.) Rose calm and comforted; had, on the whole, a good and comforting meeting, though no ministry; called on my aunt and the N. Whites. A very unprofitable day, meeting time excepted; I grow worse, I fear, rather than better. I am so dissatisfied with myself, that I dare hardly ask or expect a blessing on my labours. How cold and dead in the spirit I feel to night; but I know "we have an Advocate with the Father, Jesus Christ, the righteous," and how I need one!

(5th.) A good and comfortable night, and rose in spirits, but felt unwilling to work at my book. Dear friends called; had a kind odd letter from H. T., and so characteristic! *Made* myself finish another fable for my work, and liked it. Just come from dining at Neville W.'s with his mother and sisters—enjoyed my visit. On the whole, more satisfied with this day than the preceding one; but I am very lazy, and like in spirit to Festus, of whom I have just been reading, when he said to Paul, that he would send for him, and hear him, at a convenient season. Oh! that deferring.

(6th.) Rose, refreshed by a good night, and willing to perform my duties. Wrote some verses for a friend's album, and improved my fable of the Lapdog and the Ass. Went to the jail, and found the woman in bed: read to and exhorted her. She *seemed* in a promising state of mind. Went next to visit a poor woman, but felt she and her husband were not so much interested as when I was there before. Called on my aunt: she gave a poor account of my uncle. Poor M. B.! his interesting son Edward *worse*, and no chance of aught but a protracted life of suffering, likely to end in early death: may he be preserved in his day of trial. Have passed this evening in alternate reading and writing, but not of a profitable nature; however, I like my verses very well. This day there has been some performance of duty, but, on the whole, it marks no progress in grace. To-morrow is first day; may I keep it holy.

(7th of the month, 1st day.) A quiet night, and very satisfactory morning meeting. J. S. had to speak in rather long quotations from the Scriptures, and spoke, I think, to edification. No other ministry—felt no want of any. Afternoon meeting still, but not long, like the morning one. Read dear S. M. B. on the Sabbath; then read the first part of Mary Dudley's Life; felt true unity with her experience when first called to the ministry. What a bright course was hers! Wrote a serious letter, with Scripture quotations, to L. E., with two copies of J. J. Gurney's letter: may the gift be blessed to him! Read about eighty pages of a book lent me by Dr. Ash, called "The Grounds of a Holy Life." Believe the author to be a Friend in principle, if not in profession. Read Paul's fine address to Agrippa to the servants, and remarks on Paul's letter to Titus, by H. Tarford; hope they understood it; it explains the nature of grace, and clearly. Cough very troublesome. Now to bed, thankful for the mercies and favours of the day. The poor Duke of York! would I knew what his death-bed feelings and hopes were, and *on what grounded.*

(8th.) Rose unwell; but my mind was particularly calm. Finished M. R. Mitford's pretty book, and wrote out my new fable. After tea wrote two sheets of my new book. Heard of poor Lady H.'s death. How I feel for her childless, fond mother! and how thankful that I was permitted to live to cheer my dear father's age, and attend his dying bed, much as I have suffered, and still suffer, for his loss.

(9th.) Wrote a good deal in the morning. Lady H. *not* dead; how glad I am! Too hoarse at night to read much to the servants. On the whole went to bed rather pleased with my day, but expecting to cough.

(11th.) Meeting a very satisfactory one. C. came and sat an hour or two. Got, alas! on religious subjects; a most painful conversation; but I was made, I hope, beneficially sensible, how poor a pleader I am, as yet, in the best of causes; but I tried to do it justice. Went to my uncle's at nine; passed a pleasant evening, but was detained by a dangerous accident to H. P.'s coachman, and I waited to hear how he was. Did not get home till half-past eleven. Read to the servants, and sent them to bed. Sat up in my own room and read the second volume of A.'s, that it might not encroach on the business of the morrow. Read a psalm and went to bed, not dissatisfied with my day; but feeling how wrong it is to let a day pass without employing it really well. Mem. made a resolution not to speak slightingly again of ——— if I can *help it.* (12th.) Had a bad night, but rose with a thankful spirit, I trust. Staid at home all the morning, and wrote some of my book. Had the joy of hearing of E. P.'s safe confinement. Went to Lady J. W.'s, met several friends, and had a pleasant evening; E. M. played admirably. Read as usual, and to bed, thankful that I had passed so favoured a day. (13th.) Rose late, and was the better for my morning sleep. Wrote to several friends, and in the evening had a small party. Made two good likenesses, as they said.*

(14th.) A night of cough, but of comfort; and rose in spirits; a painfully windy walk to meeting; an agreeable surprise there. J. J. G. returned this morning unexpectedly from London. He was much favoured in his ministry to-day, morning and evening. Called on poor old B., and read the 43rd of Isaiah to him. Called on poor P. U., found her very low indeed, and no wonder; these are early times with her yet, poor bereaved being! The sight of such upsetting and destroying grief is very affecting, and I have only too much sympathy with her. We have both lost our earthly all! Was prevented, by the weather, from calling on the M.s, and it was fortunate, as the wind had brought down their chimnies in a most destructive manner, though providentially no lives were lost, as they had taken alarm and removed the children. "His tender mercies are over all his works!" A quiet evening; read to the servants; hope they understood. (15th.) Coughed all night, and unable, alas! to go to E., but when I had recovered the disappointment, passed some tranquil and agreeable hours. I read "Galt's Life of Wolsey" with interest. To bed thankful, and rather better; could only read a psalm to the servants. (16th.) Rose rather better, but not well enough to go to E.; wrote a great deal of my book, to carry to-morrow, if well enough to go. Read through my own "Temper," never saw so many faults in it before; still I like some of the remarks on detraction so well, that I think of inserting them in my new book. Shall lay

* Mrs. Opie is constantly mentioning the likenesses she takes of her various friends. It was her custom, from a very early period, to take profile likenesses, in pencil, of those who visited her. Several hundreds of these sketches were preserved in books and folios.

my head on my pillow with less self-blame for the faults of the day than usual. (17th.) Rose refreshed, and better than for many days; went to E., and enjoyed being with my dear friends again. I had a long *tête à tête* with J. J. G., and read my MS. to him, he did not approve it as a whole; thought the tone too low generally, but liked parts of it; I shall leave out and amend much. Read a psalm in my own room to my maid, and went to bed full of good resolutions, and ardent desires and prayers to be satisfied in them. (18th.) Rose refreshed, not *gay*, but very peaceful; went to meeting, very still and solemn; a time of precious, conscious favour to me. J. J. G. spoke quite to my state, the first time he rose; and I felt the force of the admonition the second time; but *I* had had *no work to do,* and left meeting, so far, with a clean conscience. I called on friends, and sat some time with my aunt, E. A.; to bed with much comfort and thankfulness. (19th.) To Earlham with J. J. G., and read my MS. to him and the sisters; they were all very encouraging; with what a thankful heart I am going to rest! (21st.) Left Earlham grateful for many happy hours spent there. Came to meeting; J. J. G. particularly favoured in his ministry; painful to me to break up. Alone all the afternoon and evening; read in the Italian Bible; am going to bed comforted and thankful; but had, at morning meeting, one of my paroxysms of regret for ill-fulfilled duties, and was brought very low; "but He helped me," and all is peace again, and I shall lie down in quiet. (22nd.) An unsatisfactory day, except as I read in my Italian Bible, and to the servants. (23rd.) Tranquil at rising, and wrote all the morning, till I went to E., where I met Lady H. G., D. G., and dear A. G.; a happy day! and am going to bed thankful. (24th.) Obliged to leave E., preferred doing so; I wanted to go home to draw U. M. for her dying lover; I succeeded entirely, they thought; felt thankful to be so enabled. (25th.) To meeting, a marriage there. I went a round of visiting invalid friends, and a poor woman; in the afternoon, went out again and visited another afflicted invalid. Felt my mind tenderly impressed with pity, and with thankfulness for my own health. Saw dear O. A. Woodhouse, glad to see him for *many* sakes; evening, wrote, and to bed at eleven, most thankful and peaceful. (26th.) Going to dine at E. with a crowd.—The party tolerably agreeable, considering its size; a day, not entirely lost, I trust. (27th.) Went to the jail, and had a satisfactory meeting with the women there. To bed not satisfied with myself. (28th.) Meeting a most favoured one; dear J. J. G. very impressive and affecting, with a view to his departure for Ireland; wrote to H. G., and received from him a most satisfactory answer, authorizing me to draw on him for ———'s wants; how kind! like him! thankful am I, that I have been the means of serving her! to bed peaceful and thankful. (30th.) Rose well and happy, and settled my weekly accounts; in the evening wrote letters. I have been comforted all day through the tender sorrowful remembrance of him who is gone; and the memory of his deep and ever-enduring and *unselfish* love, is frequently recurring and *clinging* to me; and death alone, I believe, can ever banish him from my daily and fond, grateful recollection; but, "it is well;" I can say so, from the bottom of my heart, and though I remain, I murmur not—now to bed, with thankfulness, though with tears.

(1st February, 2nd mo.) Not much sleep in the night; a pleasant breakfast, and most refreshing sweet meeting. Tears would flow, but was able to supplicate for our dear departing friends, and to return thanks for being able to part with them so cheerfully. *Two years ago,* how I should have felt it, on mine and my dearest father's account; but I feel indifferent whether he be here when *I* die, or not. * * Now to bed, calm and thankful. An *idle,* I fear, and, so far, a sinful day; gave £1 to a case that *touched* me; was I fear, too much, but could not help it. (2nd.) O. Woodhouse here; glad to feel that a son of my beloved cousin, and bearing his name, is under my roof! Our evening has been placid, part spent in talk, and part in reading. Now to bed, rather depressed that I have done nothing to-day to improve myself, except reading in the Bible—I begin to feel that my time must be made profitable, or I cannot be happy; my solitary evenings are my happiest time, and shortest, because employed! Oh! that I had earlier thought thus. Then would "my peace have been as a river, and my righteousness as the waves of the sea"—perhaps—but I am, and was, vile. (3rd.) Forced myself to go and see, and minister to the wants of, some poor people. (4th.) Meeting, a mixed one of favoured and wandering thoughts; L. A. very sweet in her ministry. (5th.) Rose cheerful, went to visit various friends. To my dear father's grave, and the other graves of those dear to me; how I wished he might see me, and read my heart. Went and read to the poor widow B., and visited others. (6th.) Rose well, and cheerful. Went to call on that wretched girl in the workhouse. She cried, but I believe she wished to see me only to get money. Mean to get the prayer-book I gave her out of pawn. The committee of the new Magdalen met here to-day. I like the matron.

On the 7th inst., Mrs. Opie went to visit her friends at Northrepps; each day has its entry. She was evidently cheered, and her spirits revived and braced by this visit. Returning home on the 23rd of the month, her last entry there is—"I leave N. C. with a heart full of grateful love to its dear possessors. Alas! to bed for the last time here this year, and, perhaps, for ever! Peace be to this house!"

(Journal resumed at home.)

(Norwich, 24th.) Had, as usual, some paroxysms of agonizing feeling, at missing the object once there to meet me, yet grateful to find kind and affectionate friends here. All things here, right and well; to bed, with a grateful heart for the mercies shewn me, and the blessings that remain. (25th.) A good night, and a thankful waking. Enjoyed meeting much, called at the workhouse, &c. Afternoon meeting silent, but I trust refreshing. Evening a comfortable reading to the servants. (26th.) A good and favoured night, rose happy. * * * Wrote letters. A time of storm and calm; one of my paroxysms of grief for the dead, and self-blame for omitted duty, succeeded by calm and peacefulness. (27th.) Paid three visits of charity. Went to the workhouse; saw the child, and thought her, perhaps obstinate, but quite an object of pity and interest; thought her, too, going into a decline; carried her coquilles and oranges. Saw P. C.; death was in her face, seemingly, and seemingly contrite; but even then, I find, she told me *a lie.* Not to be believed for a word's speaking! Oh that workhouse! "There's something rotten in the state of Denmark!" Spent a happy evening; good intentions, if not good deeds. (28th.) A good night and bright awaking. * * Dined at Earlham. Next day very pleasant. (2nd.) A good night, and much thankfulness on waking. Wrote a "Tale of Truth." To the workhouse. After a happy evening *alone,* to bed, in great peace of mind. (4th.) Meeting very still and refreshing; L. A. much favoured. Wrote several verses to the memory of Bishop Heber. (5th of the 3rd mo.) Had a good night, and peace of mind, when awake. Visited poor B., and admired his thankfulness for living where he can see the blue sky, and the birds, and a rainbow, as he lies in bed! Went to Sick Poor Committee. Monthly Meeting, too low to enjoy it. One of my sad, sad fits of regret for omitted filial duties, and for things done and undone, said and unsaid; but feel this ever recurring trial to be inflicted in mercy, and to keep me lowly and humble before my Creator. Fear, however, that the feeling increases, and that it may be a temptation. Find what H. Girdlestone said to me once, the most comforting reply to my fears of omitted duty, "You seem to have expected that a sinful being should have performed a duty perfectly; but it was not in nature to do it." Well! I have only to hope that my agonies and tears may be an accepted sacrifice, and that they may keep me humble, as they spring from a sense of my own vileness. To bed early, as I dare not risk a recurrence of my lowness, and sleep may come soon. (6th.) A good night, rose cheerful. Went to the Committee of Infant School, and took the week's visiting there. S. Rose with me in the evening. Calm and thankful. (7th.) Infant School; thought the children improved, but yet troublesome and disobedient. To the Magdalen Committee—not quite satisfied. (8th.) Rose cheerful, and eager for meeting. On the whole, satisfactory; Monthly Meeting, though, rather long. Read some books from London in the evening—did not like them; dissatisfied with *so* employing my time. (10th.) Rose early. Bought cakes for the children, and went to Infant School. Thence to the jail: found two new women there; read and talked to them seriously. Had tea alone. Cucchi called in the evening; read two psalms aloud, in Italian, to him, and translated them. (13th.) To the School: class attentive and orderly; a cake each, to the children; sale of work afterwards. Came home to dress. Both my friends looking well and in high spirits; felt thankful to see them so; all good be with them! Dined at my uncle's at six. * * * Finished reading the "Hedge of Thorns" to the servants. (14th.) To Earlham; a most happy time there. (15th.) Ditto.

(Journal discontinued, till the 13th April.)

(April 14th.) Rose low and self-abased. At the jail, read tracts to the women, and the Prodigal Son; was satisfied with the manner of two of them; but have no faith in their amendment, in one way, while the turnkeys are men, and men on business are admitted, where women could do as well; but this is, I fear, a thing which will never be remedied. * * (15th, 1st day.) A sweet, favoured meeting. Silence, I trust, blest to me; the ministry lively and touching. My Cousin R. to tea; went over his sermon with him; time went unconsciously. (16th.) Letters and calls. After dinner went to sit by poor E. D.'s bedside, read several hymns to her; she bade me, I believe, what she thought, a last farewell! She is on the Rock, and one ought not to regret her. What a sweet letter Edward Irving has written to her! * * * * To bed, thankful, instructed, I hope, and cheered. (19th.) Rose before seven, and lighted my fire; wrote till half-past eight. Meeting a favoured one.—"The fire on the altar." Called on A. B., an interesting woman, and wish I could do more for her. She has been used to such excellent society, and an object of interest and kindness to so many. She talks rapidly, and raises her voice sometimes, as all nervous people do; I wonder whether checking her, and saying "do not talk so fast!" would do her good. Not intimate enough yet to *risk* it. Lost a great deal of time to-day reading an old favourite—displeased and shocked even, at my waste of time, and my life so far spent! "God be merciful to me a sinner!" my constant and necessary close of every day's and night's prayer. (21st.) Went out on H. G.'s business. How pleasant to have to give pleasure, whether with my own or others' money! Poor —— might indeed be grateful to him. Went after a poor man, but could not find him; probably only a street beggar. Went to poor A. B.; what a sufferer! but resigned. Called on my aunt, sorry I could not stay with her. To bed, with many pleasing feelings, thankful for unmerited mercies. What a generous Master we serve!

(6th of the 5th mo.) What indolence and neglect! from 21st of last mo. not a line written in my journal! Oh for power to be more diligent in future; but how soon, through life, have I been weary in well doing! To-day, felt solemnly and deeply engaged, in secret prayer, at meeting. Yesterday —— and —— to dinner; how little either of them, poor things, seemed to think of their great change! though one is 76, the other 73. Dress, cards, the world! But let me look to my own blindness and worldliness, and not censure theirs; and to me the voice has spoken, "Come," and how have I obeyed it? Alas! Visited a sick friend and a poor *lost* girl, just released from jail; read Rutherford's letters all the afternoon: wrote for votes for a charity-boy; read to the servants, and to bed, not so dissatisfied as usual with my day's work; may I be humbled, and enabled to rise early to my work to-morrow, and may the labours of my pen be blest!

(3rd day, 7th.) Rose early; to Infant School; little boys idle and ignorant in my class! *one*, however, good and diligent; then called on A. B., found her low for her dear sister's death, but enjoyed my call. Went to the jail, have hopes of one woman; the other is sorry for detection, not for sin; but these are early times yet; her temper seems bad, *i. e.* if *expression* is to be trusted; two calls on my way home. Tired, but not displeased with my day. * * *

The Journal here breaks off, not to be renewed (as a note, added at the close, tells us) until 1829, "in another book." We shall close this chapter with an extract from a letter written in the autumn of this year, to her friends at Northrepps Cottage.

* * * How every day teems with eventful changes; F. and C., dear ones, have to inhabit a new abode; but death, *death* is the change of changes! How trumpery, how unimportant, seem all changes compared to *that;* and how *that* changes even the very look of existence to many of us! Sometimes it is almost unbearable to me; and I could run into the next room to look for what I cannot find, and cannot see again, and which yet seems blooming beside me, and cheerful, and living, and likely to live! and then I think how little I prized him while I had him with me! Oh! you know some of these feelings, and can deeply sympathize with me in what a child alone can feel. How deeply have I entered into the feelings of my estimable friend T. R., (an only child,) on the loss of his mother, who lived with him; I expressed my feelings as follows:—

At length, then, the tenderest of mothers is gone!
Her smile, her love-accents, can glad thee no more;
That once cheerful chamber is silent and lone,
And, for thee, all a child's precious duties are o'er.

Her welcome at morning, her blessing at night,
No longer the crown of thy comforts can be;
And the friend seen and lov'd, since thine eyes first saw light,
Thou can'st ne'er see again! thou art orphan'd like me.

O change! from which nature must shrink overpower'd,
Till faith shall the anguish remove and condemn,
For the change to those blest ones "who die in the Lord,"
Though to us it brings sorrow, gives glory to them.

9th mo., 1827.

CHAPTER XV.

YEARLY MEETINGS; LETTER FROM LONDON; LETTERS FROM LADIES CORK AND CHARLEVILLE; "DETRACTION DISPLAYED;" LETTER FROM ARCHDEACON WRANGHAM; CROMER; DIARY FOR 1829.

From the time Mrs. Opie joined the Friends, she regularly attended the Yearly Meetings of the Society, held in London during the month of May. At these seasons she met numerous friends and acquaintances, and had an opportunity of attending the meetings of various societies, in whose objects she sympathized, and of which the Bible, and the British and Foreign School, and Anti-Slavery Societies, were among the most valued. What cordial interest she always evinced on these occasions, and with how much animation and lively description, she loved to detail, afterwards, what she had heard and seen! Her eye kindled as she recalled the eloquent address of some friend of the wronged and helpless, and her delighted approval was a meed which a good man might well rejoice to have earned.

Shortly after the entry in her journal, with which the preceding chapter concluded, she went to London, for the purpose of attending the Yearly Meeting. Many painful regrets and memories of the past were unavoidable; but she bore up against them, and the effort was beneficial. Solitude, prolonged solitude, preyed upon her spirits, and her essentially social nature languished and pined under it. One letter to the friend before alluded to, contains some interesting particulars of her proceedings during this visit.

Bradpole, Bridport, Dorsetshire,
6th mo., 29th, 1827.

MY VERY DEAR FRIEND,

* * * Pray excuse my long silence. I know nothing of N. since I left it. I have had a feeling which has made me indifferent, not only to writing letters, but to receiving them. It was so different once; and my life, during the last three weeks in London, has realized my loss to me more than ever. I have had pleasing and gratifying things to relate; but, alas! he, to whom the relation would have given such pleasure, is gone; and even on the instant my pleasure has been swallowed up in pain;—but this is weak and earthly, and I will forbear. My life in London, during and after the Meeting, has been very happily spent. My lodgings were too far from Devonshire House; but I always got there in time, and when meeting was over, T. R. generally came home with me. Yearly Meeting was peculiarly sweet to me this year, and satisfactory to Friends. I attended the African Meeting at the Freemason's Tavern: it was this year quite thin. Spring Rice, Chas. Barclay, and the Duke of Gloucester, were among the speakers. I saw Lady S. and her daughter, and gladly acceded to their request that I would sit by them. The Duke of Gloucester spoke to them, coming and going; but though he bowed to me, I was sure he did not know me; so on his returning, I begged Lady S. to name me, and he seemed so glad to see me, and talked some time, retaining my hand in his. (I hope friends behind were not scandalized.) There was an American lady who came up and introduced herself to me, and begged me to call on her, adding that Sir W. Scott's niece was staying with her; accordingly, I called on them at Ellis's

Hotel, St. James' Street, when my new friend (sweet food for vanity, and I hope also for some better feeling) told me that my "Odd-tempered Man" had reformed a dear friend of hers, and she seemed to remember far more of it than I do. * *

I promised to call at Lady Cork's and ask leave to introduce the two ladies to her: and I did so, their footman attending me, to hear Lady C.'s reply. She sent a gracious message back, and accordingly they came, just as Lady C. Lamb had arrived, so they saw *her;* but so changed! I should hardly have known her.

On 6th day morning, I went to Lord Roden's, to hear him read and expound the Scriptures. At two o'clock every Friday he had this meeting, during his stay in London. The company was numerous, and several persons of quality among them. He is, indeed, a highly gifted man; but, my dear, I have since been at a meeting which will interest thee more. Since I came to London I have heard of many whom I left in the world, being come *out* of it; amongst the rest, Thos. Erskine and his wife. At a bazaar for the schools in St. Giles', held at the Hanover Square Rooms, (at which many of the sellers were Irish nobility,) I saw some friends, who prevailed on me to go and dine with them, and there I met Caroline Fry, with whom I talked of thee. At dinner they spoke of Mrs. Stephens, who, they said, was to expound that evening, at a friend's house near, and I consented to go with them to hear her. It was a large assembly, and I found there many of my bazaar friends. I was warmly welcomed, especially by the fair expounder. Sir James Mackintosh's daughter (the widow of M. Rich) introduced me to Lady G. Wolff. Her spouse did not come till late. Though tired with the bazaar, &c., and as sleepy as possible, that extraordinary and gifted being kept my attention fixed an hour and a half. How eloquent and touching were her words!

When it was over, I went up to her; and, as I could not express my feelings, I gave her a kiss, and she afterwards embraced me, and we promised to meet if ever we came near each other's habitation. I then stole away. It is certainly an extraordinary power, and many of the clergy who disapprove of woman's ministry, have been brought round to approve; but I do not call hers *ministry*, except in prayer. She has done this twenty-two years, and still she does not seem old. How I wish thou hadst been there!

I came here, quite knocked up; but this green flowery sequestered nest, amongst hills, and the sweet society of dear friends, will, I trust, soon restore me. Pray write to thy attached friend,

A. OPIE.

In this letter Mrs. Opie mentions having called on Lady Cork; their friendship had been of long standing, and not even the great change in Mrs. O.'s habits and opinions could estrange from her this early friend. Soon after she joined the Friends, Lady Cork wrote to her thus:—

"*Si vous êtes heureuse, je ne suis pas malheureuse*," used to be my motto to you. I must be glad that you are happy; but I must confess I have too much *self*, not to feel it a tug at my heart, the *no-chance* I have of enjoying your society again. Will your primitive cap never dine with me, and enjoy a quiet society? but really, am I never to see you again? Your parliament friend does not wear a broad-brimmed hat; so pray, pray, *pray* do not put on the bonnet. So come to me and be my love, in a dove-coloured garb, and a simple head-dress. Teach us your pure morals, and your friend of the lower House shall join us, and approve of your compliance. He will agree with me, that good people, mixing with the world, are of infinitely more use than when they confine themselves to one set. Pray treat me with a letter sometimes; and when you do write, (if you happen to think of it,) say whether your Norwich goods are cheaper upon the spot than I can get them in town—this is of no consequence. Cannot you give me one of your 200 pictures? you're welcome to my phiz, if you will come and paint it, or shall I step to you? I could fill a paper with fun, but the cold water of your last makes me end my letter. God bless you! Adieu.

Yours ever, sinner or saint,
M. CORK AND ORRERY.

What! do you give up Holkham, your singing and music, and do you really see harm in singing? Now F. sings all day long, and thinks it her duty.

Her friend Lady Charleville, too, wrote kindly and feelingly :—

London, le 10me Avril, 1828.

Pour avoir le plaisir de te tutoyer, je t'écris, ma chère, en François, ou l'on tutoye naturellement celles que l'on aime. * * *

Et je te jure que, quand tu te ferois Bramine, cela me seroit égale, tant que tu conserverais pour moi la même bonté que jadis! Le prince C. m'a parlé de la mort de ton cher père, mais il m'a assuré que je ne devois point t'écrire à ce sujet, pour te rappeller l'abîme de douleur où tu etois dans le premier temps.

Ma chère Madame Opie, j'ai partagée la douleur, et je sais ce que c'est d'être privée de l'objet qui nous est cher.

* * Pour la secte dont tu fais partie,—je la respecte au-de-là de toutes les autres. Je ne vois rien d'outré dans leur façons de penser, et je voudrais être assez bonne pour me conduire comme eux.

Viens nous voir—j'en serai trop enchantée; ton cœur n'est point changé, et je suis sure que ta costume ne te rendra pas moins intéressante pour tes amis. Comptez, ma chère, que le temps ne fait nul effet sur moi, pour changer à l'intérêt que je prendrai toute ma vie à toi.

E. M. CHARLEVILLE.

There is something in the evident truthfulness and genuine feeling of these letters, which convinces one that there were many sacrifices of feeling, and poignant regrets, to be felt, in parting from the companions and sympathies of the past.

In 1828 "Detraction Displayed" was published. Among the many acknowledgments Mrs. O. received from her friends on this occasion, was a letter from Archdeacon Wrangham, to whom she had alluded in this work. He writes:—

September 10th, 1828.

DEAR MRS. OPIE,

Having now read by snatches, as my little leisure has permitted, "Detraction Displayed," I hasten to acknowledge the pleasure (and I trust I may also add profit) which I have derived from it. It is the conscientious work of a very gifted writer, and cannot be read without producing, by God's accompanying blessing, excellent effects. The subtilty of the spirit, which you have endeavoured to lay, is such, that even the worthy, in many cases, inhale and exhale it, almost unawares;—persons who require only putting upon their guard, to avoid it scrupulously for the future. I don't believe the Greek Alphabet, if such be the probable result of your volume, and its Alphas and Betas, &c., ever accomplished a more valuable service, since the days of Cadmus, its reputed inventor. So far do morals outgo mere literature.

I cannot be insensible to your kind compliment in p. 231, and I am happy to be able to say, that none of my epigrams have had malice as their motive, though some, perhaps, a little *méchanceté* in their composition. I rejoice to see your compliment to Mrs. Hemans, who is indeed a "charming writer," and I would send you my Latin version of the two epigrams of pp. 227, 228, as, having been made some years ago, (the latter upwards of thirty,) they prove that my taste on the subject concurs with your own,—if I did not fear that it might look like pedantry. * * *

Yours, dear Mrs. Opie, most faithfully,

JOHN WRANGHAM.

In the month of June Mrs. Opie, writing from Upton, to Miss Buxton and Miss Gurney, gave them an account of her proceedings during her sojourn in town; and thus records her impressions of a scene which greatly interested her:—

* * * I wished for you both, the other evening, when I had the inexpressible delight of hearing and seeing some of the very first men in the country, assembled to celebrate the Repeal of the Sacramental Test. One of the select committee, (Henry Waymouth,) kindly saved a ticket for me; which admitted me into a gallery just over the table where they sat; a private gallery, holding only twelve. We entered our box at half-past four, before the company came, having to go through the room to it. However, the time did not seem long, although the tables were not covered till half-past six. When the company was assembled, the Duke of Sussex arrived, and many with him. Previously, however, the clapping of hands had announced some one of consequence, and this was Sir F. Burdett, who took his seat under us, and so near, that we saw him always. I never heard acclamations and applause before this evening, (I may say.) The sounds were deafening. When the Duke was seated, the gallant band and true was arranged, beside and around him. Lord J. Russell on the right hand; Lord Holland on the left. Brougham, announced by loud clapping, sat where we saw him always and perfectly; but I wished him nearer. I suppose my friend Gurney told him I was to be there, for he put his hand to his cheek, and looking up at me, gave me one of his comical looks of recognition. * * * I was disappointed at F. Buxton's not being there; however, I heard admirable speaking from Lord Holland particularly, and Brougham, Burdett, Lord Carnarvon, and every one, indeed, did well. Brougham, however, deservedly, my favourite speaker. Sir Francis spoke well, and gracefully, but with a tone. Brougham has such a voice! and his action is *perfect*, I think. In common speaking his voice is not very

sweet; but in haranguing it is exquisite. Durham, fine also; and deep. Oh! it was one of the greatest treats I ever had; and in proportion was my sadness when I remembered that I had no one to relate it to, who would, as formerly, have doubled my pleasure by reflecting it perfectly. It was *one* in the morning before the Duke departed, having well performed his duty. I had been so absorbed in attending, that I did not suppose it was eleven o'clock! I could have sat all night. We had ice, fruit, champaign, hock, tea, and coffee sent up to us; and in the lady behind me I found a most pleasant companion, and every minute told.

In the autumn of this year, Mrs. Opie repaired to her much-loved Cromer; her notes contain some poetical pieces, written during this visit, from which we select the following lines,

WRITTEN ON THE SEA SHORE.

11th mo., 1828.

Above, lo! cloud to cloud succeeds,
Below, the waves in surges roll,
Bounding and white as Grecian steeds,
That bore their monarch to the goal.

Now, his swift wings the sea bird lowers,
For well he reads the angry skies,
And ere the storm its fury pours,
For shelter to the rock he flies.

Bird of the wave! when dangers threat,
When life looks dark and conflicts roar,
Should deep remorse and vain regret
Rouse in my heart desponding fear;

May I for shelter seek, like thee,—
Shelter, which can all fears remove,
And to my rock of refuge flee;
A dying Saviour's pardoning love!

From Cromer Mrs. Opie went to Northrepps, on a visit to her friends at the Cottage, and, while there, she resumed the Journal which had for a time been discontinued.

New Year's day, 1829. Rose at seven o'clock, after a good night; feeling thankful for being once more under the hospitable roof of friends, so very dear, and so very kind. * *

At the close of the day went to my room, grateful for the enjoyment I have had; but, as far as Christian duty goes, I fear it has been a day of selfish enjoyment only,—a day for time, but what for eternity? however, if I have not performed one good action, I trust I have not committed any great offence; but then, are not sins of omission as bad as sins of commission? If so, alas for me and myriads of others!

(3rd.) Rose very thankful for a refreshing night. But my dreams were affecting in the retrospect; they carried me back to the second house I ever lived in, and where my mother died. I saw her, and my dear father, and the room so plainly! and all the past came rushing over me;—both gone! What a comfort to remember what my father said to me, when he announced her death to me: "she is gone! and may you, Amelia, never have cause to blush when you see her again!" How often, during my succeeding years, did those words of parental warning recur to me, and pleasantly! The *dearest wish* of my heart is to see both my parents again; and perhaps it will one day be gratified. Surely, where parents do their *duty*, children can never know a tie stronger, or as strong, as their *earliest* dependence on a parent's love produces! and, after the lapse of many years, how fresh and vivid still are the recollections of parental and filial love! At least, *I* feel them to be so.

(4th.) A night to be thankful for. Snow on the ground and trees, when I rose; happily, I had given up all idea of going to S. Meeting, for fear of making myself ill again. My dear friends and the family gone to church; I going to keep my meeting in my own room. The snow is falling from the trees, and taking away the beauty it gave; but the sky seems likely to bring it again. The wind is to the N.E. and high, and one cannot but fear for ships at sea; so my benevolent friends have ordered out the fishermen who look after the gun, to keep watch along the cliff. May He, who rules the waves, watch over the endangered! * * *

I have enjoyed my first day, even though I have not been to meeting. It is sweet to know one is in a worshipping family!

(6th.) Sleet and snow abounding; made drawings of three of my friends, and rode out in a snow storm, and enjoyed it. * * * To bed latish, with pleasant recollections of the day, though burdened with the sin of having desired the accession of *great wealth*—that is, of *power*, and the means of self-gratification. Who is to be trusted with such a gift? Not I, I am sure; and ought I not to know that *wishes* are a species of *murmurs*, and that "nevertheless, Thy will not mine be done," is the only proper language? (9th.) Reading Washington Irving's Columbus—how interesting! As well satisfied as I can bē, while doing nothing for the good of others. (10th.) Drove to Sheringham, and returned in a storm of sleet, just in time to keep my engagement at H. B.'s; and arrived there as *the clock struck five*, punctual, to my heart's content. * * To bed grateful for much, but most, for having been able, in some instances, during the evening, to speak according to my own moral standard, whether vainly or not. (14th.) A good night; was dressed by eight, but so absorbed in the psalms, and in making extracts from Columbus, that I did not hear the reading bell, and lost the reading, which I regretted. * * After dinner we drove out; but previously I wrote a little account of cruelty to a dog. We had a most charming drive. It was a bright afternoon, and the sky over the sea was full of tints, and such a glorious setting sun, which clothed the church steeple, and many other prominent objects in sunshine, as we came down the road from Roughton! But, welcome were our home, and our smiling fire, and welcoming friend! (16th.) Drove out to D. B.'s, to see my epitaph on the stone. Thankful to have given pleasure to the son, by these lines. Oh that, like the epitaph named by Legh Richmond, in his Young Cottager, they may be made the means of good! A happy evening, to bed thankful for much, though not satisfied with my own conduct. (17th.) A good night to return thanks for. Drove to see *that* house, where I had so often been with those most dear, now in their graves—my husband, and my cousin Olyett Woodhouse! Dear O! when he went away and sold this estate, he hoped to repurchase it, and return; but he is in his Indian grave! What a trial his death was to me! but my *last* loss annihilated, in a great measure, the sense of every other. (18th, first day.) *Grieved* I could not get to meeting, but I must bear it as well as I can. My own sitting, a favoured and comforting one. After dinner, set off to see the poor widow Green, a blind woman of 89; read to her a long time, and gave her money. Went to the cliff; the sea and sky truly interesting. * * To bed with sabbath feelings. (19th.) Went to see the skaters. Lord Suffield came up to us; and, while we admired the tints of the sky,—which were pale green over the sea, melting into pale blue, and then gradually deepening, till they became the deepest, richest, indigo and purple, over our heads,—he observed, that he had often, but vainly, tried to convince distant friends that our skies in Norfolk, near the sea, have the finest tints he ever saw, and pale green particularly.

(22nd.) A most comfortable sitting of two hours in my own room. Thought of dear N. friends, and wished myself there, (at meeting,) but was thankful for my lonely opportunity. * * * If I were not so idle, and were nearer a meeting, my happiness could know no drawback; especially when we three are alone together. (23rd.) Such a good night! We read as usual; afterwards dear A. was dragged in her hand-chair, to visit the cottages and the sea. The cold, on going out, was intense; the snow in our faces; but I got warm with walking, and enjoyed the scene and the visits. Went to the cliff, and saw, on the shore, planks and baulks, which a most angry sea had washed up; a wreck, no doubt, somewhere,the fishermen said. Fresh barley had floated to land also, and we went to a farm yard near, to see a ladder, bearing the inscription of Exmouth, Hull. My dear friend ordered the men to be on the alert, and watch, lest any vessel should be in distress on the coast, that the mortar might be used. Happily, however, we heard of none being in sight. Drew three likenesses; two, reckoned very good. Alas! it was my last evening at the dear cottage! and it was one of love and interest; and, to me, of thankfulness that I have such friends.

Of this walk in the snow, Mrs. Opie afterwards wrote a pleasing account, part of which we subjoin:—

* * * Snow had continued to fall, and I to admire; but we became impatient of keeping the house, and resolved to go out in some way or other. Accordingly, as to use the horses was impossible, I equipped myself for walking, and one of my friends for going in a chair on wheels. But when the moment for our departure arrived, I felt very loth to leave the fire-side, and envied the dear companion, who, not daring to brave the cold, was left to enjoy its cheering precincts. However, though casting "a longing lingering look behind," both on my friend and the fire, I sallied forth. The wind was a keen north-easter, and blew full in our faces, while I, though shuddering in the blast, ankle deep in snow, and with fingers in agony, romantically attempted to convince myself how delightful the walk was, by repeating a sonnet to winter, written in the days of my youth. But even my own fictions had not power to warm me; and as, with blue and quivering lip, I spouted my tuneful admiration of what was taking away my breath, and inflicting pain on me besides, I ended in a hearty laugh at my own absurdity; in which, as my companion was not sensible of what I was doing, since the wind blew my words away from her, she happily could not join, and I kept my own counsel.

I then tried to beguile my sense of cold, by admiring the group before me. Methought we should have made a figure in a landscape—not that there was aught picturesque in my dress; still, my full long cloak was blown by the wind into folds, which would, in a picture, have turned, I flatter myself, to some account; but my friend in her chair, the servants and the dogs who accompanied us, made a group which, as I said before, might have employed the pencil to advantage. Yes, we had three dogs with us, one of them was a fine black curly Newfoundland dog, called Charley; and his companion was a small terrier. The Marquise de Sevigné said of a friend of hers, that he abused the privilege which men have to be ugly—and I think poor Hefty has abused the privilege which terriers have to be so; *au reste*, he is a good dog, but, like his species, high-minded and aristocratic. Every one knows that dogs do not like the poor, or their houses; probably there is something in the smell of poverty which displeases their nice organs.

The terrier in question, when, to his great annoyance, one day, I forced him into a cottage, got under my chair, and would not stir from it while I staid, wrapping himself up meanwhile, in the train of my silk gown.

The servants were forced to keep a sharp look out after Hefty and Charley, because they knew there were plenty of pheasants and hares in the coverts, alongside of which we passed, and seemed to think a chase after them would be an agreeable pastime; while their bounding feet, ever and anon on the verge of trespassing, and the exemplary readiness with which, better taught than most children, they obeyed the calling voice to return, gave interest and cheerfulness to our walk.

The third dog was a short-legged, big-bodied, over-fed, tiny, pet spaniel, with brown ears, that almost swept the snow as he waddled along. Why he came out at all I know not, as he has no vocation for any exertion save that of eating, lapping, and barking; and, I believe, if Jackey could have spoken, he would have begged Charley and Hefty not to walk quite so fast, but wait for *him*. At last, the poor little body was so tired, that his mistress took him on her lap, and, while his really pretty head peeped over her arm, he added to the picturesqueness of our group.

We had some way to go, before we came to a habitation, and the "untrodden snow," extending on all sides, made the scene appear unusually desolate. The Parish Church, too, which we passed, added to the desolation. The greater part of it, that is, the whole body, is a ruin; but part of the nave is still entire, and able to hold the population of O——. It is, perhaps, one of the smallest churches in England, but I doubt whether there be one, in which the service is performed with more exemplary zeal and heartfelt sincerity, or where the worshippers, (chiefly fishermen and their families,) are more truly and fervently devotional. Tradition says, that every evening, at twilight, the *ghost of a dog* is seen to pass under the wall of this churchyard, having begun its walk from the church at B———, a village between Cromer and Sheringham. It is known by the name of Old Shock, and is said to be very like Charley, the companion of our walk, by those who have seen, and *felt* him; for this four-footed ghost, unlike all human ones, is not only visible, but tangible. A worthy, sensible gamekeeper, now no more, declared, and believed, to the day of his death, that one evening it ran under his hand, and "though ready to face any earth-born poacher, four-legged or two-legged, at dawn or at dusk," he owned he was so frightened, for he knew what it was he saw glide on before him in the moonlight! Its back, as he described it, was rough, hard, and shaggy.

Old Shock walks sometimes with a head, sometimes without, but, be that as it may, the villagers, when questioned, assert that his eyes are "always as big as saucers."

He is supposed to be a relic of the Danes, because Norfolk was long their abode—so long, that many Danish words are left in use amongst us, especially on the coast of which I am writing; and a similar story of a spectre dog is current in Denmark. There was one also in the Isle of Man, so long under the Northmen's sway.* This spectre dog of ours is certainly an animal of taste, to judge by his choice in walks.

The following day (the 24th instant) Mrs. Opie returned to Norwich, and the next entry in her Journal is made from her own house :—

Returned in safety to my lonely home. What a contrast to the scene I left! but I am deeply thankful for three weeks and two days so happily spent, and for the real and many comforts to which I return.

Shortly after, she records the illness and death of one of her early friends, the daughter of Mrs. Colombine, (to whom she addressed a letter of friendly sympathy, in 1803, from which an extract is given in chapter xiv.) Most tenderly did she watch beside the bed of the poor sufferer, minister to her wants, and, at length, close her eyes. A day or two after her death, she writes :—

She begged me not to leave her—but how could I? I resolved to sit up with her. I went home to my tea, and then came back. She had slept in my absence; when she woke, and saw me, she was so glad; and when I assured her I would not leave her, she kept saying, trying to smile, (a ghastly smile indeed,) "God bless you! bless you! bless you!" After a night of great conflict on her part, and deep feeling on mine, she breathed her last, at five minutes past five; and I had the melancholy office of closing her eyes. How thankful was I, as I stood by her breathless clay, to know, that she, who had shed so many tears, was gone where "tears are wiped from all eyes," and to picture the reunion of mother and daughter, where *separation* comes not! She survived her

* See the Notes to the Lay of the Last Minstrel.

mother only a fortnight—oh! what a mercy; blessed be He who willed it so to be!

Next day I rose at one, and visited the poor, bereaved aunt; staid some hours, became ill, oppressed, and nervous, and called on Dr. Ash, who prescribed for me. Met H. G., who went home with me, and staid two or three hours; and when he left me, I had not a complaint in the world! Went to bed so thankful, even for the trials of the night and day. (4th day.) Went in the mourning coach, with Dr. Sutton and J. Beecroft, to the house. How the French Church, where the dear sufferer was laid, on her mother's coffin, called back the days of my childhood, and French School! Dr. S. read the service *well.* Went to Magdalen, committee long and interesting; called at my uncle's. (6th.) Catherine G. to dinner; did *so* enjoy her company. Went to bed very happy. (7th.) My uncle's birthday, (seventy-six;) dined with him; a pleasant day; my uncle in spirits. To bed thankful and contented.

Here the Journal abruptly breaks off.

In May of this year, Mrs. Opie was, as usual, in London, and writing to her friends at Northrepps Cottage, she says:—

5th mo., 11th, 1829.

My very dear Friends,

I would write "histories" if I could, but for even short tales I have no time; and I am always led to feel myself very "infirm of purpose," when I come to London. I meant to have written down what I composed on the road, and to send it to dear Northrepps Cottage, but I have not had any adequate leisure. I was ill all the way hither, with a feverish cold, and kept the house next day; but was well enough, by dinner, to enjoy our admirable guest, Baptist Noel, and he was our only one; and we did indeed enjoy him; one word is sufficient to express him, and includes his mind, heart, manners, conversation, and character—Delightful!

In the evening came the, T. Erskines. Without any affectation, B. N. leads the conversation to religious subjects, and happy the young, as well as the old, who can frequently associate with such a man! It was a rich day. The next morning we drove to Christie's; he was very kind; and on the 23rd my pictures, which now I rather pine after, are to be exhibited, and sold, with some by Ward and Gainsborough. He advises immediate sale, as times grow worse and worse.

Henrietta Erskine having given me a reserved ticket for the Jews' Meeting, I then drove to the Freemasons' Hall, which I found nearly full. As they passed, I had an opportunity of shaking hands with F. Cunningham, Wilberforce, and Simeon. Sir Thos. Baring was in the chair; and I heard twelve speakers, and was there from twelve to near half-past five! but I was so deeply interested that I was not tired. There was much eloquence, and, what was better, a christian spirit, and christian humility, I think, pervading all, and manifested very visibly. You will read the whole proceedings in the Record, therefore I will not name the speakers. We are going now to the British and Foreign School Society Meeting.

In the month of June following, Mrs. Opie visited Paris, and spent some months there. An account of this trip is given in the next chapter.

CHAPTER XVI.

VISIT TO PARIS; JOURNAL DURING HER STAY THERE; LETTER FROM THENCE; RETURN TO ENGLAND; LETTER FROM LAFAYETTE; SONNET "ON SEEING THE TRICOLOR;" SOUTHEY'S "COLLOQUIES;" LETTER FROM MRS. FRY; "NURSING SISTERS."

MRS. OPIE had for some time been projecting a visit to Paris; and she now found an opportunity of indulging that desire for travelling, which, as we have seen, she entertained before the death of her father. With mingled emotions she anticipated revisiting a place she had formerly seen under such different circumstances, and she thus expressed her feelings on the occasion:—

It was with twofold sensations, of which, *at last*, pleasure predominated, that I decided on revisiting Paris. * * When I last saw it, I was accompanied by my husband, as well as endeared friends, and my pleasant experiences were then communicated to my beloved father. *Now* I am alone in the world, affording, not receiving, protection; and in every way my position in life is changed. Yet, while my self-consciousness and selfish feelings vent themselves in silent but heartfelt regrets, I cannot but recollect that France has undergone changes of far greater importance to itself and the world. The France which I left a Republic, in 1802, has become a Monarchy again, under the dominion of a Bourbon! and I can hardly help smiling at my own engrossing egotism. * * *

During this, and her subsequent Parisian visit, Mrs. Opie kept a daily journal, (as indeed was her wont during all her journies,) in which she recorded events of interest, and carefully noted the attentions shewn her, of however trifling a character, whether by friends or strangers. The following extracts from the journal of this second visit to the French capital, may interest the reader.

* * * * Went on board the Lord Melville steamboat, at half past four in the morning of the 10th of the 6th mo., accompanied by a young lady whom I promised to see safe to Paris. My spirits neither high nor low, and I resolved to keep recollections at bay. * * *

The passage was rough, but I did not suffer from sea sickness. The next day, after a good night, we started at nine o'clock in the diligence, and had a pleasant journey to Abbeville; one of our companions, a pretty Frenchwoman of twenty-five, surprised me by her ignorance and excessive curiosity, and interested me by her evident family attachment. She travelled without a bonnet, (in a very becoming cap,) and told me she rarely wore one, but worked, and walked, and went to mass, without. At sight of her brother, who came to meet her, her fine eyes overflowed with tears.

After a pleasant journey, the traveller reached Paris on the 12th, and, being welcomed by her friends, says:—"I shall like my *séjour* with them while I stay, and am thankful for everything—all so much more than I deserve." Next day, on the Place de

Grêve, she beheld a crowd gathering round the guillotine! a man was about to suffer death for murder.

* * * For a curious traveller it was an opportune circumstance, and we got out and drew near to examine the awful instrument; a *gendarme* told me "*d'éntrer, et faire la tour.*" I found it was the same in form and size as that *d'autrefois.* Thence we proceeded to the Jardin des Plantes, which was delightful; I saw the elephant bathe, and admired the splendid giraffe, and one bird, the *aigle destructeur,* which alone, it was worth coming to see. (1st day.) Went to the Champs Elisées, to Meeting at T. S.'s—situation charming—we met only seven persons, and sat only one hour. (15th.) Went to the Duchess de Broglie's, and had an interesting conversation with her. Thence went to the Hall of the Institute, and was much pleased. (17th inst.) Went this morning to the Marquis de Lafayette's, found him at home; was most kindly received, and presented my letter, and begged him to read it; he said he was glad to know me, and his daughters would call on, and invite me. A delightful loveable man! a handsome blooming man of seventy-two. My hero through life! How my dear father would have rejoiced in my knowing him. Came home pleased, and bought some confitures. (18th.) Had tickets for the Chamber of Deputies, and was admitted to the *Tribune des Dames* at twelve. At two the chamber assembled—noise, of the *côté droit* especially, *astonishing.* Did not understand much, but enjoyed what I did, and was excessively interested. Saw Benjamin Constant, and heard and understood him. Saw Berard. House up at six. (20th, Saturday.) Lafayette sent me tickets for the Chamber again, with an English note sealed with the head of Washington: precious! At nine went to Baron Cuvier's, and stayed till half past eleven—amused and flattered. (1st day.) To the Champs Elisées; a short, but most interesting, sitting. It was the *fête Dieu,* and we should all have liked to have seen the procession, but

could not, without giving up meeting. (2nd day, 22nd.) Went to see the glass manufactory in the Faubourg St. Antoine, and on my way saw le Café Turque, full of glasses and bouquets; it must be very pretty lighted up. At the manufactory, the largest glass 130 inches (French) long, and 63 in width. Being near Vincennes, went thither in a *cabriolet de remise,* and ascended 250 steps to the tower of the dungeon. Was repaid by the view from the top and the fine fresh air, but a tempest came on so violently we could only get to the chapel, and not to the ditch, where the poor d'Enghien was shot. Part of his monument is very fine, and the painted window very much so, the designs are from Raphael. All the way home it rained in our faces; I held *mon petit chapeau* on my lap, and put my shawl round my head, and the hat escaped unhurt.*

On the 23rd. The evening was spent at Lafayette's, where she found many Americans, to whom she was presented, and Mr. Benjamin Constant, who addressed her "politely but coldly." With her distinguished host and his family she was "delighted," and two days after, says, "I went at half past ten to Gen. Lafayette's to sit with him, while he sat for his picture to Davis; Lady Morgan was also there, and I enjoyed my visit. Returning home I went to the Luxembourg gardens, 'the gardens of Roses!' and

* She mentioned afterwards, that the driver was much amused at seeing her do this, and at last said, "really, madame, you must be very fond of your *petit chapeau,* to give yourself so much trouble about it." To which I replied, "*oui, j'aime beaucoup mon petit chapeau—c'est mon petit Buonaparte.*" Oh! what a look the man gave me! his fine dark eyes were almost fearfully bright, as, with a smile of delight, he cried, "*vous êtes une brave femme, d'avoir osé me répondre de la sorte, et je vous jure, madame, que je vous menerais même en Angleterre!*"

afterwards to La Morgue, whence I hastily withdrew, feeling that I could not bear it."

The Journal continues:—

(7th day, 27th.) To the General's, and staid till past twelve, then to the Tuilleries' palace, which much delighted me with its grandeur and beauty. My evening was spent at Madame la Baronne Cuvier's *soirée,* where I met David, and returned home by twelve, much pleased. (2nd day, 30th.) David came to me and I sat for my medal; afterwards spent the day in visiting various places.

The next few days record sittings to David for her medal, and visits to the General's, to be present while his portrait was proceeding.

(5th day, 2nd of mo.) Breakfasted at the Hôtel des Isles Britanniques, and went with my friends to *le Palais* * * * saw fine pictures, and fine furniture and rooms; and the bed where Napoleon slept, the last night he passed in Paris, and the table on which he signed his second abdication! The same day went to the Hospital for incurables, and was delighted with *Sœur Angelique, sœur de la Charité:* I must go again; it is a most perfect Institution. Went afterwards to the Maison de Santé, in the Rue du Quartier St. Denis; and dined at the Café de Paris, on the Boulevards; dinner excellent, and the room so pretty. (7th day, 4th.) Went to Père la Chaise, and being forced by rain into the chapel, saw a young woman give money to have a candle lighted; then she took a chair, and knelt on it and prayed; no doubt it was for the soul of one lost and loved! We were twenty-two in company, of all ranks and conditions, but she alone proved herself devout; soon after, as we were walking along, we saw a young lady in deep mourning, beside a newly-made grave, sobbing violently and wringing her hands, while a gentleman with her begged her to come away and be consoled. I wished to stop and ask him what friend they had lost, but *dared* not; if I had been alone, I think I should. The view of Paris from this interesting spot is delightful; I felt much interested in this singular scene, and shed many tears at sight of one inscription, in particular. I envied the *power* of planting flowers on the graves of those we love. We could not find poor George Blackshaw's grave, nor his son's. I must come again.

Short entries for several days succeed, recording the events of each day; the completion of her profile medal, by David; her visits to La B. Cuvier; to San Lazare and la Salpêtriere; to the General Lafayette's; to Sèvres and St. Cloud, &c.

(11th, 1st day.) After meeting, David took me to l'Abbé Gregoire's and I was delighted with my visit, and next day he accompanied me to Père la Chaise; we had a most interesting walk of four hours, but could not find G. B.'s tomb. In the evening I received a letter from De Bardelin, dated *Paris*, and, glad surprise! he came and took tea with us. the next evening went to Gen. Lafayette's for the last time, and he invited me to go to La Grange.

On the 17th, she went with a party of friends to Montmorency, and was charmed with the country, but "saw Rousseau's tomb and the Hermitage *unmoved!*" Each day bears a record of some visit or excursion, with the many friends who gathered around her. On one of these occasions, at Bishop Luscombe's she "met a lady whom she had known in 1806;" and beheld with much pleasure, a picture by her husband, which her friend David "thought very good, taking it for a Spanish picture; it is reckoned like Murillo." A visit to the *atelier* of the sculptor also draws forth her warm encomiums; she says, "*delighted* with his

General Foy; the statue admirable, the bas-reliefs excellent; also I liked Gregoire's bust much." Shortly after she went to see a somnambule, and was "put *en rapport avec elle—she* very complimentary—I not satisfied; am to see another; my companion was in ecstacies about nothing." Her journal continues—

(22nd.) Went to l'Hôtel Dieu, was satisfied; went next to Nôtre Dame, and saw, in the sacristy, the things used at the coronation of Napoleon; also, in boxes, the relics—*le porte Dieu,* used at Napoleon's coronation; and the *glory* of rare diamonds; also the robes of Napoleon and Josephine, and the *robes brodées en fleurs,* which he had made for the pope; and the robes of Charles X, *bleu et argent.* Went next to the Palais de Justice, and heard pleading and judgment given in the Cour Royale and the Cour de Cassation. Went afterwards to the flower market—delicious! and so home, well satisfied with my morning.

The following letter is selected from amongst several written at the time:—

Rue Cadet, 11, F. S. Montmartre.
Ce 24me., du 7me mois, 1829.

At length my too long neglected friend, I sit down to write to thee; a duty and a pleasure, which I have found it easier to contemplate in prospect, than to fulfil and procure—but *trêve d'excuses.* Here I have been six weeks! I came for *four,* but how could I quit this *beau Paris et les amiables Parisiens, que j'ai trouvés ici?* Dear friend, were I not, as I hope, too old to have my head turned, I think it would have been turned here, by all the attentions and flatteries I have received; but it was humbling, in some measure, to find that I was courted for my *past,* not my *recent* writings. The latter are not in the French style; I fear I must own that their moral standard is not as high as ours; but there are here, I fully believe, men, and women too, holy enough to save the city. My experiences have been various, and among all classes; from the sceptic who owns to me, that when he dies, he expects to go into entire nothingness; to the exemplary and pious catholic, who, believing in his own salvation, is kindly and fervently anxious for *mine;* but I wish my two Generals—one known to thee personally, the other by reputation, to be the chief heroes of this letter. After a month's residence here, I wrote to Bardelin, at St. Germain's, where I fancied he was, to tell him I was coming thither, and hoped to see him. He answered me that evening, from *Paris*, and came to see me soon after; and I find him out of the service, a Maréchal-de-camp; General chevalier décoré! How glad it made me!

The other general is Lafayette; the hero of my childhood, the idol of my youth! And I have found him far beyond my idea of him, high raised as it was! He is a handsome man of seventy-two, humble, simple, and blushing like a girl, at his own praises, with manners the most perfect possible; and his *bonhommie* is so striking, that one almost forgets his greatness and his fame. I brought a letter to him from my friend, Dr. H., which I delivered in person—I shall never forget his reception!

His daughters called on me the next day, and I had a note from him, inviting me to his *soirée.* [The letter goes on to describe what is related in the journal.] * * * The great delight was my friend M. S.'s having sent over Davis to paint Lafayette, and Davis wishing me to be present to animate the General! Accordingly I was there five mornings, having his conversation to myself. I was also at his house in the evening, five times. * * *

I have another General to tell about, one of the first men in France as to family; the Marquis de Clermont Tonnerre, (who as a boy was known to thee;) he gave me a dinner the other day, the most beautiful little French dinner I ever saw. Dusgate is a complete *savant,* shut up, studying mathematics, and, for health's sake, living on bread and water!! He is, however, very clever and agreeable. The Marquis and I were soon acquainted, and agreed to go together to see sights; we were together some hours, during which I was delighted and edified by his deep piety, (he is a *bon Catholique*,) and he gratified me by his desire, that I who am "*si bonne, et si dévouée aux bonnes œuvres*," (according to him,) should be "*entièrement Catholique*."

My next hero is no General, but a *sculpteur libéral*, the first man of his class here; who, before I saw him, was desirous of making a medal of me, for having made him *cry his eyes out* by my works. *Malgré moi*, he has made me *en medaille*, me and my *petit bonnet*, which the artists here say looks like a Phrygian helmet, and has *un air classique;* but, though young and flattered, the thing is *like*, and David satisfied.* To this gentleman I owe some of the most interesting hours I have passed here; with a mind in some respects analogous to my own, he has my husband's *poetical views* of his art. He has given me much of his precious time; we spent some hours at Père la Chaise, vainly seeking my poor friend's grave. Père la Chaise is a lovely place. This morning I have been to see an Infant School; very good. Yesterday I saw the lady who is one of the chief directors; she excels all the women I have yet seen here, the Duchess de Broglie excepted. I believe I love her already! In about ten days I expect to set off for England, by Dieppe. I shall leave Paris with regret, and deep gratitude. We have a nice quiet meeting in the Champs Elisées on the first day morning. * * Now for noble monuments, (principally by my companion,) fine trees, a blue sky, and affecting recollections.

With love, I am thy affectionate friend,

A. Opie.

The same day (the 24th) Mrs. Opie visited the Bibliothèque du Roi, and was much amused, "but too late to see the manuscripts:" the succeeding four days were spent in visiting, and on the 28th she writes:—

* The engraving which forms the Frontispiece to this volume is taken from this medal.

Up at five, and off to Fontainebleau, enjoying the day excessively; the palace almost painfully interesting, from association; splendid and beautiful; and the forest unique and delightful. It was night before we left it; on the 29th up again at five, and by six off, along the forest ride, to where we must take boat;—too soon for it, and had to walk two hours, so climbed a rock in the forest, and went to see a curious water-mill; took boat at nine, nearly constant rain, but not disagreeable; the voyage seven long hours; the coffee excellent and eggs ditto, and I got a good breakfast, and am writing on board the boat, to keep myself awake; have read nearly three books of De Lisle's poem on Imagination, some parts of it are excellent.—Reached Paris before four, the rain having ceased.

A succession of daily visits and friendly greetings followed, during the first week in August, (on the 7th she "heard the ministry was changed, and nothing talked of but this change,") and on the 13th and 14th saw the prizes distributed at the Sourds Muets, ("excessively interested") and went to a *séance*, at the Ecole de Commerce et d'Industrie, where she heard La Fitte, Charles Dupin, &c., and was much delighted. She continues:—

(11th.) Went to Nôtre Dame to see the King and Royal Family, and saw them also walk in the street. (25th.) I went to the Institute and heard two *prix de vertu* adjudged, and saw the prize given for the best poem on the art of printing; the prize poem was read by Le Mercier after the young man had received the prize, and Baron Cuvier delivered a most excellent discourse. My pleasure was increased by seeing Lally Tollendal opposite me, whom I recognised and was glad to see so young and well looking, still. Next day (26th.) Went with Victor Sauce to the Palais de Justice, and heard Dupin plead for Berton, and admirably, but he was condemned! In the evening at Gérard's, the sentence was much talked of and condemned. On 1st day to Meeting, a solemn and favoured one, to me at least. 2nd day evening to the Missionary Meeting.

Early in September she mentions the arrival of her friend Mrs. Austin, and her cousin, Mr. Briggs, with many others, in company with whom she paid visits and made excursions, each day giving a note of where and with whom, in her journal. On the 21st she paid her promised visit to La Grange, of which she writes:—

Started *par la diligence*, with a very agreeable companion, T. B., with whom on my return I am to visit the *ateliers* of artists. At Rosoy, found the General's cabriolet waiting; thought the approach to La Grange beautiful; an ancient castle, lawn *à l'Anglaise*. The General as usual, fresh, benevolent looking, and admirable, in all ways. His uncle, the celebrated Ségur, there; his daughters, son-in-law, and grandchildren all to my mind; a most happy day. (22nd.) Rose early with much thankfulness for unmerited mercies. (23rd.) At ten we assembled in the *salon;* at half-past the General led me down to breakfast, a breakfast of hot meat and pottage, wines and fruit, ending with coffee and dry toast. After breakfast the weather cleared, and the General shewed us, and many newly-arrived guests, his farm, all but the Norfolk and other cows; they were out. Enjoyed our walk, afterwards went to see *le jardin potager.* At dinner, led, and placed as usual; the evening most interesting! The General gave us an account of some of the early events of the revolution, the other gentlemen assisting. The evening ended only too soon, but I read in my own room the Memoirs of Ségur, and with a curious feeling lay down, knowing I should see him and Lafayette next day!!

(5th day, 25th.) Much pleased with Madame de L.'s schools, and walked in the park till the General admitted us into his library. What a library, full of interest! The *swords* he has, especially. The room round, and commanding his farm, as well as some beautiful willows, and points of view of home scenery. The dinner interesting, the evening not so much so: and it was my last!

Mrs. Opie's stay in Paris was extended some weeks longer, during which she appears to have enjoyed, with great satisfaction, the opportunities for intercourse with her friends, and for seeing objects of interest around her. She mentions sitting to an artist, for Galignani, and also to her cousin, H. P. Briggs. On the 20th of October, "*the saddest of anniversaries*," (that of her father's death,) she left Paris, and on the 23rd went on board the King George, for England, and after a sixteen hours' passage, arrived, "thankful for safe return," in her native country.

Shortly after her return, she received the following letter from General Lafayette:—

La Grange, November 5th, 1829.

Your kind letter, (17th of the 10th month,) dear and respected friend, for want of being directly sent to la Grange, has remained some days unreceived, and three days more unanswered, on account of an invitation to Provins, the mention of which you may have seen in the *Courier Française*, or *Journal de Paris*, November 3rd; so that I remain acquitted for the delay, and am anxious to acquit myself with a due tribute of gratitude, for these last testimonies of your indulging kindness. You don't say whether the distinguished artist, your friend, remains in town. I hope I shall have the pleasure of a personal acquaintance with him. Remember me very kindly to your young cousin. The whole family at la Grange join in friendly compliments and good wishes to him and to you, dear Madam, and I am most cordially, Your obliged friend,

LAFAYETTE.

P.S. With much pleasure I have read the appeal in behalf of the Greeks. The 200 sets of plates delivered to Doctor Temple, cannot be in better hands. The Rev. Jonas King is my particular friend. I much wish the religious zeal in behalf of Greece may have some influence on the policy of your government; when the Christian powers have it in their power, and it has become their duty, as well as their true interest, to insure, upon a large and liberal scale, the independence, liberty, and consequence, of that so very interesting nation.

We add here some verses written by Mrs. Opie during this visit; inscribed,

ON SEEING THE TRICOLOR AGAIN.

At sight of thee, O! Tricolor,
I seem to feel youth's hours return;
The lov'd, the lost, those hours restore,—
Again for freedom's cause I burn!

When last those blended tints I saw,
Napoleon's laurell'd brow they grac'd,
Ere, in despite of freedom's law,
The crown that simple badge displaced.

But now a different scene is nigh,
Lo! freedom's sons once more are met!
See, patriots lift those colours high;
Who leads them on?—their Lafayette!

See him, from dangers, dungeons, death,
Escap'd through heaven's almighty hand,
To win again the civic wreath,
And sav'd, to save his native land!

Hail! freedom's dearest, purest son,
What honours now adorn thy brow;
Thou hast the *hardest* conquest won,
The victor o'er thyself art thou!

Thy country's good thy only aim,
Thou couldst thy life's loved dream resign;—
Then take the meed thy virtues claim,
And be the world's loud plaudit *thine!*

R

Shortly before Mrs. Opie left England, she had written to Mr. Southey, who answered her in a letter which was published in his "Memoirs." In this letter he mentioned that he had sent her a copy of his "Colloquies,"—in which he had referred to her in these terms:—

"I have another woman in my mind's eye; one who has been the liveliest of the lively, the gayest of the gay; admired for her talents by those who knew her only in her writings, and esteemed for her worth by those who were acquainted with her in the relations of private life; one who, having grown up in the laxest sect of semi-christians, felt the necessity of vital religion, while attending upon her father with dutiful affection, during the long and painful infirmities of his old age; and who has now joined a sect, distinguished from all others by its formalities and enthusiasm, because it was among its members that she first found the lively faith for which her soul thirsted. She has assumed the garb and even the shibboleth of the sect, not losing, in the change, her warmth of heart and cheerfulness of spirit, nor gaining by it any increase of sincerity and frankness; for with these, nature had endued her, and society, even that of the great, had not corrupted them. The resolution, the activity, the genius, the benevolence, which are required for such a work, are to be found in her; and were she present in person, as she is in imagination, I would say to her * * Thou art the woman!"*

"The work" in which Mr. Southey was anxious to engage the sympathies and aid of Mrs. Fry and Mrs. Opie, was the establishment of Societies for

* Second volume of Southey's "Colloquies," at the 322nd page. —On reading this eloquent eulogium, Mrs. Opie observed, "It so overpowered me, that I could not read it through at first, and wept because the eye it would most have pleased, would not see it."

reforming the internal management of Hospitals and Infirmaries ; so as "to do for the hospitals what Mrs. Fry had already done for the prisons."

On her return to England, Mrs. Opie wrote to Mrs. Fry, communicating Mr. Southey's letter; she replied :—

Upton, 12th, 12th mo., 1829.

MY DEAR FRIEND,

I only yesterday heard from Catherine thy wish to have R. Southey's letter returned. I now therefore send it thee at once; being in London I could not do it yesterday.

Pray, dear friend, let me have a copy of it, because I think that there is much truth in its contents. I also wish thee seriously to weigh the subject, and if thou feelest, as well as seest, thy road to open in it, I shall be glad; because I have seen the thing wanted to be done, ever since the days of my youth. Is not London the place to begin such a work—or is the country? I think what has been accomplished in Liverpool is very important. Let me have thy sentiments upon all the points in question, and believe me,

Thy very affectionate friend,

E. FRY.

From a passage in Mrs. Fry's Life (vol. 2, p. 383) we find that, some years subsequently, her thoughts reverted to the subject; and the results are thus recorded.

"Mrs. Fry's habitual acquaintance with the chamber of sickness, and with scenes of suffering and death, had taught her the necessity that exists for a class of women to attend upon such, altogether different and superior to the hireling nurses that are generally to be obtained. Her communications with Mr. Fliedner, and all she learned from him personally, of his establishment at Kaiserswerth, stimulated her desire to attempt something of the kind in England. Her own occupations being too urgent and numerous to allow of much personal attention, the plan was undertaken, and on a small scale carried into effect, by her sister, Mrs. S. Gurney, with the assistance of her daughters and some other ladies."

Some misconception having arisen as to this institution, it was thought desirable to change the original designation of "Protestant Sisters of Charity," for that of "Nursing Sisters."

"The exertions of this little society (continues the Memoir) have been hitherto greatly circumscribed, and it may be looked upon more as an experiment, than as an object attained. The help of the "nursing sisters" has been sought and greatly valued by persons of all classes, from royalty to the poorest and most destitute."

CHAPTER XVII.

REVOLUTION OF "THE THREE DAYS;" MRS. OPIE GOES TO PARIS AGAIN; HER JOURNAL THERE.

THE fearful events which transpired at Paris, in the summer of the year 1830, deeply and painfully interested Mrs. Opie. She wrote to her friends at Northrepps in the month of August, and an extract from her letter will best shew her feelings under the excitement of the time.

Norwich, 8th mo., 2nd, 1830.

Dr. Ash shall not go to Northrepps without a letter. I think you will like to know how I am, under existing circumstances. I went to Wroxham on the election day, and should have enjoyed, even more than usual, the exquisite, and even increased stillness of that place, (as it appeared to me,) had not my calm been interrupted by the inquietude of mind, induced by the alarming news from Paris. The Chamber of Deputies dissolved for ever, and the liberty of the press abolished!! We saw the results of this news in the fearful perspective; and yesterday came the affecting tidings, that the National Guard had re-organized themselves; that Lafayette was at their head; that the Chamber had assembled, and voted their sitting *perpetual,* and had declared the throne *vacant;* that the king, ministers, court, and ambassadors, had left Paris, and were at Vincennes, or Brussels; that cannon was planted against the city; that it had fired, and killed 5000 persons, and the beautiful Rue de Rivoli was running with blood; and that they are to be *starved* into submission.

I humbly hope I shall be enabled to pray for my friends there, which is all I *can* do. "Whom the Gods mean to destroy they first make mad," says some Latin proverb, and this seems illustrated now.

You will readily believe how anxious, interested, and excited I feel. I was, and am, writing on the scenes of the Revolution in 1802, little dreaming that another was so near, in which some I love and reverence must be actors! * * *

I am reading "Lafayette en Amerique!" Such a book! it fills me with untellable wonder and admiration of him, that such *worship* should not have turned his head, and that he is still simple and seemingly humble-minded; and secondly, because his *youth* in America was evidently marked, not only by courage and talent, but by kind, generous actions, privately performed; and because it was his nature to do them. He gave them his money, I find by another work, as well as his time and exertions; therefore the gift of money and land to him, in his (comparative) poverty, was only a debt, repaid with interest. And how they honoured him! He was passed on from one State to another, almost through an unbroken chain of triumphal arches! But he always, amidst all his career, kept the Sabbath day holy. And this man, as it were miraculously preserved through two revolutions, and in chains, and in a dungeon, is now again the leading mind in another conflict, and lifting, I trust, not only an armed, but a restraining hand in a third revolution! May He who alone can save and direct, watch over and direct *him!* How many other now familiar faces, and I may add, dear also, do I see engaged in this awful struggle, and on different sides! Well, I must turn away from it as much as I can! Farewell, my dear friends.

Unable, probably, to keep the prudential resolve, with which she concludes this letter, Mrs. Opie, full of irrepressible anxiety to be on the scene of action, very shortly came to the resolution to repair to Paris. She seems to have allowed very few of her friends to know of her determination, perhaps anticipating their remonstrances and objections. Her anxiety, however, was so great as to affect her health and spirits; and after a few weeks' irresolution, her determination was made, and she was on her way to Paris. Her stay proved, in the event, longer than she had perhaps intended or anticipated. During the former part of the time she kept a Journal, from which selections are given in the following pages:—

Hôtel de Breteuil, Rue de Rivoli,
5th of 11th mo.

I arrived at this charming residence on fourth day last, and the trees had nearly lost their leaves, and the gardens their flowers. I gazed on the prospect around me with still increasing delight. On the side near me was the palace of the Tuilleries, with the tricolor flag hanging on its centre dome; and, to the right, the fine dome of the Invalides. But oh! the people—the busy people—of all ranks probably, and of various costumes, passing to and fro, and soldiers, omnibuses, cabriolets, citadines, carts, horsemen, hurrying along the Rue de Rivoli, while foot passengers were crossing the gardens, or loungers were sitting on its benches, to enjoy the beauty of this May-November! But what was become of the Revolution? Paris seemed as bright and peaceful as I had left it thirteen months ago! And the towns too, through which we had passed on our road, bore no marks of change. We did not see the tricolor till we reached a village on the morning of our second day's journey, (it was the *féte* of Le Toussaint,) when I remarked, not only the tricolor flag, on a pump in the middle of the small *place* opposite the inn, but the colours, exhibited with no little grace and coquetry, on a very handsome youth, probably the *beau* or *coq* of the village.

As to the country, it appeared to me even less populous than ever; and I almost wondered where there could ever be found hands enough to cultivate the wide spreading hills and vales. "Well, but to be sure we shall see some obvious changes in Paris," my travelling companion and I observed to each other; but alas! we did not reach Paris till two in the morning, when even its lowest and fiercest inhabitants might be expected to be asleep; and, without any let or hindrance, we arrived at the Messagerie; and, at three in the morning, a commissioner conducted us on foot to the Hôtel de Lisle, Palais Royal, the only one open. "And we are going to the Palais Royal! the very focus of everything!" observed my companion (who was a Royalist) bidding me at the same time remark the tricolor floating behind us on the Palais d'Orléans. I did so, but my attention was soon directed to another quarter; I saw two men advancing, as we crossed the Place Royale, who were singing the new national song, by Casimir de la Vigne, called the "Parisienne;" and just as they drew near, they sung the most interesting line in the whole song, to me.

"Pour briser leurs masses profondes,
Qui conduit nos drapeaux sanglants?
C'est la liberté des deux mondes,
C'est Lafayette, en cheveux blancs!"

What a thrill of emotions those words excited in me! how many recollections of former days and former friends those few words recalled! recollections of those dear ones, who had first taught me to love the name, and admire the character, of Lafayette; and who would have enjoyed, like me, the brightness of that setting sun, which they had hailed at its dawning! And how long was the course of time which those little words marked out! "*Lafayette en cheveux blancs!*" And what a number of years did I, unconsciously to my companion, retrace in a moment! But why, as I thought on the man of two worlds, and recollected what and where he now was; why was my pleasure overclouded with sadness? because, though still in the splendour of his fame, that of his days was past; and though still Lafayette, it was Lafayette "*en cheveux blancs.*" I cannot describe the feelings with which I have always read those words; but now that I heard them, I felt them still more; and then, by a very natural process, I began to imagine the feelings of the General himself, when he hears them: but he, I dare say, hears them with less emotion than I do—his well poised mind, satisfied with being at what he believes to be the post of duty, looks back on the past with thankfulness, and to the future with hope.

But how I have wandered from the Hôtel de Breteuil! As I stood on the balcony, gazing with admiring eyes, my obliging landlady told me that many ladies, English and others, having first closed the *croisées*, had stood there to see the battle of the three days. As the balcony is *au troisième*, they could do so no doubt without danger, except from the *mitraille;* still I did not envy them their post, and earnestly desired, in my time, no such awful scenes might pass beneath the windows.

"Well," (said I to myself when I was left alone,) "here I am, actually at Paris! and alone at Paris: few of my friends in England knew I was coming, and none in France know that I am here! A new and strange position; but the *incognito* is not without its charms!" And, though excessively fatigued, for two nights, I felt an extraordinary elevation of spirit, as well as a sense of deep thankfulness; not only because I was in the most interesting of all cities, at the present moment, but because I was capable of feeling enjoyment in being alone, and alone in a strange land, *alone in Paris!* But I was conscious that my trust was placed in Him, whose protecting eye is everywhere; and though my thoughts might recur affectionately and frequently to the dear relatives and friends whom I had quitted, the uneasiness of mind, and indisposition of body, which had attended my irresolution whether to stay at home, or depart, had entirely vanished; and the future seemed arrayed in smiles.

Having dined early, I sallied forth to the Boulevards, just as the sun was beginning to sink behind the trees of the gardens; and, though I was walking towards the east, when I reached that pleasant spot, the western rays were so beautifully reflected on the upper part of the white buildings before me, that, for a little while, I was unconscious of the loss of the trees on the Boulevards; but, suddenly recollecting myself, I stopped to look round in painful astonishment, till I remembered it was for *la patrie*, and to save lives;—then I could regret no longer! I was on my way to M.'s to subscribe to his library; and on my expressing to his wife my regret at missing the fine trees, I found that her patriotism was strong enough to console her; and I believe that I shall not pay my court well, to the residents on the Boulevards, by expressing any regret for the sacrifice which was required for the cause of liberty and the country. I next bent my steps to the gardens of the Tuilleries, in hopes to overtake the setting sun. The seats were many of them still occupied by well dressed men and women, three of whom I observed reading by the red and sinking light. I do not remember to have seen such a sight in my own country; and I should have stopped and lingered to observe the group, had I not been impatient to renew my acquaintance with the statues on the Pont Louis quinze; but I arrived too late to distinguish their countenances, though the grand outlines were clearly to be seen. I was disappointed also to observe, that thirteen months of exposure to the air, had deprived them of that striking whiteness, in complete contrast to the dingy hue of the surrounding stone, which had formerly given them in my eyes (at the hour of twilight) the appearance of unearthly beings—the ghosts of the departed great, standing there to watch over the destinies of that country for which they have laboured both in arts and arms!

I looked on the *Condé* of my friend David with added pleasure, from having recently heard its merits so eloquently described by Lady Morgan; and lingered long on the bridge, watching the last beams of the setting sun, till I saw I was alone, and remembered I had some way to walk. I found the gardens nearly deserted on my return, except by a few soldiers on duty; and therefore hastened to my new home, refreshed by my walk, pleased with my new position, and saying to myself, "How difficult should I find it, to make some of my friends in England believe that I could be walking alone in Paris, at twilight, in perfect peace and security."

The next day, after *fifteen* hours' repose, I awoke refreshed, (as I well might,) and resolved that I would still keep my arrival in Paris unknown to my friends.

I proceeded to walk out, accompanied by Manuel, *a valet-de-place de l'hôtel.* My first visit was to the Louvre, not to see the pictures, but to inquire concerning *le Suisse*, or porter, who was so civil and attentive to me last year. I had thought it only too likely that he had been amongst the killed, when the Louvre was assailed; and could hardly speak, from strong emotion, when I saw him alive and well, and looking as if nothing had happened! I expressed, as calmly as I was able, my fears for his life, and my joy to see him as I had left him. He seemed gratified; and thanked me in a manner very creditable to himself.

I have always observed a civility in the lower orders in France, as remote from coarseness as from servility, which did not, I suspect, distinguish them previous to the revolution of 1789. "If our revolution has done nothing else for us," said General Lafayette last year, "it has, at least, done this; it has taught men to look their fellow-men in the face, and feel their own dignity."

I next went to see the ravages which civil war had made, and which are now nearly repaired; but my valet pointed out the mark, yet remaining, of a bullet, fired by one of the Swiss, from a window of the Louvre, which hit one of the columns of the Palais des quatre Colonnes, across the water. We were, at that moment, standing on the *nameless, unhonoured* graves of the Swiss who had fallen in the action, and by the ornamented and hallowed graves of their victims. "Take your hats off," was the cry, as the latter were approached;

and there stood men of all ages, with their heads uncovered, (besides rows of women and children,) all gazing, with mournful interest, on the place where lay the ashes of those *morts pour la patrie*, on the memorable three days!

My next course was to the Palais Royal, which seemed as when I last saw it; its beautiful fountain was still playing, its shops looked as tempting as ever; but the Tricolor floated on the Palace of the King, and the National Guard (a large detachment) were on duty there. I must confess to looking on these men with great complacency; they had so recently shewn their forbearance in the midst of great provocation; they really reasoned, and joked, and wheedled the agitators in the late tumult, into quiet and dispersion. The citizen was not forgotten in the soldier;—theirs was the victory of good sense and self government, over the excitement of ignorance and passion; —and be their country's confidence and gratitude their well-earned reward!

* * * This morning I have received a note of welcome, like herself, from Sophie de V. She will not invite me to the Saturday *soirée*, at the Jardin des Plantes, (Baron Cuvier's) which takes place every week, because she says, "*vous êtes invitée née*"—a compliment prettily expressed.

(7th day, 6th of November.) A bright day; the statues in the Tuilleries gardens looking *so* white, and what remains of the foliage on the trees so richly tinted! The right side of the prospect (that is, the Invalides and other lofty buildings) is clothed in sunshine; the palace is in shade—but even while I write the scene is changing, and all behind the palace is becoming a sheet of silver! May this be emblematical of the future prospects of its present owner, and of all to whom he belongs! * * * *

The light has now passed entirely away from the *côté droit* to the *côté gauche;* a little breeze is getting up, and the gorgeous autumnal leaves are waving in it to and fro.

Then * * * * * but I will not indulge my fancy—a truce to metaphors and types; my object is matter of fact. I have just read the speeches of our Parliament, in the *Journal des Débats.* How entirely I agree with Lord Grey; but the bare *possibility* of war with France is insupportable! I cannot hate and condemn war more than I do, else this fear would make me. Brougham does not mention such a possibility, and I think his opinion nearly as good as Lord Grey's.

I have engaged lodgings for a month, at the Hôtel de Douvres; my apartment looks on the Rue de la Paix, and I can also see the Boulevard des Capucins! an excellent situation, but the rooms so small!—Well! a month is soon gone, and at the end of it I may be gone too; who knows?

I dine at five, and at eight shall go to M. Cuvier's * * * Though I went early, the room was full enough to make me feel a wish I had come earlier; most of the faces were unknown to me. By half-past nine the room was almost full, of, I believe, persons all distinguished in some way or another. "Who is that gentleman?" said I, "Oh! nothing particularly distinguished, he is only *un homme d'esprit*," "only *un homme d'esprit!*" replied another, what a compliment! when wit is so scarce. * * * *

Soon, Baron de Humboldt was announced, and I was looking eagerly round for my old and valued acquaintance, when M. Cuvier led him to me. I was very glad to see him, but sorry to hear he was going to England. We had not met for sixteen years. "You find him then grown grey," (said la Baronne.) True, but he was embellished, for he was grown fat, and really is now good looking.

Another pleasure awaited me, in the entrance of my friend David, who did not know of my arrival; he was indeed surprised, but hurt, (and perhaps with justice,) that I had not let him know I was come or coming.

David speaks highly of the king, and says, while mounting guard the other morning, he saw him in his night-cap, walking on the terrace. Poor man! I dare say he cannot sleep much!

"Happy low, lie down,
Uneasy lies the head that wears a crown."

David has sent me the bust of Lafayette,* and some other things to England! Well! they will be there, I trust, to cheer me when I return, (if in mercy permitted to do so,) and have bidden to Paris a probably eternal adieu!

"By all means go to Lafayette's on Tuesday," (said two or three gentlemen to me.) *Nous verrons,*—he does not receive at his own house now, but in his staff house, in the Montblanc. * * * I certainly much enjoyed la Baronne's party, and her tea, and her cakes. I came home a little past midnight.

(1st day, 7th.) A night of wind! a day of rain! went to the Champs Elisées. Our sitting was still, and, I trust, favoured.

I expect to be alone all to day—what a great privilege it is, not to feel solitude a trial, but a pleasure! The first thing I heard on waking this morning was *la Parisienne,* sung, I concluded, by passing soldiers. I checked the internal reproof rising to my lips, on remembering that the military band plays, as it returns with the soldiers from church, in my own city, and in all others; and most probably these soldiers were returning from early mass.

(2nd day, 8th.) I cannot but wonder at my own stillness, and the stillness of all that surrounds me in this busy city; the depository at this moment probably of all the springs and agencies, which, set in motion, must act upon, and decide, the destinies of Europe! At this moment (10 o'clock) even the Tuilleries are deserted; the fountain played yesterday, but it is quiet to-day; it only works on a Sabbath day! The morning is dark, and the view therefore is not as lovely as usual; I can sit by my fireside, instead of going to my balcony; so much the better, as I must leave it to-morrow, for a less lovely prospect. * * * * A sense of my inability to do the subject justice has alone kept me from committing to paper what passes in my mind, and is always uppermost in it, on the subject of politics, but I must relieve my mind by doing so very soon. The *Journal des Débats* has, to-day, some

* This Bust she left in her will to T. Brightwell.

admirable remarks (in my opinion) on the liberty of the press. * * *

How impossible it is to know what is usually going on in any country without being in it, and even then how difficult! I see and feel, even from my short and limited experience, more of the real state of Paris at this moment, than I could have taken in, for months, at home!

I thought while I was observing, the other day, the mark of the bullet on the column of the Palais des quatres Nations, and saw the eagerness with which my *valet-de-place* pointed it out to me, how wise it would be to efface that striking provocation to a continuance of popular resentment; and rejoiced to see the other traces of civil war disappearing so fast.

I spoke and felt like a lover of peace, and a hater of all discord and all war; and I was painfully convinced how right I was in my ideas on the subject, by hearing a reputed Jacobin say, at M. Cuvier's, "how sorry I am to see the traces of our three days so quickly disappearing! I wish them to remain for ever, to keep up the *spirit of just indignation in the people!*" I heard, sighed, and shuddered, and then, as well as I could, combated the frightful and fearful observation. The speaker was one of the National Guard, and in that Guard how many may there not be whose desire is for war, rather than peace; and republicanism, before royalty, even though the king be a citizen king! And there are pictures of Napoleon, at all ages of his life, exhibiting at the Luxembourg, with other pictures, for the benefit of the widows of the wounded: and Napoleon brought on the stage at the minor theatres, and applauded, and extolled, and mourned and wept over, on his bed of death and in his grave! If I were a royalist, and an intriguist, I would bring forward and support this Napoleon drama, which will, no doubt, end by bringing the young Napoleon before the minds of the people.

(3rd day, 9th.) I and my baggage arrived, this morning, at my new apartments, at the Hôtel de Douvres. * * *

I have bought an orange tree full of flowers! how it embellishes and perfumes my little room! it is quite an acquisition! At eight I shall go to the General's, to catch him before he is *entouré*, if possible; but alas! he receives at the État Major of the *Garde Nationale* now; I shall feel as if going to court! * * * * * * Dressed all in my best, and going off! the house is only across the Boulevards —my valet seems rather pleased, I think, to be going to Lafayette's; he is a most pleasing servant, and it is as cheap, and certainly better, for me to have a valet than a maid-servant. * * * Well;—the *fiacre* is here—not a word more till to-morrow.

(4th day, 10th.) * * Though, at one period of my life, I was accustomed to follow my name into rooms filled with lords and ladies, and perhaps princes,—the confidence which custom gives was so annihilated in me by long disuse, that, as I ascended the wide staircase of the splendid hotel of the État Major, I desired that my name might not be announced; and I was the more satisfied that it was not, when I found the general was not arrived, and there were many gentlemen whom I did not know, assembled in both the apartments, or (as the French call them) *les salons de reception.* I know not when I have felt more ill at ease; and, feeling myself in a sort of Court, and waiting the appearance, if not of a king, of a much greater man, and one whose influence was nearly supreme over France—I sighed, as I looked at my simple Quaker dress, and considered whether I had any business there; and shrunk into a corner,—for the first time in my life wishing the apartment I was in less brilliantly lighted. The ladies of the family, as the General dined out, did not think it necessary to come as early as usual, and thus was my painful solitude, in the midst of a crowd, unusually lengthened; at length a small door, at one corner of the room opened, and the Commander-in-chief appeared; a sort of circle instantly formed around him, he shook each individual of it by the hand, and then made his way up to where I stood, and welcomed me most kindly to Paris; but he could not tarry with me, and was soon again surrounded. A young man, (name unknown) feeling for the awkwardness of my position, then entered into conversation with me, and I was contentedly chatting with him, when Madame G. Lafayette, and the rest of the General's amiable and lovely family came in, and I went forward to meet them. Soon after, the room was filled; the officers of the National Guard, Americans of both sexes, deputies, ladies, men of letters, artists—the distinguished and the non-distinguished, thronged both the saloons; while the General passed from room to room, with a smile and a proffered hand to each in turn. I felt the scene a royal one, as it were, but there was one marked difference to those at which I have been present, when I met the late king, (then Prince of Wales and Regent,) in the London assemblies. The prince never went to the company, *they* came to him; Lafayette, on the contrary, assumed no state, but was as simple-mannered as usual, and apparently as unconscious of his increased consequence, as he was in his assemblies of last year; and I believe that there was scarcely an eye present, that did not follow him with love, nor a heart that did not rejoice in the seeming perfection of his strength, and the enduring freshness of that cheek, which a life of temperance and usefulness has preserved in lasting freshness.

I know not when I have seen so much beauty in the youth of both sexes, as I saw last night. The young men, particularly those in the National Guard, looked so very animated, so very happy! and their uniform was so simple, and so becoming therefore; but, plain as it generally was, that of the Commander-in-chief was plainer still. The evening was only too short and pleasing. I felt elated, but at the same time overwhelmed, with the kind attentions and flatteries, which, as a woman of letters, I received; and again queried whether I ought to be there; but I knew I had a duty to fulfil, a sort of commission to execute, and I resolved not to leave the house till I had done it.

Accordingly, when it was past midnight, I watched the General to a seat, and begged an audience of him, putting into his hand a little paper, containing an extract from a letter, (from a dear friend of mine, a member of our society,) wishing Lafayette to request the abolition of slavery and the slave-trade, and also an expression in writing, of my valued friend Fowell Buxton's wishes, that he would lend all his powerful aid to this great cause.

He took my paper and assured me he had already talked with the minister *de la marine* on the subject; and that they were going to declare the trade *piracy*, as we had done in England, and as the Americans had done also. Alas! how little is this! and we know how the law is evaded! I took my leave, saying, that while liberty was in so many places the order of the day, and would probably be over all Europe, I did hope that the cause of Africa would at length triumph also—but when?

I feel, and own, that France has yet much work to do at home, and interests nearer and dearer to attend to; but I, for one, shall be sadly disappointed if she does not ultimately take up this long-neglected cause, and set a great example to other nations.

Amongst the crowd I saw, for a moment, Benjamin Constant; and saw, with pain, that his truly valuable health has suffered since last year, but his noble mind seems as vigorous as ever! how just are his views, and how eloquent his expressions of them!

Among those also present were the Baron de Humboldt, General Carbonnel, David the sculptor, Le Brun the dramatic poet, &c., &c.

Having executed my commission to the General, and also given him the purse, I had felt such pleasure in netting for him, I withdrew; his son attending me to my coach.

(4th day, 10th.) Soon after I had breakfasted, General de B. called to ask me to go with him to the Luxembourg, to see the exhibition of pictures there, for the benefit of the wounded. I gladly complied, and we set off in a *fiacre* the driver of which told us the *ex-ministers* were expected: we did not believe it, but it gave me a queer sensation.

How fine the day was! how bright the sun! how blue the sky! It was curious to see a large square place in the gardens, just before the front of the palace, absolutely filled with men, women, and children, of all ranks, sitting on benches and chairs, and on the ground, crowded together, enjoying the winter sunshine!

The exhibition was a curious one also. The walls of the long vaulted gallery were covered chiefly with pictures of Napoleon; Napoleon in situations the most interesting and recommendatory to the nation; conquering at Aboukir, Marengo, and Austerlitz; saving the life of a whole family at Cairo; visiting the sick in the hospital of Jaffa; in short, there he was, usually as large as life, surviving in his military glory, on the animated canvass, and recalling to the Parisians the splendour of their arms under their victorious leader; but the most interesting picture was Napoleon on his death-bed, or rather, Napoleon dead; the different expressions of the grief of the bystanders was well expressed. The likeness of Antommarchi (the only one I could judge of) was striking, and I daresay so were the others: above it hung the picture of his tomb, from the hand of Gérard.

Coming home I heard, with pain, the news from England! Our monarch and his queen, so justly popular, to be kept from going to the city feast, to receive the respect due to them, by the unpopularity of a minister! Oh! shame! * * * Again alone, but busy, and happy therefore.

(6th day, 12th.) My birthday! I dare not be guilty of the egotism of committing to paper my feelings, when I recollect that on this day, so many years ago, I saw the light; and that the recollection comes over me that I heard my dearest father say, on his death-bed, it was the happiest day he had ever known! To *one* being, then, it had been an important day; but *he* is gone, and what is it now become? of consequence to no one; and I shall spend it alone in a foreign land! unwelcomed and unheeded, save by myself. But these feelings have been succeeded by wiser and more beneficial ones! Oh! that the resolutions I have this day formed, may make my next birthday, if I am permitted to see one, a day of less condemnatory feelings! * * * Went out to the Jardin des Plantes, and found only la Baronne at home. She made an observation, the result of experience. Speaking of the new animals which had lately been sent, as a present, to the menagerie, and mentioning the excessive tameness of one of the tigers, she said that it would allow her brother-in-law to play with it, and even would court his caresses. "I should, notwithstanding, be much afraid of a *coup de patte*," said I. "Not with as much reason," she replied, "as if you were caressing a ruminating animal; they are much more dangerous and difficult to tame; besides, when a wild animal grows tired of you, he lets you know it, by a certain restlessness and little cry that he makes, therefore you are on your guard; but with the others there is no preparation, and one of the stag species did a very serious injury the other day."

(7th day, 13th.) At eight I went to to the Jardin des Plantes, in my muff and tippet, and most winterly gown. Found Sophie in muslin, and wondering at my Siberian appearance. "Come," said she, speaking in my ear, "I must name to you all the celebrated persons present." De Humboldt I knew, but I should vainly tax my memory to name the rest; one of them, a handsome delicate-looking young man, with brown and curling hair, was, I found, Mignet, author of the "History of the French Revolution," in 2 vols., which I have bought, and which made the delight of my last winter's solitude. Another of the circle was Salmady, one of the Chamber of Deputies, and whose conversation was so eloquent and animated, that Baron Cuvier said, with his meaning and intelligent smile, *voilà la jeune France.*"

(1st day, 14th.) A wet Sabbath day, but I contrived to walk to the Champs Elysées; to bed *not* satisfied with myself, but in peace with all the world, I trust.

(6th day, 19th.) Quatrefuges had procured tickets for the

Chamber of Deputies, and as the business between Ch. de Lameth and the Procureur du Roi was to come on this day, I was very glad to go, and he was to call me.

When ready expecting him, I heard a ring at the door, and concluded it was he, but was most agreeably surprised to see, on entering the *salon,* David and *Cooper,* he whom I so much wished to see! I was very glad, but sorry I was going out directly. C. had only time to promise me that he would come and see me whenever I liked, and would introduce me to his wife. * * * Went to the Chamber, too late for choice places, but heard and saw well. Much pleased with the change in the new Chamber, in the situation of the Tribune des Dames; it is now near the Tribune. The debates were very interesting; the first was on the liberty of the press. Count de T. charmed me, both by his delivery and sentiments. The next debate, relative to the Procureur du Roi, was opened by a paper, read by Benjamin Constant, with whose opinions I have usually much unity; the question seemed to me to lie in a small compass, but it occasioned long discussion. The result was that Ch. de L. was *right* in not obeying the summons of the Procureur du Roi, and the latter, not meaning to attack the privileges of the Chamber, was *not wrong* in summoning him!!! We got away at a little past five.

(7th day.) Prepared for my company; the room looked neat and comfortable. Dr. Bowring and his wife came first, followed by other friends. In the evening to B. Cuvier's.

(1st day, 20th.) A very comforting Meeting; called on the Bowrings again; saw where a bullet on the 29th of July had broken a pane in the window, just after he had shut it! Description of the dying and wounded beneath them, most affecting! At six some friends came, with whom I had a sitting after tea; to *me,* a favoured one. Read to them afterwards some lines of mine, serious enough to end the evening satisfactorily; to bed with a thankful heart for all the favours of the day.

(2nd day, 22nd.) Had engaged to go to David's *atelier,* and to Antommarchi's, to see the mask of Napoleon, when

C. Moreau called early to say he had intended to take me to call on Madame de Genlis, who had promised, if it was fine, to dine with him, but as it rained, he feared she would not come; however, we could call on her. I told him I was engaged till four, but would then call at his house, to go or not as he pleased. Went to D.'s and was delighted with all I saw. Goethe, General Foy, and a brilliant, &c., &c. Went to A.'s *au quatrième*—very high and fatiguing; but remembered the reward of my toil—the cast, and the fine view from his windows, the cast was there, the view gone, walled up! poor man! I would not, *could* not stay there; the cast more than ever recalled to me Napoleon when First Consul! There was also there a fine print from the picture of Napoleon on his death-bed. Antommarchi so like! I then drove to Moreau's; the weather was become fine, and we went to la Comtesse de Genlis'; she received me kindly, and I, throwing myself on my feelings, and remembering how much I owed her in the days of my childhood, became enthusiastically drawn towards her, very soon. She is a really pretty old woman of eighty-seven, very unaffected, with nothing of smartness, or affected state or style, about her. We passed through her bed-room (in which hung a crucifix) to her *salon*, where she sat, much muffled up, over her wood fire; she had dined at three o'clock, not expecting to be able to go out; but as the weather was fine, she soon consented to accompany us, but she laughing said, she must now go without "*sa belle robe.*" We said in *any* gown she would be welcome; she then put on a very pretty white silk bonnet and a clean frill, and we set off. I set them down at C. Moreau's, and came home to dress, but long before the dinner hour, I was at C. M.'s again, and took my post at the side of Madame de Genlis. A party of distinguished men came to dinner. The table was spread with a mixture of excellent English as well as French dishes; roast beef, boiled turkey, plum puddings, and *mince pies!* the latter the very best of the sort! Madame M. is an Englishwoman. As usual, St. Simon, and his preaching and doctrines were discussed, and at my end of the table, laughed at. Madame de G. did not talk much at dinner, but by her attention to what passed, and an occasional remark, it was evident nothing was lost upon her. After C. Moreau had given her health, with a most appropriate and flattering speech, wishing her to live many, many years, Julien, l'Encyclopèdiste, gave the health of the King.

I thought Madame de G. conducted herself on this occasion with much simple dignity; yet it was a proud moment for her. She murmured something (and looked at me) about wishing the health of Madame Opie to be drunk; but no one heard her but myself, and I was really glad. When we rose from table, most of the gentlemen accompanied us. The room now filled with French, English, and Americans; many were presented to the venerable Countess, next to whom I sat, and then to me; she seemed to enjoy a scene, to which for some time she had been a stranger. I found, while I was conversing on some interesting subjects, she had been observing me. Afterwards she said, "*Je vous aime!*" she then added with an archness of countenance and vivacity of manner, the remnant of her best days, "*je vous sême,*" (imitating the bad pronunciation of some foreigner.) At half-past ten I saw C. Moreau lead Madame de G. out, and I followed them, and paid her every attention in my power, for which she was grateful; when I had wrapt her up, and put on her bonnet for her, my servant got a coach, and C. M., another gentleman, and myself, conducted her home.

CHAPTER XVIII.

LETTER ON THE DISTRIBUTION OF PRIZES AT THE CATHOLIC SCHOOLS; CONTINUATION OF JOURNAL; LETTER GIVING AN ACCOUNT OF HER VISIT TO THE FRENCH COURT.

Mrs. Opie's next entry in her journal contains an account of the distribution of prizes at the Catholic Schools of the *Halles aux draps*, in the 4*me arrondissement*. The accompanying letter enters into some particulars of this visit, and gives other details of interest.

Hôtel de Douvres, Rue de la Paix,
11me mo., 30me, 1830.

This *shall* be a letter-writing day, my dear friend, and I will at least begin my letter to thee, though it will not go till sixth day by the ambassador's bag. I was truly sorry not to see thee before my departure, and equally so not to be able to write thee.

Hitherto all has prospered with me, and I trust will continue to do so; we are more quiet here than you seem to be in my dear native land; even the ex-ministers seem forgotten, the people threaten them no longer—audibly at least. It is thought they will soon be transferred to the Luxembourg, guarded by several troops of the National Guard; when there, I should not be surprised if the duty of watching over them became a very difficult and anxious one; but *nous verrons;* violent excitements, if not kept alive, soon wear themselves out. I had such an interesting morning yesterday at *les Halles aux draps!* It was the distribution of prizes at the boys' and girls' schools. I went alone, and had time to contemplate, with great interest, the young population before me! The boys were dressed in a dark brown tunic a little *à la Grecque*, and this added to the illusion, when I fancied that I beheld a race of young republicans. "*Voyez vous cette jeune population?*" said an old man near me, "*et en quinze ans ils seront hommes!*" It was only a truism, but it made me think; and when, after a very good liberal address from the mayor of the *arrondissement*, in a tricolor sash and scarf, those young voices burst into songs of joy and praise, I felt my eyes fill and my heart beat! * * * Interrupted by Quatrefuges du Fesq, *Commandant de la Garde Nationale, du département du Gard!* a protestant gentleman of large estates. He came to take me to the Chamber of Deputies, but, as I dine out, and go to Lafayette's, (if a cold will let me,) I refused to go, and after a visit of an hour and a half he has just quitted me; he seems a worthy man, and has lavished on me a great deal of useless eloquence to persuade me not to go out at all, and threatening to keep guard always at my door! he was in his full military dress, and when two plain Friends came in, to call on me, they looked so surprised to see such a warlike man by my side! I said, "*que je présente un homme de paix à un homme de guerre!*"—I was glad to find that he belongs to a Bible Society *chez lui;* and he is going to present me to its president. He is delighted at being one of my agents, and I have met two English clergymen who are equally willing. To go on with my schools—the Comtesse de St. Aulaire, one of the committee, introduced herself to me, and hoped I approved what I saw and heard; I was glad to be able to express my unqualified approval. When the crowns of flowers and greens, and the books, were all distributed, a letter from Appert was read, announcing one prize from the Queen, which was given to the girl who had already gotten the prize for good conduct, and she came looking so meek and pretty in her crown of white roses. One child who got a prize, was, the Comtesse told me, only six years old! When the Mayor told them, at the close, that their industry should be rewarded by ten days of holidays, the little girls clapped, and shouted "*Vive le Roi!*"—"The boys did not do that," said I to a gentleman near me. "No, but it was in their hearts to do it," he gravely replied.

I then drove to Bowring's lodgings, where I found the wife of the Spanish General Mina; she was on her way to him; he has been very ill. In the evening I saw Napoleon's Count Bertram; which completed the pleasurable sights of the day. I had the pleasure of presenting to the dear General two members of our Society, J. B. and his young nephew, and H. S.; they were much pleased.

I have dined at de Bardelin's twice, and yesterday I met him at Mrs. D.'s. One of the dishes was a *canard aux olives;* very peculiar, but very good. I live *quite to my mind;* I have my dinner from the *restaurateur* belonging to the hotel, which is the cheapest way, as firing is very dear, and I should have a dinner's worth expended in the kitchen; but I have a kitchen to myself, and the whole floor, that is, the *entresol* to me exclusively; a great comfort. The parties on a seventh day eve, at the Jardin des Plantes, (Baron Cuvier's,) are pleasanter than ever; ambassadeurs, savans, sages, deputés, historiens, &c., &c. The Paris intellectual world runs just now after a new sect, (a new religion, as they call it,) the Saint Simoniennes; the founder is a St. Simon, of the Duc de St. Simon's family. His disciples preach up equality of property. The thing is, I suspect, more political than anything else, in its object; but on a first day there is religious preaching, and the room overflows; so it does on a week-day evening, when there are only lectures. The room is very near me, but I am in vain urged to go. "What a triumph it would be to them," (said a Frenchman to me at Cuvier's,) "to get off that little cap, and see it exchanged for their large black hat and feathers!" (the costume, with a blue gown, of the women.) But I, at present, hold out; because I have, in the first place, as I tell them, a scruple against going to any place of worship from curiosity merely; and also because I have vainly tried to read their book of doctrine—I could not get on with it; but as they agree with Friends on two points, I am sometimes tempted to go one evening;—*nous verrons.* * * *

(12th mo., 1st, 1830.) I passed a most pleasant day at Major M.'s; the only guest beside myself was a General Ferguson, well known for his sufferings in the cause of liberal opinions, as he was imprisoned through the jealousy and suspicion of the Austrian government some years ago, and liberated with great difficulty, by Canning. I do not remember his story, but it was before the House. My friends here have persuaded me to be at home on one particular day; so on the seventh day morning I receive from one to five, and I have *beaucoup de monde.* Farewell, till to-morrow.

My friend E. M. is arrived. How good are her objects, how bright her zeal! She is a Christian indeed, and she says much good is doing; even that the St. Simoniennes are overruled for good. She wishes me to go one evening. She says one or two pious preachers mean to go and answer them, (for they put questions on a week-day, and *wish* for discussion.)

With love to all, I am, thy very affectionate,

A. Opie.

The Journal continues:—

I went in the evening, at eight o'clock, to Lafayette's, and had a kind reception from the dear and venerated host; the rooms were very full, and some Americans were introduced to me. The officers of artillery and cannoneers, bearing their plumed caps all the evening, have an odd effect.

(24th of the mo.) Received some visitors unexpectedly this morning; one of them, in conversation, mentioned a remark by Prudhomme, the editor of a Jacobin journal, in former days, which struck me; "*Les grands sont hauts, parceque nous sommes à genoux! levons nous!*" what an axiom! My evening solitary, but pleasant; occupation is not only happiness itself, but it makes one forget unhappiness.

(26th.) Went to St. Cloud. It is a splendid place, but I thought not of its last owner, but of Napoleon; and while I gazed on its magnificence, and thought of that and other palaces, and of supreme and imperial dominion being so suddenly, as it were, obtained by a soldier of fortune,—it seemed as if I was contemplating not a reality, but a dream; and yet it happened in *my* time. If then I, who know it *did* happen, and who even saw some of the splendours of the Consulate, have difficulty in believing that such things were, I must think the next generation will suppose the accurate historian, even, writes with the pen of exaggeration. And then to leave it all as suddenly! Were he not exhibited here in public, in pictures in the morning, and on the stage at night, even his memory perhaps would pass away like a tale that is told! The column on the Place Vendôme is, however, his most enduring monument.

Returning to Paris, we drove to the Palais Royal, and dined at Richard's in the grand *salon*. The charge there is two francs per head, wine included; but if you drink no wine, you are allowed another dish: we drank no wine, therefore were allowed a third dish for our two francs; but we finished with a bottle of champagne, price five francs, (4s. 2d. English.) Still, our dinner did not cost us much, and it was varied and excellent. To bed delighted with my day. How I wish, where it is not the custom to introduce, that every one was ticketed.

(28th.) Went to Meeting; we had a comfortable sitting. Dined at the Champs Elysées; read aloud two letters from a pious book; after tea we fell into silence unexpectedly, and sat near an hour; a great comfort—pleased with my day.

(4th day, 1st of 12th mo.) Ill, and at home all day alone; had a most welcome and unexpected visit from E. M. Her account of the state of the religious world here was cheering; I am so glad! May her hopes for this great, but, on some points, *blind* country, be realized; and may the prayers of her Christian heart be fulfilled! There are many labourers in the field, oh! may it really be white for the harvest. Wrote letters, and to bed unwell, and rather depressed.

C., the Italian, called to thank me; poor man! he is welcome to my money, but not my time; besides, I hate to be thanked.

(7th day.) Rose refreshed, and comparatively well. I had several callers; F. remained after the rest, and gave me a curious account of the causes of the difference which I observe in the American accent, or dialect. He himself has no accent, (a Philadelphian,) nor had F. Cooper, (a New York man,) and the inhabitants of New York are said to speak better English than those of other cities. Enjoyed my quiet evening alone.

(1st day, 5th.) To Meeting: a quiet refreshing sitting. Went afterwards, with my friends, to call on l'Abbé Gregoire;* found him looking so well and bright! He was eighty the day before, and said he had not slept much in the night for thinking of his father and mother, and of the hope to be reunited to them soon, in another world. He said he did not go out, except to visit the sick, or he would call on me; he also goes to walk in the cemetery of Mont Parnasse, where he shall himself lie. We left him, much pleased with our visit; and then drove to my hotel, and dined together. I read to them a MS. of mine. Before we parted, we fell into silence, and sat an hour; and then I read two psalms. The day a very satisfactory one.

(2nd day, 6th.) Went to St. Sulpice, to hear a charity sermon, preached by l'Abbé Faisan, for the benefit of the schools of St. Nicholas. The beginning of the discourse was

* The Abbé Gregoire, who, with Lafayette, and thirty-eight more, is the only survivor of the twelve hundred (I think) who formed the first National Assembly. I knew him twenty-seven years ago, here.—A. O.

excellent, the end extraordinary. He said if he had his choice of the power and will, to give alms or to work miracles, he should prefer the former, because the latter would not do him good; but the former would win the favour of God, and procure him heaven! Almsgiving alone was the means of salvation—not the blood of Christ! poor man! M. Guizot and V. de L. held the bag at the door; we gave our mite, and afterwards went to the cemetery of Vaugirard. It was a touching spectacle! how many tricolor flags were waving, like so many butterflies, over the graves of those killed, in their country's cause, on the memorable three days! Suddenly the sun burst forth from a cloud, and darted its golden rays on some of the white tombs and columns; the effect of the catching lights was indescribable! The abode of death was suddenly illuminated, emblematic, as it were, of those hopes of immortality which illumine the bed of death of the pious: and, as the flags waved in the breeze triumphantly, (as fancy thought,) they seemed indicative of that victory which has robbed death of its sting. And close by us stood a father and mother, weeping over the grave of their son, a boy of fourteen, and weeding his flowery turf! and he had been dead nine months! I thought they would be relieved by talking of him, so I spoke to them; and I found he was such a wonder of learning, for he could read and write so well, and he was so good! I wished that He who could alone comfort them might be near them; they said I was '*très honnête*'.

(Third day, 7th.) Went to the Musée Grec. What changes had taken place in thirteen months! Many beautiful things had been removed, because the glass of the frames which held them had been broken by the bullets, and others for fear they should be so. There was a meaning smile (which I returned) on the faces of the attendants, while I asked reasons for such and such a change. We went to see where the people had entered, and the damage done. It was very little, considering; and as we were looking out of the window, we found we were over the graves which I had visited the day after my arrival; and there, as usual, stood men uncovered, and women and children. They were now surrounding a tricolor flag, newly raised to one of the victims; the groups were picturesque, and the feeling that had assembled them was honourable! but what a shuddering sensation, what painful thoughts of *civil war;* what *horrors* did the sight occasion.

In the evening I accompanied Madame M. to Lafayette's. I cannot reconcile myself to the *cannon* at the door; but they were made for the general, and presented to him by the people of Paris, since the Revolution of this year, as the engraving on them states.

We could scarcely enter the second room, it was so full! and the military caps and plumes in the midst of it were like a forest! Count de L. came up to us, "Observe the Prince de Salms," said he, "in a splendid scarlet and silver uniform: he is come to pay his court to the General; he wants to be king of Belgium!" I *did* see him, a lively-looking, short young man, dazzling in silver embroidery. How different the costume of a Polish Palatine, who soon after entered! dignified in his carriage, but looking like a priest, rather than a soldier; his tunic was black; the tops of the sleeves were full; round his waist was a girdle of gold lace, full four inches deep; and I think his gold-handled sword and dagger were fastened with something of gold fringe. His hair, of a reddish brown, was cut square on the forehead, and hung *squared* also, below the nape of his neck; he was young and remarkable looking, and the tone of his voice deep, rich, and sweet. I should have liked to have talked to him, and tell him I knew Kosciusko; I saw *my* dress excited his curiosity as much as *his* did mine. The evening was interesting. I talked with Americans who were named to me, and with Frenchmen, who neither knew me nor I them; but we were jumbled together in the crowd, and politics and the *great days* are themes which naturally occur. I saw also, with interest, the Prince of Moskowa, the eldest son of Marechal Ney. We did not get home till twelve.

(4th day, 8th.) Went in search of lodgings; called at poor

B. Constant's house, to inquire for him, as I heard at the General's he was in danger. I heard he was worse; what a loss to France! * * * *

B. Constant is no more! I hope to have the melancholy satisfaction of attending his funeral.

(1st day, 12th.) Breakfasted at De B.'s to see the funeral procession pass; I gave up going to Père la Chaise, as I could not be easy to give up Meeting, and said I should be at the Champs Elysées by half-past twelve; it was *impossible.* The convoi, which set off at ten, from the Rue d'Anjou, did not pass our windows till one; there were at least 80,000 men in it! Had it not been first day, I should have taken a coach, and followed it to the Temple, and to Père la Chaise.

(14th.) In the morning Cuvier's lecture; in the evening with some Friends to Lafayette's. The General received us in his usual kind manner; they were pleased, and so surprised at his youth and beauty! It was a gratifying evening to me. A number of Americans were introduced to me, who had read my works, and admired them, particularly the book on *Lying;* and a young lady said, "our youth bless your name, you have done us so much good!" I was affected, and, as usual felt but half gratified, because my dear father could not know it also.

(1st day, 19th.) After Meeting went to call on la Comtesse de Genlis; enjoyed my interview, and met a French lady who had read my works in English; was flattered, as usual. The trial of the Ministers is going on, and disturbances are feared.

(20th.) Fenimore Cooper called on me; a most interesting interview! I read him a manuscript. He is a charming man; he said things looked gloomily at the Luxembourg. * * * *

(12th mo., 21st.) Rose at half-past seven. I went to the T.s to dinner, and heard, from undoubted authority, (that of Le Dieu, editor of the "Revolution,"—a journal so called,) that there were serious disturbances expected at the Luxembourg; and that, not only the prisoners, but the peers were in danger; however Le D. had promised to come in the evening, if he could, and tell us what was passing in that quarter. Anxiously did we look towards the door, whenever it opened; however, when we had dined, and were talking over the cheerful fire, ceasing to watch for his entrance, he was announced, and we crowded round him. His news was indeed alarming! He was just come from the Luxembourg; the people had assembled in thousands, had made three attacks on the gates; had at last "*enfoncé la Garde Nationale*" and forced the gates. They could not, however, make their way to the prisoners or the peers, because the National Guards had, instead of forming in lines, fallen back in a mass before the doors, holding their arms as when exercising; the people then attempted to seize their arms, but they said, "take care! we will not fire, but, if you do not desist, we will use the bayonet." Soon after, some one (probably to produce a change of place and object) said, "while you are stopping here, the Peers will escape the other way;" this produced a diversion, and they dispersed. Le D. then went on to say, that the people continued to increase, till, he believed, there were 60,000, and 30,000 *Gardes nationaux;* that the guards had formed cordons round certain streets and *quais* to keep off the people, and that he had advised some one to propose sending off the prisoners to Vincennes in the night. He said he had had conversation with the chiefs of the people, who were deliberating together in some Café; and that their demand is, that the Chamber of Peers should be *dissolved,* as well as the prisoners condemned. He added he had advised the people to assemble in the Champs de Mars, and decide to petition the King for justice and redress; that at last they were angry with him, and accused him of being the friend and defender of the criminals; that he eagerly repelled the charge, and that promising his friends to return at eleven o'clock, he came to us! I staid listening to his various anecdotes, some grave, some gay, till near eleven o'clock, and returned home to my new apartments, anxious for the results of to-night and the prospects of the morrow.

(21st.) Could not sleep. The *Journal des Débats*, which I had at half-past eight, was at once alarming and tranquillizing; it confirms the dangers and disquietudes of yesterday, but, at the same time, it assures us that very strong means are taken to resist the revolutionary spirit. It says that Lafayette went to the Luxembourg, and put himself at the head of the *Garde Nationale*, and was well received. Le D. represented him as become very unpopular, and his excellent "*ordre du jour*," (which is on the walls,) as having been torn down and trodden underfoot.

I wonder whether he will receive this evening! Perhaps the ladies will receive, whether he be there or not, that the rooms may appear lighted up, as if there was not much to fear. General de B. came just now, in kindness, to advise me not to go out to-day. I want to go to the lecture, but I could not get him to say positively whether he thought it probable, or possible, for Cuvier to lecture to day, as that quarter of the town is the disturbed one; if the cordon be there, that was there yesterday, no *fiàcre* can pass, but whether or not, he advises my staying at home. I cannot yet determine what to do. The people and their leaders in this *mouvement* (that is the word in use) do not consider the chamber of peers as a legal body according to *existing circumstances;* they consider it as a child of the Restoration, and think it should have followed its parent, and *disappeared.* Nor has the conduct of the peers, on this trial, done aught but considerably increase their unpopularity. The people have their spies in the chamber; and, in reply to my observation—"they are anticipating the judgment of acquittal, was it not time enough to act when it was given?"—he said, they knew from their friends how things were going; they felt themselves betrayed, and therefore could forbear no longer, and nothing but their dissolution, as a chamber, can satisfy them. If *now* they dissolve themselves, they may yet be saved! I think I shall venture out at two; and towards the rue St. Jacques. * * H. L. came at two, to say that he dared not take me thither, the streets around, and that where the Baron lectures, being filled with men and soldiers, and that it might be difficult to get back. We went however to the État Major, to ask whether the General received that evening.—Not allowed to enter the gates, and found that the État Major was no longer there; that seemed answer sufficient. To bed, "anxious for to-morrow's dawn."

(4th day, 22nd.) At eight o'clock Manuel knocked at my door, and told me that judgment had been pronounced the preceding evening, and that Polignac and Peyronet were condemned to death, and the others to exile! It was a terrible moment! and I dressed myself hastily, and in no small emotion; but my mind was relieved when I saw the *Journal des Débats*, and saw that P.'s death was only *mort civile.* While reading the deeply interesting narrative of their being carried to Vincennes, I heard the drums beating in an unusual manner, and found it was the *Générale* calling all the soldiers to arm and assemble in haste. At eleven I sallied forth to call on the Coopers, and spent a most agreeable hour with him and his wife. I left them, to go to the Duchess de Broglie's; and he was going to see what was passing at the Palais Royal, for the continued beating of the *Générale* was alarming. When I reached the Rue de Rivoli, I saw General Fergusson, who advised me, on second thoughts, as he said, not to go to the Rue de l'Université, but to defer my calls till next week; and, as the Duchess might be fearing for her husband's life, I thought my call, long deferred, might be deferred a little longer. I then went to the Place du Carousel, and saw an awful scene to me: national guards, bivouacking before the Tuilleries palace, and the people looking at them through the *grille,* in silence but not in love; disappointment and deep resentment seemed lowering on their brows—I never saw such expression before! Tears filled my eyes as I gazed on them! In the place itself there was a considerable number of soldiers also, and the people were outnumbered. I had satisfied my curiosity, and I retired, and next traversed the whole garden of the Tuilleries alone! Near the terrace, to the west, I saw the *Garde Nationale* stretching in a line before the *Garde Meuble*, and others exercising, as I believed. Soon after, I saw a very long line of guards coming along the *quai*. I was pursuing my walk; and, by the time I got to the gates and the streets, this body of men passed me; and, as I was crossing to go to the hotel Bretuil, I was stopt, and a little alarmed by seeing a long line of men approaching, *en habit bourgeois*, and on their meeting the guards I heard violent shouting, but I knew not what it was! I stood by while they passed—they walked, the tricolor in the midst, and in great order, and on their hats was a card or paper, and they were all young. I was told they were the different schools, but whither they were going, and why, none knew; still I thought they looked too happy to be insurgents and "*jeunes insensés*," as I heard them called. Being told the Place Vendôme was full of soldiers, I resolved to get home as fast as possible, and it was near four o'clock. I found the guard bivouacking in the Rue Castiglione, and their fires along the street; but in the Place Vendôme there was no crowd, only soldiers preparing to bivouac. I learned that the young men were the scholars, who, having been falsely accused of conspiring and insubordination, had come forward, begging to have arms and uniforms, to give the lie to their accusers. This was quite a relief to my mind, and I found the dear young men did not look so happy for nothing. After dinner C. M. came to take me out, and shew me Paris. I said "it is now too late"—"not if you will venture;" it was nine o'clock, and the weather rather rainy; but I am a curious and sentimental traveller, and I went.

(5th day, the 23rd.) Now to relate my adventures of last night—went first to look at the bivouacs on the Place Vendôme; was forcibly reminded of Salvator Rosa's pictures of banditti, as the fire-lights glanced on the helmets and fire-arms, and the faces of men were seen in shadow—passed on—(no one was suffered to linger there) and went to the Place du Carousel. Along the Tuilleries were fires and soldiers; and, while we were warming ourselves at one of them, a horse *patrouille* passed us, some of whom cried, " *Vive le*

Roi!" but, (as I observed,) "*j'ai entendu mieux crier.*" The people, chiefly boys, with us, at one of the deserted fires, did not join the cry—poor things! they seemed to enjoy the warmth. We then went to the Palais Royal, our steps constantly impeded by companies of soldiers: as we approached this focus of *émeute,* we saw the surrounding houses were, in a measure, illuminated. When we got to the outside *grille,* we saw women and men clinging to it, while inside and outside were continued and loud cries of "*Vive le Roi!*" and we found he was shewing himself in the balcony. Soon after, it was said he was coming out, and to-day I find he did come down amongst them. Once the gates opened, and we found it was the Duke de Nemours, going out with the cavalry guards to *patrouiller* the city. Redoubled shouts now greeted a coming body of men, and they proved to be the schools I had seen in the morning. At length we went through a shop into the galleries (as they are called) of the Palais Royal; they were lighted up as usual; but in the square of the fountain were various fires for the bivouac, and round them were soldiers of the line and National Guards intermixed, dancing *à la mode,* and singing the songs of liberty! The people outside were looking on delighted. We soon entered the lighted and vaulted passage which leads out of the Palais Royal; and at length, through new and beautiful passages, (where we saw many *gens d'armes* and National Guards, quietly reading the papers and taking refreshments,) we reached the Boulevard through the passage Panorama; quite convinced that order for *that night* was re-established. On the Boulevard we met one of the *aides de camp* of Lafayette. My companion stopt and introduced him to me, as the very man who conducted the transfer of the prisoners to Vincennes; what a pleasing opportunity for me! I asked him how they looked? He said they looked "*défaits, pâles, abattus, et comme des hommes qui s'attendaient à chaque instant d'être mis en morceaux;*" and so, added he, they *would have been,* if we had set off half an hour later. He described the awful moment thus:—"*A la petite porte du guichet, au petit Luxembourg,* there was *no one;* there the *Garde Nationale* formed '*une haie;*' it was three in the afternoon, the judgment not given. There the *calèche* with two horses drove up, the prisoners were waiting at the *guichet,* and we put them in the *calèche.*'" "*En silence?*" "*Oui, Madame, tout c'est passé dans le silence le plus profond.* At a certain distance the *calèche,* and the fifty guards who accompanied it, set off '*au grand galop.*' In the villages we were recognised, and terrible cries of vengeance were heard; but we went too quick to be stopt, else all would have been over with them. So sure indeed were they, that they should not reach Vincennes alive, nor quit Paris alive, that they made some arrangements before they set off; and the happiest moment of their lives was that of their arrival at their prison, '*pour n'en plus sortir!*'" It is curious that this gentleman was one of those whom Polignac had set down in the list, to be arrested, and probably condemned. He is the editor of a journal, and wrote against the Ordinances. He said he had not had his boots off for days and nights, and was then going back to mount guard. "But all is quiet now, all is *over,* all danger?" "All is *reprimé maintenant,*" was his answer, but his countenance was *triste,* and the word *reprimé* did not satisfy *me.*

When we came again in sight of La Place Vendôme, which we left full of soldiers, we went to ascertain the fact of their being there no longer, and so it was; only two or three soldiers remained to see that the fires were put out. One woman was collecting some of the fire into an iron pot: "it would be lost, you know, (she said) if I did not take it," and an officer (as I believe he was,) came up and said, "*elle fait bien.*" In reply to our inquiries, he said:—"All is far from being *terminé. Ah Madame! demain à trois heures, je vous conseille de rester chez vous, et de ne plus sortir de toute la journeé: bon soir! voilà un petit avis que je vous donne!*" I went home almost sorry to have received this *rabat joie.*—

However, though (from reading the journal of to-day) I am almost sure the man only wished to alarm me, or perhaps to reprove my venturous walk of last night, I have given up my intention of going to walk in the gardens, where yesterday I saw ladies and gentlemen *as usual.*

(Christmas day.) Had many visitors—several Americans—dined with my friends on turkey and plum pudding. Went at half-past nine to the Cuviers'; how I repented going! I had seen in the *Journal des Débats* the discussion, relative to the Commandant Generalship, and felt it an intended blow to General Lafayette—the discussion being such that it would lead him to resign; and lo! M. de M. came, and said a most important event had taken place, which might have *de grand résultats;* M. de Lafayette had sent in his *démission!* This was accompanied with remarks and a manner which gave me a feeling not only of sorrow but of speechless indignation! Came home uneasy, angry, and anxious. What a Christmas evening! however, I had a pleasant dinner with kind friends.

(3rd day, 28th.) Found Lafayette had positively refused to continue, and was to receive at the rue d'Anjou. There are different opinions on the subject, as usual; I think him quite right. His speech in the tribune on the subject, was admirable, and its *truth* undoubted. Went to the rue d'Anjou; the room crowded to excess, the street also; 1000 persons at least, first and last—he *en habit bourgeois*—calm, dignified, kind, as usual. I felt pleased to see the General so *clung to.*

(4th day.) Q. came and persuaded me to go with him to the Hotel de Ville, to see, and be introduced to, that admirable man, Odillon Barrot. I went, and was much pleased with him, and promised to go to a *soirée* next fifth day.

(5th day.) Rose anticipating much enjoyment, but heard almost the most overwhelming news I could receive, from England. My eldest and almost my dearest friend, Joseph Gurney, dead in a moment, and in his wife's presence! but to him what a merciful dispensation! On her sorrow I cannot dwell.*

(6th day, 31st.) I did not go out the whole day. Had some callers at night. Went with Manuel to see the shops, and buy some presents on new year's eve. At five o'clock, while I was dining, C. M. came in to tell me poor Madame de Genlis was that morning found dead in her bed!! How I regretted not going to see her last first day!

(New Year's day.) Had many cards, and sent many also. Some callers; several Americans; I gave some my autograph, and lines to Lafayette. * * * What a longing though I fear vain desire do I feel, to do good to those over whom I have any influence. J. J. G.'s "Letter"† was my new year's gift both to men and women.

(1st day, 2nd.) Went to Meeting, afterward to see poor Madame de Genlis in her coffin! Happily arrived too late! was introduced to some dear friends of the deceased, who for her sake received me *à bras ouverts,* because she loved me! I promised to go to her interment.

(3rd day, 4th.) Went to meet the mourners assembled for poor Madame de Genlis' funeral; General Gérard was presented to me. At night went to Lafayette's as usual, and was introduced to many persons.

(5th day, 13th.) Went to see the diorama of the three days; got there just as Lafayette left it!—In the evening to Mark Wilks's; a delightful evening! met the Duchess de Broglie.

(28th.) Had a brilliant party of distinguished persons. I was rich in characters; Baron Cuvier, Gérard and his wife, Firman Rogier, the Belgic deputy; General Pépé, the famous Neapolitan chief, who brought with him Count de Almeyda,

* One of the "Lays for the Dead" (page 63) commemorates this event.

† Mr. J. J. Gurney's "Letter to a friend on the Authority, Purposes, and Effects, of Christianity." This Tractate Mrs. Opie had translated into French during her stay in Paris.

a Portuguese minister to Donna Maria; Cooper, Koseff, the witty physician of Talleyrand; H. Chuter, a man of letters, Colonel de Kay, a young and gallant *chef d'escadre*, who distinguished himself for his skill and bravery in Buenos Ayres. There were persons of ten nations present. It was a choice party and pleasant evening; I hope I was not improperly elated, and was certainly thankful for this, amongst other favours.

(6th day, 4th.) In the evening Firman Rogier called; it was near ten. "What news from Belgium?" "None to-day, I expect dispatches to-morrow." "Who will be king?" "No doubt the Duke de Nemours."—He staid till half-past ten, then said he was going to make another visit.

(7th day, 5th.) The first thing I saw in the papers to-day was, that at *six* the preceding evening, the telegraph had announced that the Duke de Nemours was elected king! and the Belgic Envoyé knew it *not*, but was making calls! how strange! he must explain this to me when we meet. Had nearly twenty callers. Unwell.

* * * * * *

We shall not pursue the Journal further, but conclude this chapter with a letter, in which Mrs. Opie relates her visit to the French court.

Hotel de la Paix, 3rd mo., 7th, 1831.

* * * At least I will begin a letter to thee, my dear friend, to day, *reste à savoir* whether I shall be able to finish it. I am amused (yet that is not the word) at seeing the formidable appearance which the little disturbances here make in the papers. I, living in the Rue and Hôtel de la Paix, know nothing of them, therefore they are certainly local, and nothing of consequence. We are most anxiously expecting the news from Poland. One of my most agreeable associates here, Count de Platen, left Paris, as he said, for London; but he is fighting at Warsaw! having been obliged to enter Poland in disguise. I am glad now I was not at

home when he called to take leave. * * But to a less painful theme.—I had the pleasure of spending the evening of last first day week, seated *en famille* by the side of Marie Amèlie, Reine des François, in other words, I have been to court; and, as the phrase is, most graciously received. La Marquise de D., *dame d'honneur de la Reine*, came to my morning reception the day before, and told me the Queen desired to see me the next evening. I said I went nowhere on first day, but this should be an exception to a general rule. She replied, that if I had a scruple, she would ask the Queen for another day; I told her I had *no* scruple, for I felt sure there would be less company than usual. "No one scarcely, but the family." This was just what I hoped and wished, and we parted.

I wanted to go at half-past eight, but my man was so sure they could not be risen from dinner, that he persuaded me not to set off till twenty minutes before nine, by which delay I failed to see the King, who, tired out with business, was gone to bed before I arrived. I was *alone*, and I really thought the long suite of rooms would have no end. At last I was shewn into a long room, at the end of which I saw some ladies sitting round a table; as I entered, an English lady, coming out, caught my hand, and said, "I must speak to you." I returned the pressure, saying, "I remember thee;" and then saw la Marquise de D. coming to meet me. "*Je viens à vôtre secours*," said she, and we approached the table, on which the Queen, and la Princesse d'Orleans, rose, and said, "*bon jour, Madame Opie*," the Queen adding, "Sit down by me, I am glad to see you, I have read your works,"—and so forth. My friend, the Marquise, sat on the other side; round the table, sat two of the princesses, and some *dames d'honneur*, and the Dukes of Orleans and Nemours were standing near it. I cannot tell thee all the conversation that ensued, nor all the interesting questions which I had to answer; but I found the Queen a very pious-minded woman, and thou wilt think so, when I tell thee one of her *most favourite works*, and one she has given to her daughters, is the life of Mary Fletcher, the methodist, lately translated into French. The Queen, at length, resumed her work, (making a sort of silk *charpie* or lint, to stuff *chauffe pieds* with.) "As it is Sunday (said she) I cannot do any other work; but I do not like to sit idle, and when one works it is pleasant to know one is working for the poor—this is for a lottery for the poor." I asked the Marquise the name of the lady I had met going out. "Walker." "Then I was right," I cried. "*Oui Madame Opie*," said the Queen, "I knew her well." "And she was one of my most intimate friends," said Mademoiselle d'Orleans. "And she was very good to me," said I, instantly recollecting (what I did not choose to mention, namely,) that being in the habit of singing Italian duos formerly, with that very lady, and going one night, by invitation, to a musical party at her house, when I entered, she came up to me, saying, "Oh! my dear, I am so sorry: I invited you this evening in order to present you to the Count d'Artois, (Charles Dix,) I wanted him to hear you sing, but he is ill, and can't come!" I do not know how *many* years afterwards, and after a long separation, I met my singing friend, her daughter, in the palace of Louis Philippe! * * * *

I am thine, with love to distribute,

A. Opie.

CHAPTER XIX.

INFLUENCE OF CHRISTIAN FELLOWSHIP; MRS. OPIE RETURNS TO ENGLAND; GIVES UP HOUSEKEEPING; JOURNEY INTO CORNWALL; LETTERS AND JOURNAL DURING HER RESIDENCE THERE.

Some of Mrs. Opie's most sincere and attached friends felt a degree of anxiety, lest her protracted sojourn in the gay capital of France, where she was surrounded by admirers, and found so much to gratify and charm her taste and feelings, should be injurious to her best and highest interests. They feared lest she should be "drawn away from the simplicity" of faith and manners, which must characterize the true Christian, in his intercourse with the world. These anxieties were natural, and the expression of them salutary. The knowledge that such care was felt on her behalf, that such watchful eyes of love were upon her movements, awakened her gratitude, and influenced her conduct. The union that subsisted between her and the Friends, with whom she had "cast in her lot," was a true and beneficial one; exerting an abiding and useful influence, and having a hold upon her affections, as well as her principles. In her journals, she continually refers to the happy and comforting experiences of her first day services, with the "two or three," who met together for religious fellowship and sympathy; and her heart yearned towards those whom she had left behind in her dear native city, when "vexed" with the ungodliness and carelessness of heart which she saw around her.

But her nature was many-sided and elastic; she could, and did, take a living interest in all the varied forms of life and society; and could be *in* the world though she was not *of* it. She was able to turn with undiminished interest, from scenes of high excitement, to small and apparently uncongenial subjects. To each claim she responded in turn, and the tale of every human heart had power to interest her. Hence, when she returned to her solitary home, and the quiet and comparatively monotonous life she led there, she lost none of her spring, nor appeared in the slightest degree less keenly alive to all that claimed her attention. The society of her friends, and the works of charity which she had relinquished for a season, were returned to and resumed with warmth and diligence. She was especially interested about this time, in the cause of the Ladies' Branch Bible Society, in Norwich. Mr. Charles Dudley was anxious to effect an improvement in its management, and there were meetings and committees at the Friends' meeting-house, at which Mrs. Opie assisted. She also took a district, and visited among the poor, receiving their weekly pence as a collector, and thus coming into contact with many scenes of sorrow and want, that awakened her kindly feelings, and found employment for her charitable dispositions. She mentions, in her diary, the pleasure she felt at being welcomed on her return after her long absence, by the poor people whom she met. This was a reward quite after her own heart!

In the year 1832, Mrs. Opie sold her house in St. George's, which she had been desirous to do from the time of her father's death. During Dr. Alderson's life, many of Mr. Opie's pictures were in his possession, and adorned the walls of the rooms in which he lived. There were two of large size over the mantel-piece in the dining and drawing rooms; one, the well-known picture of the Secret Correspondence, or Love letter, the other was the Shepherd Boy, in Gainsborough's style. There were beside these, many others, including the portraits, which formed the subjects of six of her "Lays for the Dead."—The latter Mrs. Opie retained in her possession, taking them with her when she went into lodgings, and eventually to her house on the Castle Meadow.

Having completed all her arrangements, disposed of her house, and dismissed her servants, she resolved to give up housekeeping for some time, that she might be entirely at liberty to wander at will; and, in the autumn of this year, at length found herself able to accomplish a desire, which (she said) had for many years been near her heart; viz. to visit Cornwall, her husband's native county, intending to make her stay there as long as she found desirable; and on the 20th of September she left London for Falmouth, *viâ* Plymouth. On finding herself in Cornwall, she wrote:—

I cannot describe the sensation I felt at being in my poor husband's native county, which I had so often heard him lavish in praise of; but *his* part of the county was bold and rocky, and without trees; *this* was rich and wooded, though rocky, and the low walls, made of a red stone, appeared to me particularly picturesque. Indeed, at every moment, scenery of increasing beauty presented itself to the view. Before we arrived at Truro, I was extremely pleased with a long dell, called the Forest, extending to a considerable length; across this dell very large forest trees bent over, forming a natural bower, beautiful and magnificent, and, as I concluded must be the case, a fine stream ran through the hollow, and, at its termination, there is a gentleman's seat; I fear that I *envied* the owner his delightful residence.

Rocks, woods, and river, were the constant succession of objects which my delighted eyes gazed on, as we proceeded on our way; and the vale of Perran fully equalled my expectations, though I could not explore its heights and look down on its lovely valley. Penryn is a striking scene, from the business going forward there, and the romantic scenery around its river. Next came the beautiful harbour of Falmouth, on which we looked down as we drew near; it fully realized my high-raised expectations!

At the inn, I found my friend awaiting my arrival; he drove me up an almost perpendicular street, which reminded me of Whitby, where the streets are all precipitous. When I reached W. Place, and the kind inhabitants introduced me into the house, I was *overpowered*, as it were, by the sense of beauty with which the view from the window impressed me! The bay was blue as heaven! and there seemed nothing between us and that, but a gently undulating lawn, enamelled with flowering shrubs. To the left, rose the castle of Pendennis, on its high and verdant prómontory, and the whole was so like an Italian scene, that I could scarcely fancy myself in England. I felt deep thankfulness when I retired to my charming room at night, not only for my safe arrival, but that the lines were fallen to me in such pleasant places!

Mrs. Opie, after remaining a month at Falmouth, left her friends there on the 22nd of October, and proceeded to Perran, on a visit to another branch of the same family, and from this time she seems to have kept a journal, from which we purpose making occasional extracts. On her way to Perran she visited a mine, which she describes thus:—

There is here the largest steam engine, perhaps, in Europe; when I entered the room I went up to see the immense beam, or bob, that opened and shut, and looked like a great whale, opening its jaws to devour me. The whole thing was vast, even to sublimity. We then went below, and a little steam was let off, for me to hear the roar; they went on to increase it for my amusement, but I had enough at the *third* roar, which, from its extraordinary noise, made me feel ready to faint; a fourth increase of sound would, I believe, have made me fall to the ground. We then went to see the women at work. The first sight of the mining district exceeded all my ideas of its desolation—a desolation only equalled by its population.

On the 21st, (she says,) I bade a sorrowful farewell to dear Perran, and drove off with a heavy heart, at leaving my friends, to St. Agnes. The drive was interesting while the light lasted, and I was kindly welcomed on my arrival, by my worthy relatives.

From hence she wrote the following letter:—

TO SARAH ROSE, BRACONDALE, NORWICH.

St. Agnes, 11th mo., 26th, 1832.

MY VERY DEAR FRIEND,

I shall begin by what is uppermost with me just now. Last night, in the papers, I had the shock of seeing the death of Lady Stafford, at Brighton! what a loss! what a wide-spreading loss! What did she die of? how sudden her removal! but it is those who are left who have to mourn. One cannot think but all is well with *her*, poor dear! I used to lament I knew so little of her, but now I rejoice! I am sorry to think, dear friend, what a gloom the death of this noble and excellent lady will cast over thy circle, and, consequently, over thyself. * * *

I am here, with my poor husband's nephew, and his wife and family, which consists of Edward Opie the painter; a boy of ten; and of a gentle and pleasing young woman, named Amelia, after me, at the desire of my poor sister. They have just lost a lovely, gifted girl, of thirteen, whose loss has sunk deep into the hearts of her parents. The whole family have soft pleasing manners; in short, I like them all. From the summer house in the garden, there is a view of rock and ocean, seen over a thick wood, which I should always like to look upon; but alas! the parlour window looks only on a narrow road, and a high house opposite. Such an exchange for beautiful Falmouth bay and harbour, and Perran vale, whence I now come! Yesterday I dined at Harmony Cot, where my husband and all the family were born and bred. It is a most sequestered cottage, whitewashed and thatched; a hill rising high above it, and another in front; trees and flower-beds before it, which in summer must make it a pretty spot. *Now*, it is not a tempting abode; but there are two good rooms, and I am glad I have seen it.

I have here the most delicious bread, butter, and clotted cream, possible. I have luxuriated in this latter article since I reached Cornwall, and also in sweetwort, at Falmouth. A kind old friend there always keeps a store ready for me; for, strange to say, one can buy it at Falmouth a penny per pint, and the man brews almost every day. I was at Falmouth one month, at R. W. Fox's, and at his mother's at Perran and Falmouth another month, and came hither last fourth day from Redruth monthly meeting, and I go to Truro next fourth day, to stay till the beginning of next month, when I go to Burncoose, and I *hope* to take up my abode, in lodgings of my own, at Penzance, by the second of the next year, if not before—but I have so many invitations! I was, on fifth day, up St. Anne's beacon. Such a magnificent sea view! We hope to get to Perran Path, to see rocks and caverns, on second day. * * * Enter a *sweet giblet pie.* Farewell.

After dinner.—When I am at Penzance I mean to go on excursions from that town; the neighbourhood is very interesting, and rocks and sea do not lose, but gain, in beauty and sublimity, from rough weather.

How many persons have died even during the short time of my absence! and I *have* had to fear for dear Dr. Ash! I am truly thankful he is restored. I have good accounts of my aunt and J. Sparshall and of all (save Henry Bidwell) in whom I am interested. May such accounts continue! I have had a letter from Lady Milman to-day; like herself, admirable! In much love, and with messages of love to Whites, yourselves, Beecrofts, and Anne Bevan,

I am, thy ever affectionate friend,

A. Opie.

How I wish I were, what I am not, and fear I never may be, *weaned* from the pleasures of this life, and given only to preparation for another! I sometimes reprove myself for the happiness I feel; and my health so perfect!

The Journal proceeds:—

(7th day, 1st of 12th mo.) Went to see the market, and institution or museum. *En route* met the Wesleyan minister, and went to his house to ask C. Cook's address at Paris, and to speak to him on the necessity of a Temperance Society at St. Anne's, as spirits are the universal drink among *temperate* people, and who see not the danger of such a habit. Had letters from J. J. G. and H. G. Wrote to the latter, for the *last* time by a frank to him!

(1st day, 2nd.) Got to meeting; snowy. In the evening came on an awful storm; thunder loud, lightning vivid! When it subsided, W. T. opened the windows for me to see what he called his *illumination.* It was the large Methodist meeting house lighted up, and towering in radiance in the valley on the left!

(3rd day, 4th.) Monthly meeting day—time to go and prepare. * * A most satisfactory meeting; much dropt that was interesting and instructive.

(4th day, 5th.) Quarterly meeting. A full attendance of Friends from all parts of the country. S. and C. Abbot, to me unknown before, amongst them. The meeting still, and evidently *owned.* Several friends spoke to great edification; but C. A., for voice, manner, and matter, delightful! Such sweetness of voice, united to such compass, I never heard before; and then her communication! I wish I could hear her often. The meeting well attended in the evening. Next morning our friends left, with a solemn, sweet, though short, parting benediction.

(1st day, 9th.) Heard a good account of dear M. Fox and her children. Lodgings suitable procured for me, at Penzance; much pleased to hear it. Walked after dinner up the hill beyond the house, to see to advantage the remarkable and sublime appearance of the clouds, which resembled the glaciers, and formed ridges of ice, like those on the Mer de Glace! It was a sublime spectacle; and, if it had not left us, we should have found it difficult to leave *it.*

(6th day.) Shocked to find that Gurney and Ker had lost their election! Heard from S. Austin. Rolfe in for Falmouth; good! P. W. drove me to see the pit where Wesley preached; a hallowed spot—now made into a circle of turf seats, and will hold 12,000 persons. Interesting indeed!

On the 10th of January, (1833,) her Journal continues:—

Rose at five, and off at seven for Penzance; a day of incessant wind and rain! looked for the mount and its bay to the *right,* but happening to turn to the left window, I just did so in time to see it in all its glory, and quite near me, the billows lashing its rocky sides! Kind Lord de D.

has procured me the means of sleeping there at the next full moon! * * My lodgings pleasant; a good drawing-room, a decent bed-room, and a fine sea view, are my possessions here, and *leisure*. May I employ it well! Dear S. and A. Fox! they were so kind, that I was *very* loth to quit them! but here I am.

A touching mention follows of the tidings she received of the death of a sweet child of some of the friends she had left.

(11th.) Walked on the shore after dinner—the Mount very dark when we first saw it, then it was sunlit, then dark and misty, then light again, and green as an emerald was the flood swelling against it, and edged with snow-white feathers. Beautiful Mount, I long to be better acquainted with thee!

(18th.) The day lovely; walked to find the tombs of my cousins. Such a walk! the air balmy, the bay blue and gold, the Mount darkly grand! saw it almost all the way. The churchyard pretty; the tomb simple; in its railing is another like it, over a mother and son, *friends* of Philothea.* On our return the Mount was bright—saw the granite rocks: and the sea was first green and then a bright blue! so lovely! not at all tired. Enjoyed my walk and my dinner. Wrote in the evening to General Lafayette and E. M.

TO SARAH ROSE, BRACONDALE, NORWICH.

Regent's Terrace, Penzance,
1st mo., 14th, 1833.

It is long since the receipt of any letter has given me so much pleasure as the one I received to-day from thee, my beloved friend. * * * I intend to write to my friend, Judith Beecroft, but I defer writing till

* In her "Lays," p. 72, there are some lines "on a mother and daughter, relations of mine, who died at Penzance within a short time of each other;" beginning:—

Pure, lovely, learned, gifted, pious, wise,
Here, by her mother's side, Philothea lies.

I have visited St. Michael's Mount. She and Laura, who have passed a night with the monks, at the convent of Great St. Bernard, will still look down on poor me, who shall, when I write, have passed a night in that *rocky wonder.* But I am to enjoy the great pleasure of visiting the rock and ramparts by moonlight, and I am to sleep there;—*par conséquent,* I shall also see the sun rise and set there—a great privilege; whether I may have the bells set a ringing or not, I can't tell, but I should like to judge of all the effects *possible* in that unique spot.

I have lately been staying at Lord de Dunstanville's, and he it was who wrote to Sir John St. Aubyn's housekeeper, desiring a bed to be prepared for me, whenever I chose to go; and that is at the *next full moon,* (a suspicious circumstance, *n'est ce pas?)* But, dear me! how should there be any moon where there there is *no sun?* only once have I seen the latter since I came hither, last fifth day, the 10th. Wind, rain, and no fish! and I usually *live* on fish; but then in two minutes I can be on the beach, and see the Mount. * * * Oh! what a blessing is leisure, and its promoter, solitude! I can say, with deep thankfulness, that I have been only *too* happy with my dear Cornish friends; *too* happy, because, I have been idle and useless; but, much as I have enjoyed this very precious society, I cannot express my delight at feeling that I have fourteen hours before me when I rise, or more, to do what I will in, and write and read as I choose.

* * * At Paris the glass is many many degrees below freezing point; here, there is rain and wind, but no frost. I fear, indeed *know,* that you have frost, but I hope thou feelest it not. I will add that my health is perfect, and I need the sorrows of my friends to *sober* my spirits. My drawing-room commands the bay, and on one side the town and hills of N., washed by the sea.

Now to talk of thyself. I am cheered much by thy letter, and I humbly trust that the best of all cheerfulness, that which results from entire resignation, is thine now, and will be to the end. "If we live to the Lord, we shall also die to the Lord;" and I believe persons afflicted with incurable complaints are permitted to live on and suffer, that they may be made profitable examples. * * * To-morrow I am going to dine and sleep at Sir Rose Price's. I have many letters yet unacknowledged; I like to put my friends in *my debt.* I am paying off mine; I sent seven yesterday to the post. Farewell! remember I must hear from thee again.

Thine affectionate friend,

A. OPIE.

(5th day, 24th.) A bright and dazzling sun, silvering over the bellowing sea, like great wit and talent, throwing a lustre over turbulent passions, under an agreeable surface. This day four months I came to dear Falmouth; what happy months! Blessed be His goodness who willed them so to be. I hope for some letters to day * * * one from S. Rose, franked by H. Jerningham, the first catholic frank I have had. Poor dear Mary White! H. K. W.'s mother. She is gone, full of years and honour; and no doubt gone to glory! What a meeting will hers be with her blessed son, if, (as I trust,) the "raised again" know each other. (1st day, 27th.) To meeting; silent, as usual, both morning and afternoon, still it was refreshing. In the evening read some pages of S. Crisp's Sermons—admirable! Read Newton's "Cardiphonia,"* and in the Acts; an edifying evening, still to bed discouraged, though much enabled to pray during the day. (28th.) A disturbed night, but woke with "My grace is sufficient for thee" on my lips. Hoped it was an answer to prayer. Slept again, and woke with the same text. Rose encouraged. * * * This evening went on with my remarks on the sons of Eli and the Rechabites. Read Carne's "Letters from the East," which, though not new to me, were most pleasing; so absorbed with his accounts of the Holy Land, I could scarcely quit them to go to bed.

* In one of Mrs. O.'s notes, she writes, "Of all the books I ever read, Newton's 'Cardiphonia' (the Bible excepted) did me the most good."

(5th of 2nd mo.) * * * * Received a very good and civil note from the housekeeper. (4th day, 6th.) Packed up and ready at a quarter before ten, for Marazion. Meeting satisfactory. Sent my parcel before me to the Mount. Ascent very steep; surprised at the difficulty and pain of the effort. Housekeeper very civil. Saw all the *prime* of the house. Walked round the ramparts. No moon; she rose, however, and was fine at midnight. A bad night, but enjoyed the novelty of my situation.

TO THOMAS BRIGHTWELL.

Regent Terrace, Penzance.
2nd mo., 11th, 1833, evening.

MY DEAR FRIEND,

If I were now at my dear old house at Norwich, I should, perhaps, have the pleasure of passing this evening with thee; but as we are separated by a distance of nearly 400 miles, this pleasure I cannot have. I am therefore desirous to make myself amends for a privation which I frequently regret, by holding with thee that communication, imperfect though it be, I *can* enjoy through the medium of pen, ink, and paper. * * * One of the most interesting sights that I have seen, is THE PIT where Wesley, almost at the hazard of his life, addressed the Cornish men, for the first time. It is now an immense punch bowl of green turf, cut into circular seats from the top to the bottom; steps, left to ascend and descend, dividing the area into four parts; at the top of the last one are two posts of granite, on which, when any one preaches, there is laid a board, to support whatever the preacher may require. On every Whit Sunday one of their most distinguished ministers holds forth to an immense congregation—immense indeed! for the place holds above 10,000 persons, and it is often quite full. I could fancy, as I stood there, those thousands of uplifted faces, wrapt in devout attention, and, as I hope, drinking in waters from the well of salvation.

The greatest sight, and perhaps one of the most unique in Europe, is St. Michael's Mount, as it is stupidly called, for the term *mount*, gives one no idea of *vastness*, but the contrary; and who would expect to find a place called a mount —a rock, a mountain, and a castle? Yet, such is St. Michael's Mount; one of the seats of Sir John St. Aubyn; where I passed two days and two nights *alone*, last week; and where I had leave to stay as long as I liked, but I felt a scruple against taking possession of a man's house in his absence, and putting his housekeeper to the trouble of waiting upon me, and cooking for me; she said she wished me to stay a week, but I thought she would, in her heart, be very glad to get rid of a crazy old gentlewoman, who came to look at the moon from the ramparts of the castle, as if she had no moon in her own country! and I don't doubt but she fancied me moonstruck, which idea was, I dare say, confirmed, by her catching me drawing the faces and figures I saw in the fire; a new, but I assure thee, a very amusing occupation. I advise Lucy to set about it directly. The sea is closed round this magnificent mountain, with its masses of rock frowning midway down its verdant sides, during greater part of the day, and such a sea as it is in winter! They are shipless waters, for no vessel could live in them; and I did enjoy to see the waves of the Atlantic rolling proudly on, on one side of the castle, telling of greater and more fearful power beyond, where my eye could not penetrate. The first night I was there, the weather was so rough, that I went to bed supposing the moon would not shine; but when the tide *unclosed*, as the saying is, the moon shone, and I, on waking past midnight, saw her light, but could not see her; so the next night I sat up till she rose, and, leaning on the balcony, witnessed her fight with the wind and rain, and her ultimate victory. Such was the roughness of the sea, that the white foam made the "darkness light about it," without the aid of the moon; but where she did not shine on their jutting points, dark as Erebus were the turrets, the ramparts, and the walls of the castle; while the little town at the foot of the mountain, and the more distant town beyond, lay in a sort of half tint of moonshine, and the noble rocks over which I leaned, were softened into beauty by the mellowing rays that rested on them! It was interesting to watch the lights from the habitations, far and near, as they gradually disappeared; and to feel that I, probably, was the only being awake and moving, in that vast space of land and water. I walked and gazed, and leaned on the ramparts, till the consciousness of my solitude became oppressive to me, and I hastened along that corridor, so often trodden, in times long past, by the monk or the warrior, to my repose. This castle was once a monastery, and I entered a dungeon which was found, a few years ago, bricked up, and the skeleton of a large man in it, no doubt that of an offending monk, left there to die by inches. * *

Thy attached Friend,

A. Opie.

(2nd mo. 10th.) A day of storm and rain. To meeting, which was still and solemn, though a very small gathering. I was there *first*, and enjoyed the opportunity of solitary worship. Anne T. was favoured much in her ministry. It was a privilege which it is long since we enjoyed before. At three, to meeting again; a notice given to those not in society with us; afterwards all came to me—a pleasant evening. (13th.) Went to meeting, a quiet one, only four persons present. Afternoon netted, and sat watching the sun, and the heavens, and the sea; the sun setting in radiance though not in glory; rain, like hail, pattering against the window at the same time, and the wind roaring as loud as the foaming sea.

(15th.) Rose early, and again worked on my Lays. Letters. Shocked to hear of my dear friend, Sarah Rose's death; but, a mercy to her! Still, I *grieve* to see her no more, a friend so long attached. I long to hear more, and expect to learn that she had *more* than a peaceful end. (17th.) Can't sleep after five, till time to rise; a bad habit. Forgot it was the day of Marazion meeting, so I went *here;* quite alone, but I did so enjoy it! Wrote *all* my Lays on my six pictures—very poor, but hope to improve them. To bed much cheered.

(19th.) Finished my purses—packed up; a day of fearful wind and rain! forced to have a chaise to get to the coach for Falmouth. Felt glad, on arriving, to be in this kind home again. Drew all the evening.*

After a short stay with her friends, Mrs. Opie returned to her solitary lodging, and in her diary, records her progress with her "Lays," and some short pieces; there are frequent notices too of the domestic joys and sorrow of friends with whom she corresponded, and verses addressed to them on these events. The weather was exceedingly stormy during the latter part of her stay; she writes:—

(2nd mo., 28th.) Rose amidst such a storm of wind and rain; the maid fears for the chimney, so do I! The sea a succession of foaming billows, and the white horses galloping towards us. * * What a change since the scene of an hour ago! The sea a succession of circling green waves, seemingly flowing the *other* way; and the sun in dazzling brightness, edging every wave with silver. Oh! the ever-varying beauty of the ocean. I think I must live near it whenever I fix again. If the brightness did not make my eyes ache, I could not keep from the window. * * The beauty all gone again. Now to work on my Lays. I have added to, and corrected, and written in my book, all my lines on my portraits; 192 lines of blank verse; and I think I must add a few more to those on my dear father. I fear no one will read them! * * The wind, rain, and hail are all abroad again, spite of the moon and stars. * * No, there they are again, making the bay so bright! * * To bed peaceful, *grâce à Dieu.* (1st day.) A good night, but dared not go to the meeting, so went here,

* Likenesses of her friends.

knowing I should be alone—enjoyed it. Rain again! "The rain it remaineth every day!" (2nd day.) Went to the workhouse and jail; found one of the committee there, who was very civil, and, with the governor, went about with me. The workhouse well-conducted and comfortable indeed—mad patients there also; saw one poor woman. In the prison not *one* person, but a woman debtor—going out soon. Gave 5s. to the fund and 2s. 6d. to the poor woman; they promised to send me an account of the average expense of the establishment per week, to the fund collected by poor's rates; he thinks it not more than two shillings and a few pence, each person. This gentleman called to tell me that what I had given, with a little added, would give the poor people a treat of cake and tea, at five, next fourth day, and asked me to go and see them enjoy it. It was kindly meant, but I should think it ostentatious. * * Went to the shore, to see the Mount by moonlight. I saw that poor young Irishman, A., at No. 1, walk to day, and I met him; he looks thinner and weaker, but, his colour grows more and more brilliant! how I wish I dare speak to him, and ask him how he does; he comes from the north of Ireland. It is a comfort his brother is with him. I have read through "Anecdotes of the Court of Napoleon," some of them true, I doubt not, but many disgusting! To bed, so low, and haunted with painful images. (5th.) Read the paper of yesterday; what times! what speeches! admired many, but most Sir R. Peel's, I think. Still, am incompetent to judge on the propriety, or rather absolute necessity, of the Irish Bill. (6th.) An almost sleepless night, the storm raging! Thought of the poor souls at sea; hoped Captain Rosewall had not sailed. A day of incessant rain and howling. This weather is very trying to the nerves, and will reconcile me to leaving Penzance! The sounds of wind and rain are bad companions for a lone person, and impede one's progress in anything; still I am sometimes too much absorbed to mind them. (9th.) A fine, blue, windy, frosty day. Went to the Land's end, to the Logan-rock first, a magnificent amphitheatre of rocks indeed! walked up to it with my nephew,

Tom Opie; ascended, and proved it. The position and the movement, make this piece of rock (which weighs 92 tons) very curious; but the fine sight is the mass of varied rocks around! The Land's End in *sea,* was a grievous disappointment; no swell at all; the wind blew from land, but the sea was green and blue and beautiful, and Cape Cormorant grand; and the strange rock in the sea, called the Prisons, very fine; and the the very *Land's End,* and its rocks—oh! it was very fine; and I consoled myself on hearing that had there been a great swell and wind, we could not have approached as we did. We then drove to Whitsand bay; the hills that guard it are strewed with immense pieces of rock, some worn round like a bowl; I never saw grander desolation. The sand there is *white,* and the little shells which abound there are beautiful. (19th.) Set off in a heavy, dark, dirty vehicle, with Thomas Opie, for St. Ives! day bright, but cold; hills steep, rocky, rugged! car jolting; horse going a foot's pace; and two hours and a half going through a barren, rocky country, full of mines, and desolate. Sublimely ugly! Halstown, a curious place; four and thirty double cottages of white stone, abodes of miners, placed in shelves on the edge of a rocky, steep, high hill. The bay and sea at St. Ives lovely. (22nd.) My last day at Penzance! I felt quitting a spot so endeared to me by hours of refreshing, and, I trust, beneficial solitude. A pleasing note from poor young B. A., (the lame invalid I saw daily from my window,) returning my books and regretting my departure.*

Mrs. Opie returned from Penzance to Falmouth, where she remained for some weeks, visiting her

* He afterwards corresponded with Mrs. Opie on religious subjects; and she lent him books, and wrote, giving him christian advice and instruction. He eventually died in Cornwall, and there is reason to believe that her efforts were not in vain, and that she was instrumental in leading him to the only "hiding place from the wind, and covert from the tempest."

friends, and enjoying their kind hospitality and true friendship. She makes daily entries in her Journal, and details the domestic every-day life, and the occasional *fêtes* or troubles of her friends. Especially she dwells, with evident delight and cordial satisfaction on the religious services of the Friends, and expresses her "entire unity" of sentiment with them.

At length, on the 29th of April, she writes:—

Alas! the day of my departure from dear Cornwall, therefore unwelcome. I bade a reluctant adieu to all my dear Cornish friends, deeply thankful for the happiness I had enjoyed, during seven months, in this interesting county, and with this interesting family and others; and endeavouring to prepare mentally for other scenes and other persons.

She spent a few days with friends, at Combe, on her way to Bristol, where she arrived on the 4th instant, and closes her diary, shortly after, thus:—

Here ends my Journal of my Cornish visit, (and its appendix at Combe,) for the health, safety, benefit, and enjoyment of which, I feel deep thankfulness to the Giver of all good!

CHAPTER XX.

RETURN TO NORWICH; EXTRACTS FROM HER DIARY; DR. CHALMERS AND MRS. OPIE AT EARLHAM; LINES ADDRESSED BY MRS. OPIE TO DR. CHALMERS; "LAYS FOR THE DEAD;" VISIT TO LONDON; JOURNEY TO SCOTLAND; HER JOURNAL THERE; THE HIGHLANDS; HER VISIT TO ABBOTSFORD.

AFTER her long absence, Mrs. Opie, on her return to Norwich, took up her abode in lodgings, in St. Giles' street. We find her note book with its daily entries, from which we give a few extracts:—

Arrived at 70, St. Giles' street, on fourth day, 25th of the 6th mo., 1833; having paid for my fare, (from London,) £2, and for coachman and guard, 8s. 6d. Breakfasted and went to bed, thankful for my safe arrival, and also that I did not feel *not* coming to my own home and servants. At three, I rose, and went to call on my aunt, whom I found drest to go out, and looking well and happy; then went to the Sparshalls' and E. Martineau's, thence to the Willetts', and found them well; gave her the handkerchief and bag, and left the dandy pocket handkerchief for Joseph S.; then went to the burying-ground; found my dear father's grave well done, and the "Forget-me-not" on it, in full bloom! thankful for that; next I went to my uncle's; home tired, and went to bed; on my way, I was kindly greeted by some poor people, and welcomed home. I must call on poor Lizzy's parents as soon as I can—her death *me tient au cœur:* I know she was well cared for in temporals, but more I know not. (5th day, 26th.) Went to meeting; a full attendance. Friends very kind in their welcome home. R. Dix stood some time, and afterwards was engaged in prayer. R. Holmes spoke a few words, and dear Lucy Aggs, both in the meeting for worship and discipline, was highly favoured indeed. Dined at the Grove. Sat by H. Birkbeck at dinner, according to his request and my own inclination —a pleasant day. Went home by the Ashs', and learned there the death of poor S. J.; how thankful I am that before I went away I put her under the care of C. A. and M. G., so I know all was done for her that she needed. She was a truly pious Methodist, and needed not the preparation of a death-bed, I believe, to fit her to meet the Lord. (3rd day evening.) Having dined, I went out at seven, took tea at my own dear *ci-devant* house! and saw the improvements—it is now perfect. (28th, 7th day.) A letter franked; a note from Lady Cork, enclosing one from Mrs. T. Read M. Henry's Life; drank tea at Dr. Ash's; calling at S. Wilkin's and T. Brightwell's *chemin faisant;* enjoyed my visit; to bed thankful, but low. (1st day, 29th.) Rose after a restless night; Meeting at the Gildencroft; felt favoured, still, and encouraged. Went with S. Mackie to visit the graves; forbad the culture of that yellow flower (name unknown to me) on them, in future. After dinner called on A. Bevans, surprised and pleased to find her so well in body; her mind is always well. He is the great Physician of souls! Fire in my room; read again M. Henry's Life. (2nd day, 30th.) H. Girdlestone called; wrote to Paris; room north and cold; I have a fire. Called on poor —— at her desire; she thought I should do her good. I did my best, having asked Divine assistance; sent her Wesley's Hymns for all states, and Worthington on "Self-resignation." What a dreadful feeling for any one to feel themselves spiritually deserted and unable to pray! but then the case is one of physical, as well as moral disease. May I be permitted to do her good, by leading her to throw herself wholly on her Saviour.

Called on my dear old friends, the Rogers. (3rd day 1st of mo.) Went to the Infant School, called on the Whites, the Candlers, and the Wagstaffes. To tea at the Martineaus. (5th day, 3rd.) Came to the Grove for a week. * * * *

The "Lays for the Dead," many of which had been written during her stay in Cornwall, were now completed and prepared for publication. Among them are many which have reference to friends and events connected with the history of her life through successive years, and some are very touching tributes to the memory of those she had loved and lost. This little volume concludes with a series of "Sketches of St. Michael's Mount," inscribed to Lord de Dunstanville and Sir John St. Aubyn. When it was published, she wrote, "I have humbly endeavoured to school my mind against the trial of its failure, by meditation and prayer; sadly monotonous it must be; the St. Michael's Mount Lays are less gloomy, but all are tinged."

In the month of July, of this year, Mrs. Opie enjoyed the great pleasure of meeting Dr. Chalmers, who was then on a visit to Mr. J. J. Gurney. In his Journal, Dr. C. gives a pleasing account of this occurrence, from which we select an extract.*

"Friday, July 26th. * * * Last of all, I must mention another lady, who dined and spent the night—one who, in early life, was one of the most distinguished of our literary women, whose works, thirty years ago, I read with great delight—no less a person than the celebrated Mrs. Opie, authoress of the most exquisite feminine tales, and for which I used to place her by the side of Miss Edgeworth. It was

* See "Memoirs of Dr. Chalmers."

curious to myself, that though told by Mr. Gurney in the morning, of her being to dine, I had forgot the circumstance; and the idea of the accomplished novelist and poet was never once suggested by the image of this plain-looking Quakeress, till it rushed upon me after dinner, when it suddenly and inconceivably augmented the interest I felt in her. We had much conversation, and drew greatly together, walking and talking with each other on the beautiful lawn after dinner. She has had access into all kinds of society, and her conversation is all the more rich and interesting. I complained to her of one thing in Quakerism, and that is the mode of their introductions: that I could have recognised in *Mrs. Opie* an acquaintance of thirty years' standing, but that I did not and could not feel the charm of any such reminiscence, when *Joseph John* simply bade me lead out *Amelia* from his drawing-room to his dining-room. I felt, however, my new acquaintance with this said Amelia to be one of the great acquisitions of my present journey; and this union of rank, and opulence, and literature, and polish of mind, with plainness of manners, forms one of the great charms of the society in this house. Had much and cordial talk all the evening; a family exposition before supper, and at length a general breaking up, somewhere about eleven o'clock, terminated this day at once of delightful recreation and needful repose.

"Saturday, July 27th. Mrs. Opie left us early, and we parted from each other most cordially."

Mrs. Opie was much gratified with this meeting, and afterwards addressed these lines

TO DR. CHALMERS.

On reading his description of Dr. Brown, in his Chapter on the connexion between the Intellect and the Will.

When Eve (by Milton's magic muse pourtray'd)
In the clear stream her new-born self survey'd,
Surpriz'd she gaz'd, with admiration fir'd,
Nor knew she *was* the being she admired;

X

And while describing what had charm'd her view,
Suspected not, she her own portrait drew.
Chalmers, however strange the thought may be,
To our first mother I resemble *thee!*
In what, with all thy generous warmth of praise,
Thy pen lamented Brown's vast powers displays;—
Paints him, diffusing Fancy's genial hue
O'er the cold paths philosophers pursue;
Intent to bid round Reason's thoughtful brow
Imagination's varying garlands glow,
Till "Intellectual Power" attention lends,
And from its "awful throne" soft "smiling bends;"
Paints him, on mind's most "arduous" summit plac'd,
The scene still decking with the flowers of taste
As if, call'd forth by wand of fairy elf,—
Then, trust me, Chalmers, thou describ'st *thyself;*
And all the charms which in Brown's picture shine,
By thy unconscious hand pourtray'd, are *thine.*

Mrs. Opie's health was already impaired, and she suffered from attacks of the disorder which afflicted her throughout the remainder of life. She walked *lame*, and was under medical treatment; but still her spirit was buoyant, and she wrote, "I am full of hope; and after all, it is no bad thing for any of us to feel the time for positive preparation come. Life, indeed, ought to be a constant state of preparation for death; but few make it so, and I feel I have not so done."

In the spring of 1834, she went to London.

I do love home better than any other place, and also solitude, (she says,) which is indeed a mercy, considering my lone condition; and I almost dread the idea of London, but "such is the sweet pliability of woman's spirit," that I dare say, when I get there, I shall be pleased. * * * This winter has been one of much physical trial, but I believe I can say, without affectation, it has been one of the happiest and most beneficial of my life.

Sir B. Brodie's opinion, that there was no radical disease, relieved "her mind of its burden;" although she still suffered from pain. "But, (she says,) Yearly Meeting is an excellent cordial; I forget all my ailments there, and could almost wish life itself were one Yearly Meeting!"

The month of August found her on her way to Scotland. Eighteen years had past since she was there, and it had been a long-anticipated purpose some day to revisit it, and to see the Highlands. On the 9th inst. she went on board the "Monarch" steamer; her Journal gives an amusing account of the scene she witnessed when she woke up during the night, and of the inconveniences of the crowded vessel. The next day was the sabbath, and service was performed by a clergyman on board. "Afterwards, (she says,) I read some psalms, and have been in spirit with my afflicted friends the Candlers, at their mother's interment, and have thought of them and other friends there; I hope I too have been thought of and remembered before the throne of grace." The terror of sea-sickness was upon her, but a quiet and refreshing night restored her; and in the afternoon of the day the Scottish coast was visible. On arriving at Edinburgh, she established herself in lodgings, and writes thus in her note book:—

Deeply thankful do I feel for the mercy that has hitherto attended and watched over me! Oh, that beautiful and sublime castle and rock, on which I gaze from my sitting-room window, how I delight to see them again!

On the 14th she left Edinburgh to attend a General Meeting of Friends, at Aberdeen.

Seven miles from Edinburgh we took boat and steamed over the beautiful Forth into Fifeshire; thesky blue, the water calm, the hills fine, and the corn golden. Before we reached Dundee, we had to cross another water; it was the Firth of Tay; one of my fellow travellers, who had lived many years in India, said it reminded her of the Ganges. (16th.) Had a beautiful drive to Aberdeen, through corn fields sloping down to the sea; their golden hue finely contrasting with the deep blue waters. The approach to Montrose very lovely—a succession of pretty cottages on one side, standing in gardens full of flowers, and the blue waters behind them. As we passed along we saw many gentlemen's seats; the distant hills formed a fine back ground. The Dee was now the river in sight, when we lost the Firth of Tay.

After attending General Meeting at Aberdeen, Mrs. Opie proceeded to Stonehaven, from whence she says:—

I walked to Ury, a long two miles, but the walk is beautiful, and Ury is a lovely place. M. B. drove me to S. to take a boat and go to see the ruins of Dunotta Castle, but we sailed past it, and went out to sea to tack, in order to view a most magnificent ridge of rocks, where the sea fowl live. I was wrapt in a sort of devout astonishment at the size and height of the rocks—the highest on the coast—and pleased with the novel sight of the countless sea anemones, just under the waves, like a varied flower garden, pink, lilac, purple, white, yellow, orange, and variegated. Nor was the sound of the birds, as they winged their flight over our heads, without its appropriate charm in such a scene. I was too tired to visit the Castle that day; Captain Barclay dined with us, and was kind and agreeable. (21st.) The Laird with us. Saw the Apologist's study; and leaned on his cane. Drove to Dunotta Castle. The ruins grand and vast, and the rock, of which they form a part, sublime.

Returning to Aberdeen, our traveller started again, by the "Highlander" coach, for Braemar.

Words *can't* do any justice to the magnificence of the drive by the Dee all the way after the first fifteen miles. The Grampians, and "their dark Lognegan," sung by Lord Byron in his first poems, defy description.

(24th, 1st day.) Went to kirk; interesting to see the groups of men and women in the highland costume, and children also. I was impressed and pleased with the whole scene. The lords and ladies sat in the gallery—I below. The sermon was excellent, the preacher evidently zealous—it was a keeping holy the sabbath day. Next morning I set off again, after giving good advice to the Scotch girl, Agnes Mackay, who waited on me.

The most remarkable objects on my way were the immense rocks and mountains around; the Grampians in all their magnificence! Oh! it was at times a fearful pass! the road wound round the edge of a precipice spirally, and there was no fence! (at least at the worst part there was none.) They were, however, so sublime, that I was sorry to part with them for tamer scenery. The Spittal of Glenshee is a desolate, wild, savage looking place indeed! nothing could make me like to abide there, except the wish to do good to some one. (26th.) Rose cheerful, and thankful, and hopeful. Drove to Craig Hall. The scenery is just what I like beyond all other. Steep, rocky banks, wooded by the hand of nature, enclose a clear, rapid stream, breaking over rocky masses as it rolls, and forming tiny cataracts. The walk is a mile long, and ends in a semicircle of rocks, shutting the valley in. It moved my envy more than anything I ever saw. I was sorry to come away.

* * * * From Blair Gowrie I went on to Dunkeld. At length the Grampians reappeared, and at first in *bare* grandeur, but ere we reached D., which lies sweetly at their feet, they became feathered with trees up to the top. * * What an agreeable surprise! Sir Charles Lemon is here

—he tells me the Lord Chancellor will be here to-morrow; I hope to see him too; he also is on his way to Taymouth. It is a refreshment to see well-known faces anywhere—especially when alone, and far from home—but two such men! That *is* a treat. To bed, pleased and thankful. (27th.) Set off on my return to D.; next day left for Perth, rest and fire welcome, when I arrived—landlady a Norfolk woman, glad to see me for my *county's* sake and my *own*, as she knows my works. (29th.) Went to see Scone in a gig. The *Old Cross* to be seen where the kings were proclaimed. Only a doorway remains of the old Palace; but the furniture and bed and cabinets *all* used in the new one, which is built of pinky granite, beautiful to my eye. I saw a bed and a screen worked by poor Mary when a prisoner at Lochleven, and her odious son's bed, &c. Went next to Kinfauns, a beautiful place built of a white and better granite; but I prefer the other. There is a terrace here, and beautiful and grand wooded rocks to be seen from it, and from the windows, and the Tay glides through the vale beneath. The house too is evidently built and furnished by a man of taste and virtu. I am sure I remember Lord Gray, by his *picture*, an officer at N. when I was quite young—*not out.* I saw, and lifted with great difficulty, the sword of W. Wallace. My landlady sent me in, a Norfolk paper; I have cut out S. Wilkin's affecting letter to show John Sheppard, if I see him at Edinburgh. (30th, 1st day.) Heard, from one of the waiters, that there were Friends opposite; wrote a note to invite myself to sit with them, as the man said they met privately. They received me, and we sat an hour and more, in silence; I think they expected I had a religious concern to visit them.

This has been a ruinous week! shocked at the amount of my bill, and I so abstemious too!

The next day I committed the great imprudence of going in an open carriage to Crieff, and got wet through; but I was a little comforted by seeing the paragraph in the paper on *myself!* * * * Thence I posted to Loch Earne Head, the most beautiful of drives—thence to Callander, but could not get taken in there. (3rd day, 1st Sept.) Embarked on Loch Katrine, and after visiting the Isle resumed our boat, and soon landed at a point whence we had a walk of about four miles, returning very wet and weary, but *delighted.*

At this point Mrs. Opie became really ill; the cold she had taken was succeeded by fever, and her night was one of "pain, choking, and distress." Happily some benevolent strangers (Dr. now Sir J. Richardson, the well known arctic traveller, and his lady) came to her assistance, and rendered her all necessary succour. She mentions that Professor Whewell walked ten miles, giving her his seat in a carriage, and at length she reached Callander again; "deeply thankful for the aid received." Her Journal continues:—

Off, on the fourth, at six, for Stirling; in the coach were some Americans, who overwhelmed me with thanks and praises for the good derived from my works. I was fool enough to be pleased! Stirling Castle on the whole disappointed me. Took boat for Edinburgh at twelve.

She remained at Edinburgh about three weeks, and records in her note book many events of interest; visiting Dr. Chalmers, pleasing meetings with numerous friends, &c. On the 22nd of September she departed, to carry into effect her proposed journey to the Highlands. A few extracts from her note book will enable the reader to trace her route.

On the 22nd of September I left Edinburgh for Glasgow, and dined at the house of Sir W. Hooker, with whom I had the pleasure of renewing acquaintance at the Scientific

Meeting at Edinburgh, a short time previously. My day at Glasgow is dear to my recollection. Next morning I set off, per steam boat along the Clyde, to Dumbarton; from thence, by coach, to Loch Lomond. How glad was I to find myself at last gliding up that "Lake full of Islands." One of these is appropriated to the use of harmless insane people, who are permitted to wander about it at will: had I known this at the time, my interest would have been greatly enhanced. * * * It was a lovely afternoon, the sky was blue, and the clouds floated in silvery brightness above the mountains, and even the lofty head of Ben Lomond was unveiled! As I gazed upon his grandeur, and listened to the gentle ripplings of the waters of the lake as they broke against the shore, I felt a soothing calm and a devotional enjoyment.

When a girl, I had delighted to read "Gilpin on Picturesque Scenery," and particularly had admired the coloured print of the Castle of Inverary, with the sun setting behind it: now I had come to see it! As we rowed over the clear and lovely waters, skirting the proud domains of the house of Argyle, how busy was my memory! The waters were so transparent that I could see to the bottom, which in the mid-day sun, seemed paved with emeralds, and I could also see shells and seaweed of varied sorts.

* * * * The morrow came, and what a lovely scene did I gaze upon when I entered my sitting room. The sea was so smooth that the vessels on it, though all the sails were up, appeared quite motionless, when first beheld. The top of Mull was cloudless, but the mists of night were slowly and gracefully unwinding themselves from the verdant sides of Morven, and I was indeed gazing on the Western Isles, so often imaged to my fancy, so full to me of Ossian and poetical associations. But regret mingled with my pleasure, as I knew I was come too late in the year to visit Staffa and Iona. Still it was satisfaction to look at them, and I could not long keep away from the window.

* * * As we steamed past "rocky Morven" it was clothed in lights, shadows, and tints which no pencil could

paint, nor pen describe. I gazed, almost spell bound, as I floated by. There was an unearthly hue over the western side of the scene, which would soon have assisted the fancy to trace on it the forms of the heroes of Ossian. The declining sun, while scattering over surrounding objects the brightest tints, threw, at the same time, over the Western Isles, and their lofty boundary of rocks, a mysterious, faintly coloured mantle of ever vanishing, yet ever renewed, vapour; the rippling waves were bright with gold and silver; the black shadows of the rocks of Morven were reflected in the glassy bosom of the sea; and the magic colouring of the western vales, mountains, and waters, rendered me insensible to the attractions of the eastern shore, till there was pointed out to me the land of "Selma and of song."

* * * * It was a bright, blue, and nearly cloudless day, and the waters of Lochleven, though motionless, glistened in places, with the rays of the early morning, as I approached the darkly frowning entrance of Glencoe, which reminded me of that of Borrowdale; but Glencoe is formed of higher rocks, and shapes more strangely fantastic. How congenial to such scenes are the deep solitude and stillness that reigns here! In the Glen of the massacre especially, the ruined walls, and cottages destroyed, and the absence of the once cheerful population, tell, without language, a tale of death and destruction, on which silence and desolation are the heart-touching comments! I could apply to Glencoe, with justice, the description "beauty in the lap of horror!" I was in the midst of precipitous and bare mounts, and of peaked rocks, some of which shewed indelible marks of mountain torrents; while below them were gracefully swelling hillocks, which appeared to smile away the gloom of the awful creations above them. The recollection of the horrible crime committed here, thrilled through my heart. Why is it one lingers, as if reluctant to leave a scene of powerful and even painful emotion? It must be from the love of excitement; a love which few outgrow.

* * * * From Dalmally I retraced my steps to Strongmachran. My way lay up a very steep, high hill, called the "hill of surprise," from whence I beheld Loch Awe, with its twenty-four islands, lying in its watery grandeur before me. It *was* a surprise, and I was sorry that I was unable to stop, and visit some of the ruins on the Islands: I was on the wrong side, too, for seeing the magnificent pass of Awe.

The notes of this Journal are closed with the following lines:—

How congenial to the Highlands are solitude and silence! We may deplore the present desolateness and depopulation of those most interesting scenes, but they certainly increase their beauty and solemnity. I always admire the ocean most when there are no vessels whatever on its waves; and the solitude, stillness, and depopulation of the Highlands, were to me, heighteners of their charms.

Mrs. Opie also visited Abbotsford, and thus describes what she saw and felt:—

Eighteen years had passed since I first crossed the Tweed; and Abbotsford, an entirely new creation since that time, was already without inhabitants, and the burial-place of the Scotts, already tenanted! "Well, (said I to myself,) I will see the wonderful man's house in life, and his house in death." And at length, at six o'clock on a misty wintry morning, I reluctantly bade farewell to the kindest of friends, and set off for Melrose, where, as soon as I arrived, I ordered a post-chaise and drove to Abbotsford.

It was with considerable emotion that I beheld the gates of this far famed, but now untenanted, house!—but the mind of Walter Scott still seemed to pervade everything around. All the objects, all the furniture, spoke of him, and realized, as it were, all the creations of his pen—nay, evidently had helped to create them. It was action and reaction. He began to write with warlike weapons, and things of auld lang syne about him, and these stores, accumulating, impressed themselves powerfully on his imagination, and his imagination in turn stamped them upon his paper, till his pages resembled his rooms, and his rooms resembled his pages.

How much was I interested in examining the varied curiosities which the rooms contained—the beauty of the apartments themselves—the pictures—the gate of the Tolbooth and its massy keys—the silver vase, the gift of Lord Byron, containing the ashes of the Greeks, found under the walls of the Acropolis—and the various other objects around me!

But the sight of all these things did not tend to elevate my spirits, and I quitted the place with feelings suited to a scene more melancholy still. As I drove past Melrose Abbey, the rain prevented me from stopping to see those picturesque ruins again; but they seemed changed since I saw them in 1816, and less in size—nor was I mistaken, for part of the ruin had fallen down. I also thought that the red colour of the stone was faded; but then, when I saw them before, they were lighted up by a summer sun, and now I beheld them through a thick-falling rain in winter.

The fatigue of my journey from Edinburgh had disposed me to sleep, but I was aroused from my slumbers by a strange sensation, like that produced by the motion of a steam vessel. We were fording the Tweed, and going against a very strong current, and, in spite of my admiration of that river, I did not relish the idea of being drowned, even in its classic waters; not that there was any real danger, but the tide rolled darkly and powerfully along, and I was tired and depressed.

I soon found a guide to the ruins,* and followed her along a narrow path covered with fallen leaves, the emblems of decay; a fitting carpet for the road to the abode of death, which now met my view in unmitigated dreariness. For

* Dryburgh Abbey.

though the carved roof of the crypt remained entire in its beauty, the sides of the ruin were open to every wind that blew. The graves of Sir Walter and Lady Scott, raised several feet from the ground, were placed immediately beneath the arch of the building, and therefore, in a degree, sheltered from the weather. But not one blade of grass grew on those graves of clay; and, giving the unconscious dead my own feelings, I was weak enough to wish, while the rain fell and the wind whistled around, that their last dwelling had been warmed, at least, by a covering of vegetation. To my judgment, this seemed indeed an idle desire, but feeling, or rather folly perhaps, was predominant. It was with many affecting associations that I gazed on the grave nearest me, that of Sir Walter Scott, and it was some minutes before I could prevail on myself to quit the spot, and go to the burying-ground of Lord and Lady Buchan, where I experienced an absurd feeling of satisfaction in finding that their remains were deposited under stones of memorial, and in a building covered in from the weather. But the sight of these tombs did not call forth in me either regret or emotion. Their inhabitants had died at a good old age, surviving even the usual term of man's existence; but their far-famed neighbour, in the abode of death, had fallen a victim to premature decay! * * * *

CHAPTER XXI.

JOURNEY TO BELGIUM; VISIT TO GHENT; JOURNAL OF HER TRAVELS; LETTER FROM THE RHINE FALLS; HOMEWARD JOURNEY; ARRIVAL AT CALAIS.

In 1835, Mrs. Opie again visited the Continent. As on former occasions, she kept a daily Journal, which is written in very fine characters and in pencil. Her route was directed through Bruges and Ghent to Brussels, where she was to join her friend Madame M., with whom she purposed making a trip up the Rhine.

The earlier part of this Journal, giving an account of her visit to the various charitable institutions in the city of Ghent, Mrs. Opie published in *Tait's Magazine* for 1840. From Ghent, she proceeded to Brussels; and at this point of her journey we invite the reader to accompany us, as we follow her steps; occasionally making an extract from her note book. Her friend not having arrived, Mrs. Opie, awaiting her coming, established herself at the Hôtel de France; she says:—

(First day, 2nd of 8th mo.) I have not been out, and perhaps shall not stir; yesterday I read a good deal of dear Mackintosh's life. How rare is truth! *All* relative to me, except M.'s strictures and opinion of my Memoir of my husband, *is erroneous.* W. Ashburner, called my cousin!—the "Forget-me-not," which I wrote years after W. A. died, and I was a wife, said to be addressed to him! That song was written to *no one.* It is a most interesting memoir, and Sir J.'s praises and just appreciation of my husband delight me; his praise of me is welcome also; but I shed tears while I read, for past joys, and for those who live no more! How have I wept over what I could not but turn to, an account of the dear man's death. Yes! it is, I am sure it is, satisfactory. He was no daring sceptic, but a *seeker* to the last, and fully do I believe he *found* and was accepted in the Redeemer! And he was kind to every one;—oh! so truly kind. He loved to give pleasure certainly, and those who do this, have *something* at least, that was in Christ Jesus.

Who that reads these last touching words can fail to apply them to the dear, loving, and beloved writer? alas! now those who loved her must weep, because she, too, lives no more.

Madame M. having arrived, they went by the *chemin de fer*, (which they did not find so swift a passage as they expected,) to Anvers, and next day, (the 8th) proceeded to visit the citadel, and walked over every part of it, and also saw the Scheldt and its banks, Flemish and Dutch; thence to Nôtre Dame to see the pictures by Rubens.

Words cannot express (she says) my feelings at sight of the Descent from the Cross, *in the light* which it was painted for probably. What grand conception! What motion in all the figures! The scene, the subject, the sense of surpassing genius, and the living effect of everything, quite overcame me, even unto tears.

On Sunday, after a "sitting," in her own room alone, she went with her friend to see several churches, and at one of them the *concierge*, on their approaching the altar,

* * * made a dreadful noise, with something in his hand, to forbid it, and as we did not immediately leave the church he cried "*allez!*" and when we came to the door, which he held in his hand, his look at me was fierce and appalling, and in Flemish (as I suppose) he said something which seemed to me *trembleurs; il avait l'air si menaçant que, si javois tardé de quitter la porte, je crois qu'il m'auroit donné un coup quelconque, ses lèvres etoient pâles, comme la mort!*

From Antwerp the travellers returned to Brussels, whence they started on the 12th, for Namur, going "unconsciously by the road, *not* over the plain of Waterloo—a disappointment, but we saw distinctly the mound and the white lion on it, which mark the *spot.*" From Namur, they proceeded to Huy and Liège, and on the 13th, visited Chaude Fontaine, with which Mrs. Opie was rather disappointed, and "one thought of dear Scotland" dimmed the beauty of this pretty vale in her eyes. Of the cathedral at Liège, she says, "the roof curious, the whole a grandly simple edifice, sculpture in wood excellent; pictures good for little."

On the 16th they were at Spa, of which she writes:—

This is a lovely spot indeed; to me, how does it bring back my earliest recollections! Poor Amisant used to give me *bons bons* and toys from Spa, and tell me stories of it! dined at the *table d'hôte;* forty persons present—good company. Next day went to see a famous cascade; the drive thither through a deeply wooded ravine, was beautiful; the cascade itself trumpery. We came back by Malmedy, a pretty town in Prussia, picturesque in buildings and lovely in situation. On the 20th we were to have seen a curious grotto, but could not get horses on account of the odious races. Well! money saved, and fatigue avoided; a hundred persons dined at the *table d'hôte.*

They left Spa for Aix la Chapelle, on the 21st, and though disappointed in the country around, were surprised at the width of streets and beauty of the buildings in Aix. Of the cathedral at Aix, Mrs. Opie writes, "outside, in parts, it is beautiful, light, and imposing; and the Hôtel de Ville, old and grand, (when *entire*,) as a palace. The fountain opposite to it, with a statue of Charlemagne, in complete armour, with the crown on the head, is curious and interesting, but the passages for the water are small, and have a bad effect." On the 23rd, her Journal proceeds :—

Rose depressed, Sunday no sabbath for me! This is an odious place. I enjoyed my quiet sitting at home, and was with my dear and endeared brethren and sisters at N. meeting in spirit; in the afternoon drove to Louisberg, an exquisite drive and beautiful walks, commanding the forest *des Ardennes,* (no doubt that of the Duke, Rosalind, &c.,) a splendid view; saw, too, the ever-boiling fountain at the village called Bouille; I hope it was not a profanation of the sabbath to go to these places. (24th.) All noise, bustle, and carriages, come in for the races. No one seems to think of anything but *les courses.* We have *bitten* all nations now, with this vicious folly! We went to see the *Trésor* at the cathedral; the relics encased in gold; was glad to see them, but the priest was evidently disappointed at not seeing any marks of homage and reverence about me, for what I saw! Afterwards went to see the church; but was led away from attention to things of man's creation, by the sight and hearing of a man, in a blouse, who was kneeling before the altar, and in a loud voice doing penance, his arms extended in the form of a cross; so he remained at least half an hour, and from the gallery above

I watched him; as he went out, he passed us, pale and feeble from his exertions. M. M. says she has seen such a sight in Ireland, and that when he paused, there were persons answering him from behind the confessional. (25th.) Went to the cathedral, to see, and sit in, Charlemagne's chair. The man there again, *doing as before:* the sacristan said it was no penance, it was a voluntary action; and he had an idea of getting by that means to paradise, and that he *came every day* and staid near an hour! This sight interests me much, be it how it may. After dinner went to shew myself, and be *described* at the passport office. Alas! could not get places in the diligence for Cologne, till sixth day. Two more days in this sink of dissipation! Really I turn from the scenes of gambling, vice, and evil around me, with a feeling of comfort, to the poor, *mistaken*, but pious man, and penitent conscious sinner, in the cathedral!

On the 28th the travellers proceeded to Cologne, and next day the Journal proceeds:—

My window looked on the river, and I rose at half-past four to gaze at the Rhine; the sun was breaking behind a church, with fine towers, and the water reflected objects. No one seemed waking but myself. It was a still, sublime, and solemn moment. At seven we came on board the steamer, where I now write; the Rhine, broad and rapid, spreading around me. The banks are tame, and fog hides the hills, but the voyage is truly pleasant, and we are on the Rhine!

Landing at Bonn, they proceeded to Godesberg, lying at the foot of the Drachenfels, which they ascended on asses, on the 1st of September; she says:—

It was an exquisite day, and exquisite was the ascent. I enjoyed it, in spite of the disagreeable way of going. We were so high, that the many, and I may say, tall, vineyards, which we had passed on our way, looked only like a carpet beneath us. The lights on the mountains and on the river were very fine, and Rolandseck and Roland tower were the finest features in the scene. On the 2nd we were towed across to the island of Nonningwerth, where was the nunnery, a fine establishment for nuns indeed, and one for noble ladies. It would have delighted me to have passed some time there, making excursions on the Rhine from thence.

I had forgotten to mention our most interesting visit to Kreuzberg, a high hill, rising near Bonn. There we saw the buried monks, in a vault near the church; their bodies in a wonderful state of preservation; the lids of the coffins are decayed, and there they lie by each other's side, some with the nails, toes, and fingers, still fleshed, and so are parts of the knees and legs. I do not remember to have seen any features perfect. It was a curious sight, but did not affect me as I expected it would have done. One thing strikes me on recollection, which I did not think about at the moment, viz: the great length of the limbs. We stay here a day to rest. The students are very picturesque in their appearance, but they have not long hair, at least, we have seen none. Oleanders are everywhere here, like meaner flowers elsewhere, and so fine; one of the students whom I saw, wore a straw hat, with bunches of oleander stuck in it; this, with the naked throat, looked so effeminate! I write this in a chair in the garden. Two days of rain chilled the air, but then it *laid the dust.* There is always in the physical, as well as in the moral world, some good coming out of evil! (4th.) Took the steam-boat for Coblentz, my heart full of thankfulness; after a *glorious* voyage we arrived, when it was quite dark. Our chambers looked on the Rhine, and the moon shone on it, and the lights of the city on the opposite shore (for we were at Ehrenbreitstein, whose grand fortress towered behind us) added to the beauty of the scene. I was loth to go to bed.

After two days' stay at Coblentz they proceeded by the Rhine to Bingen, and on the 7th ascended the

Rüdesheim mountain, from the summit of which they had "a glorious view indeed of the mighty river, into which the river Nahe was seen sending its pale brown waters, contrasting with the soft pale green of its superior neighbour. Eleven green islands in the Rhine were visible from this high point." Thence their way led to Mayence; they stopped at one place to change horses, when Mrs. Opie says: "I strolled down to the Rhine, where were peasants gaily dressed, *en bateau*, singing and chorussing their national air, and then raising a cry like that of our harvestmen, only sweeter." Next day they saw Mayence, and proceeded on to the Duke of Nassau's palace, which she calls "exquisitely handsome;" thence to Wiesbaden. On the 14th they were at Frankfort, and went to church twice, being "charmed with the preacher, Bonnet;" and after two days exploring in this city, they proceeded on the 16th to Heidelberg, where, the Journal continues,—

We arrived late, after an exquisite drive; the castle grows on one, the more one looks at it; its vastness is surprising, and the beauty of its site, and trees, and gardens, and terraces, is striking; but the Neckar, though pretty, is not large enough for such an edifice, it should have been the Rhine. One view, up the river, is the most advantageous to the castle. * * * The great tun is not worth seeing by English persons, who know there are such things as brewers' tuns so much larger! Came home delighted with all our sights. On the 19th to Manheim, a lovely drive, the Rhine in all its beauty. We stopped at Schwetzingen, to see the beautiful gardens; at M. we saw the grand Duke's handsome palace, 400 rooms in it; we did not see all, certainly. (20th, Sabbath day.) Alas! at home till after dinner. (21st.) At Carlsruhe. (23rd.) Set off at eight for Baden, the approach to it is beautiful! that evening I drest and walked to the post, and found a letter telling me of the death of E. B.; oh! her poor mother. We then walked to Chabert's, and sat under the portico, and ate ice; and saw, but scarcely entered, the grand room, where, all day, men and women are playing *rouge et noir*. English most of them! (22nd.) Walked after dinner to see a waterfall, the walk was exquisite along the edge of what is, and in what was, the Black Forest. High indeed were the mountains and rocks on either side, and on one towered the black pines of the far-famed forest; the path was steep but gradual, along a narrow murmuring torrent, which in a wet season must have been very fine. After a mile's walk, at least, we reached the wooden bridge and the cascade, which was well worth coming to see, and we did indeed enjoy our walk. (29th.) To church; it was nearly full of English; a good sermon by an English gentleman. After service walked in the burying-ground; the place was full of crosses, fancies, and flowers, and of some pretty memorials. After dinner at the *table d'hôte*, went to my room. (28th.) Went to see the chateaux; the first, that of the Duchess Stephanie; nothing remarkable externally, but there, beneath, were the chambers of the secret tribunal! Alas! our guide was a youth who could only speak German; however, he knew what we wanted to see, and taking a lantern himself and giving us a candle, he led us from the bright rooms and daylight into utter darkness! we saw the *oubliette*, the room of judgment, and the tribunal, or rather, place of it; the massy stone doors; the dark airless cells; and what Mrs. Trollope has so well described. We then drove to the ruins on the rock, a painfully steep ascent for the horses, but they did it well! It is an exquisite ruin, and from its top we beheld the valley of the Rhine, lying shining and winding beneath, and to the east a mass of beautiful mountains.

On the 30th the travellers left Baden, in company with friends, (and friends and acquaintances they met at every turn,) and on the 1st of October reached Friburg; with the interior of the cathedral they were much struck, and its "windows, all of painted glass, such as I never saw before;" the Journal proceeds:—

From thence we set off for Boldbach, *en route* to the Falls, and soon turning into a valley, went up, on foot, a very steep, narrow, rocky defile, the river rolling and talking beneath, the rocks and mountains so high, that in the carriage it was difficult to see to the top, the vale was so narrow! It was sublimely grand to look back, and so repeatedly did the road wind, that it seemed we were blocked in by rocks! this was the Black Forest, and the famous *gorge d'enfer*. The next thing, worthy of equal admiration, was the Black Forest itself, through which we passed, and the latter part of it we had the moon to light us through. Before we reached the forest, we saw the Alps, and, for *some time*, some nearer and plainer than others. Oh! it was glorious!

(3rd of 10th mo.) Rose at five, but not off till past seven; and I was going to the Falls of the Rhine! At length I heard them roar, and saw them smoke! and as soon as the *voiture* stopped at the inn, I ran off to the Falls.

TO THOMAS BRIGHTWELL.

Hotel of the Rhine Falls,
10th mo., 3rd, 1835.

I think, my dear friend, thou wilt not be sorry to hear a little of my goings on. * * Thou didst not come as far as this spot, and my journey has been extended much beyond my original plan; but I am so delighted with the Rhine, that I could not resist the temptation and opportunity—one which cannot occur again—of seeing it in its wondrous beauty here. Three times have I visited the Falls to-day, and, if the moon rises bright, I am to visit them again. We came yesterday from Friburg, and to that place we went from Baden Baden

—a beautiful spot, but there is no water except in the environs, and I admire no place where water is not. Friburg Cathedral is most beautiful; they say Strasburg is finer —*nous verrons.* From F. our route lay through a very steep mountainous country, and through the Black Forest, that haunt of banditti in former times, and the scene of so many tales and romances. It is sublime in its dark-browed beauty still, and a fine moon added to the solemn calm of the scene. But the Alps! long before we saw the Forest the snow mountains were in sight—and also long before we were in Switzerland, Swiss cottages, Swiss chalets, and Swiss costumes, met our eyes at every turn. We went, just after we left Friburg, up a steep rocky defile, and up mountains, and through forests, to the top of which our eyes could scarcely reach, and in which the exquisite beauty of foliage and colouring went *de pair* with sublimity—and from the top of these passes the snow mountains first met my eager gaze. This morning we set off at six precisely; we are at present travelling in a returned carriage—which holds us and our luggage, and we find such modes of conveyance the cheapest and best. It was half-past twelve when we reached this hotel: *chemin faisant* I heard the roar of the Falls, and saw them smoke, and while my friend staid to eat her breakfast, I (who had had coffee before starting) could not delay my visit to this long-desired scene, and I hurried down a steep path to it, which, if under less powerful influences, I should have cautiously trodden—but I arrived safe at a railing near the fall, and was awhile satisfied! but I soon changed my place, and walked till I came in front of the mighty torrent. Oh! those busy restless waters—no one can fancy what they are! they must be seen to be conceived of! Some persons are disappointed when they see them, and, in one respect, so should I have been, had not prints prepared me for what I was to expect. I am used to see and admire cascades that fall from a height, over one narrow rock, and then over another—and perhaps over another still; but *this* is, I may say, like Niagara, a *table* or flat fall. It is a wide river, coming to an edge or wall of rocks, and leaping over them—then gracefully rolling on, like liquified *aqua marine*—that beautiful green stone of such exquisite tint and clearness. The *chute* itself is like the purest snow; but, ever and anon, as the sun shone on it, some of the tumbling masses, falling over the rocks below the great fall, were like liquid sapphires and of the palest purest blue. Still the Rhine here is, as a river, unlike its usual self, of the full green blue, like the precious stone named above. In its *best* dress, where the boats go, thou mayst remember, it is of that undefinable light, pale-blueish green, the colour of Dresden china. When it flows smoothly on at this place, it turns up a narrow channel, and glides along through richly wooded rocks, and is seen no more! Oh! it is a glorious river! and had it no banks, I should love it for itself alone! There is something awful in the constant roar and eternal motion of these waters! The sea is sometimes calm, and its roar becomes a gentle murmuring, but these rolling waterfalls seem to know no change, but fall and roar for ever, exempt from the common doom of created things, which is to alter and to end. There is an inhabited castle on a rock beside the Rhine-falls; I should like to know whether its inhabitants have, of necessity, acquired the habit of speaking so loud as to break the drum of the ears of their acquaintances!

We go on improving in our enjoyments. I mean, the natural beauties we see, go on increasing in sublimity and charm; and so they had need, to console me for my trying absence from my religious duties and opportunities, and my religious friends—my sabbath days—ah! there is the trial. But I dare not repine, I have put myself in the situation, and I often say to myself, like the man in the play, "*tu l'as voulu, George, tu l'as voulu!*" but I never contemplated so long a tour. We did mean to go back by Holland, but have given that up. * * I am very, very, home sick; however, if permitted to return in health and safety, I shall do so with a deeply thankful heart, and I can also add, with a heart still more attached to the friends I have so long deserted. We have associated occasionally with some pleasant men and women, and have occasionally travelled with them, but I have not desired to form acquaintances. We have mounted the Niederwald, and we visited the Brunnens. We liked Heidelberg much; we were there five days. Chaude Fontaine we liked; but Spa, Weisbaden, and Aix la Chapelle, I *hated;* they are sinks of dissipation, gambling, and vice, and even English ladies game there, at the public table and the public rooms, at all hours; and nowhere, and by *none,* is the first day of the week kept holy. True, the English as well as the Germans, go to church, after the Lutherans and Catholics are come out of it; but *cela suffit.*

We occasionally see an English newspaper, or rather, *Galignani's Messenger,* and are amused at O'Connell's progress, but alarmed at Spanish affairs. * * Farewell, till I return from my walks, or find I cannot go. I hear the waters roaring most invitingly. * * Just returned—the moon shewed herself *de temps en temps,* but not enough; however, I dare say she is now gilding the waters well; but I had no right, I thought, to keep my poor guide out of his bed for my pleasure, so I came away, having seen her rays sparkling on one side of the river, but I doubt whether her beams would ever reach the fall so as to convert it into diamonds; thus I console myself. Farewell, with love to your circle; let my aunt, E. Alderson, know of this letter from her vagrant, and as yet far distant, niece. I thought of you all in the Bible week, and wished myself with you. I shall write to my dear friends, the Sparshalls and Willetts, and my beloved friends at Earlham and the Grove. I hope J. Fletcher and wife are well, &c.

Thy truly attached friend,

A. Opie.

From the Falls the journey was continued to Zurich, ("a noble lake, the banks all studded with country houses and gardens,") and Lucerne. Her Journal continues:—

Arrived by twilight (on the 5th) at beautiful Lucerne! The Righi was before us, unveiled almost all the way, and now we found him on the banks of the lake, *as it seemed;* on either side were snow mountains, in rows, one behind another, filling up the lake in one place, so as to make it seem impassible by boat. The moon was rising—the sun setting—a neck of green land covered with flowers, was shooting into the lake, near where I was, and the whole scenery was lovely beyond description. Our inn was eight stories high! my room five, but then it commanded the lake and its beauties, and I was never tired of looking out of my window. From the balcony I saw the moon rolling its flood of light into the bosom of the lake, the Righi in deep shadow, the snow hills of a ghostly white, and the rays just catching on some of their sharp peaks. (6th.) Mont Pilate, which rises just behind our hotel, is the most beautifully outlined and grandest mountain I have yet seen. We rowed on the lake to where the rocks and hills formed a complete cross; four cantons at the end of the four arms, Uri, Friburg, Unterwald, and Lucerne; the wooded rocks come down straight into the lake, and the effect is fine, but there is no walk on the banks, as at Zurich. Dined at the *table d'hôte,* dinner excellent; in short this hotel both in rooms, situation, attendance, and fare, is perfect. In the morning we went to see the famous lion, sculptured in a rock near, from a model by Thorwaldsen; the model is *exquisite.* We went then to the fair, and were amused with the different costumes. In the twilight we walked along the lake, and through the cloisters of the church of the Jesuits, and lingered on the shore as long as we could. (7th.) Saw the sun rise at six, behind the Righi, from my window, and fill the lake below with crimson light; oh! it was glorious; but so fleeting! It was beautiful to see the mists rolling off the mountains. We were very sorry to come away.

The next two days rain and mist prevailed, and the mountains were closed in; no Jungfrau visible! At Berne, at the *table d'hôte*, Mrs. Opie found herself placed beside a *marquise*, whom she supposed from her accent must be English; "she said she was born English, but was the widow of a French peer, the Marquis Lally Tollendal!" At length, on the 10th, the sun shone; it was Sunday, and after attending church, the travellers walked on the ramparts, and saw a "piece of the Jungfrau, and one or two snow hills, but no more." On the 11th, weary of waiting, they proceeded to Thun; but were still pursued by rain and mist. However, at Interlachen, a gleam of sunshine lighted up the prospect, and they saw the distant Alps "in beautiful and glorious succession—a scene never to be forgotten." On the 14th, Mrs. Opie was greatly distressed at reading the announcement of Mrs. J. J. Gurney's death, in Galignani. Of this painful event she writes:—

A most afflicting and unexpected event! the death of my beloved young friend, Mary, the wife of my dearest and best friend, J. J. Gurney. I had learnt to love her dearly; by constant and never-failing experience I knew the generosity of her heart, and the openness of her hand in giving! Her will to do good, was even greater than her power! To her husband she was the heightener of his joys, the soother of his trials, the sharer, and I may say assistant, of his literary labours; to his children she was a most affectionate, kind, and judicious mother; to me she was ever a kind, attentive friend, and I looked forward to her as one of the comforts of my old age! but she is gone before me, and has left a blank which cannot be filled up. Alas! how many are mourning with me for her loss! but it is my misery to deplore her alone in a foreign land! deplore—I mean for the sake of others; for she, I can have no doubt, is gone to glory! to that Redeemer through whom alone she hoped for acceptance, and for the joys of the world to come!

Mrs. Opie ceased to make any entry in her Journal for many days after this. She proceeded to Basle and Friburg, and thence to Strasburg and Manheim, where she found letters that cheered and relieved her. Here she enters in her note book:—

So thankful to be here! To-morrow I hope to be on the Rhine, and my face turned towards home. May I not be disappointed! I hope fearfully, and I trust humbly.

On the 22nd they were at Mayence; thence they went on board the boat. She says:—

We went down into the handsome cabin, but were most civilly requested to leave it, as it was engaged for the Princess of Saxony. We went on board again, and I soon forgot even my sorrow, in the lovely scenery around. On the deck I had a flattering *rencontre* with the Princess, who, attracted by my singular dress, opened a conversation with me. At last she asked my name; and when I said Amelia Opie, "Madame Ôpie," she exclaimed, "*quoi! auteur célèbre!*" and then she was kinder still, had one of her own stools brought for me, and made me sit beside her.

At Cologne she took her leave of the Rhine:—

I rose (she says) in the night to look at the river, &c., and for the last time gazed on its beauty, from the spot where I first saw it. How much had I undergone of trial, in many ways, since I saw it last! I felt humbled, but resigned and contented, and, I trust, *taught.*

On the 27th they reached Brussels, and the next day, Ghent. On the 1st November the two friends parted at Lisle, and Mrs. Opie, travelling all night, reached Calais, where she closes her Journal with the following words:—

So ends my Journal of my journey; would it were a better record of better things! But I am returned; *good things* more endeared to me than ever; and when I saw Calais to-day, and remembered what I was when I first saw it, in 1802, I felt overwhelmed and humbled with a sense of being richer, wiser, and happier, in one sense, than I was then; for I had learned to know my Saviour, and not as a teacher and a prophet only, but as the Redeemer, as He who died that I might live, and through whose merits alone I am to be saved. Glory be to the most High for this greatest of all His mercies!

A. O., 2nd of 11th mo., 1835.

CHAPTER XXII.

MRS. OPIE'S REMOVAL TO LADY'S LANE; LETTERS, VISITORS, AND WRITING; SPRING ASSIZES OF 1838; MEMOIRS OF SIR. W. SCOTT; VISITS TO LONDON AND NORTHREPPS; DEATH OF FRIENDS; ANTI-SLAVERY CONVENTION; WINTER AND SPRING OF 1840-41; VISITS TO TOWN AND LETTERS FROM THENCE IN 1842-43; ILLNESS; CLOSE OF 1843; LETTER OF REMINISCENCES OF THOMAS HOGG.

Mrs. Opie returned from her trip up the Rhine at the close of November, 1835. This was her last journey; from this time her absences from home were never of long duration, but limited to a few weeks in London, and occasional visits to friends in the neighbourhood of Norwich. She did not remain many months in the lodgings in St. Giles' Street, but transferred herself to Lady's Lane, where she had commodious apartments, and in which she remained until her final removal to the Castle Meadow House. In this home she settled herself, surrounded by her Lares, the "Portraits," which hung around her, and appeared to great advantage, when lighted up, at night, by wax-lights in branch lamps. The most beautiful of them, the portrait of herself, is not described by her pen. It was painted soon after her marriage, and was engraved (though very indifferently) for the No. of the "Cabinet," in which Mrs. Taylor's memoir of her appeared. This picture is certainly very charming, and is also admirable as a work of art.

Bright colours Mrs. Opie delighted in, and she had a sort of passion for prisms. She had several set in a frame, and mounted like a pole-screen; and this unique piece of furniture stood always in her window, and was a constant source of delight to her. "Oh! the exquisite beauty of the prisms on my ceiling just now, (she writes) it is a pleasure to exist only to look at it. I think that green parrots and macaws, flying about in their native woods, must look like that." Flowers, too, were her constant companions; she luxuriated in them, and filled her window-sills with stands of them, and covered her tables with bouquets; their most luscious scents seemed not too strong for her nerves. Light, heat, and fragrance, were three indispensables of enjoyment for her.

It has been said, with truth, that her mornings, during the latter years of her life, were spent in an almost constant succession of receiving visitors, and writing letters. Everybody who came to Norwich sought her; old friends, acquaintances, and strangers hastened to pay her their respects, and she loved to welcome all, and to give a cordial greeting to each. The extent of her correspondence was such, that it would have been a burden, had it not been a delight. In a letter written, in 1849, to her friend, Miss Emily Taylor, she said, "if writing were even an effort to me, I should not now be alive, but must have been *absolument epuisée;* and it might have been inserted in the bills of mortality—'dead of letter-writing, A. Opie.' My maid and I were calculating the other day, how many letters I wrote in the year, and it is not less than six in a day, besides notes."

Her pen was also diligently employed in writing articles for various periodicals of the day. She regretted afterwards that she had not kept a list of the publications to which she had sent contributions, as she was frequently applied to by friends, anxious to identify her verses, &c. The "reminiscences," to which reference has been occasionally made, published in Tait and in Chambers, were written about this time.

The year 1836 seems to have been unproductive of change. We find her recording visits to Keswick, to Northrepps, to Swanton Morley; and (as always) to Earlham. In the following year, her revered friend, J. J. Gurney, went on a religious visit to the United States, and was absent nearly three years. On his return he printed, for circulation among his friends, an account of this journey, "described in Familiar Letters to Amelia Opie." This interesting volume is very scarce, as only a limited number of copies was printed, and given by the author to his friends. This year Mrs. Opie mentions the arrival of Bishop Stanley and his family in Norwich, as "a great acquisition;" and their friendship proved indeed a source of much happiness to her.

The farewell letter from her venerable friend Lady Cork, written in the spring of this year, will be read with interest.

London, March 15th.

One thousand, eight hundred, and thirty-seven. Thanks dearest dear friend, for your cordial letter. Yes, thank God! 91 is quite well in health, and if my beloved friends enjoyed the same blessing, would be perfectly content in mind. Nephews and nieces whom you are not acquainted with, are suffering. They are folks whose virtues you must esteem, and some whose wit you would admire. Oh! why do you not come to town earlier in the season? Our dear Lady Frederick is not yet in town, but there are many of your playfellows. Yesterday dined with me, Rogers, Sydney Smith, Granby, and more wits and worthies, such as you would relish. * *

The picture of Hannah More is by Gainsborough; I think it a little like her; when she was young she could not afford to have very fine, *long, diamond* ear-rings; nor were they the fashion when I saw her flirting with Garrick; however, all the connoisseurs agree that it is an excellent painting. N.B. There is a ring on the wedding-finger, which does not resemble blessed Hannah.

Poets are springing up like mushrooms, but the novels are sad trash. Lord Carnarvon's new publication much admired.

Yours more than words can express, says,

OLD M. CORK.

A short note in her pocket book written by Mrs. Opie about this time, so much illustrates one of her peculiar excellencies, that we venture to give it.

J'ai toujours attaché une importance extrême à ce qu'on appelle vulgairement les petites choses; des attentions delicates, quand elles sont persistantes, prouvent la constante occupation de la pensée. "Take care of the pence, and the pounds will take care of themselves," says the proverb; and it is applicable to everything, I think, and particularly to human conduct, and the formation of character. Take care of indulging in little selfishnesses; learn to consider others in trifles; be careful to fulfil the *minor* social duties; and the mind, so disciplined, will find it easier to fulfil the greater duties, and the character will not exhibit that trying inconsistency which one sees in great, and often in pious, persons.

At the Spring Assizes (1838) Mrs. Opie was, as usual, in the Nisi Prius Court, she writes:—

Much did I enjoy it; one day I was there eleven hours, and all one cause, so that I could not leave it; the next day I was in from nine to seven again. Baron Parke was the judge, and an admirable one he is; and he was very kind to me, having a place saved for me, and I was admitted through the private room. I remembered *the days of Judge Gould.* Baron Bolland was equally civil, but to his court I could not get before the last day; and grandly beautiful does he still look, though he has had a paralytic stroke.

In July, writing from London, she says:—

I am here in perfect health, and much enjoying myself; yesterday we dined at S. Hoare's. The other day I went to call on the Miss Berrys, the wits and beauties of former days, at their cottage at Richmond, and they made me stay dinner, tempting me with Lord Brougham. I had really a delightful day!

The autumn and winter, however, brought returns of her malady, and her medical attendants said that she must expect such attacks, in which she acquiesced, saying, "no doubt I must." A confinement of some weeks to her bed-room, was found so irksome, that she gladly had recourse to an ottoman couch bed, on which she could recline, and receive her visitors, as she said, "in state."

The "Memoirs of Sir Walter Scott" were published at this time, and with deepest interest did Mrs. Opie peruse these records of one whom she had so much honoured and admired. Among her papers is one containing some remarks upon them, written shortly after, from which we select a few passages.

No pages of fiction, not even his own, ever excited in me more deep interest than did the sixth and seventh volumes of the Memoirs. I knew he was aware while writing his journal, that it would one day meet the eye of the world, and that therefore it must have been written with caution and under some restraint; yet, it had to me the charm of unfettered ingenuousness. There is through the whole of it a mournful reality, which I could not read without intense sympathy. It is a remarkable circumstance that he should have begun it almost at the time when he first had reason to suspect that his commercial engagements might possibly involve him in difficulties.

I own that in spite of the drollery, the bursts of jollity and mirth, the wit, the humour, and all its pleasing variety, the journal is rarely divested to me of the signs of secret suffering. It reminds me of the royal castle at Baden Baden, where all is splendour and gay decorations above, while beneath lie the deep dark dungeons, concealed from the eye of day, telling of the terrors of the secret tribunal.

After that awful year, 1825, marked in the commercial world by the ruin of thousands, the diary becomes more a work of art, through which nature still forces itself. He writes gaily, but feels more and more joylessly. Never after 1826 and '27, could any one fancy it, in my opinion at least, the journal of a happy man. Certainly he was not warmed by his own brilliancy, nor enlivened by his own pleasantries; and though it was a relief to him to write his journal, and it might be an accurate transcript of his own sad feelings, there was "a lower deep," a deeper current still, which he did not allow any human eye to penetrate, that was bearing him on its fatal tide, to imbecility and death.

I may be wrong, but I believe Sir Walter Scott's horrible dread of the trials hanging over him and others, had an instantaneous effect on his mind, and that his judgment was impaired, and his power of self-control gone, while his imagination and invention remained in full vigour.

Judgment is the quality which enables us "to decide on

the propriety, or impropriety of an action," and had not Sir Walter's judgment been weakened, he never could have sinned so much against propriety, (to use the gentlest word,) as to pen down so many oaths in his diary; but had the irritation of the moment led him so to err, he would have effaced the offensive words, and regretted his want of self-government, if his power of judgment had not been obscured. It his said he never swore with his *tongue*, but in his Journal he frequently swore with his pen, wounding alike the pious and the refined.

But, as I attribute this fault to an impaired judgment and a weakened power of self command, the consequences of his bitter trials, my conviction of the depth of his religious feelings remains undiminished. He somewhere says, that such was his fear of "becoming an enthusiast," that he was very careful over "the state of his mind," (or words to that effect,) whenever, while in a time of affliction, he was in "communion with his God"—a proof that such communion was well known to him; and I humbly trust that "lower deep" to which I have alluded, was illumined and cheered by that blessed influence which devotion is permitted to shed over the broken and supplicating heart. The satisfaction with which he listened to the Scriptures, his strong desire to have them read to him in his last days, and his parting words to his son-in-law, are chiefly valuable as indications of previous religious convictions, surviving, though in a shattered state, the wreck of mind; and are precious as are the broken pieces of carving from off some fine marble column in ruins, because they give evidence of its perfection in former days.

Early in 1839 Mrs. Opie visited her beloved friends at Northrepps, and on her return wrote:—

I had a pleasant journey home; found my page waiting with a fly, a fire in my chamber, and a "Sally-Lunn" cake and tea ready, and the last number of Nickleby, such a treat!

besides the *Evening Chronicle,* full of amusing speeches. I have much enjoyed my visit to you;

> A circle may be still complete
> Although it be but small!

That summer, one of these friends, Miss Buxton, died; and long and lovingly was she remembered. This event was followed by the death of her cousin, Mrs. Briggs, which occurred in the month of September, of the same year. Mrs. Opie was with her during her last hours, and her distress and grief at this painful loss were very great. She says;—"these are the trials which make lengthened life, or long life, so undesirable; but it is the Lord, let him do that which seemeth him good"

In the spring of 1840, writing to Miss Gurney, who was at that time in Rome, she says:—

My mind ever since your departure, has been dwelling on Peter and Paul; till I have quite convinced myself that, were I to go to Rome, my first desire would be to see the house where Peter lived, the place where he was crucified with his *head downwards,* and then the house where Paul lived with the soldier, and the rest of his *locale:* they both suffered in 66. I love Peter better than I do Paul; and I cannot read without tears those words of our Saviour, where He foretells his having to undergo a violent death. Peter, by his occasional lapses, seems to me to be the David of the disciples. * * * I am reading with delightful interest and edification a new "Memoir of George Fox," the introduction to it is said to be written by Samuel Tuke.

The month of June, in this year, was the time appointed for the Meeting of the Anti-Slavery Convention in London; the announcement of this proposed Meeting had excited great interest in the friends of Abolition, and more than four hundred delegates assembled on the occasion. Mrs. Opie was present, and among her papers is one giving an account of the proceedings in the first day's sitting, in which she enters at considerable length into the addresses of the various speakers, and the measures they proposed, and ends by saying:—

Thus concluded the first day's meeting, and if the benefits resulting from it be in any proportion to the intense interest which (as I believe) it excited in all who were present, then

Millions yet unborn may bless
The meeting of that day.

The introductory remarks prefixed to her account of the second day's sitting of the Convention are interesting, as they contain her own personal impressions of some of the actors in the scene, in short and graphic sketches, she writes thus:—

I entered the Hall of the Convention at so early an hour this morning, that I was able to obtain the same advantageous situation as on the preceding day.

By arriving so early, I was enabled to see each delegate take his seat, and I observed the entrance of some of the Americans with more interest than I did the preceding day, because I had learnt more of their personal history.

To Henry Grew my attention had been particularly drawn on the first day of the meeting, even before he had addressed the chairman; because the arrangement of his hair, and the expression of his countenance, realized my idea of the Covenanters of old, and his speech did not weaken this impression; therefore I was not surprised when I was assured, by a countryman of his, that he not only resembled in appearance one of those pious men, but that, under similar circumstances, he would probably have acted and died as they did.

But, till this second morning, I did not know, that in Wendell Phillips, the young Secretary with the pale golden hair parted on his open forehead, I beheld "the very young speaker" mentioned in the "Martyr Age" of America, "on whose lips hung, for the space of three minutes, the fate of the Abolitionists in Boston." The dark eyed, dark bearded, intelligent looking young Secretary opposite to him, was pointed out to me as being one of the fifty young men, students in the Lane Seminary at Cincinnati, in Ohio, who left that College, because the president and professors thought proper to prohibit all free inquiry among the students in their leisure hours, and had more particularly forbidden them to discuss the question of Slavery.

In J. G. Birney, the American gentleman sitting to the left hand of the President's chair, with the thoughtful brow, the dignified and manly bearing, and with an expression of calm deliberate firmness in his countenance, I now knew that I beheld one of whom his country might indeed be proud. He was once a slave-holder; but, being convinced, at an early age, that the religion of Jesus forbade him to remain so, he emancipated his slaves and had them educated; and when, on the death of his father, he became entitled to half of the paternal inheritance, he chose to take that half in the slaves his father had left; and when they became his, he emancipated them also.

"But who is that," said a friend to me, "with the dark, thick, curly hair, and a plain brown frock coat, who, though he looks somewhat like a Quaker cannot be one, because he answers to the title of Colonel?" "That is," replied I, "Colonel Jonathan Miller, from Vermont, who, though he looks like a man of peace, in some measure is, or has been, a man of war, as he fought for the Greeks at Missolonghi, and has in his possession the sword of Lord Byron. That broad, brown beaver hat of his, might be worn by a plain Friend; still, I must say that I have seen him wear it on one side, in a manner rather unusual in our meetings; but I have looked upon that hat with much respect, as well as on himself, since I have been informed that he wears it in order that a runaway slave in his own country may know, if he sees it, that he has a friend, and protector nigh."

It were tedious to enumerate all those whom I was now able to point out to others, and was interested in observing myself; among these, however, I must name the learned Professors Deane and Adam, and J. C. Fuller, an Englishman by birth, but now an American citizen; a delegate, whose short, but shrewd and pithy speeches often amused the hearers. Nor can I omit to mention, with more especial notice, Captain Charles Stuart, one of the delegates from Jamaica, with his fine picturesque head, covered with clustering curls of iron grey, and his deep toned powerful voice, sounding like a minute gun, when he rose from his distant seat, and said, "No," or "Chair;" but when he spoke at some length, his voice seemed to be a sort of musical thunder. He is honourably distinguished as being one of the most devoted friends of the oppressed. There was, sitting near this gentleman, one from Ohio, whom I had long known and esteemed; a tall, mild looking man, with finely chiselled features, and an expression which, in that convention at least, seemed often to denote he had less communion with earthly things, than "with things above." He, and the serious, sensible looking man beside him, a minister, and his colleague, came over to England more than a year ago, to plead in behalf of the Oberlin Institute: a blessing has attended their labours; and humble as their demeanour is, there were no men in that meeting more worthy to be welcomed by their oppressed countrymen, as friends and benefactors, than William Dawes and John Keep.

Mrs. Opie afterwards sat to Haydon, who was then painting his picture of the Convention. In the life of the painter we find the following entries in his diary:—

"(July 31st.) A. Opie sat, and a very pleasant hour and a half we had. (Again, the following day,) A. O. sat, a delightful creature; she told me she heard Fuseli say of Northcote, 'he looks like a rat who has seen a cat.'"

Mr. Haydon, as he looked at the assemblage of portraits in this picture, pronounced it to be his opinion that "such a number of honest heads were never seen together before."

The winter and spring were passed by Mrs. Opie much as usual. While suffering from occasional attacks of pain, nevertheless her constant thought and care were exerted in behalf of others. That she sometimes felt these claims too much, is evident from many of her notes. In one of them dated 3rd mo., 1841, she says:—

I am weary of having to give the little time I may have yet to live, to the business of others; it saddens me. (And again.) Two letters, involving me in writing and trouble; but be it so! it is a favour to be made useful to others, and my life here seems passing away in writing letters on others' business; well, the time may soon come, when I cannot work.

That this was not imaginary pressure, was abundantly evident to those who saw her day by day; and among her papers, after her decease, were found an inconceivable multitude of applications for charity, or acknowledgments of favours received, &c., &c.

During her customary visit to London this year, she wrote home:—

33, Bruton Street, Berkeley Square,
5th mo., 14th, 1841, night.

MY DEAR C. L.,

* * * * * * We had such a charming meeting at Exeter Hall last second day, (Monday,) Lord John Russell in the chair! it was the British and Foreign

School Meeting. I never saw or heard Lord John to such advantage, and all the speakers (except Clay, the M.P. for the Tower Hamlets) spoke exceedingly well; indeed Lord John was excessively applauded, and he felt it at his heart, I am sure. Even Burnet, the witty and sarcastic, was courteous on this occasion; and, with tact and courtesy, contrived, while returning thanks to the Duke of Bedford for his annual £100, and eulogizing the late Duke for the same, and the House of Russell generally, to let the audience know that the Duchess of Bedford was present, in one of the galleries; on which she was cheered and applauded, and had to rise and curtsey, and she was cheered again when she went away.

I have dined with Sydney Smith at the Bishop of Durham's, and breakfasted with him at Miss Rogers', (breakfasts are the *ton* now,) and he, Rogers, and Babbage kept up a pleasant running fire. I sat between S. S. and his more charming brother, and wished to hear the latter, but in vain. At my cousin Edward's, I sat by Lockhart, who is always charming in my eyes, and was then, particularly agreeable. To-day was the Anti-Slavery meeting, to which I looked forward with interest, mixed with dread; and not without reason, for Chartists were there, and some climbed upon the platform, and one was allowed to speak. The last speaker had to be silenced by a policeman; at length, generally called for, rose O'Connell, in his might and majesty, and the magical music of his voice hushed the jarring elements to peace. He is a marvellous person! But how I took myself in; I had a ticket for a side gallery, and I chose the one nearest to that side of the platform where O'Connell usually sits. Alas! when the *thunder* proclaimed his approach, I saw him come in at the other side. He never sat there before; and he had a lady with him, his own dear daughter. However, when he spoke, he came near the middle of the platform; but, had I been in my usual place, I should have always seen him and heard every word, which I could not do to-day. He certainly must have been ill, though he looks blooming; for he is excessively shrunk: but he looks all the better for it. He spoke admirably, but I thought his voice less powerful than usual. To-night he holds, at the Crown and Anchor, a meeting for Repeal. He said several unguarded things, but still the charm predominated.

I found a friend at the door when I went out, who took me to see the Reform Club House, that splendid erection, which will cost £70,000, and the first person I saw there was O'Connell! To be sure we had a cordial meeting and shaking of hands. He said he had seen me at the meeting, and I had heard him, as well as seen him. By the bye, Lucy, he would have made such a fine drawing! He had wrapt a cloak round his manly form; and his loss of flesh (of which he had far too much) makes his neck look longer; and his cheeks being less round, his face appears less flat; the nose is much handsomer than I thought it was. I reckon on hearing him again on the 17th, at the Aborigines' Protection Society.

On the 18th I dine at Lord Stanley's, (of Alderley,) and on the 19th Yearly Meeting begins, and will probably last nine days or ten. I have now been well some days. I threw physic to the dogs last week, and felt my lassitude go with it; and now, I trust, the fatigues of our Holy Week will prove none to me; but that it will be as reviving and welcome as the Holy Week, at Rome and Edinburgh, to those who keep it holy, and are, during its term, devoted to their duties.

Farewell! Please, Miss, to answer this.

Affectionately thine,

A. Opie.

Again, June 26th, she wrote:—

* * * I was at the House of Lords. The Queen's reading was more perfect than ever, and her quiet, self-possession, her grace and dignity, are beyond praise. She wore a circlet of diamonds only, no crown, and she looked so well! It was pretty to see Prince Albert hand her up and down the Throne, and lead her in and out. There were seventy-six Peeresses. It was a fine sight altogether.

In the spring of 1842 Mrs. Opie was again in London. Her notes give a lively record of the two months she spent there. Yearly Meeting she attended as usual; and on the 10th May she writes:—

I dined to-day in company with Lord Brougham, and sat between him and my cousin Edward; he was in high spirits, and talked incessantly and well, and was very entertaining and interesting: I never saw him pleasanter. We were, indeed, evidently so merry and happy at the bottom of the table, that those at the top sat silent, and endeavouring to catch the words that fell from the eloquent man's lips. Again. (6th mo., 11th.) Every night this week I shall have dined out, and in parties of a most agreeable description; of my visit to the Duke of Sussex, and our interesting *tête a tête*, I can't write. The Duchess shewed me all over the Palace, and the long row of Bibles. The room is fifty feet long, and the Bibles are in all languages.

Shortly after (June 24th) she wrote, referring to the general state of want and suffering then prevalent:—

Appeals to national generosity, for aught but national distress and starving populations, in our three countries, ought, in my opinion, to be now suspended, and speculations, however benevolent, also; we are, I think, accountable to our distressed countrymen for expenditures of the sort. The accounts from Ireland, which I read the other day, brought tears into my eyes.

This summer Mrs. Opie paid her usual visits to the coast, and, after her return home, we find in one of her notes the following entry:—

The weather seems so hot here! I pine almost for the fresh sea breezes. I like the book I borrowed, (Lives of Physicians,) it delights me to read how generous those great physicians were; how patriotic, and full of care for others! I feel proud of the faculty!

This is quite a characteristic touch. She was almost jealous for the credit and good name of the medical profession; and very anxious that its members should be held in high esteem, and their services liberally remunerated.

The winter of this, and the early spring of the following year, found Mrs. Opie occasionally suffering from her disorder; but enjoying the supports and consolations of christian faith and trust.

In one of her notes she says:—

My trials are afflictive to nature; but I have long known and experienced that there is support in entire submission to God's will, in little as well as in great trials; and, when I can buckle on that armour, I feel as if I could walk erect and securely.

In May she was, as usual, in London; and, writing thence, says:—

Yearly Meeting has engrossed me as much as ever, for I never missed *one* sitting since I obtained the great privilege of belonging to it; one which I feel more and more every year, is the last thing increasing age will cause me to forego.

In a note, dated July 12th, she says:—

I have struck up a friendship with "Sam Slick," alias Judge Haliburton; but, alas! one of the American delegates carries away with him a large piece of my heart! It is grievous to make acquaintances with people, learn to love and admire them, and then bid them farewell for ever! Almost all the American delegates, and their wives, came to me on the 10th, to tea and supper. I had Colonel Thompson, and Serjeant Thompson, and an Andalusian traveller to meet them, and willing to be pleased, they were so.

This summer seems to have been a very happy and busy one; the following extract, from a note, gives a peep at one of her mornings:—

(8th mo., 16th.) I have seemed lately to want for many necessary and proper purposes, the most precious of all things —time. Other people's business, and my own pleasures have prevented my writing before. At ten I must be out shopping; at eleven to the Magdalen; at two I must drive to see my aunt and say farewell! and then I am off to Ketteringham, to a five o'clock dinner, as E. Sidney lectures at seven.

At the close of the year, she suffered again from an attack of her old disorder. One of her latest notes, (12mo., 11th,) says:—

Alas! I am in my room still, forbidden to leave it. Dr. Hull attributes my relapse to my efforts of last week; I had hoped I was out of the wood, but no such thing. Long live Don Jorge! he is my delight both night and morning, and my happiest hours are spent in his society.*

The following letter of "Reminiscences" was written to her friend at Northrepps at this time:—

Norwich, 12th mo., 16th, 1843.

MY DEAREST. A.,

* * * * I will begin, if I do not finish my account of poor Thomas Hogg, in whose christian end I rejoice. I think it was in 1816, '17 or '18, that Lady Cork

* The "Bible in Spain" was published this year.

was full of a sort of holy man, a poet, whom she had picked up in a ditch, a poor, half-starved man, whom she and Mrs. B. invited to their houses, and fed and clothed; and Lady C. prevailed on him to come to London, and she made up a bed for him in her stables.

He did come, and his arrival was made known to me. He had written a poem on Hope, in heroic verse, and I was to see it. I think he was a hedger and ditcher, and made verses while he worked. I had, then, the worldly custom of receiving company on a first day morning, after I returned from church; and a full *levée* I had, consisting of persons on their way to the parks and gardens, whither, on that day, I never went myself. Well, my friends were beginning to come, on first day, when my astonished footman (a better sort of butler) came up to me, and said, "Ma'am, here is Lady C. has sent her footman with a man in a slop, who is, she says, to come up and see you." Quite right, (said I,) shew him up; and I told my wondering guests who was coming.

The poor man entered; he was a short, thick, middle-aged, ruddy looking man, clad in a very handsome slop of unbleached linen, very handsomely worked round the neck and at the wrists; and I received him very kindly, and seated him by me. Perry, of the *Morning Chronicle*, was one of my visitors, and some half dozen ladies and one or two gentlemen, who seemed inclined to laugh. Perry and Hogg nodded at each other, and P. said, "I have just been seeing Mr. Hogg at Lady Cork's; and Mr. H., I find has a kind of divining power—he knows who persons are, by their countenances. On the Countess of Mornington's (Duke of W.'s mother) asking him what he thought she was, he said she was, he saw, a woman of great courage. 'I am the mother of a *Hero*,' was her reply." Still I saw Hogg did not like Perry, and he soon interrupted him, saying to me, "I am come to read you a poem of mine, for I hear you are a poet—a poem on Hop." (I ought to say his dialect was quite new to me.) "Oh! by all means," I replied, "ah! a poem on *hops;* you are a Kentish man perhaps." "No," he thundered out, "on Hop,

Hop."—and I had then wit enough to understand he meant *Hope.* "Better and better, (said I,) where is your poem?" "I will go fetch it—it is outside the door;" and he went for it. When he was gone, Perry took his seat, by me, and we were talking of this strange visitant, when he returned, and instantly exclaimed to P. "that's *my* place;—what do you mean by taking it? get up!" and really, had P. resisted, it seemed likely that a blow would have followed the words; but Perry obeyed, and while Hogg was reading his manuscript, I went to the chimney-piece and took down a large bottle of lavender water, which, as it was a hot day, I carried round to the company, and then offered it to him also, to smell at. "No, no," said he, "if I took any it would be in a glass;" evidently taking it for a dram: and I had difficulty in keeping my guests from indecorous mirth; at last the poor man (in whose bright eye I thought I read more than incipient insanity) began to read; but with such difficulty, (for it was not in his own hand-writing,) that I humbly requested to be allowed to read it for him, and he consented; and I did read it, and really was surprised to find how good many of the lines were; and I own, I did improve some of them, when the measure halted, by adding words. He seemed much pleased, poor man, and we got through the whole. Some of the guests who were there at the first, stole away, 'ere I had done; and others coming in, I pointed them to a chair, while they listened, and looked, in utter astonishment! It was a scene indeed! When the MS. was returned, my servant came up to tell Mr. H. that Lady Cork had sent her servant to see him back to her house; "tell the fellow I will not go yet, and I can go alone;" and he re-seated himself. Not long after, came in my cousin T. A. The servant had told him Lady C. had sent a poor crazy man to me, and I could not get rid of him; so he hastened up, to rid me of the guest he supposed to be forced on me, by the Countess; but when I met him smiling, and told him Mr. H. had come to read me a pretty poem, he with difficulty suppressed a laugh, and sat down meekly. But soon after came up another message, "Madam, Lady C. has sent another servant for Mr. H., and says he must come directly!" "Must! I won't come; I know my way," was Hogg's reply; and the bard of Hope had almost thrown me into Despair—the despair of getting rid of him,—when I bethought me to try to convince him civility obliged him to go to Lady C., as I was sure she wished much to introduce him and his poem to others of her friends; and, at last, I prevailed on him to go, my cousin most politely seeing him downstairs. I saw him no more; and, I think, two days afterwards, the poor man, sick to death of London, and of being made a show of, took French leave, one morning early; and I believe he took with him both Lady C.'s gifts, the *blanket* and the *blouse.*

It was a pleasure to me, in after years, to read an account of the poor wanderer's having found pious friends in the last days of his life, and that he died the death of a Christian.*

* In the 23rd volume of the "Christian Observer," No. 1, there is a "Brief Memoir of Thomas Hogg," giving an affecting account of this poor and pious man's end: he died in great want, but full of christian hope and peace in believing. That he was no common man, is apparent from the few details there recorded. One remark he made may, perhaps, be deemed worthy of record here. The divisions unhappily prevalent in the Church of Christ, being lamented in his hearing, he said, in his native sprightly manner, "No matter, there are two sides to the river." Some parts of his Poem are given in the article from which we quote. He died at the age of 65, in 1818.—E.

CHAPTER XXIII.

DEATH OF MR. BRIGGS; SUMMER ASSIZES, 1844; "REMINISCENCES OF JUDGES' COURTS;" "REMINISCENCES OF GEORGE CANNING."

THE spring of the year 1844 was overclouded by domestic affliction. Mr. Briggs, the much esteemed relative of Mrs. Opie, had, for some time past, been suffering from pulmonary disorder; and as he expressed a desire to see her, she was prepared to expect the summons, which was not long delayed. On the 9th of January she wrote:—

I do so enjoy my home. In a morning I am only too full of company; but when at nightfall I draw my sofa round, for a long evening to myself, I have such a feeling of thankfulness!—and so I ought. It is well to see how the burden is fitted to the back by our merciful Father. I have been a lone woman through life; an only child! a childless widow! All my nearest ties engrossed by nearer ones of their own. If I did not love to be alone, and enjoy the privileges leisure gives, what would have become of me!—but I love my lot, and every year it grows dearer still—though parting with beloved friends throws, for a while, a deep shadow over my path. * * *

And even now the shadow was upon her. Six days after she writes:—

I go on my melancholy journey to-morrow, scarcely expecting to see my poor cousin alive; but he wishes to see me, and it is therefore my duty to go.

She remained with him to the last, and touchingly describes the closing scenes. When all was over, she said:—

Going into his gallery of pictures, where so many, alas! are unfinished, reminds me so powerfully of bygone days, when I stood in my *own* gallery, where finished and unfinished pictures abounded!

This melancholy visit was the last Mrs. Opie paid to the metropolis for a long period. During the next four years she was closely engaged in attendance upon her aged aunt, Mrs. E. Alderson, and seldom left Norwich for more than a few days at a time.

After her return home she wrote to Miss Gurney:—

5th mo. 7th.

MY DEAREST A.,

* * * I fear that I shall feel the loss of London and the Meeting, but at present I do not; for the duty and necessity of staying where I am, is more evident every day, because my aunt is become so dependent upon me, that I could trust no one to attend to her wants but myself. I have sent a large box full of repository purchases to M. G. to-day. I kept shop.* I have seen A. Hodgkin at Meeting and at the Grove; her husband had a public meeting last night, and has again to-morrow. *Such* ministry as J. H.'s last night is what is *rarely* heard, and never, I believe, but in a Friends' Meeting! It was soul-searching; and I only wished hundreds could have heard it. * * *

* This alludes to Mrs. Opie's keeping a table at the yearly sale of the Repository, for the Norwich Sick poor Society; this she did during many years, and an admirable saleswoman she was. On one of these occasions she wrote to a friend, "Simeon's Life is most precious to me. I have had extracts from it made, and printed, to be sold at the Repository."

Mrs. Opie was present in court, during the summer assizes of this year. She writes:—

I heartily enjoyed the Courts, the Judges, and the High Sheriff, and every part of my *entourage.* I was more in the Nisi Prius Court than in the Criminal; but the last morning I found myself let in, to hear a woman tried for poisoning her baby with laudanum. I should have fled instantly, had I not been assured, by the chaplain of the jail, and others, that, on the plea of insanity, she would be found not guilty; and, to my speedy relief, the Judge would not allow the trial to go on. By the bye, he is a very pleasing and clever Judge, (Williams,) and cordially humane; and, though a little man, he has a remarkable degree of dignity in his appearance and manner on the Bench; his eye, too, is very fine in shape and expression. In the year '20 I said to Sir G. Phillips, at a party at his house, "who is that little man in the window-seat, with those very fine eyes?" "That little man, it is expected, will prove himself a great man to-morrow; for he is the third counsel employed to defend the Queen, and his turn comes to-morrow morning." I then little thought I should see him here so frequently as Judge.

The other evening, while Baron Alderson and the High Sheriff and I were talking together, in the Judges' room, (they waiting for the other Judge's finishing a trial he was engaged upon,) Sir E. asked me how I was going home? on which the High Sheriff, seizing my hand, said, "Oh! she shall go with us, we will take her home." I drew back, of course, not believing he could be in earnest! but the Judge said "yes! let us take her." I still resisted, but Edward pulled me on, saying "come brother Opie!" as he tucked me under his arm; the High Sheriff led the way, and into the carriage I jumped, ashamed, but pleased; and I sat by my cousin, and the astonished chaplain sat opposite the Judge, wondering and laughing. We set the Judge down first, then the High Sheriff set me down, and went back for Justice Williams. Little did I think I should ever ride behind four horses, harnessed, and two outriders, with trumpets, &c.! But I must own that the Judge ordered the trumpets to remain behind, as they were not going in state, and to drive fast in order to come back soon. So much for the escapade of a grave Judge and High Sheriff.

Here is a note in which Mrs. Opie invited the writer to accompany her to the scene she afterwards described.

MY DEAR C. L.,

The Judges always, as I believe, go to church first, and take the sacrament afterwards. But I *always* go early, to be sure of a good seat, so I mean to call thee at nine, and we can talk there as well as here—and the time will soon fly! I went in a chariot-fly to see them come in. Farewell! little dear; I fear thou art a lazy-bones—but *indeed*—by ten I have often seen the best places filled. Often, *how* often, both as a young and old woman, have I been in that court by half-past seven in the morning—was this time twelvemonth.

A. O.

Among Mrs. Opie's papers left in an unfinished state, was one headed "Reminiscences of Judges' Courts," written in 1844. It was probably intended for publication, but never completed; in the following pages the reader will find the principal parts of it.

Hark! the bells are ringing their loudest, merriest peal, and at intervals are heard the deep tones of trumpets! Those sounds proclaim that the Judges have entered the city, and are about to open their Commission in the Court of our ancient Castle, and that the next day they will begin their momentous task.

Alas! I lament that the ringing of bells, which usually proclaims a wedding, and other joyful events, should be employed to welcome those who come to fulfil the painful office of sitting in judgment on their fellow creatures, and condemning many of them, perhaps, to long imprisonment, exile, or death.

Would that this custom were always discontinued, and trumpets heard alone; because the sound of the latter is *not* that of rejoicing, but of solemn preparation. It is *a call*, a summons, and one sometimes of fearful augury.

It is calculated also to excite in the minds of the prisoners salutary emotions, and prepare them for the scene that awaits them; while the joyful peal, which makes itself heard into their cell, drowning all other sounds, and seeming to insult their misery, calls forth in them feelings of indignant bitterness.

Let me add, that while the higher orders seem to consider the assize week as a time for public amusements, though many of the lower classes are undergoing every variety of anxious suspense, and some perhaps awaiting the terrors of the Law, the consciousness of this painful truth may have a hardening effect on the surrounding population, whose sympathies are with their poorer brethren at the bar, not with those in the theatre or the ball-room; and whatever has a tendency to excite, among the former, a belief that their sufferings are forgotten, or viewed with indifference by their superiors, may lessen that love and confidence in the higher ranks, on which so much of the safety of society depends.

That week has always possessed for me an attraction of an intellectual kind, which at present I still feel irresistible; I mean attendance in the Nisi Prius Court—a love for which has "grown with my growth, and strengthened with my strength;" and certainly it has not become weaker since I have had the gratification of seeing on the judgment seat a near and dear relative, and sometimes also a highly esteemed friend.

The interest excited by the Criminal Court is often painfully strong, even though such a blessed change has taken place in the penal law.

Horace Walpole (who hated capital punishments) says in one of his letters, that whenever he heard any one was being tried for his life, he always earnestly desired he might be acquitted; and so strongly do I compassionate the prisoner, that I never attend a trial for murder, and am only at my ease in the Civil Court. And there I am, at a very early hour, in order to secure my favorite place in it, and before any preparations for business are begun. Nor is it without interest that I look round the empty Hall, and at the large table covered with green cloth, where the barristers and attornies sit, and think that soon the vacant seats will be filled with busy, anxious life, and the stillness exchanged for the hum of many voices! and absorbed and amused in the contemplation of the coming scene, I find the time of waiting pass almost imperceptibly away. But at length the solitude ceases—the necessary preparations are made by the attendants, and soon the bells and trumpets announce the approach of the great functionaries. To greetings, and the hum of voices, succeeds the silence of expectation; for silent become the bells and trumpets; and, in another moment, the Judge is in the Court; the barristers rise, as he courteously salutes them, and the business begins.

After a short process, twelve jurymen are sworn in—to me a most disagreeable ceremony—though the oath is repeated now with less rapidity than it used to be; still I always rejoice when it is over.

The leaders now take their places—a cause comes on—the junior counsel employed in it reads aloud to the jury the particulars of the case. The leader then rises, explains and comments on its merits, artfully warning the jury against the eloquence and sophistical arguments which his learned brother will, he knows, bring forward for the defence; but which he is very certain of proving vain and nugatory by the witnesses whom he can, without fear, expose to the powerful battery of his learned brother's cross-examination. After a long and often eloquent speech, the counsel for the plaintiff calls his witnesses; by each of them, when called into the witness box, the oath is taken, and each in his turn is subjected to the fiery ordeal of cross-examination. Then rises the counsel for the defendant, hoping, and sometimes very justly, that cross-examination has shaken the testimony of the plaintiff's witnesses; he tells the jury that though his own eloquence has been so warmly lauded by his obliging and learned brother, he has himself too mean an opinion of it to presume to rest on *that* his client's cause; nor does he rest it on his arguments alone, though they are not sophistical, as his learned friend calls them. No! his only weapon will be the force of truth; for he shall bring forward *facts;* facts which he shall prove by witnesses, whose evidence not even his brother's well-known power of cross-examination can shake; and he shall also prove that, whether from unintentional inaccuracy in their statements, from defective memory, or an utter disregard to truth, the plaintiff's witnesses have borne testimony which was utterly *false;* he is *sure*, he says, to obtain a verdict for his client. Then comes "the tug of war," and such a view of the case is presented, that it changes, no doubt, the opinion of many minds, (my own, for instance,) and of the probable result we form a very different expectation to what we previously entertained. But the first speaker, having left himself a right to reply, then rises again; after having opened on the defendant's witnesses, the formidable field-piece of his cross-examination; and, that done, he is doubtless, not the less warm and powerful in argument, now that he feels his client's cause is in more danger than when he opened the case, and that for the last time he fights for ultimate victory; at length he sits down, expressing his certainty of obtaining it!

Oh! bloodless fights! would that we should never hear again of any battles but these!

But now another interesting period has arrived—the judge is about to speak: he has not been silent during the proceedings; but has made many observations, and asked questions of the witnesses on both sides; and now, much to the refreshment of short memories, he sums up the whole proceedings, and delivers his charge to the jury; going over every tittle of the evidence with surprising accuracy. The Clerk of Arraigns then says, "Consider your verdict, gentlemen!" the jury then turn their faces to the wall, and form so peculiar a group, that were an artist to draw them, no one could imagine, I think, what they were meant to represent, unless well acquainted with courts of justice. * * *

There are certain persons at the barristers' table, whose position is calculated to excite the sympathy of observers, and who have often awakened mine on their behalf; namely, the young lawyers, who have, perhaps, gone circuit after circuit, and still remain briefless barristers. This must be a painful situation; and I have been much gratified, when it has occasionally happened to me to see a usually unemployed barrister, with flushed cheek, opening, it may be, his first brief in that court, and, with beating heart, preparing to enter the legal arena. Gratifying indeed must it be, to a young man of talent, when at length some fortunate circumstance gives him the long-desired opportunity to distinguish himself, which was all, perhaps, that he required to rise in a short time to the head of his profession; and how enviable must be his feelings, when he looks back to departed hours, passed in vain expectation of business, sitting unobserved at that crowded table, making to himself employment by nibbing his pen, or cutting his pencil to write notes to a brother barrister, at a distance; and then, contrasts with that trying period, his present position, when he has scarcely time to sit, except when his opponent in a cause is speaking. Now, he is the "observed of all observers," and feels that on his skill in argument, and on his powers of elocution and persuasive appeal, depend, perhaps, the future well being and happiness of many of his fellow-creatures, who have entrusted to him the vindication of their rights, and sometimes of their reputation. Anxiety must indeed be felt by barristers on every circuit, even whether they have attained, or not, the greatest eminence; since it is as necessary for them to retain, as to gain, that eminence. The advocate, therefore, pleads for his own as well as his client's cause, when he puts forth all the energies of his voice, his gesture, and his mind, on the legal stage; and could address his audience in the words of the poet: "Alas! I feel I am no *actor* here!"

One of the attractions in the Nisi Prius Court is the agreeable surprises which one experiences in it. I have known a cause, promising at the beginning, to be very dull and uninteresting, become, as it went on, one of great interest and entertainment; for instance, a horse case, where the warranty of the horse is the subject brought forward, and many amusing witnesses are examined; or a right of way cause, as I believe it is technically called.

On such occasions I have seen the old, and even the infirm, put into the witness box to give evidence, neatly dressed in their Sunday clothes, and seeming to enjoy their temporary importance; and I have gazed with interest, which at length, perhaps, became painful, on the sharpened features, almost seeming prepared for death; and listened to the feeble voice striving in vain to perform the required task, and make the testimony it bore heard by the judge.

I have often asked myself why it is that I, and many others, can sit from early morning till evening in a court of justice, with still increasing interest? and the answer has been, that it proceeds from that general and enduring passion, the love of excitement.

Those courts are epitomes of human life, and their walls, within their bounded space, contain beings full of the passions, infirmities, resentments, self-deceits, self-interests, fears, hopes, triumphs, and defeats, incident to our common nature, and the proofs and results of which are there painfully brought before us.

A court of justice may be likened to a stage, the principal performers on which are the barristers; and happiest are they who have the most frequent opportunities of moving the feelings, and influencing the convictions, of that respectable audience—a British jury.

A Nisi Prius cause is a new drama, brought before the

jury as the audience; but with this great difference between a play and a cause—the actors in it, on one side only, are interested in its success.

One great advantage which assize courts possess over the theatre, is the certainty we have, that all the emotions we behold are real, not acted, and springing from the exigences of the moment; that the eloquent energy of the pleaders, the replies of the witnesses, and, alas! the fearful perjury sometimes elicited by cross-examination, together with every outbreak of tongue, are not only like the representations of great actors, "faithful to nature in the mimic scenes," but are nature itself!

There is another reason why, in my opinion, the interests in a Court of Justice come more forcibly to the heart than that of representations on the stage It is that, while contemplating the dramas of real life, as exhibited in a Court of Law, we have an undefined consciousness that we are liable to be ourselves, one day, performers in similar scenes, and worried by the same difficulties, experiencing, either in our own person or that of those dear to us, the trials and anxieties we see there endured by others.

My theories on this subject may be deemed fanciful and untrue, and the charge may be a just one; but, whatever be the cause of the pleasure which I take in attending Courts of Justice, I hope it is an innocent gratification, and no undue waste of time, as the opportunities occur only twice in the year, and rarely last longer than a week. It is also my conviction that whatever brings us acquainted with, and interested in the affairs and well being of our fellow creatures, in their varied stations and positions in society, may have a beneficial influence on our hearts, minds, and characters.

Another short "Reminiscence," which was written about this time, will show how her thoughts went back to the days of her youth, and with what tenacity her memory retained the most minute details of bygone scenes and events.

I was never (she writes) so fortunate as to be in company with that celebrated man George Canning, but at a very early period of his life and mine, he was brought, by circumstances, under my admiring observation. An aunt of his was married to a clergyman in Norwich, and lived there, and when he was at Eton he used to pass part of his holidays at her house.

He had already distinguished himself by his poetical talents, and the Eton boy had given promise of what the man might be. During one of his visits to his aunt, there was a benefit concert given at our Assembly Rooms, to which I was *chaperoned* by an old lady of my acquaintance. Till the middle of the first Act we were able to hear and enjoy the music, but then our attention was disturbed by the entrance of George Canning's aunt, with a large party. Unfortunately, they took their seats before us, and instead of listening to the music, began to converse, as if nothing was going on. I was not so much annoyed as I otherwise should have been, because I was told that the young man before me was the Eton boy, whose productions had been so much admired. I was, therefore, interested in examining his countenance, and was pleased to hear his voice, though exerted during a violin concerto!

But I shared at length in the displeasure of my companion, who, finding the predestined orator becoming more and more vociferous, gave him a rap on the shoulder with her fan, and when he turned round, astonished at the blow, shook her head at him reproachfully. He understood the appeal, and bowed his head gracefully and respectfully in return; nor did he offend again, but evidently reproved the talkativeness of his party. This delighted my old lady and still more myself. The feeling and well-bred youth, did not yet think he had made sufficient amends; and as soon as the Act was concluded he came up to my aged friend, and, with an ingenuous blush on his cheek, he said, "I am very sorry, ma'am, that I interfered with your pleasure by my talking just now, and am really ashamed of myself, pray excuse me; I assure you I will not offend again." The old lady received the apology as graciously as it was made; and my young heart rejoiced to find that this boy, in spite of the head-turning honours which were his at this early period, was possessed of, what a long life's observation has taught me to believe is almost the rarest quality, namely, a due consideration for the rights of others in *little things.* From that time he possessed a higher *niche* in my esteem, than his successes at Eton could have given him.

Many years elapsed before I saw him again; for though I became rather intimate with his aunt, he never visited at the house while I happened to be one of the guests; and at an early period of my life, the family quitted Norwich. But I saw him soon after he obtained a seat in Parliament, (1793,) and when the Pitt administration had won the young orator from his early political friends, and ranked him amongst their adherents. At the time to which I allude he was standing on Windsor Terrace, bare headed; his cheek evidently flushed with pleasurable emotion, and listening to George the Third, who, with the Queen, and the Royal Family, was taking his evening walk there. The Royal party stopped some time before the young member, and it was with an emotion of pleasure that I saw him thus publicly distinguished by his Sovereign.

The last time I beheld him, was in the Hall of Buckingham House, when the Queen and Regent received at that palace, and he was returning from a *levée.* With what increased interest did I then behold him; he was then in middle life, but I saw the same character of face, and features, as when I was interested in the Eton boy. How different was now his bearing; how different the character of his person altogether! There was a degree of dignity in his mien, and a loftiness in the carriage of his head, which a well-founded consciousness of his importance in the scale of society would naturally give, at the same time, there was a slight expression of sadness in his smiles; yet he might be justly called the child of prosperous ambition! His talents had raised him to the highest offices of the state; his eloquence was the delight of his friends, and the terror of his enemies; he had formed a high and happy connexion in marriage; he was admired by his opponents, and loved by his intimates; and it seemed as if this world could bestow on him nothing more!

But even then, the corroding cares of public life and their awful responsibilities, were, no doubt, preparing to fasten on his heart, and gradually destroy the functions of life. Stormy grew the political horizon during the years that ensued; though on the whole, he may be said (to use his own words) "to have weathered the storm;" and, at the period of his untimely death, he seemed to have overcome every prejudice against him; and when he fell a victim to his public duties, a universal lamentation attended his exit, and a universal plaudit!

Among his mourners, none was more sincere than myself, and rarely, even yet, do I pass his statue, without breathing a sigh to his memory, and exclaiming, as I gaze on that sculptured form, "Oh rare George Canning!"

CHAPTER XXIV.

THE SEVENTY-FIFTH YEAR; NOTES AND INCIDENTS, IN THE YEARS 1845-46; DEATHS OF MR. J. J. GURNEY AND OF DR. CHALMERS; LETTER FROM CROMER; DEATH OF MRS. E. ALDERSON; MRS. OPIE'S VISIT TO LONDON IN THE SPRING OF 1848; LETTER FROM THENCE.

MRS. OPIE was now entering upon her seventy-fifth year; confinement and pain were her portion during a large part of her remaining days; and yet, on the whole, she was remarkably free from most of the infirmities, bodily and mental, usually attendant upon such an advanced age. Her sight was perfect, and even excelled in keenness; so that she read without difficulty the finest print, and wrote in the same minute and delicate characters to the last. Her sense of hearing, too, though less acute, was not perceptibly impaired; and her carriage was as erect, and indicative of vigour and energy, as of yore. But it was her soul—the mind within her—that never felt the frosts of age. Her heart beat warm, her eye kindled with living joy, her spirit responded like a well-tuned lyre, to every breath that passed over it; and she was, too, such a very woman in all her sympathies and antipathies. Such quick sensibilities and vivid perceptions, such appreciation of little attentions, and cordial interest in that which touched the hearts of others—no wonder the young loved her! Perhaps, never were so many young and fair faces seen clustering around an old one, as were to be found in her room, week after week. They came, and made her their confidante;—and she liked so well to hear the tales, and to enter into the hopes and pleasures of youth!

Her love of fun,* too, her merry laugh, her ready repartee, made one forget that she had numbered three-score years and ten. If we should ask, whence came this bright and joyous old age? we may trace it partly to natural temperament; her nature was genial, her temper sweet, and, until a late period, her health was excellent. But, great as these natural advantages were, more yet was owing to religious principle, and self-discipline. She was not kind and forbearing merely because her temper was sweet: she was so on principle; in obedience to the great command of the gospel, "Love one another." Her readiness to pass by an unkind or slighting action, did not spring from easy indifference; none was more keenly sensitive to these things. When she was deeply wounded on one occasion, and could find no excuse for the offender, she looked sad and disquieted, and at length said, "I hope I shall be able in time to *forget* this." It pained

* She patronized the old custom of sending valentines, (which is much kept up in Norwich,) and on one occasion, wrote some droll verses, which she got copied and sent to some young friends, who, presently after, hastened with their puzzling *billet-doux* to her, that she might help them to guess who could possibly have sent them! She did so enjoy the fun of mystifying them with her guesses!

her to think otherwise than well of any one; it was a real *pang* to be obliged to believe that he had acted unworthily. She wept over the misdeeds of others, and rejoiced when they acted well and nobly. She was "tender-hearted" towards the failings of others, and *would* not believe an evil report. There was really nothing which roused her anger so much as for any one to spread a report to the disadvantage of another; it seemed an offence done to herself: and is not this the spirit of Christianity, akin to the "mind that was in Jesus?"

It were easy to give instances proving these to be no exaggerated statements. It may be permitted to mention one illustration of her humble-minded ingenuousness in acknowledging herself to have done wrong. The writer of these lines was one day calling on Mrs. Opie, when some one who was very deaf, and talked in a loud, harsh voice, was visiting her. After he had left the room, chancing to refer to something that had passed, she repeated the words of her visitor in his dissonant tones—in fact, mimicked him to the life! Almost immediately after reaching home, the writer received a note from Mrs. O., saying how much self-reproach she was suffering, in the thought of the "unchristian and vulgar action" of which she had been guilty, and begging it might be forgiven.

We have seen that the loneliness of her lot was felt increasingly, as her years multiplied, but happily, most happily for her, she was sustained by the consciousness of the Divine presence; and it was this which cheered her lonely hours, and inspired the sentiment with which we find her entering upon the new year; she thus writes:—

2nd mo., 4th, 1845.) I can say with truth that I am never *less* alone than when alone: home is becoming daily more and more the place that suits me best. I have many cares and some trials; but I feel, in the depths of my heart, that all is right; and that all has been, and will be, for my good. "Shall not the Judge of all the earth do right?"

This month occurred the death of Sir T. F. Buxton, causing another gap in the circle of Mrs. Opie's intimate friends. She had been long and greatly attached to him, and all his family; and cordially united in his views for the abolition of slavery, and in his desires and plans for the improvement of Africa.

During the storms of the winter, great inroads had been made at Cromer by the sea, and referring to this she wrote to her friend at Northrepps, at this time, saying:—

I am very sorry for that dear West Cliff,

"Where once my careless childhood strayed, a stranger yet to pain."

There used to be, I am sure, a field before one comes to S. Hoare's field, where I used to gather the blue bugloss, and deck myself out in it. Such is my love of Cromer, I sometimes think, when I lost my dear father, I should have settled myself there, or very near it, (on the West Cliff, most probably,) had I not joined Friends.

In the same letter she speaks of several books she was reading, and says:

* * * I have read two volumes, (the last two, I think,) of Lord Malmesbury's Diaries, and with intense interest. I knew so many of the men he writes about, and lived on the spot where they acted. But, be not angry, as well as surprised, when I tell thee, that, of the fourth volume, William Pitt is my hero, and eke George III; their characters and

powers come out there in such high relief! * * I am also reading Carlyle's history of the French Revolution—full of genius, pathos, and pictures; with all its faults, (and it has great ones,) still, I can hardly lay it down!

Shortly after, recurring to the subject of the weather, she wrote:—

I try not to be impatient of the duration of this winter, and I rejoice at the belief, (probably, however, an erroneous one,) that my *only* tree, an elm, in my south garden, into which my sitting room looks, is budding! It is a pain to me to think of the sufferings of inanimate nature, as well as of human nature. I grieve for the cruel sea's inroads at Cromer! But, as almost all things "work together" for some "good," these dangers give rise to circumstances, honourable to one's species; for instance, the pious child that would not be saved till his father's safety was secured. Generally speaking, I have long thought that in these days filial piety was at a low ebb; but, in this instance, assuredly, the high tides have floated it into my good opinion again. I am just returned from Earlham, where I have been passing a happy day and a half, with J. J. Gurney and Eliza; no other guest there but myself. We called at dear W. Forster's door on our way home.

Mrs. Opie made frequent visits, in the course of this year, to her friends; and mentions with peculiar pleasure meeting Mr. Hallam, during her stay at Ketteringham. Although occasionally suffering from accesses of her old disorder, she was, upon the whole, free from pain. Her notes refer to the great enjoyment she felt in attending various religious meetings, and also the course of lectures at the Museum, delivered by Professor Sedgwick.

On the return of the autumnal season her malady

distressed her much, and during her stay at Northrepps she was quite confined to the house; "never quitting it after I entered it, till I got into the carriage which took me away; but though unwell during the eighteen days I spent there, I had much enjoyment." In October of the following year, writing to her friend there, she said:—

Oh! how sorry I am that I cannot come to thee next week, even in a carrier's cart; but I cannot. Dr. Hull says "it would be madness;" and Mr. Crosse says, "he hopes my finger may allow me to go to Keswick;" but I have so much cold and cough besides, that I fear I shall not be able to leave the house at all. It *is* a disappointment to me not to have paid my usual visit to Cromer, and to feel there the gratitude due to Him who has in unmerited mercy spared me, that I might have been enabled once more to enjoy the society of my dear friends at that place, so full to me of early and pleasant recollections.

In the course of the summer of 1846 she was cheered by a visit from Mrs. Backhouse, the daughter of Mr. J. J. Gurney, (whom Mrs. Opie always called her grandchild,) bringing with her her infant son, who was greeted as great-grand-child, and pronounced a darling. "I love all babies," she said, "but this one excels them all in my eyes." Her cousin, Mr. R. Woodhouse, also visited her in the month of August. But amid all her cheerful and sympathizing enjoyment, she suffered grievously. A sorrowful note, written about this time, tells how much.

* * * You will be glad to hear I am better. This day week I was in great pain for hours! How thankful I ought to be; nothing can have exceeded Dr. Hull's attention; he

came twice every day to me; and I am sure his medicines have done me much good.

P.S. Sir R. Peel's heart has stolen *mine*; that exquisite self-oblivion, and that prompt sympathy with poor Haydon's sorrows, even only four days before his death: and then the feeling and immediate reply to the hopes of the poor suicide in his letter in his dying moments; and the prompt help, and the promised succour of his purse and influence at a future time, and when he (Sir Robert) was not himself lying on a bed of roses! Oh! he is a good, as well as a great man, and God's blessing must rest on him.

On the 4th of January, 1847, died Mr. J. J. Gurney. Three weeks before, he had been thrown from his pony, while crossing Orford Hill. At first he appeared not to have sustained much injury; and, with thoughtful love, he hastened to Lady's Lane to inform his dear friend of the accident, saying that he could not bear she should hear of it from any other but himself, that he might assure her with his own lips of his safety. Alas! how little did either of them imagine that ere that moon had waned he would be sleeping the sleep of death! but so it was. This was indeed a heart-blow; and, shortly after, his beloved daughter, Anna Backhouse, followed him to the grave. It was an entire breaking-up of the much and long-loved circle at Earlham. Mrs. Opie attended the funeral of her friend. She saw him laid low in the midst of his usefulness; cut down while there was, as yet, no shadow o'er his path to tell of coming night. Honoured and beloved he was, and a blessing to thousands. Doubtless in her heart she said, "would God I had died for thee!" but she remembered her favourite text, "shall not the judge of all the earth do right;" and bowed, and worshipped in silence and submission.

There is no dwelling on these things. Each one, as he passes along on the road of life, experiences like sorrows, and learns from his own trials to realize the feelings of his fellow sufferers.

The following note, written shortly after this event, shews her state of mind.

Norwich, 1st mo., 29th, 1847.

My dear C. L.

* * * * Thanks for thy kind inquiries, and still more for thy graphic description of the Cambridge show; it made me long to have been there! thy account of the behaviour of the students carried me back to 1810, when I was at Oxford, at Lord Grenville's installation, and was excessively amused by the thundering and hissing of the students for some time; but the third day I grew tired of the noise. The Proctors *there* were treated, one excepted, with great indignity. How I did rejoice in the first wrangler's success; when I found he was a boy of obscure birth, educated by a benevolent individual on whom he had no claims, and that he had been enabled to repay his benefactor!

The dear Bishop came yesterday afternoon, and was so kind and sympathizing! I *could* see him, for I was in my drawing-room again. My doctors are just gone. I hope I am improving, and expect to be allowed to get out next week to see my aunt; but I shall be slow in returning my calls, and slower still in paying any visits. I do so *dread* the convincing myself, when I go out, that there is one whom if I look for him, I shall never, *never* find! But no more of that, I can't bear it.

Believe me, thy ever attached friend,

A. Opie.

Her grief did not, however, prevent her taking an active interest in the sorrows and sufferings of others. She was engaged in collecting for the relief of the poor Irish, and says:—

Oh! the horrible state of things in that country; without our aid they say the poor people must perish! I am collecting for the Ladies' Committee at Dunmanaway, near Cork; a very distressed district, but small and with few rich residents in it, therefore the more needing help. I let no day pass without having, in the course of it, begged of some one. I take sixpence or a shilling with thanks; and I have accepted twopence from a little boy, who sent it to me because he knew what it was to be hungry himself. I have a humble agent at work to procure small sums, as my Irish ladies advise; and have a little money still in hand, which I hope to make more. We shall one day perhaps know scenes here like those in Ireland, and trials which *wealth* cannot help us to avoid or remove, but "shall not the judge of all the earth do right?"

In the spring of this year Mrs. Opie paid her usual visit to Cromer. While there, the tidings of Dr. Chalmers' death reached her. She wrote home requesting to have the lines she had addressed to him in 1833 sent to her; and acknowledged the receipt of them in the following letter:—

TO MRS. BRIGHTWELL.

Cromer, 6th mo., 5th, 1847.

MY DEAR FRIEND,

* * * I do not exactly know to whom I was indebted for the great kindness of copying for me my lines to poor dear Dr. Chalmers,* but perhaps the same pen

* The lines alluded to in this letter are given in chapter xx. Mrs. O. had forgotten that she had written them until reminded of them by her friend.

(it was thine I think) would do me the same favour again. I am very desirous of having them, though ashamed of troubling thee.

Poor dear man! on his way home to Edinburgh he could not be easy without going to Darlington, to see dear J. J. Gurney's daughter once more. In his letter to me he said that he hoped one day "to see him *before the throne*," or words to that effect; how soon (as I trust) the hope has been fulfilled.

I am here in such a lovely lodging! my sitting-room has a bay-window that looks *on* the sea and *up* the shore and on the jetty and the breakwater. I am at Randall's bath house, and the hot bath is delightful indeed! I think I am better, in spite of visitors. I have had eleven callers already, since ten o'clock!

When I came, the sea was beautiful! yesterday it was awful to look at! the white horses, the cavalry of the sea, were all out yesterday. Alas! their appearance was signalized by death; a boat was capsized, and a poor old man drowned, in sight almost of my window. At twilight I looked on the sea, which appeared terribly sublime! The hue grew darker and darker, as the mass of waters seemed sloping *upwards* as they went, till they looked like a dark mountain bounding forth to engulph us—and I retreated almost in fear. I hope this evening to see the sun set from the western cliff. How beautiful, in my eyes, were the hedges as I came! such a profusion of germander, bright red bachelor's buttons, the golden furze, and broom, in luxuriant blossom, and the may, only too much laden with flowers; Farewell; with love to thy spouse and bairn,

Thy attached friend,

A. OPIE.

Mrs. Opie returned from Cromer in the middle of June; in her notes we find the following entries:—

I am come home, not the better for the sea and baths, though *much* so in mind and feelings for the great attentions and kindnesses I received. A lame old woman is, however, best at home. Poor dear Dr. Chalmers! he passed four or five as happy days as he *could* pass there, with the daughter of J. J. G.; he would not rest without going, and was so charming! he died two days after. He left Darlington well, but went home as it proved—to die! He was every day, when there, going to write to me, and I was just about to write to him, from Cromer, when he died. (6th mo., 18th.) In the year 1809 I began to write lines to Mrs. Lemaistre, on her birthday, and ever since, from 1809 to the fifth of this month, 1847, I have never omitted writing the accustomed verses. I wonder whether any king's laureat ever wrote so many to one potentate; perhaps Colley Cibber did to George III. (19th.) I have been reading the life of Sarah Martin; it made me shed many tears, from the sense of her superior virtue, and my own inferiority. What an example she was, and how illustrative her life, of what that of a humble, but real, and confiding Christian should be! and her end was one of intense bodily suffering! as Pope says of some one:—

> "Heav'n, as its purest gold, by torture tried—
> The saint sustain'd it, but the *woman* died!"

W. Allan's admirable Life I have read quite through, with delight, and, I hope, instruction.

Mrs. Opie visited her friends at Brooke in the following month, and writing shortly after to Miss Gurney, she says:—

* * * I received, before I went to Brooke, a very valuable present from Lord Brougham, which he had ordered to be sent two months ago, and I expected. It arrived at last, and is a folio volume, two nails thick, containing the evidence before the select committee of the House of Lords, appointed to inquire into the execution of the criminal law, especially respecting juvenile offenders and transportation. It interests me, and I daresay I shall read it through. When I came home I found a very interesting letter from Lord B.—

that letter I am answering to-day. I am glad he has renewed correspondence with me; he often wrote during last autumn, and he is one of the pleasantest recollections of my early days, when I was first in London society.

My head is full of this horrible, *most* horrible of murders, at Paris! I am glad I do not know the parties concerned. I earnestly hope that if he must die, he will be allowed no privileges on account of his rank; the people would not bear it! and the Most High "is no respecter of persons." We purse-proud English are a sadly aristocratic nation, and want humbling. * * * If my aunt's health allow, I intend to go to the Birkbecks' ere long for a few days, but yesterday I conceived an alarm concerning her, poor dear, and I must talk to her medical man on the subject.

This alarm proved to be well grounded. Mrs. E. Alderson sank gradually, and at length expired on the 10th of January, 1848. Mrs. Opie says:—

When I looked upon my dear aunt, just after I had closed her eyes, she was, to me, the image, almost, of my father.

The time was now come, when Mrs. Opie was able to carry into effect an intention she had long entertained. She felt very desirous to have a house of her own; it had become, indeed, necessary to her comfort; and, after long consideration, at length she fixed upon the house on Castle Meadow, which she inhabited during the remainder of her life. Before removing, or rather preparatory to doing so, she went up to London, to spend some months there, according to her old usage. Four years had elapsed since she visited the Metropolis, and the present occasion proved one of much enjoyment. She bade adieu to Lady's Lane on the 6th of April, and journeyed to town, availing herself there of the cordial invitations given her by her friends in Russell Square and Langham Place.

Much occurred, during her stay, to interest and cheer her, of which she wrote accounts to her friends at home. She made short excursions to Hampstead, Hornsey, Wandsworth, and Tottenham, and went to hear the speeches at Harrow. She also attended all the Friends' Meetings, and was present as well at the Missionary and Bible Meetings, in all which she took a lively interest. Her letters shew that she still retained much of her wonted energy, and interested herself in the stirring events going on around her. In one of them she refers, very characteristically, to the alarm excited by the threatened outbreak of the Chartists —

I *would* come home (she says) from Wandsworth on the Sabbath day night, because I could not bear the anxiety I should feel while being six miles from the scene of action on the Monday. How agreeably disappointed every one was who was not disaffected! Nothing ever was better managed: and I hear that the Duke of Wellington was so delighted because all was effected without a single soldier's having been seen! but great was the alarm, particularly of the Ministers. It is now clear that the respectable middle classes are *not* with the ultra chartists. It was an interesting sight to see noblemen and their sons, artizans, and men of all grades in society, sworn in as special constables, and patrolling the streets.

The following letter is selected from among others, written at this time, as being of most general interest:—

TO THOMAS BRIGHTWELL.

Russell Square, 5th mo., 22nd, 1848.

MY DEAR FRIEND,

I have been intending to write to thee for some time past, but was prevented. My career has been a very pleasant one, spite of occasionally *great* lameness; but though

I always limp, I am not always in pain; and I find it possible to bear, with patience, the ill which can't, I fear, be ever cured.

I will, as briefly as possible, give thee a sketch of my goings on; a dinner at Lord Denman's was my pleasantest; I met Lady C. L., Lord N.'s daughter, a dear old friend of mine; Mr. Justice Earle, the new judge; and Mr. Warren, the author of "Ten Thousand a Year." These gentlemen and my host talked *across the table* and most pleasant were the dinner hours, as well as those which succeeded. * * * More of this when we meet, if I am permitted to return in health and safety. The next prosperity, was, my going to a private view at the Society of Arts and Sciences, in the *Adelphi,* where Barry's pictures were lighted up, and the rooms opened to receive so many and *no more;* that is, twenty noble Ladies got leave to have so many tickets each, to give, in order that the wonderful and beautiful specimens of new English arts and manufactures, might be seen and known, to those able and willing to purchase; and it was to be, that unusual thing, an evening private view, beginning at ten o'clock. My kind friend, Lady C. B., gave me a ticket, and after *hours* at the Bible Meeting, and a dinner at Baron Alderson's, I went to the place of rendezvous; I was the first person there, so I could survey all the lovely things, and exquisite pictures, long and well known to me, before any one came: but the room filled at length, and the Bishop of Norwich told me he never saw more of the nobility assembled. I saw many old acquaintances and made many new * * *

Once, as I was walking round the room, the Duchess of S., leaning on a gentleman's arm, curtsied to me, (for the first time in her life,) with a most sweet smile. I acknowledged her curtsey, regardless of the gentleman with her, and, indeed, not seeing him; but he said, "what! do you not choose to see and acknowledge an old friend?" I started, and beheld Lord Morpeth! Surprized, and thrown off my guard, I exclaimed, "Oh! *dear* Lord Morpeth! how glad I am to see thee!" eagerly accepting his proffered hand. "Then you have not forgotten old times?" * * * I then told him

I had heard him speak in the morning, and we talked of the meeting, as very interesting: "but," I said, "I thought it was rather *venturesome,* if I may so say, to allude so much to the state of affairs in France." He gave me a look I did not quite understand, but replied, "perhaps there was somewhat too much of that;" and I was told by the Bishop of Winchester, (with whom I dined the next day) that Lord M. in his speech, had *given the tone* to the other speeches; but Lord M.'s speech was not such, as to have drawn forth what I disapproved,—the speeches of La Harpe, and others; however, everything was approved by the meeting, and the French goings-on *delighted* in, as leading to an increased spread of the Bible! We then talked a little more, and parted Lord M. insisting on it, that I used to be at Milcham School with Mathews, the great ventriloquist, and I saying, "no, no, I disown Mathews entirely!" Long have I wished to renew acquaintance with this *good* man, and at last I have, under pleasant circumstances. At the B. and F. School Meeting, where he was chairman, I sat nearly under the chair, and had a most kind bow from him, which I as cordially returned.

Last sixth day (yesterday week) I dined at Sir J. Boileau's, and met Guizôt, the American Ambassador, and our Bishop. After dinner, we all went to the Royal Institution, to hear a Lecture on the Greek Anthology, by a Mr. Newton, and I had the pleasure of taking the Bishop with me, in my carriage.

Lady C. B. and I sat on a form near the lecturer; in front of him was another chair, for the President, the Duke of Northumberland; and on a chair, placed on his *right* hand, was Guizot; on his left the American Ambassador—*par conséquant,* we conceived this was meant as a compliment to Guizot, who seems much noticed. The private view of the Exhibition I rejoiced in, till the people came, (but I believe I wrote an account of all this to Lucy,) Sir R. Inglis followed up his kindness to me there, by calling; and Lady Gurney, myself, and Russell, were there this day week; a most pleasant evening to me, for I met old friends, and among them, the British Minister, Morier, and his family, whom I first knew at Paris, as Consul-General, and afterwards, as our Envoy at *Berne*.

Now, to finish with my visit at Claremont. The ex-Queen fixed the day and hour, by Madame de Montjoye, her Lady; I hired a clarence and two horses, and borrowed J. Bell's servant; and, in a broiling day, set off on my fifteen miles' journey! Madame de M. came to me *first*, and said the Queen would soon come to me; she did, and I cannot express my feeling, when I thought of the change in her position since we met! I could scarcely speak, while she pressed my hands most affectionately, and called me "*ma chère, bonne Opie, que vous êtes bonne, de venir me voir!*" at last, she sat, and desired I would do the same. Madame de M., had previously told me they had heard of the Duchess of Orleans that day, and that she was in Germany. I can't *now* tell you all the conversation. The first question was, "I hope you are writing? you know I read and like all you write." I replied that I did *not* write, and so on. * * * After half an hour, she rose, and said she was very sorry to go, but she must, because she had letters to write, which were to go to Paris that morning; again she took my hands and pressed them to her heart; I not being able to speak, from rising tears. At length I got out, that "*les paroles me manquoient et que je ne pouvais pas exprimer les sentiments que j'eprouvois;*" and I almost wished to kiss, as well as press the hand I held; as she disappeared, she said, "*souvenez vous, et ecrivez encore, ecrivez toujours!*" Madame de Montjoye gave me her arm, to the other room, and we parted most cordially. * * *

Thy attached friend,

A. Opie.

Mrs. Opie's stay in London was cut short by her increasing indisposition. She had prepared to go on a visit to Mr. S. Gurney, when (on the 7th July) she had a severe access of her disorder, and Sir Benjamin Brodie recommending rest and quiet, after a week's nursing, she returned to Norwich.

CHAPTER XXV.

THE CASTLE MEADOW HOUSE; INDISPOSITION; INCREASE OF CRIME; RUSH'S TRIAL; SUMMER ASSIZES OF 1849; DEATH OF BISHOP STANLEY; SUMMER AND AUTUMN OF 1850; FAREWELL VISIT TO LONDON; THE GREAT EXHIBITION; SUMMER OF 1852; RHEUMATIC GOUT; NOTES; LAST VISIT TO CROMER; THE SPRING AND SUMMER OF 1853; SUDDEN ILLNESS, OCTOBER 23RD; PATIENCE AND CHEERFULNESS; INCREASING SICKNESS; LEAVE TAKING; DEATH.

RETURNING from London on the 14th of July, 1848, Mrs. Opie took possession of her new house, on the Castle Meadow. She looked back with pleasure upon the time she had passed in town, and said, "never indeed, did I have a more gratifying reception, than I met with from all my friends, of different ranks, this time of my being there." Fortunately her choice of an abode proved satisfactory, she thoroughly liked it from the first, and conceived the happy idea that Dr. Alderson would have been pleased with it, "for (she said) he would have enjoyed this lively scene, and he often wished to have a house in this locality." When she had become quite settled in it, she wrote:—

* * * * I am every day more charmed with my new house and home. I feel it a very desirable house to die in, that is to be ill in; a "pleasant cradle for reposing age;" and I do so love to look at my noble trees and my castle turrets rising above them; and when the leaves fall off, I shall still have

the pleasure of seeing the green and grassy mound of the Castle. From one of my drawing room windows I see the woods and rising grounds of Thorpe. I neither hear nor see the cattle on market days, and I am quite happy in my choice, and deeply thankful that "the lines have fallen to me in pleasant places." Indeed I have no *désagrémens* at all, that I am conscious of, in my new abode.

In the month of October, Mrs. Opie made a short stay at Lowestoft; but the fatigue brought on a return of her malady, and in one of her notes she says:—

I came from Lowestoft apparently well, but soon became ill, and was obliged to send for Dr. Hull, who was, at first, alarmed at my symptoms; but I was not, as he kept his fears to himself. My sufferings were great indeed, and I never was so conscious of his judgment, as while observing the truly efficacious manner in which he treated me. I rallied directly, and was able, with his leave, to go to Sir J. Boileau's to stay two days and nights. I was charmed with M. Guizot, who was one of the guests; his manners are very simple, and he played at "*jeux de societé*" with us *young* people, at night, and enjoyed it as much as we did! It is, indeed, a great favour to be permitted to enjoy life still, so much as I do, in company; but it is a far greater one to be able to enjoy equally my lonely hours. * * * How fearful is the state of things on the Continent, and who knows what the result will be? but I read the 46th psalm, and remember who reigneth, and I trust in Him, and am at peace.

At Michaelmas, of this year, Mrs. J. J. Gurney left Earlham Hall for the Grove, and before she removed, Mrs. Opie went over to take a last look at the place which was endeared to her by the recollections of so many bygone years. During the two years longer that Mrs. Gurney remained in England, Mrs. Opie had the comfort of her society, and it was with sorrow that she bade her farewell when she departed for America, in the summer of 1850.

A note, written shortly after this time, refers to the fearful crimes which were committed during that autumn. She says:—

I heard, at that *blessed* City Mission meeting, which I attended the other evening, that our county is reckoned one of the worst for crime and ignorance. Now comes that murder, by wholesale, at Stanfield, and every week I read of two or three murders. Still, as Dean Swift sarcastically wrote,

"And hell, to be sure, is at Paris or Rome,
What a blessing for us, that it is not at home."

France and Ireland do not, I think, much suffer in comparison with us. Truly, we English improve rapidly in virtue!

Mrs. Opie, latterly, took a somewhat morbid view of the existing state of things, supposing that instead of improving they became worse. She read the daily papers, in which the same crime is repeatedly brought to notice, week after week; and became possessed with the idea that murders and horrors were multiplied in proportion to the publicity given them. In the month of March she went to visit Miss Gurney, and returned from Northrepps on the morning of the Lent assizes, when Rush's trial came on. She did not attend on that occasion, adhering to her constant determination, never to be present in the Criminal Court in a capital case. But in one of her notes she gives a lively picture of her feelings while the trial was going on:—

I know not what to do to-day except look at the castle and watch the crowds on the plain, and the people continually passing, few walking, but most running, as if too much excited to do otherwise. Rush is on his defence! * *

I dread to hear the verdict, and yet I wish all was over. (The evening of the second day.) On my castle turrets, to the west, the sun set gloriously this evening, converting it into a mass of red granite; and while I write the moon is shining into my room, "looking tranquillity." But what is passing within those castle walls? A man, fierce as a tiger, is struggling for life at the awful bar of justice. * * * *

What hundreds are passing to and fro; and what various sounds I hear! now children and boys laughing and shouting; then men, congregated under my windows, and talking: but always, within those walls, *I* see that wretched man, writhing in mental agony, and against what, I fancy, he now *believes* inevitable doom!

In the Summer Assize Mrs. Opie was in her usual place in court, and with how much lively interest she watched the proceedings, is evident in the following letter:—

Castle Meadow, 8th mo., 4th, 1849.

Well C. L. how art thou? * * * * and so thou hast trodden where Robin Hood did! He was one of my heroes when I was young; and at sixteen, when driving through Sherwood Forest, I insisted on getting out, to walk through it, and tread where he and his merry men had trodden. Thy papa has been very kind to me; he gave me his arm, and saw me safe home, when I walked, two evenings together, from the Shirehall, where I, the poor, limping invalid, (no *appropriate* name that,) was, from nine to six, on the sixth day, and from nine to nine the following day; that is, twelve hours on Saturday, and without refreshment of any kind save two gingerbread cakes; but I wanted nothing, so completely did mind conquer matter. It was *one* cause only which lasted from twelve on Friday, to six that evening, and the next day from nine to nine; and so interesting it was to me, my attention never flagged a minute, and when I got home I was quite as able and bright as when I went into court. It was Lord W. Poulett's action against our Railway Company for damage done to his property and his tenants', by the fire emitted from the train. I never saw a clearer case proved. I had no bias either way; if I had any leaning it was to the Norwich persons, the defendants; but I felt sure the verdict was a just one. It was for the plaintiff. The fire may be kept in, but they must take more trouble and go to more expense; and I believe this action will save property if not *lives.* Byles spoke admirably, and the judge was excellent also. I assure thee this calling up of all my energies has done me great good. Except in my lameness, I am as well as ever I was in my life; and at the Palace, the other evening, (last Wednesday,) I walked across that room, and to my fly, hold of Arthur Stanley, and did not limp. I heard thy father's voice last evening, but did not see him; for I was just getting into bed at nine o'clock: but the last time I saw him, he walked off, at half-past ten o'clock, from my house, with a pretty young lady hanging on either arm, to their hotel. I was at Paris when the sister of these ladies was married, and was present at the wedding, and a pleasant sight it was. The marriage took place at the ambassador's chapel, and the bride and her husband were a sight to see, as they knelt before Bishop Luscombe, picturesque from his fine face and large sleeves!

It is, to my feelings, so cold a day, that I am sitting by a large fire in my smaller drawing room * * * * There, my letter is longer than thine, and I have written four besides this, so hasten to conclude.

Thine faithfully and affectionately,

A. Opie.

In August Mrs. Opie spent a week in Cambridgeshire, visiting some kind friends at Melbourne-Bury, and returning home shortly before the lamented death of Bishop Stanley. This was a grief which, (as she herself expressed it,) cast a shadow over the remainder of her days, and to which she could never refer without deep emotion. How many hearts grieved when the solemn sound of the bell announced to the inhabitants of the city this melancholy event! Every one felt that it told of a general loss, and that a good and holy man had been taken from amongst them. And when, in compliance with the wish of the honoured and beloved prelate, his remains were brought to rest in that cathedral where his voice had so often been heard, there was a mournful satisfaction in the conviction that his heart had loved the people for whom he had laboured, with an unfailing charity, and with a ceaseless zeal.

Several references are made in Mrs. Opie's notes to this event. At the time it happened she was surrounded by a large circle of her relatives, and while they remained with her she said—" I was taken from myself; but now regret is uppermost again. How I feel for the dear bereaved ones!" Again she says:—

(9th mo., 20th.) * * I cannot reconcile myself to this great loss to me; and as yet can scarcely believe I am awake and not in a delirium. I can't believe he can be gone for ever! he came to take leave of me, and I am recalling all his looks and words. I followed him to the top of the stairs; he said he was to be gone a month, and that he wanted *rest*—and I would not call him back if I could; he was weary, and is gone to his rest—the rest of the people of God.

In the course of this autumn Mrs. Opie paid several short visits to her friends in the neighbourhood of Norwich; the last of which was to Keswick Hall. On her return home she was attacked with a severe inflammation of the right eye, which caused her much pain, and compelled her to sit in a darkened room. During this confinement, (and indeed during the latter period of her life,) she was much indebted to the kind offices of her friend, Miss Brownson, who was indefatigable in reading to her, and otherwise ministering to her comfort.

On the 6th of April, (1850,) Mrs. Opie went to Lowestoft to spend a few days with her young relatives, the children of Mr. Briggs; and this visit she spoke of with much satisfaction. On the 25th she proceeded to Northrepps, where she remained until the 16th of May.

At the Midsummer assizes, Baron Alderson and Mr. Justice Patteson being on the Norfolk circuit, Mrs. Opie went into court, accompanied by some of her relatives; and, not being able to walk, (from her increased lameness,) was carried in a sedan chair. It was her last visit to that court in which for so many years she had been present! She did not neglect on this occasion to make her usual offering of a bouquet to the judge.

In September she attended the Annual Meeting of the Bible Society in St. Andrew's Hall; and in November she was present at the meeting of the City Mission. These meetings cheered her spirit, and she "closed another year very happily."

In 1851, after a visit at Keswick, Mrs. Opie, on the 7th of May, travelled to London, and took up her residence with her friends in Russell Square. During her stay she attended several meetings at Devonshire House and Westminster Meeting, and paid numerous visits to her friends and acquaintances. She felt that it was her *last* visit, and seemed desirous to take a farewell look at all her old haunts; she would go to the various shops she had been wont to frequent, and at every turn was met by some one who recognised and welcomed her. (At Swann and Edgar's she saw the Duchess of Orleans.)

Her visit to the Great Exhibition was quite a delight to her. She was among the few privileged persons who, from age or infirmity, requiring chairs, were admitted an hour before the usual time. She saw there many whom she knew; among others, her very old acquaintance, Miss Berry, also in a wheel-chair. Mrs. Opie's carriage attracted the notice of her friends, by its superiority. The wheels had a coating of Indian-rubber, and sprang forward at a touch. At length Miss B. exclaimed, "where did you get that chair Mrs. Opie? I quite envy it;" on which Mrs. O. playfully proposed a chair race! After the public were admitted, she remained sitting in the Transept an hour, enjoying the sight of the many hundreds who rushed in; among whom were several of the Society of Friends, and others known to her, who gathered around her chair and cordially greeted her.

Mrs. Opie left Russell Square on the 19th June for Ham House, (Mr. S. Gurney's,) where she staid two days. Her homeward journey was rendered uncomfortable by some derangement of the railway engine; so that they were twice stopped on the road, and had to change carriages. On arriving safely at home, she expressed her gratitude for journeying mercies; and added, "these alarms have been warnings to me, that in my infirm state I must not venture on the line again. So, railway, farewell!"

In the course of the autumn Mrs. Opie paid short visits to her friends in the neighbourhood of Norwich, (at Berghapton, Ketteringham, Brooke, and Keswick,) and, though almost constantly in pain, was bright and cheerful. The death of Lady Charleville, which happened about this time, much affected her; this event was probably hastened by a severe domestic calamity, which occurred early in the same year, on which occasion Mrs. Opie wrote:—

My dear old friend of forty-one years, Lady C., has lost her son by her first husband, and she has written me a *touching* note indeed, and as well composed as in her young days, pious too, and satisfactory; and the day after this beloved son's death, was that of her 89th birthday! She is a wonder, and yet, as her amiable daughter wrote to me, "there she is, still well and intellectual, and even capable of business!"

She said on one of these occasions, "it is a heavy trial to be called on to survive so many dear ones, some younger than myself; it has been my fate to do so, and seems likely to continue to be so; but still I think and feel, that He doeth all things well, and I hope to be always able to say with the Patriarch, 'though He slay me yet will I trust in Him.'"

Mrs. Opie attended (for the last time) the Annual Meeting of the Bible Society, in St. Andrew's Hall, in the month of September, and says:—

I had been nursing for it two days, and was so glad to be able to go. I did so enjoy it, in spite of certain reminiscences of auld lang syne! The Bishop's speech was charming and judicious, and to me, so affecting, that it brought me to tears. He paid a just and touching tribute to the memory of Andrew Brandram. Last year he (A. B.) came to me, while I waited for my chair, and I congratulated him on his good looks: he looked ten years younger than when I saw him last: and there was I, yesterday, years older than himself, sitting there, in health, (though not with my once active limbs,) and *he* was in his grave!

In November her last visit to Northrepps Cottage was paid. On the 2nd of January following, (1852,) she was attacked with rheumatic gout in her feet, which confined her to her bed two months, and never afterwards entirely left her.

The following note to Miss Gurney, written shortly after this time, shows her happy resignation and cheerful spirit amid increasing infirmities.

Castle Meadow, 3rd mo., 5th, 1852.

MY DEAREST A.

I was very sorry not to be able to see R. yesterday; but I was denied to every one while Mrs. F. Kemble was with me, as I had much to say to her. The cold of this day has kept me in bed, and one of my feet has been very painful. I much enjoyed F. K.'s conversation. She is gone to-day on her way to London. How many things I want to say to thee, but can't say them! but I am very thankful for what I *can* do, and I do not repine at what I can't do; and life flies only too fast. I do not see, at present, any chance for my speedy recovery; but life has still its charms. I am so glad to have an excuse for lying in bed all day: it is so troublesome to move from bed to chair, and thence to sofa.

Thine ever, most affectionately,

A. OPIE.

A few passages from her notes will be read with pleasure.

(4th mo. 18th.) My prisms are, to-day, quite in their glory. The atmosphere must be very clear, for the radiance is brighter than ever I saw it before. Surely the mansions in heaven must be draped with such unparalleled colours! (5th mo. 4th.) Oh! Captain Gardener and his crew! how I have cried over their death; and yet how enviable was the state of their minds; how meek and entire their resignation how blessed their entrance into the Redeemer's kingdom, and their awaiting welcome there! I have read it through three times, as though fascinated.—Poor John Dalrymple, cut off when he had *attained* the height of his profession! (5th mo. 18th.) No one surely ever had so many kind friends as I have! I can truly say that I have every alleviation of my suffering that I can have, and have every comfort that I desire, and I do not want any nursing but what I have. Mine has been a lonely lot through life; but I have never felt it painfully so; and I believe the happiest persons are those who have the fewest wants. The great I AM, is more even-handed than we think Him.

In the month of September, Mrs. Opie made her last visit to Cromer. She remained there for a fortnight, and had two rooms on a ground floor of the house in which she lodged, where she could lie in bed, and watch the billows as they rolled. Numerous friends flocked around her; amongst them her very old and valued ones, Mrs. and Miss Hoare, whose daily visits cheered her; and many were the little kindnesses she received, which, small in themselves, were yet valued as tokens of love; and they were mentioned with grateful remembrance. On reaching home she was carried upstairs in her basket-chair, never to go down again!

Shortly after her return she wrote to Miss Gurney,

9th mo., 26th, 1852.

Dearest Anna,

I had a pleasant journey home, arriving safely at my own door; but not quite so pleasant an one as I went upstairs. * * It grieves my heart to think that I am not any nearer at present than I was to get to the Bible Meeting, and my *Quarterly* Meeting! but I find I am not up to the exertions necessary. It is heart-breaking to me, almost, to miss a Bible Meeting; this is the *first* I ever omitted, and I did not with any certainty look forward to another; I can truly say that I give it up most unwillingly, but "His will be done!"

I am come home with a cold, but nothing to make me regret one hour spent at Cromer; so many dear friends to see, some new ones to welcome, and more enamoured of Cromer than ever. Farewell! I must lie down and hope to sleep.

Thy ever affectionate,

A. OPIE.

Three months later she wrote:—

I shall probably never be able to go out again; and the idea of being confined to my bed is anything but disagreeable, what a mercy this is! but thankfully as well as reverently, I can repeat, "His mercies are new every morning." I must, however, own, that being unable to go to meeting is a continually recurring trial; but I hope by spring, if I live so long, I may have contrived a way to get there again. All I ask is to be made more and more resigned to the Divine will, whatever it may be.

In January, 1853, her long-loved and honoured friend, Lucy Aggs, died; she writes of this event in one of her notes:—

(1st mo. 23rd, 1853.) She is indeed *gone home;* this morning she slept her last, like a wearied child; how sudden her removal! This day month she was with me, and at meeting twice! how trying to me and to others is this event; but how blest to her. I am grieved more than I can express; and am almost selfish enough to forget that our great loss is her abundant gain.

During the course of the summer many of Mrs. Opie's relatives visited her; their presence seemed greatly to cheer and comfort her; and she frequently spoke of the pleasure it gave her to see them all; on one occasion particularly, she remarked, "I know not how it is, but my cousins and friends seem as though they felt their leave-taking were the last. My cousin R. W. came back twice to shake hands with me. Would that the Baron had been with them!"

The strong feeling of family attachment which characterized Mrs. Opie through life, was retained to the last. She evinced the deepest sympathy with her beloved cousin, Lady Milman, whom she knew to be dying, (and who, in fact, survived her but a very short time,) constantly inquiring for her, and suggesting anything which occurred to her mind as likely to contribute to her comfort, expressing her joy that the confidence of this dear relative was like her own, placed in the blessed promises of the gospel, and thus secure for eternity.

We add a few closing passages from her notes.

(5th mo. 30th.) Again I am forced to feel the pain of not being able to go to Yearly Meeting, a great loss to me; and I have lost an opportunity of seeing H. B. Stowe; but I heartily rejoice in the reception she has met with: well has it been deserved, in my opinion; and well has she performed the work delegated to her from above. I am very glad dear H. Birkbeck has a son; and very glad also, that dear L. B. will soon be home; for I had feared I should not live to see her again. I rejoice, too, to hear such good accounts of the dear Cunninghams.

Another note, dated 7th mo. 18th, records the visit of her cousin, Mrs. Vincent Thompson, with warm affection, and expresses the happiness she had experienced in her society, concluding, "I am indeed delighted to have seen her once more." Shortly after this time she mentions the expected departure to America of the lamented William Forster; he had been her friend and counsellor; one to whom she looked for help and support; and from whose lips she had drunk in truth and wisdom. It did indeed cost her heart a severe pang to part from him; and the more so, as she felt she "should see his face no more." She writes:—

(7th mo. 28th.) How very much I feel the return of this season, this year. The dead have been more present with me than the living; but that is very natural. I am writing in bed, the place I love best. Alas! to the house of the Lord I *cannot* go, and that is an evil. Dearest W. Forster! going away, not to return again, I fear, till I am no more; but I shall not own that to him.*

On the 21st of October Mrs. Opie appeared much as usual; during that morning she received several friends, and was highly interested by a visit from Lieutenant Cresswell, who had recently returned to England with dispatches from the Investigator, to tell of the discovery of the north-west passage, though not, alas! of the finding of Sir John Franklin. His communications excited her lively sympathy; and, as the grandson of Mrs. Fry, his presence alone awakened the slumbering remembrances of the past.

The following day she was evidently somewhat fatigued, but was able to write several notes. In one, addressed to Miss Gurney, after expressing her joy at hearing a good account of her dear friend Mrs. Hoare,

* He died soon after in Tennessee, while on a mission on behalf of the slave.

she mentions the pleasure she had enjoyed in seeing Mrs. Cunningham and Mr. John Gurney, who had dined at her house, and attended the Bible Meeting; she says:—

> I could not accompany them, nor can I perhaps expect to go out again. Well! all good and all *evil* here will soon be over with me now. I am abundantly thankful for everything; for I feel that "His mercies are new every morning." How I wish thou and dear Lady Buxton could have been my guests yesterday. It was really a very enjoyable time, and the only drawback was my being unable to go to the meetings, and to dine below stairs.

The next day was Sunday; early in the morning she was taken ill; and her maid, S. Nixon, observing symptoms unusual with her mistress, sent immediately for Dr. Hull, who desired she might be kept perfectly quiet.

The writer of these memoirs had been in the habit, since Mrs. Opie's confinement to the house, of spending an hour with her, on Sunday morning. On that day there was not the usual influx of visitors, and she seemed to enjoy having a quiet chat. The usual call was made that morning, but the mandate of the doctor was communicated, and, of course, obeyed. It was with a strange feeling of alarm, that turning away from the door-step, the writer began to think over the past few months. Yes, there had certainly been some tokens of enfeebled powers— a partial failure of memory—an occasional loss in the thread of her conversation; and at times an inability to express clearly her meaning. For the last few weeks the newspapers had been neglected; and, once or twice, an ominous sentence had been dropped, that startled her friends. "When I am gone."—"I feel I shall not be here long." To her faithful friend of many years' standing, the Rev. H. Tacy, she had said, shortly before, "Do not be long before you come again; for I am on the wing!"—But, her aunt had lived more than ninety years, and Mrs. Opie was so cheerful and bright, her carriage so erect, and she looked so much as she had long done, that, after all, these occasional symptoms were probably merely the inevitable results of advancing age, and her foreboding expressions the effects of confinement and seclusion!

So whispered Hope; and the writer, for one, did not realize the idea that the end was at hand. On the evening of that Sunday, a message from Dr. Hull was sent to her friend and professional adviser, Thos. Brightwell. Mrs. Opie was very ill—might not, perhaps, survive many hours; and, as she had desired, in case of any sudden attack of illness, that "Thomas Brightwell and Mary Brown" should be sent for, he had felt it his duty to inform them of her condition.

In a few hours, however, the alarming symptoms subsided, and the gout appeared externally, and fixed itself in the right heel.

Mrs. Opie survived nearly six weeks from that day, being unable to leave her bed, and suffering greatly. At first, there was much of her usual cheerfulness and buoyancy of spirit about her; and she evidently entertained no apprehension of the fatal nature of the attack. She took an interest in the events occurring around her, and frequently made inquiries and remarks that shewed her sympathies were lively, and her recollection unimpaired. Her constant patience and endurance under suffering, were truly exemplary To one friend who asked her, after she had been talking with great vivacity, whether she suffered much pain; she replied, "Oh! yes, I am scarcely ever free from it, and it is often severe; but I am so used to pain, I have learned not to mind it;" and, on another occasion, when her sufferings were spoken of, she said, she thought "more of her mercies than of her trials." During the last three or four weeks of her life, she became greatly worse; her weakness increased; she took little nourishment, and suffered much distressing pain in the hip and in the heel. Throughout this trying season, her kind, gentle, and watchful friend, Mary Brown, remained in constant and unwearying attendance beside her, ministering to her wants, and answering the numerous inquiries, personal, and epistolary, of her friends. Having, like herself, joined the Society of Friends, she was the more able to sympathize with her feelings; and to *her* it was, that she expressed her constant adherence to the religious tenets of Friends, and the satisfaction she experienced in looking back upon the time when she joined their communion.

The frequent presence and devoted attention of her cousin, the Rev. R. Alderson, was another great comfort to Mrs. Opie; happily, he was able to give much of his time to her; and she missed him if he left her, and anxiously inquired when he would return. It was doubtless, a great satisfaction to him to render these last and important services to his honoured relative.

Mrs. Opie had expressed, on more than one occasion, the hope that her friend William Forster, would be with her during her last hours. But this wish was not granted her. His sisters, who were then in Norfolk, assiduously visited her, as did also Mrs. Birkbeck; and John Shewell, a Minister of the Society, paid her a religious visit, shortly after the commencement of her illness, and was enabled to speak to her comfort and satisfaction; and her kind and highly esteemed friend, the Rev. J. Alexander, saw her, and his spiritual aid was "refreshing" to her. But, soothing as are the offices of friendship, and precious the prayers of the righteous under such circumstances, how unavailing is all human ministry when heart and flesh are failing! *Then* the soul realizes her independence, and the inefficiency of earthly help, and feels with whom she has to do; and knows that for herself, and alone, she must stand in the presence of the Holy One. And so it was, in this instance. Alone, in the night season, her voice was heard in supplication, pouring out the desires of her soul to her Redeemer. The pathetic utterances of resignation, amid pain and anguish, were heard, by those who watched beside her couch; "what am I (she said, thinking aloud) that I should expect to escape suffering? this, also, is meant for my good." Often too, she was heard repeating to herself texts of Scripture, and hymns; and on more than one occasion, she called for her Bible, and for Wesley's Hymn Book, (her much used copy of which is full of her marks, and turned down at her favourite hymns,) and, sitting up in her bed, read aloud to her maids, as it had been her constant habit to do.

Mrs. Opie often spoke of the kindness of her friends, and evinced the most tender interest in them; weeping as she mentioned the proofs of their affectionate remembrance, and sending touching messages in reply to their inquiries. "Tell them (she said) I have suffered great pain; but I think on Him who suffered for me."—"Say that I am trusting in my Saviour, and ask them to pray for me." And when told by one of those who visited her, that many prayers were offered for her, she said (and a tear glistened in her eye) "it were worth while to be ill, to have the prayers of our friends."

Latterly there was a striking change in her personal appearance. So completely was her countenance altered, that it would have been impossible for any one, even of those who knew her best, to recognize her. The only vestige remaining of her former looks, was a peculiar uplifting of the eye, accompanied by a slight shake of the head. Her articulation also became so imperfect, that it was very difficult to distinguish what she said; and for very weakness, her head lay, bent sideways, apparently powerless, on the cushion.

Her debility prevented her seeing more than two or three most intimate friends; and one of the last visitors she received, and the sight of whom evidently afforded her the most heartfelt satisfaction, was the friend of her early days, Mrs. Gurney, of Keswick; who, herself an invalid, made a considerable effort to reach her bedside and bid her farewell. "How much she loved me!" was her whispered expression, when she afterwards mentioned this interview. Shortly before her death, the Rev. H. Tacy called to see her, not knowing of her illness; and little thinking that the words she had spoken when they last parted, were so soon to be fulfilled. His visit, painful as it was, was opportune, and appeared to comfort her much. On another day, she desired that parts of the Litany and the other prayers should be read to her, which was done; Mrs. Opie, with clasped hands, repeating all the responses.

Her debility now visibly and rapidly increased. She refused almost all nourishment, and seemed to crave no other refreshment than "cold water," for which she frequently called. It was evident that her end was approaching.

On the last Sunday of Mrs. Opie's life, (the 27th November,) the writer of these lines accompanied her father to pay a farewell visit to the bedside of their dying friend. She lay propped up on pillows and cushions, extremely feeble, but perfectly clear in her intellect, calm, and composed. She had become conscious of her danger, and anticipated her approaching departure. This she intimated by saying "the last few days I have been preparing to go."* In reply to the inquiry, what she meant to convey by these words, she said, "why, to die, child, to be sure!" "You have long been prepared to die, we hope." "I hope so indeed," she replied, "there is only *one* way."

There she lay! helpless, dying, alone. Could all those whom she had loved and served been permitted to gather around her couch, what a cloud of witnesses,

* The preparation to which she referred had reference to some small directions she had dictated to her maid a few evenings before, to be communicated to her executor; at the close of which she said, "I should have liked to give little remembrances to all my friends, and have taken leave of them, but I have done the best I can."

circle within circle, had thronged that small chamber with looks of tender sympathy! Impelled by some such thought, the writer bent over her and said, " it is a great thing to be loved as you are loved. How many ask anxiously for tidings of you." She raised her eyes to those of the speaker, and seemed as though awaiting confirmation of the assurance, and looked satisfied on receiving it. She responded too, with evident earnestness of feeling, to the expression of the hope that she was soon about to rejoin those dear ones whom she had loved so well, and who were gone before.

From time to time she uttered a few broken words; and once, with a piteous look, said, " I am very thirsty; but her weakness was too great to allow of more than an occasional sentence. It was truly distressing to gaze upon her entirely changed countenance, and exhausted frame, and to feel the sad conviction that one was looking on her for the last time!

At the former part of her illness, Mrs. Opie's natural warmth of affection, and lively interest in those whom she loved, seemed to induce her still to cling to life; and while she said that on looking back and contemplating the past, the time seemed long in the review, yet she intimated it would be sweet to live a little longer, if permitted to do so, " were it not still better to depart." But, as the end approached, there appeared to be a gradual giving up her hold on the present life, and the few words she uttered shewed that her thoughts were on heavenly things.

On the night of the 30th she said to her cousin "all is peace;" and afterwards, when Mr. S. Gurney was present, she gave it as her dying testimony "all is mercy."

During the last five days of her life her sufferings were protracted and severe. Hers were "the groans and pains and dying strife" of a mortal conflict. But her faith and patience failed not; and at length the Angel messenger came, and she was released!

At midnight, on Friday the 2nd of December, 1853, Amelia Opie breathed her last.

CONCLUSION.

"DEATH is something so strange, that, notwithstanding all experience, one thinks it impossible for it to seize a beloved object; it always presents itself as an incredible and unexpected event; and this transition, from an existence we know, to one of which we know nothing, is something so violent that it cannot take place without the greatest shock to survivors."

Who has not experienced, to some extent, the feelings thus expressed by Goethe? The immediate results of death, no less than the actual event, excite the most perplexing and distressing ideas. All is unwonted and unnatural. One's thoughts are compelled to take a new and strange turn. They are occupied henceforth, about that which *was*, and is not; it is the "history of a life," not a living, sentient, beloved being, that occupies them now. Fancy, having tried in vain to "paint the moment after death," gives place to Memory and Love, which busily go o'er the past, and trace, again and again, each step.

One glance at the forsaken "tabernacle," lately the dwelling-place of that soul beloved, renews the sad conviction, that what you once had, you have no more, and ne'er can have again. Then, after a time, the sarcophagus—the chest, that shuts in and confines what loved to be free, and *would* not be held in durance;—it is all unnatural! the result of some infringement of the original intent.

So felt the writer when next she entered the house on the Castle Meadow; now no longer Mrs. Opie's house; for she lay dead therein. Yes! she lay dead; placed in her coffin, in the lower chamber, beneath the one in which she had breathed her last; surrounded by the portraits of her friends, which, hanging upon the walls of the room, used so often to attract her notice, and win from her some expression of remembrance and regard. Men of all views, political and religious, were there; all known, and having earned a niche there, by some superiority of natural or acquired excellences. There Lafayette, Cooper, David, Madame de Staël, and others, of her foreign friends, hung side by side. There J. J. Gurney and his brother, Elizabeth Fry and Lucy Aggs, and close by them the Bishops of Norwich and Durham, and Professors Sedgwick and Whewell; there the poets and statesmen, whose genius had charmed her; and last, though not the least, Mrs. Siddons, in her glory, as Queen Catherine.

It was an affecting and instructive sight to look upon—very sad; and yet, after a time, reason and faith suggested soothing and happy reflections. She, who lay there, had died in a good old age, full of years and honour; had finished her earthly course in peace, and now, the end was known, and all was "well." She had died in the faith and hope of the gospel; her feet had not fallen, for God had held up her goings; and her spirit, though no longer permitted to sojourn among the living, had joined the "great crowd of witnesses," which is ever multiplying its hosts, and securely awaiting its ultimate completion and triumph.

The 9th of December was the day appointed for the funeral of Mrs. Opie; she was interred in the Friends' burying ground, at the Gildencroft; in the same grave with her father. About two hundred persons, assembled in solemn silence, stood there to meditate: one voice alone was heard; that of a venerable Friend, who uttered a few simple scriptural words. It seemed strange to miss from among the sorrowing group around, so many who had loved and honoured her. But the eye had only to glance over that green enclosure, and one was reminded that they lay *there*, beside and around her. Rich, indeed, is that small plot of ground. The good, the honoured, the lovely, and beloved, lie there;—some of the best of men and saints, whose prayers drew blessings down from heaven,—awaiting the day when "the secrets of all hearts shall be made known." It is a hallowed spot; consecrated to holy memories.

Should any wanderer, at some future day, desire to visit the grave of Amelia Opie, he will find, at the extreme left side of the ground, beneath an elm tree that overshadows the wall, a small slab, bearing the names of James Alderson and Amelia Opie, with the dates of their births and deaths.

Among those present on this occasion, was one, long and well-known to Mrs. Opie, and of whom she has spoken in terms of warm praise, in one of her notes; Mr. Hodgkin, a minister of the Friends, who, addressing those around, invited them to accompany him to the Meeting House; where, after a short time spent in silence and in prayer, he rose, and spoke, in words very pleasant and judicious, of the dear departed friend, whom they had lost. He had known her, he said, from his own earlier days, and when she was very different from what she afterwards became. He believed that the ruling principle in her mind, and that which, being implanted there by Divine grace, had remained the dominant one in her soul, was the love of Christ; constrained by the sweet influence of which, she had been enabled to maintain much consistent Christian deportment, amid snares and temptations of peculiar fascination for one, endowed by nature, and trained by early habit, as she had been.

Much more he added, of a nature to impress his hearers with a deep sense of thankfulness for the Divine goodness, and to urge them to pursue, with humble and pious zeal, the path of Christian devotedness and obedience.

It may seem natural and desirable that a few words should be said touching the personal appearance of the subject of these memoirs, during the latter period of her life.—How difficult, and indeed *impossible* it is, to satisfy yourself, when attempting to portray the form and features of those you know most intimately, and have been constantly in the habit of seeing! This you feel in trying to describe the members of your own family; in the mind's eye their image lives, 'tis true; but it is rather as a *consciousness;* something, as it were, that is interwoven with the secret and hidden ideas of your soul. In a degree, this is the case with all those most familiar to you; and perhaps the reason is, that the whole idea of their personality has been formed by degrees—shade after shade, as the events of passing years have left their impress upon them.

Be that as it may; the difficulty is known, and will be acknowledged. Yet, for the sake of strangers, rather than to assist the recollections of the friends of Mrs. Opie, the following slight sketch may be permitted.

She was of about the standard height of woman; her hair was worn in waving folds in front, and behind, it was seen through the cap, gathered into a braid; its colour was peculiar—'twixt flaxen and gray; it was unusually fine and delicate, and had a natural bend or wave. Her Quaker cap was of beautiful lawn, and fastened beneath the chin with whimpers, which had small crimped frills: her dress was usually of rich silk or satin, often of a fawn or grey colour; and over the bust was drawn a muslin or net handkerchief, in thick folds, fastening into the waist, round which was worn a band of the same material as the dress; an apron, usually of net or muslin, protected (or *adorned*) the front of the gown. Her feet, which were small and well formed, peeped out beneath the dress. On her hands she wore small, black, netted muffatees, (she sometimes repaired them while talking to her friends,) and the cuffs of her gown were secured by a small loop at one corner, which she wore passed over the thumb, so as to prevent them from turning back or rucking upon the arm; her figure was stout, the throat short; her carriage was invariably erect, and she bore her head rather thrown back, and with an air of dignity. Her countenance, in her later years, lost much of that fire which once irradiated it; but the expression was more pleasing; softer, more tender, and loving. Her eyes were especially charming; there was in them an ardour mingled with gentleness, that bespoke her true nature, and occasionally they were raised upwards with a look most peculiar and expressive, when her sympathy was more than usually excited. Her complexion was fair, and the kindling blush mantled in her cheek, betraying any passing emotion; for, like her friend Lafayette, she "blushed like a girl to hear her own praises." Altogether she attracted you, and you drew near to her, and liked to look into her face, and felt that old age, in her, was beautiful and comely.

Often, very often, has the writer, while listening to her lively anecdotes, and watching her animated countenance, drawn her chair closer and yet closer, and at length, slipping down, rested on one knee, in order the better to see her; and after bidding her farewell again and again, returned to the same position and "staid a little longer."

How lively were her narratives; and with what minute touches she gave the details of the scene she was describing. What spirit and life did she breathe into the portraits of those whom she admired! Certainly her conversation was superior to her writing; perhaps the charms of manner and voice aided to enhance the effect of her words.

The peculiar virtues and excellencies of Mrs. Opie's character have been manifested (as it were unconsciously) in the notes and diaries given in these pages; and it would be unbecoming, and is unnecessary, for the writer to enumerate them. Her foibles, too, are shewn by her own hand; and happy they who have so few; happier still, they, who exercise the same watchfulness against their easily besetting faults. In one of her earlier notes, she says, "My practice every night is to examine all my actions, and sift all my motives during the day, for all that I have said or done. I make sad discoveries, by that means, of my own sinfulness; but I am truly thankful that this power has been given me, and lay my head on my pillow with much gratitude."

Seneca accounted the remembrance of his departed friends amongst his solemn delights; not looking upon them as lost, for, he said, "the thought of them is sweet and soothing to me; while I had them I expected to lose them; and having lost them, I still feel that I have them;" and if it were so with the pious heathen, with how much more confidence may the Christian cherish delightful thoughts of the friends he has lost; and, indeed, it is the will of God, and part of the favour which He has promised to His servants, that "the memory of the just shall be blessed."

To many the remembrance of Amelia Opie will long be dear. Would that these memorials of her life, (imperfect alas! and unsatisfactory as they are,) might be the means of animating some by her example, to pursue the things "which are true and lovely and of good report."

THE END.

FLETCHER AND ALEXANDER, PRINTERS, NORWICH.

A CATALOGUE
OF
NEW WORKS IN GENERAL LITERATURE,

PUBLISHED BY

LONGMAN, BROWN, GREEN, AND LONGMANS,

39, PATERNOSTER ROW, LONDON.

CLASSIFIED INDEX.

CLASSIFIED INDEX.

Natural History in general.

1-Volume Encyclopædias and Dictionaries.

Religious & Moral Works.

Poetry and the Drama.

Political Economy and Statistics.

The Sciences in General and Mathematics.

Rural Sports.

Veterinary Medicine, &c.

Voyages and Travels.

Works of Fiction.

ALPHABETICAL CATALOGUE

OF

NEW WORKS AND NEW EDITIONS

PUBLISHED BY

Messrs. LONGMAN, BROWN, GREEN, and LONGMANS,

PATERNOSTER ROW, LONDON.

Miss Acton's Modern Cookery-Book.—Modern Cookery in all its Branches, reduced to a System of Easy Practice. For the use of Private Families. In a Series of Receipts, all of which have been strictly tested, and are given with the most minute exactness. By ELIZA ACTON. New Edition; with Directions for Carving, and other Additions, Plates and Woodcuts. Fcp. 8vo. price 7s. 6d.

Adams.—A Spring in the Canterbury Settlement. By C. WARREN ADAMS, Esq. With 5 Illustrations. Post 8vo. price 5s. 6d.

Aikin.—Select Works of the British Poets, from Ben Jonson to Beattie. With Biographical and Critical Prefaces by Dr. AIKIN. New Edition, with Supplement by LUCY AIKIN; consisting of additional Selections from more recent Poets. 8vo. price 18s.

Arnold.—Poems. By Matthew Arnold, Author of *Poems by A.* A New Edition, greatly altered: With a Preface. Fcp. 8vo. price 5s. 6d.

*** *More than one-third of the contents of this volume consists of Poems now first published.*

Austin.—Germany from 1760 to 1814; Or, Sketches of German Life from the Decay of the Empire to the Expulsion of the French. Reprinted from the *Edinburgh Review;* with large Additions. By Mrs. AUSTIN. Post 8vo. [*Nearly ready.*

Joanna Baillie's Dramatic and Poetica Works, complete in One Volume: Comprising the Plays of the Passions, Miscellaneous Dramas, Metrical Legends, Fugitive Pieces (several now first published), and Ahalya Baee. Second Edition, including a new Life of Joanna Baillie; with a Portrait, and a View of Bothwell Manse. Square crown 8vo. 21s. cloth; or 42s. bound in morocco.

Baker.—The Rifle and the Hound in Ceylon. By S. W. BAKER, Esq. With several Illustrations printed in Colours, and Engravings on Wood. 8vo. price 14s.

"Mr. Baker has a loving relish of the beauties of nature, a keen eye for the antecedents of wild animals, and the coolness to observe them when face to face in a deadly struggle. He has also graphic powers of no mean order, whether as regards landscape, its living denizens, or the sportsman's actions. Some of his descriptions of scenery and wild creatures may vie with anything Wilson or Audubon could produce."

SPECTATOR.

Balfour.—Sketches of English Literature from the Fourteenth to the Present Century. By CLARA LUCAS BALFOUR. Fcp. 8vo. 7s.

Bayldon's Art of Valuing Rents and Tillages, and Tenant's Right of Entering and Quitting Farms, explained by several Specimens of Valuations; with Remarks on the Cultivation pursued on Soils in different Situations. Adapted to the Use of Landlords, Land-Agents, Appraisers, Farmers, and Tenants. New Edition; corrected and revised by JOHN DONALDSON. 8vo. 10s. 6d.

Lord Belfast.—Lectures on the English Poets and Poetry of the Nineteenth Century. By the Right Hon. the EARL of BELFAST. 8vo. price 6s. 6d.

Banfield.—The Statistical Companion for 1854: Exhibiting the most Interesting Facts in Moral and Intellectual, Vital, Economical, and Political Statistics, at Home and Abroad. Corrected to the Present Time; and including the Census of the British Population taken in 1851. Compiled from Official and other Authentic Sources, by T. C. BANFIELD, Esq., Statistical Clerk to the Council of Education. Fcp. 8vo. price 5s.

Berkeley.—Reminiscences of a Huntsman. By the Honourable GRANTLEY F. BERKELEY. With Four Etchings by John Leech (one coloured). 8vo. price 14s.

Bewley.—Decimal Interest Tables, calculated at 5 per Cent. from 1 Day to 365 Days, and from 1 Month to 12 Months, on from £1 to £40,000: To which are added, Tables of Commission, from ⅛ per Cent. to 5 per Cent. advancing by Eighths. By JOHN BEWLEY. 8vo. price 21s.

Black's Practical Treatise on Brewing, Based on Chemical and Economical Principles: With Formulæ for Public Brewers, and Instructions for Private Families. New Edition, with Additions. 8vo. price 10s. 6d.

Blaine's Encyclopædia of Rural Sports; Or, a complete Account, Historical, Practical, and Descriptive, of Hunting, Shooting, Fishing, Racing, and other Field Sports and Athletic Amusements of the present day. A new and thoroughly revised Edition; with numerous additional Illustrations. The Hunting, Racing, and all relative to Horses and Horsemanship, revised by HARRY HIEOVER; Shooting and Fishing by EPHEMERA; and Coursing by Mr. A. GRAHAM. With upwards of 600 Woodcuts. 8vo. price 50s. half-bound.

Blair's Chronological and Historical Tables, from the Creation to the present time: With Additions and Corrections from the most authentic Writers; including the Computation of St. Paul, as connecting the Period from the Exode to the Temple. Under the revision of Sir HENRY ELLIS, K.H. New Edition, with Corrections. Imperial 8vo. price 31s. 6d. half-morocco.

Bloomfield.—The Greek Testament: With copious English Notes, Critical, Philological, and Explanatory Especially formed for the use of advanced Students and Candidates for Holy Orders. By the Rev. S. T. BLOOMFIELD, D.D., F.S.A. New Edition. 2 vols. 8vo. with Map, price £2.

Dr. Bloomfield's Additional Annotations on the above. 8vo. price 15s.

Bloomfield.—College and School Greek Testament: With shorter English Notes, Critical, Philological, and Explanatory, formed for use in Colleges and the Public Schools. By the Rev. S. T. BLOOMFIELD, D.D., F.S.A. New Edition, greatly enlarged and improved. Fcp. 8vo. price 10s. 6d.

Dr. Bloomfield's College and School Lexicon to the Greek Testament. Fcp. 8vo. price 10s. 6d.

Bode.—Ballads from Herodotus: With an Introductory Poem. By the Rev. J. E. BODE, M.A., late Student of Christ Church. 16mo. price 5s.

Bourne.—A Treatise on the Steam Engine, in its Application to Mines, Mills, Steam Navigation, and Railways. By the Artisan Club. Edited by JOHN BOURNE, C.E. New Edition; with 30 Steel Plates and 349 Wood Engravings. 4to. price 27s.

Bourne.—A Catechism of the Steam Engine, illustrative of the Scientific Principles upon which its Operation depends, and the Practical Details of its Structure, in its applications to Mines, Mills, Steam Navigation, and Railways: With various Suggestions of Improvement. By JOHN BOURNE, C.E. New Edition. Fcp. 8vo. price 6s.

Bourne.—A Treatise on the Screw Propeller: With various Suggestions of Im provement. By JOHN BOURNE, C.E., Edito of *The Artisan Club's Treatise on the Stea Engine.* With 20 large Plates and numerou Woodcuts. 4to. price 38s.

Brande.—A Dictionary of Science, Literature, and Art; comprising the Histor Description, and Scientific Principles every Branch of Human Knowledge; wit the Derivation and Definition of all th Terms in General Use. Edited by W. BRANDE, F.R.S.L. and E.; assisted by D J. CAUVIN. The Second Edition, revise and corrected; including a Supplement, an numerous Wood Engravings. 8vo. 60s.

The SUPPLEMENT, separately, price 3s. 6

Bull.—The Maternal Management Children in Health and Disease. T. BULL, M.D., Member of the Roy College of Physicians; formerly Physicia Accoucheur to the Finsbury Midwife Institution. New Edition. Fcp. 8v price 5s.

Bull.—Hints to Mothers, for the Mnagement of their Health during the Peri of Pregnancy and in the Lying-in Roo With an Exposure of Popular Errors connexion with those subjects, &c.; a Hints upon Nursing. By T. BULL, M. New Edition. Fcp. price 5s.

Bunsen.—Hippolytus and his Age; Or, Doctrine and Practice of the Church of Rome under Commodus and Alexander Severus: And Ancient and Modern Christianity and Divinity compared. By C. C. J. Bunsen, D.D., D.C.L. A New Edition, corrected, remodelled, and extended. 7 vols. 8vo. [*Nearly ready.*

1. Hippolytus and his Age; or, the Beginnings and Prospects of Christianity. New Edition. 2 vols. 8vo.

Separate Works connected with *Hippolytus and his Age*, as forming its Philosophical and Philological Key:—

2. Sketch of the Philosophy of Language and Religion; or, the Beginnings and Prospects of Mankind. 2 vols. 8vo.

3. Analecta Ante-Nicaena. 3 vols. 8vo.

 I. Reliquiae Literariae;

 II. Reliquiae Canonicae;

 III. Reliquiae Liturgicae.

Bunsen. — Egypt's Place in Universal History: An Historical Investigation, in Five Books. By C. C. J. Bunsen, D.D., D.C.L. Translated from the German, by C. H. Cottrell, Esq. M.A.—Vol. I. containing the First Book, or Sources and Primeval Facts of Egyptian History: With an Egyptian Grammar and Dictionary, and a complete List of Hieroglyphical Signs; an Appendix of Authorities, embracing the complete Text of Manetho and Eratosthenes, Ægyptiaca from Pliny, Strabo, &c.; and Plates representing the Egyptian Divinities. With many Illustrations. 8vo. price 28s.

*** The second Volume is preparing for publication.

Burton.—The History of Scotland, from the Revolution to the Extinction of the last Jacobite Insurrection (1689—1748). By John Hill Burton, Author of *The Life of David Hume*, &c. 2 vols. 8vo. price 26s.

Bishop Butler's General Atlas of Modern and Ancient Geography; comprising Fifty-two full-coloured Maps; with complete Indices. New Edition, nearly all re-engraved, enlarged, and greatly improved; with Corrections from the most authentic sources in both the Ancient and Modern Maps, many of which are entirely new. Edited by the Author's Son, the Rev. T. Butler. Royal 8vo. price 24s. half-bound.

Separately {
The Modern Atlas of 28 full-coloured Maps. Rl. 8vo. 12s.
The Ancient Atlas of 24 full-coloured Maps. Rl. 8vo. 12s.

Bishop Butler's Sketch of Modern and Ancient Geography. New Edition, carefully revised, with such Alterations introduced as continually progressive Discoveries and the latest Information have rendered necessary. Edited by the Author's Son, the Rev. T. Butler. 8vo. price 9s.

The Cabinet Gazetteer: A Popular Exposition of all the Countries of the World; their Government, Population, Revenues, Commerce, and Industries; Agricultural, Manufactured, and Mineral Products; Religion, Laws, Manners, and Social State: With brief Notices of their History and Antiquities. From the latest Authorities. By the Author of *The Cabinet Lawyer*. Fcp. 8vo. price 10s. 6d. cloth; or 13s. calf lettered.

The Cabinet Lawyer: A Popular Digest of the Laws of England, Civil and Criminal; with a Dictionary of Law Terms, Maxims, Statutes, and Judicial Antiquities; Correct Tables of Assessed Taxes, Stamp Duties, Excise Licenses, and Post-Horse Duties; Post-Office Regulations, and Prison Discipline. 16th Edition, comprising the Public Acts of the Session 1853. Fcp. 8vo. price 10s. 6d.—Supplement, price 1s.

Caird.—English Agriculture in 1850 and 1851; Its Condition and Prospects. By James Caird, Esq., of Baldoon, Agricultural Commissioner of *The Times*. The Second Edition. 8vo. price 14s.

The Calling and Responsibilities of a Governess. By Amica. Fcp. 8vo. 4s. 6d.

Calvert. — The Wife's Manual; or, Prayers and Thoughts on Several Occasions of a Matron's Life. By the Rev. William Calvert, Rector of St. Antholin, and one of the Minor Canons of St. Paul's. Post 8vo. [*In the press.*

Catlow.—Popular Conchology; or, the Shell Cabinet arranged: being an Introduction to the Modern System of Conchology: with a Sketch of the Natural History of the Animals, an account of the Formation of the Shells, and a complete Descriptive List of the Families and Genera. By Agnes Catlow. New Edition, with numerous additional Woodcuts. Post 8vo. [*In the press.*

Cecil. — The Stud Farm; or, Hints on Breeding Horses for the Turf, the Chase, and the Road. Addressed to Breeders of Race Horses and Hunters, Landed Proprietors, and especially to Tenant Farmers. By Cecil. Fcp. 8vo. with Frontispiece, 5s.

Cecil. — Records of the Chase, and Memoirs of Celebrated Sportsmen; Illustrating some of the Usages of Olden Times and comparing them with prevailing Customs: Together with an Introduction to most of the Fashionable Hunting Countries; and Comments. By CECIL. With Two Plates by B. Herring. Fcp. 8vo.

Cecil. — Stable Practice; or, Hints on Training for the Turf, the Chase, and the Road; with Observations on Racing and Hunting, Wasting, Race Riding, and Handicapping: Addressed to Owners of Racers, Hunters, and other Horses, and to all who are concerned in Racing, Steeple Chasing, and Fox Hunting. By CECIL. Fcp. 8vo. with Plate, price 5s. half-bound.

Chalybaeus's Historical Survey of Modern Speculative Philosophy, from Kant to Hegel. Translated from the German by ALFRED TULK. Post 8vo. [*Just ready.*

Captain Chesterton's Autobiography.— Peace, War, and Adventure: Being an Autobiographical Memoir of George Laval Chesterton, formerly of the Field-Train Department of the Royal Artillery, subsequently a Captain in the Army of Columbia, and at present Governor of the House of Correction at Cold Bath Fields. 2 vols. post 8vo. price 16s.

Chevreul on Colour. — The Principles of Harmony and Contrast of Colours, and their Applications to the Arts: Including Painting, Interior Decoration, Tapestries, Carpets, Mosaics, Coloured Glazing, Paper-Staining, Calico Printing, Letterpress Printing, Map Colouring, Dress, Landscape and Flower Gardening, &c. By M. E. CHEVREUL, Membre de l'Institut de France, etc. Translated from the French by CHARLES MARTEL. Illustrated with Diagrams, &c. Crown 8vo. [*In the press.*

Conversations on Botany. New Edition, improved; with 22 Plates. Fcp. 8vo. price 7s. 6d.; or with the Plates coloured, 12s.

Conybeare and Howson.—The Life and Epistles of Saint Paul: Comprising a complete Biography of the Apostle, and a Translation of his Epistles inserted in Chronological Order. By the Rev. W. J. CONYBEARE, M.A., late Fellow of Trinity College, Cambridge; and the Rev. J. S. HOWSON, M.A., Principal of the Collegiate Institution, Liverpool. With 40 Engravings on Steel and 100 Woodcuts. 2 vols. 4to. price £2. 8s.

Copland. — A Dictionary of Practical Medicine: Comprising General Pathology, the Nature and Treatment of Diseases, Morbid Structures, and the Disorders especially incidental to Climates, to Sex, and to the different Epochs of Life; with numerous approved Formulae of the Medicines recommended. By JAMES COPLAND, M.D., Consulting Physician to Queen Charlotte's Lying-in Hospital, &c. Vols. I. and II. 8vo. price £3; and Parts X. to XVI. 4s. 6d. each.

The Children's Own Sunday-Book. By JULIA CORNER, Author of *Questions on the History of Europe*. With Two Illustrations. Square fcp. 8vo. price 5s.

Cresy.—An Encyclopædia of Civil Engi-neering, Historical, Theoretical, and Practical. By EDWARD CRESY, F.S.A., C.E. Illustrated by upwards of 3,000 Woodcuts, explanatory of the Principles, Machinery, and Constructions which come under the direction of the Civil Engineer. 8vo. price £3. 13s. 6d.

The Cricket-Field; or, the Science and History of the Game. Illustrated with Diagrams, and enlivened with anecdotes. By the Author of *Principles of Scientific Batting*. Fcp. 8vo. with 2 Plates, 5s. half-bound.

Lady Cust's Invalid's Book. — The In-valid's Own Book: A Collection of Recipes from various Books and various Countries. By the Honourable LADY CUST. Fcp. 8vo. price 3s. 6d.

Dale.—The Domestic Liturgy and Family Chaplain, in Two Parts: The First Part being Church Services adapted for Domestic Use, with Prayers for every day of the week, selected exclusively from the Book of Common Prayer; Part II. comprising an appropriate Sermon for every Sunday in the year. By the Rev. THOMAS DALE, M.A., Canon Residentiary of St. Paul's. Second Edition. Post 4to. 21s. cloth; 31s. 6d. calf; or £2. 10s. morocco.

Separately { THE FAMILY CHAPLAIN, 12s.
THE DOMESTIC LITURGY, 10s. 6d.

Davis.—China during the War and since the Peace. By Sir J. F. DAVIS, Bart., F.R.S. late H.M. Plenipotentiary in China; Governor and Commander-in-Chief of the Colony of Hongkong. 2 vols. post 8vo. price 21s.

De Felice.—History of the Protestants of France, from the Commencement of the Reformation to the Present Time. Translated from the French of G. DE FELICE, D.D. Professor of Theology at Montauban, by E. WEST: With a Supplemental Chapter, written expressly for this translation by Dr. DE FELICE. 2 vols. post 8vo. price 12s.

"The work of Professor de Félice is one of the most valuable additions which have been made of late years to the history of that great crisis in Western Christendom which goes by the general name of the Reformation......Of this work two rival translations have simultaneously made their appearance; one condensed by typographical cramming into one volume, the other occupying two handsomely printed octavos. The difference, however, in the value of the two translations is by no means confined to the external appearance of the respective volumes. The version which has the name of the translator on the title-page, though a respectable performance, yet bears traces of the carelessness and haste incident to the manufacture of cheap literature; while the other version, authenticated only by the translator's initials at the end of his preface [Mr. West's translation] is manifestly executed with greater care, and with a more correct appreciation of the niceties of the idiom in which the original work was written. The latter translation has, moreover, the advantage of being executed with the sanction and, apparently, the co-operation of the author, and it continues the history down to a later point than the former; a supplementary chapter, written expressly for this translation by M. de Félice, being added, which, in the other translation, is altogether wanting, and which possesses a more than ordinary interest, being occupied with the history of the Protestants of France under the new *regime* established by Louis Napoleon."

JOHN BULL.

Delabeche.—The Geological Observer. By Sir HENRY T. DELABECHE, F.R.S., Director-General of the Geological Survey of the United Kingdom. New Edition; with numerous Woodcuts. 8vo. price 18s.

Delabeche.—Report on the Geology of Cornwall, Devon, and West Somerset. By Sir HENRY T. DELABECHE, F.R.S., Director-General of the Geological Survey. With Maps, Woodcuts, and 12 Plates. 8vo. price 14s.

De la Rive.—A Treatise on Electricity, in Theory and Practice. By A. DE LA RIVE, Professor in the Academy of Geneva. In Two Volumes, with numerous Wood Engravings. Vol. I. 8vo. price 18s.

Discipline. By the Author of "Letters to my Unknown Friends," &c. Second Edition, enlarged. 18mo. price 2s. 6d.

Eastlake.—Materials for a History of Oil Painting. By Sir CHARLES LOCK EASTLAKE, F.R.S., F.S.A., President of the Royal Academy. 8vo. price 16s.

The Eclipse of Faith; or, a Visit to a Religious Sceptic. New Edition. Post 8vo. price 9s. 6d.

A Defence of The Eclipse of Faith, by its Author: Being a Rejoinder to Professor Newman's *Reply*. Post 8vo. price 5s. 6d.

The Englishman's Greek Concordance of the New Testament: Being an Attempt at a Verbal Connexion between the Greek and the English Texts; including a Concordance to the Proper Names, with Indexes, Greek-English and English-Greek. New Edition, with a new Index. Royal 8vo. price 42s.

The Englishman's Hebrew and Chaldee Concordance of the Old Testament: Being an Attempt at a Verbal Connection between the Original and the English Translations; with Indexes, a List of the Proper Names and their occurrences, &c. 2 vols. royal 8vo. price £3. 13s. 6d.; large paper, price £4. 14s. 6d.

Ephemera.—A Handbook of Angling; Teaching Fly-fishing, Trolling, Bottom-fishing, Salmon fishing; with the Natural History of River Fish, and the best modes of Catching them. By EPHEMERA. Third and cheaper Edition, corrected and improved; with Woodcuts. Fcp. 8vo. 5s.

Ephemera.—The Book of the Salmon: Comprising the Theory, Principles, and Practice of Fly-fishing for Salmon; Lists of good Salmon Flies for every good River in the Empire; the Natural History of the Salmon, all its known Habits described, and the best way of artificially Breeding it explained. With numerous coloured Engravings of Salmon Flies and Salmon Fry. By EPHEMERA; assisted by ANDREW YOUNG. Fcp. 8vo. with coloured Plates, price 14s.

W. Erskine, Esq.—History of India under the House of Taimur (1526 to 1707). By WILLIAM ERSKINE, Esq., Editor of *Memoirs of the Emperor Baber*. The First Volume,—History of Baber; His Early Life, 1483-1526; his Reign in India, 1526-1530. The Second Volume,—History of Humayun, 1530-1556. Vols. I. and II. 8vo. [*Just ready*.

Faraday (Professor).—The Subject-Matter of Six Lectures on the Non-Metallic Elements, delivered before the Members of the Royal Institution in 1852, by Professor FARADAY, D.C.L., F.R.S., &c. Arranged by permission from the Lecturer's Notes by J. SCOFFERN, M.B., late Professor of Chemistry in the Aldersgate College of Medicine. To which are appended Remarks on the Quality and Tendencies of Chemical Philosophy, on Allotropism, and on Ozone; together with Manipulative Details relating to the Performances of Experiments indicated by Professor FARADAY. Fcp. 8vo. price 5s. 6d.

Forester and Biddulph's Norway. — Norway in 1848 and 1849: Containing Rambles among the Fjelds and Fjords of the Central and Western Districts; and including Remarks on its Political, Military, Ecclesiastical, and Social Organisation. By THOMAS FORESTER, Esq.; and Lieutenant M. S. BIDDULPH, Royal Artillery. With Map, Woodcuts, and Plates. 8vo. price 18s.

Francis. — Annals, Anecdotes, and Legends: A Chronicle of Life Assurance. By JOHN FRANCIS, Author of *The History of the Bank of England,* "Chronicles and Characters of the Stock Exchange," and *A History of the English Railway.* Post 8vo. price 8s. 6d.

"Nothing in the whole range of fiction or romance can exceed the marvellous incidents and events which are detailed here, and have the additional value, like all Mr. Francis's previous productions, of being strictly and historically accurate. The book will well repay perusal, and while furnishing abundant matter both of interest and excitement to the general reader, will form, for many years to come, a standard work upon the rise and progress of assurance societies in this country." OBSERVER.

The Poetical Works of Oliver Goldsmith. Edited by BOLTON CORNEY, Esq. Illustrated by Wood Engravings, from Designs by Members of the Etching Club. Square crown 8vo. cloth, 21s.; morocco, £1. 16s.

Mr. W. R. Greg's Contributions to The Edinburgh Review.—Essays on Political and Social Science. Contributed chiefly to the *Edinburgh Review.* By WILLIAM R. GREG. 2 vols. 8vo. price 24s.

Gurney.—Historical Sketches; illustrat-ing some Memorable Events and Epochs, from A.D. 1,400 to A.D. 1,546. By the Rev. JOHN HAMPDEN GURNEY, M.A., Rector of St. Mary's, Marylebone. Fcp. 8vo. 7s. 6d.

Gosse. — A Naturalist's Sojourn in Jamaica. By P. H. GOSSE, Esq. With Plates. Post 8vo. price 14s.

Gwilt.—An Encyclopædia of Architecture, Historical, Theoretical, and Practical. By JOSEPH GWILT. Illustrated with more than One Thousand Engravings on Wood, from Designs by J. S. GWILT. Second Edition, with a Supplemental View of the Symmetry and Stability of Gothic Architecture; comprising upwards of Eighty additional Woodcuts. 8vo. price 52s. 6d.

The SUPPLEMENT separately, price 6s.

Sidney Hall's General Large Library Atlas of Fifty-three Maps (size, 20 in. by 16 in.), with the Divisions and Boundaries carefully coloured; and an Alphabetical Index of all the Names contained in the Maps. New Edition, corrected from the best and most recent Authorities; with the Railways laid down and many entirely new Maps. Colombier 4to. price £5. 5s. half-russia.

Hamilton. — Discussions in Philosophy and Literature, Education and University Reform. Chiefly from the *Edinburgh Review;* corrected, vindicated, enlarged, in Notes and Appendices. By Sir WILLIAM HAMILTON, Bart. Second Edition, with Additions. 8vo. price 21s.

Hare (Archdeacon).—The Life of Luther, in Forty-eight Historical Engravings. By GUSTAV KÖNIG. With Explanations by Archdeacon HARE. Square crown 8vo. [*In the press.*

Harrison.—The Light of the Forge; or, Counsels drawn from the Sick-Bed of E. M. By the Rev. WILLIAM HARRISON, M.A., Rector of Birch, Essex, and Domestic Chaplain to H.R.H. the Duchess of Cambridge. With 2 Woodcuts. Fcp. 8vo. price 5s.

Harry Hieover. — The Hunting-Field. By HARRY HIEOVER. With Two Plates—One representing *The Right Sort;* the other, *The Wrong Sort.* Fcp. 8vo. 5s. half-bound.

Harry Hieover. — Practical Horseman-ship. By HARRY HIEOVER. With 2 Plates —One representing *Going like Workmen;* the other, *Going like Muffs.* Fcp. 8vo. price 5s. half-bound.

Harry Hieover.—The Stud, for Practical Purposes and Practical Men: being a Guide to the Choice of a Horse for use more than for show. By HARRY HIEOVER. With 2 Plates—One representing *A pretty good sort for most purposes;* the other, *Raythor a bad sort for any purpose.* Fcp. 8vo. price 5s. half-bound.

Harry Hieover. — The Pocket and the Stud; or, Practical Hints on the Management of the Stable. By HARRY HIEOVER. Second Edition; with Portrait of the Author on his favourite Horse *Harlequin.* Fcp. 8vo. price 5s. half-bound.

Harry Hieover.—Stable Talk and Table Talk; or, Spectacles for Young Sportsmen. By HARRY HIEOVER. New Edition, 2 vols. 8vo. with Portrait, price 24s.

Haydon.—The Life of Benjamin Robert Haydon, Historical Painter, from his Autobiography and Journals. Edited and compiled by TOM TAYLOR, M.A., of the Inner Temple, Esq.; late Fellow of Trinity College, Cambridge; and late Professor of the English Language and Literature in University College, London. Second Edition, with Additions and an Index. 3 vols. post 8vo. price 31s. 6d.

"It is difficult to say in which sense the work before us possesses the greater interest,—whether as a contribution to the critical history of art in England, during the first half of this century, or as an illustration of high moral truths, enforced by a terrible conclusion. In either point of view its value can hardly be overrated. The artist and the moralist may alike pore over its pages, and learn from it lessons at once stern and profound. The editor has performed his difficult and delicate task in a manner which does him the highest credit." JOHN BULL.

Haydn's Book of Dignities: Containing Rolls of the Official Personages of the British Empire, Civil, Ecclesiastical, Judicial, Military, Naval, and Municipal, from the Earliest Periods to the Present Time; Compiled chiefly from the Records of the Public Offices. Together with the Sovereigns of Europe, from the foundation of their respective States; the Peerage and Nobility of Great Britain, and numerous other Lists. Being a New Edition, improved and continued, of Beatson's Political Index. By JOSEPH HAYDN, Compiler of *The Dictionary of Dates*, and other Works. 8vo. price 25s. half-bound.

Sir John Herschel.—Outlines of Astronomy. By Sir JOHN F. W. HERSCHEL, Bart. &c. New Edition; with Plates and Wood Engravings. 8vo. price 18s.

Hill.—Travels in Siberia. By S. S. Hill, Esq. 2 vols. post 8vo. with Map. [*Just ready.*

Hints on Etiquette and the Usages of Society: With a Glance at Bad Habits. By Αγωγός. "Manners make the man." New Edition, revised (with Additions) by a Lady of Rank. Fcp. 8vo. price Half-a-Crown.

Lord Holland's Memoirs.—Memoirs of the Whig Party during my Time. By HENRY RICHARD LORD HOLLAND. Edited by his Son, HENRY EDWARD LORD HOLLAND. Vols. I. and II. post 8vo. price 9s. 6d. each.

Lord Holland's Foreign Reminiscences. Edited by his Son, HENRY EDWARD LORD HOLLAND. Second Edition; with Facsimile. Post 8vo. price 10s. 6d.

Holland.—Chapters on Mental Physiology. By Sir HENRY HOLLAND, Bart., F.R.S., Physician-Extraordinary to the Queen; and Physician in Ordinary to His Royal Highness Prince Albert. Founded chiefly on Chapters contained in *Medical Notes and Reflections* by the same Author. Fcp. 8vo. price 10s. 6d.

Hole.—Prize Essay on the History and Management of Literary, Scientific, and Mechanics' Institutions, and especially how far they may be developed and combined so as to promote the Moral Well-being and Industry of the Country. By JAMES HOLE, Hon. Secretary of the Yorkshire Union of Mechanics' Institutes. 8vo. price 5s.

Hook.—The Last Days of Our Lord's Ministry: A Course of Lectures on the principal Events of Passion Week. By WALTER FARQUHAR HOOK, D.D., Chaplain in Ordinary to the Queen. New Edition. Fcp. 8vo. price 6s.

Hooker and Arnott.—The British Flora; Comprising the Phaenogamous or Flowering Plants, and the Ferns. The Sixth Edition, with Additions and Corrections; and numerous Figures illustrative of the Umbelliferous Plants, the Composite Plants, the Grasses, and the Ferns. By Sir W. J. HOOKER, F.R.A. and L.S., &c., and G. A. WALKER-ARNOTT, LL.D., F.L.S. 12mo. with 12 Plates, price 14s.; with the Plates coloured, price 21s.

Hooker.—Kew Gardens; or, a Popular Guide to the Royal Botanic Gardens of Kew. By Sir WILLIAM JACKSON HOOKER, K.H., D.C.L., F.R.A., and L.S., &c. &c. Director. New Edition; with numerous Wood Engravings. 16mo. price Sixpence.

Horne.—An Introduction to the Critical Study and Knowledge of the Holy Scriptures. By THOMAS HARTWELL HORNE, B.D. of St. John's College, Cambridge; Prebendary of St. Paul's. New Edition, revised and corrected; with numerous Maps and Facsimiles of Biblical Manuscripts. 5 vols 8vo. price 63s.

Horne.—A Compendious Introduction to the Study of the Bible. By THOMAS HARTWELL HORNE, B.D., of St. John's College, Cambridge. Being an Analysis of his *Introduction to the Critical Study and Knowledge of the Holy Scriptures.* New Edition, corrected and enlarged; with Maps and other Engravings. 12mo. price 9s.

Howitt (A. M.)—An Art-Student in Munich. By ANNA MARY HOWITT. 2 vols. post 8vo. price 14s.

"Since *Bubbles from the Brunnens of Nassau* we have had no local handbook so airy and buoyant, so effervescent and diaphanous, as this young lady's Munich experiences. No vulgar German vi and, made up of questionable ingredients, is here; but a *vol au vent* of choice and delicate materials. Wonder, delight, girlish enthusiasm, deep and varied emotion, sudden transitions from the picturesque and pathetic to the playful and familiar, scenes of artistic blended with those of domestic Bavarian life, keep the reader in a perpetual participation of the fair student's own genuine enjoyments." GLOBE.

Howitt.—The Children's Year. By Mary HOWITT. With Four Illustrations, engraved by John Absolon, from Original Designs by ANNA MARY HOWITT. Square 16mo. price 5s.

William Howitt's Boy's Country Book; Being the Real Life of a Country Boy, written by himself; exhibiting all the Amusements, Pleasures, and Pursuits of Children in the Country. New Edition; with 40 Woodcuts. Fcp. 8vo. price 6s.

Howitt.—The Rural Life of England. By WILLIAM HOWITT. New Edition, corrected and revised; with Woodcuts by Bewick and Williams: Uniform with *Visits to Remarkable Places.* Medium 8vo. 21s.

Howitt.—Visits to Remarkable Places; Old Halls, Battle-Fields, and Scenes illustrative of Striking Passages in English History and Poetry. By WILLIAM HOWITT. New Edition, with 40 Woodcuts. Medium 8vo. price 21s.

SECOND SERIES, chiefly in the Counties of Northumberland and Durham, with a Stroll along the Border. With upwards of 40 Woodcuts. Medium 8vo. 21s.

Hudson.—Plain Directions for Making Wills in Conformity with the Law: with a clear Exposition of the Law relating to the distribution of Personal Estate in the case of Intestacy, two Forms of Wills, and much useful information. By J. C. HUDSON, Esq., late of the Legacy Duty Office, London. New and enlarged Edition; including the provisions of the Wills Act Amendment Act of 1852 (introduced by Lord St. Leonard's). Fcp. 8vo. price 2s. 6d.

Hudson.—The Executor's Guide. By J. C. HUDSON, Esq. New and enlarged Edition; with the Addition of Directions for paying Succession Duties on Real Property under Wills and Intestacies, and a Table for finding the Values of Annuities and the Amount of Legacy and Succession Duty thereon. Fcp. 8vo. price 6s.

Humboldt's Aspects of Nature. Trans-lated, with the Author's authority, by Mrs. SABINE. New Edition. 16mo. price 6s.: or in 2 vols. 3s. 6d. each, cloth; 2s. 6d. each, sewed.

Humboldt's Cosmos. Translated, with the Author's authority, by Mrs. SABINE. Vols. I. and II. 16mo. Half-a-Crown each, sewed; 3s. 6d. each, cloth: or in post 8vo. 12s. 6d. each, cloth. Vol. III. post 8vo. 12s. 6d. cloth: or in 16mo. Part I. 2s. 6d. sewed, 3s. 6d. cloth; and Part II. 3s. sewed, 4s. cloth.

Humphreys.—Sentiments and Similes of Shakspeare: A Classified Selection of Similes, Definitions, Descriptions, and other remarkable Passages in Shakspeare's Plays and Poems. With an elaborately illuminated border in the characteristic style of the Elizabethan Period, massive carved covers, and other Embellishments, designed and executed by H. N. HUMPHREYS. Square post 8vo. price 21s.

Industrial Instruction.—The Report o the Committee appointed by the Council o the Society of Arts to inquire into th Subject of Industrial Instruction: Witl the Evidence. 8vo. price 5s.

Jameson.—A Commonplace Book o Thoughts, Memories, and Fancies, Origina and Selected. Part I. Ethics and Character Part II. Literature and Art. By Mrs JAMESON. With Etchings and Wood En gravings. Square crown 8vo. [*Just ready.*

Mrs. Jameson's Legends of the Saint and Martyrs. Forming the First Series c *Sacred and Legendary Art.* Second Edition with numerous Woodcuts, and 16 Etching by the Author. Square crown 8vo. price 28

Mrs. Jameson's Legends of the Monasti Orders, as represented in the Fine Art Forming the Second Series of *Sacred an Legendary Art.* Second Edition, correcte and enlarged; with 11 Etchings by tl Author, and 88 Woodcuts. Square crow 8vo. price 28s.

Mrs. Jameson's Legends of the Madonna, as represented in the Fine Arts. Forming the Third Series of *Sacred and Legendary Art*. With 55 Drawings by the Author, and 152 Wood Engravings. Square crown 8vo. price 28s.

Lord Jeffrey's Contributions to The Edinburgh Review. A New Edition, complete in One Volume, with a Portrait engraved by Henry Robinson, and a Vignette View of Craigcrook engraved by J. Cousen. Square crown 8vo. 21s. cloth; or 30s. calf.

*** Also a LIBRARY EDITION, in 3 vols. 8vo. price 42s.

Bishop Jeremy Taylor's Entire Works: With Life by Bishop HEBER. Revised and corrected by the Rev. CHARLES PAGE EDEN, Fellow of Oriel College, Oxford. In Ten Volumes. Vols. II. to X. 8vo price Half-a-Guinea each — Vol. I. comprising Bishop Heber's Life of Jeremy Taylor, extended by the Editor, is *nearly ready*.

Johnston.—A New Dictionary of Geo-graphy, Descriptive, Physical, Statistical, and Historical: Forming a complete General Gazetteer of the World. By ALEXANDER KEITH JOHNSTON, F.R.S.E., F.R.G.S., F.G.S., Geographer at Edinburgh in Ordinary to Her Majesty. In One Volume of 1,440 pages; comprising nearly 50,000 Names of Places. 8vo. price 36s. cloth; or half-bound in russia, 41s.

Kemble.—The Saxons in England: A History of the English Commonwealth till the period of the Norman Conquest. By JOHN MITCHELL KEMBLE, M.A., F.C.P.S., &c. 2 vols. 8vo. price 28s.

Kippis's Collection of Hymns and Psalms for Public and Private Worship. New Edition; including a New Supplement by the Rev. EDMUND KELL, M.A. 18mo. price 4s. cloth; or 4s. 6d. roan. — The SUPPLEMENT, separately, price Eightpence.

Kirby and Spence's Introduction to Entomology; or, Elements of the Natural History of Insects: Comprising an account of noxious and useful Insects, of their Metamorphoses, Food, Stratagems, Habitations, Societies, Motions, Noises, Hybernation, Instinct, &c. New Edition. 2 vols. 8vo. with Plates, price 31s. 6d.

Kirby.—The Life of the Rev. William Kirby, M.A., F.R.S., F.L.S., &c., Rector of Barham; Author of one of the Bridgewater Treatises, and Joint-Author of the *Introduction to Entomology*. By the Rev. JOHN FREEMAN, M.A., Rector of Ashwicken, Norfolk, and Rural Dean. With Portrait, Vignette, and Facsimile. 8vo. price 15s.

Laing's (S.) Observations on the Social and Political State of Denmark and the Duchies of Sleswick and Holstein in 1851: Being the Third Series of *Notes of a Traveller*. 8vo. price 12s.

Laing's (S.) Observations on the Social and Political State of the European People in 1848 and 1849: Being the Second Series of *Notes of a Traveller*. 8vo. price 14s.

Dr. Latham on Diseases of the Heart. Lectures on Subjects connected with Clinical Medicine: Diseases of the Heart. By P. M. LATHAM, M.D., Physician Extraordinary to the Queen. New Edition. 2 vols. 12mo. price 16s.

Mrs. R. Lee's Elements of Natural His-tory; or, First Principles of Zoology: Comprising the Principles of Classification, interspersed with amusing and instructive Accounts of the most remarkable Animals. New Edition, enlarged, with numerous additional Woodcuts. Fcp. 8vo. price 7s. 6d.

L. E. L.—The Poetical Works of Letitia Elizabeth Landon; comprising the *Improvisatrice*, the *Venetian Bracelet*, the *Golden Violet*, the *Troubadour*, and Poetical Remains. New Edition; with 2 Vignettes by R. Doyle. 2 vols. 16mo. 10s. cloth; morocco, 21s.

Letters on Happiness, addressed to a Friend. By the Author of *Letters to My Unknown Friends*, &c. Fcp. 8vo. price 6s.

Letters to my Unknown Friends. By a LADY, Author of *Letters on Happiness*. Fourth *and cheaper* Edition. Fcp. 8vo. price 5s.

Lindley.—The Theory of Horticulture; Or, an Attempt to explain the principal Operations of Gardening upon Physiological Principles. By John Lindley, Ph.D. F.R.S. New Edition, revised and improved; with Wood Engravings. 8vo. [*In the press.*

LARDNER'S CABINET CYCLOPÆDIA

Of History, Biography, Literature, the Arts and Sciences, Natural History, and Manufactures: A Series of Original Works by

SIR JOHN HERSCHEL,	THOMAS KEIGHTLEY,	BISHOP THIRLWALL,
SIR JAMES MACKINTOSH,	JOHN FORSTER,	THE REV. G. R. GLEIG,
ROBERT SOUTHEY,	SIR WALTER SCOTT,	J. C. L. DE SISMONDI,
SIR DAVID BREWSTER,	THOMAS MOORE,	JOHN PHILLIPS, F.R.S. G.S.

AND OTHER EMINENT WRITERS.

Complete in 132 vols. fcp. 8vo. with Vignette Titles, price, in cloth, Nineteen Guineas.
The Works *separately,* in Sets or Series, price Three Shillings and Sixpence each Volume.

A List of the WORKS *composing the* CABINET CYCLOPÆDIA:—

1. Bell's History of Russia...... 3 vols. 10s. 6d.
2. Bell's Lives of British Poets.. 2 vols. 7s.
3. Brewster's Optics............ 1 vol. 3s. 6d.
4. Cooley's Maritime and Inland Discovery .... 3 vols. 10s. 6d
5. Crowe's History of France.... 3 vols. 10s. 6d.
6. De Morgan on Probabilities .. 1 vol. 3s. 6d.
7. De Sismondi's History of the Italian Republics.......... 1 vol. 3s. 6d.
8. De Sismondi's Fall of the Roman Empire............ 2 vols. 7s.
9. Donovan's Chemistry .... 1 vol. 3s. 6d.
10. Donovan's Domestic Economy, 2 vols. 7s.
11. Dunham's Spain and Portugal, 5 vols. 17s. 6d.
12. Dunham's History of Denmark, Sweden, and Norway ...... 3 vols. 10s. 6d.
13. Dunham's History of Poland.. 1 vol. 3s. 6d.
14. Dunham's Germanic Empire.. 3 vols. 10s. 6d.
15. Dunham's Europe during the Middle Ages .... 4 vols. 14s.
16. Dunham's British Dramatists, 2 vols. 7s.
17. Dunham's Lives of Early Writers of Great Britain .. 1 vol. 3s. 6d.
18. Fergus's History of the United States .... 2 vols. 7s.
19. Fosbroke's Grecian and Roman Antiquities .... 2 vols. 7s.
20. Forster's Lives of the Statesmen of the Commonwealth, 5 vols. 17s. 6d.
21. Gleig's Lives of British Military Commanders.......... 3 vols. 10s. 6d.
22. Grattan's History of the Netherlands .... 1 vol. 3s. 6d.
23. Henslow's Botany............ 1 vol. 3s. 6d.
24. Herschel's Astronomy........ 1 vol. 3s. 6d.
25. Herschel's Discourse on Natural Philosophy .... 1 vol. 3s. 6d.
26. History of Rome.............. 2 vols. 7s.
27. History of Switzerland .... 1 vol. 3s. 6d.
28. Holland's Manufactures in Metal .... 3 vols. 10s. 6d.
29. James's Lives of Foreign Statesmen .... 5 vols. 17s. 6d.
30. Kater and Lardner's Mechanics, 1 vol. 3s. 6d.
31. Keightley's Outlines of History, 1 vol. 3s. 6d.
32. Lardner's Arithmetic .... 1 vol. 3s. 6d.
33. Lardner's Geometry.......... 1 vol. 3s. 6d.
34. Lardner on Heat .... 1 vol. 3s. 6d.
35. Lardner's Hydrostatics and Pneumatics .... 1 vol. 3s. 6d.
36. Lardner and Walker's Electricity and Magnetism ...... 2 vols. 7s.
37. Mackintosh, Forster, and Courtenay's Lives of British Statesmen .... 7 vols. 24s. 6d.
38. Mackintosh, Wallace, and Bell's History of England........ 10 vols. 35s.
39. Montgomery and Shelley's eminent Italian, Spanish, and Portuguese Authors . 3 vols. 10s. 6d.
40. Moore's History of Ireland .. 4 vols. 14s.
41. Nicolas's Chronology of Hist. 1 vol. 3s. 6d.
42. Phillips's Treatise on Geology, 2 vols. 7s.
43. Powell's History of Natural Philosophy................ 1 vol. 3s. 6d.
44. Porter's Treatise on the Manufacture of Silk .... 1 vol. 3s. 6d.
45. Porter's Manufactures of Porcelain and Glass .... 1 vol. 3s. 6d.
46. Roscoe's British Lawyers .... 1 vol. 3s. 6d.
47. Scott's History of Scotland .... 2 vols. 7s.
48. Shelley's Lives of eminent French Authors............ 2 vols. 7s.
49. Shuckard and Swainson's Insects, 1 vol. 3s. 6d.
50. Southey's Lives of British Admirals .... 5 vols. 17s. 6d.
51. Stebbing's Church History.... 2 vols. 7s.
52. Stebbing's History of the Reformation .... 2 vols. 7s.
53. Swainson's Discourse on Natural History.............. 1 vol. 3s. 6d.
54. Swainson's Natural History & Classification of Animals .. 1 vol. 3s. 6d.
55. Swainson's Habits & Instincts of Animals .... 1 vol. 3s. 6d.
56. Swainson's Birds .... 2 vols. 7s.
57. Swainson's Fish, Reptiles, &c. 2 vols. 7s.
58. Swainson's Quadrupeds ...... 1 vol. 3s. 6d.
59. Swainson's Shells and Shell-fish, 1 vol. 3s. 6d.
60. Swainson's Animals in Menageries .... 1 vol. 3s. 6d.
61. Swainson's Taxidermy and Biography of Zoologists.... 1 vol. 3s. 6d.
62. Thirlwall's History of Greece.. 8 vols. 28s.

Dr. John Lindley's Introduction to Botany. New Edition, with Corrections and copious Additions. 2 vols. 8vo. with Six Plates and numerous Woodcuts, price 24s.

Linwood.—Anthologia Oxoniensis, sive Florilegium e lusibus poeticis diversorum Oxoniensium Græcis et Latinis decerptum. Curante GULIELMO LINWOOD, M.A. Ædis Christi Alummo. 8vo. price 14s.

Dr. Little on Deformities.—On the Nature and Treatment of Deformities of the Human Frame. By W. J. LITTLE, M.D., Physician to the London Hospital, Founder of the Royal Orthopædic Hospital, &c. With 160 Woodcuts and Diagrams. 8vo. price 15s.

"Dr. Little's labours have largely contributed to the extension and perfection of the modern methods of healing the deformities of the human frame. In all that relates to the pathology and cure of these affections he is second to none as an authority, and the present edition will enhance his already high reputation. We unreservedly commend Dr. Little's production as the best treatise on the subject in any language."

THE LANCET.

Litton.—The Church of Christ, in its Idea, Attributes, and Ministry: With a particular Reference to the Controversy on the Subject between Romanists and Protestants. By the Rev. EDWARD ARTHUR LITTON, M.A., Vice-Principal of St. Edmund Hall, Oxford. 8vo. price 16s.

Lorimer's (C.) Letters to a Young Master Mariner on some Subjects connected with his calling. New Edition. Fcp. 8vo. 5s. 6d.

Loudon's Self-Instruction for Young Gardeners, Foresters, Bailiffs, Land Stewards, and Farmers; in Arithmetic, Book-keeping, Geometry, Mensuration, Practical Trigonometry, Mechanics, Land-Surveying, Levelling, Planning and Mapping, Architectural Drawing, and Isometrical Projection and Perspective: With Examples shewing their applications to Horticulture and Agricultural Purposes; a Memoir, Portrait, and Woodcuts. 8vo. price 7s. 6d.

Loudon's Encyclopædia of Gardening; comprising the Theory and Practice of Horticulture, Floriculture, Arboriculture, and Landscape Gardening: Including all the latest improvements; a General History of Gardening in all Countries; a Statistical View of its Present State; and Suggestions for its Future Progress in the British Isles. With many hundred Woodcuts. New Edition, corrected and improved by Mrs. LOUDON. 8vo. price 50s.

Loudon's Encyclopædia of Trees and Shrubs; or, the *Arboretum et Fruticetum Britannicum* abridged: Containing the Hardy Trees and Shrubs of Great Britain, Native and Foreign, Scientifically and Popularly Described; with their Propagation, Culture, and Uses in the Arts; and with Engravings of nearly all the Species. Adapted for the use of Nurserymen, Gardeners, and Foresters. With about 2,000 Woodcuts. 8vo. price 50s.

Loudon's Encyclopædia of Agriculture: comprising the Theory and Practice of the Valuation, Transfer, Laying-out, Improvement, and Management of Landed Property, and of the Cultivation and Economy of the Animal and Vegetable Productions of Agriculture; Including all the latest Improvements, a general History of Agriculture in all Countries, a Statistical View of its present State, and Suggestions for its future progress in the British Isles. New Edition; with 1,100 Woodcuts. 8vo. price 50s.

Loudon's Encyclopædia of Plants, in-cluding all which are now found in, or have been introduced into, Great Britain: Giving their Natural History, accompanied by such descriptions, engraved figures, and elementary details, as may enable a beginner, who is a mere English reader, to discover the name of every Plant which he may find in flower, and acquire all the information respecting it which is useful and interesting. New Edition, corrected throughout and brought down to the year 1854, by Mrs. LOUDON and GEORGE DON, Esq., F.L.S. &c., 8vo. [*In the Spring.*

Loudon's Encyclopædia of Cottage, Farm, and Villa Architecture and Furniture: containing numerous Designs, from the Villa to the Cottage and the Farm, including Farm Houses, Farmeries, and other Agricultural Buildings; Country Inns, Public Houses, and Parochial Schools; with the requisite Fittings-up, Fixtures, and Furniture, and appropriate Offices, Gardens, and Garden Scenery: Each Design accompanied by Analytical and Critical Remarks. New Edition, edited by Mrs. LOUDON; with more than 2,000 Woodcuts. 8vo. price 63s.

Loudon's Hortus Britannicus; or, Cata-logue of all the Plants indigenous to, cultivated in, or introduced into Britain. An entirely New Edition, corrected throughout; With a Supplement, including all the New Plants, and a New General Index to the whole Work. Edited by Mrs. LOUDON; assisted by W. H. BAXTER and DAVID WOOSTER. 8vo. price 31s. 6d.—The SUPPLEMENT separately, price 14s.

Mrs. Loudon's Amateur Gardener's Calendar: Being a Monthly Guide as to what should be avoided as well as what should be done, in a Garden in each Month; with plain Rules *how to do* what is requisite; Directions for Laying Out and Planting Kitchen and Flower Gardens, Pleasure Grounds, and Shrubberies: and a short Account, in each Month, of the Quadrupeds, Birds, and Insects then most injurious to Gardens. 16mo. with Woodcuts, price 7s. 6d.

Mrs. Loudon's Lady's Country Companion; or, How to enjoy a Country Life Rationally. Fourth Edition; with Plates and Wood Engravings. Fcp. 8vo. price 5s.

Low.—A Treatise on the Domesticated Animals of the British Islands: Comprehending the Natural and Economical History of Species and Varieties; the Description of the Properties of external Form; and Observations on the Principles and Practice of Breeding. By D. Low, Esq., F.R.S.E. With Wood Engravings. 8vo. price 25s.

Low.—Elements of Practical Agriculture; comprehending the Cultivation of Plants, the Husbandry of the Domestic Animals, and the Economy of the Farm. By D. Low, Esq. F.R.S.E. New Edition; with 200 Woodcuts. 8vo. price 21s.

Macaulay.—Speeches of the Right Hon. T. B. Macaulay, M.P. Corrected by Himself. 8vo. price 12s.

Macaulay.—The History of England from the Accession of James II. By Thomas Babington Macaulay. New Edition. Vols. I. and II. 8vo. price 32s.

Mr. Macaulay's Critical and Historical Essays contributed to The Edinburgh Review. Four Editions, as follows:—

1. Library Edition (the *Seventh*), in 3 vols. 8vo. price 36s.
2. Complete in One Volume, with Portrait and Vignette. Square crown 8vo. price 21s. cloth; or 30s. calf.
3. A New Edition, in 3 vols. fcp. 8vo. price 21s.
4. People's Edition, in course of publication, crown 8vo. in Weekly Numbers at 1½d. and in 7 Monthly Parts, price One Shilling each.

Macaulay.—Lays of Ancient Rome, with Ivry and the Armada. By Thomas Babington Macaulay. New Edition. 16mo. price 4s. 6d. cloth; or 10s. 6d. bound in morocco.

Mr. Macaulay's Lays of Ancient Rome. With numerous Illustrations, Original and from the Antique, drawn on Wood by George Scarf, Jun., and engraved by Samuel Williams. New Edition. Fcp. 4to. price 21s. boards; or 42s. bound in morocco.

Macdonald. — Villa Verocchio; or, the Youth of Leonardo da Vinci: A Tale. By the late Diana Louisa Macdonald. Fcp. 8vo. price 6s.

Sir James Mackintosh's History of England from the Earliest Times to the final Establishment of the Reformation. Being that portion of the *History of England* published in Dr. Lardner's *Cabinet Cyclopædia* which was contributed by Sir James Mackintosh. Library Edition, revised by the Author's Son. 2 vols. 8vo. price 21s.

Mackintosh. — Sir James Mackintosh's Miscellaneous Works: Including his Contributions to The Edinburgh Review. A New Edition, complete in One Volume; with Portrait and Vignette. Square crown 8vo. price 21s. cloth; or 30s. bound in calf.

M'Culloch. — A Dictionary, Practical, Theoretical, and Historical, of Commerce and Commercial Navigation. Illustrated with Maps and Plans. By J. R. M'Culloch, Esq. New Edition (1854), adapted to the Present Time; and embracing a large mass of new and important Information in regard to the Trade, Commercial Law, and Navigation of this and other Countries. 8vo. price 50s. cloth; half-russia, 55s.

M'Culloch.—A Dictionary, Geographical, Statistical, and Historical, of the various Countries, Places, and principal Natural Objects in the World. By J. R. M'Culloch, Esq. Illustrated with Six large Maps. New Edition; with a Supplement, comprising the Population of Great Britain from the Census of 1851. 2 vols. 8vo. price 63s.

M'Culloch. — An Account, Descriptive and Statistical, of the British Empire; Exhibiting its Extent, Physical Capacities, Population, Industry, and Civil and Religious Institutions. By J. R. M'Culloch, Esq. New Edition, corrected, enlarged, and greatly improved. 2 vols. 8vo. price 42s.

Maitland.—The Church in the Catacombs: A Description of the Primitive Church of Rome. Illustrated by its Sepulchral Remains. By the Rev. Charles Maitland. New Edition; with many Woodcuts. 8vo. price 14s.

Mrs. Marcet's Conversations on Chemistry, in which the Elements of that Science are familiarly explained and illustrated by Experiments. New Edition, enlarged and improved. 2 vols. fcp. 8vo. price 14s.

Mrs. Marcet's Conversations on Natural Philosophy, in which the Elements of that Science are familiarly explained. New Edition, enlarged and corrected; with 23 Plates. Fcp. 8vo. price 10s. 6d.

Mrs. Marcet's Conversations on Political Economy, in which the Elements of that Science are familiarly explained. New Edition. Fcp. 8vo. price 7s. 6d.

Mrs. Marcet's Conversations on Vegetable Physiology; comprehending the Elements of Botany, with their Application to Agriculture. New Edition; with 4 Plates. Fcp. 8vo. price 9s.

Mrs. Marcet's Conversations on Land and Water. New Edition, revised and corrected; with a coloured Map, shewing the comparative Altitude of Mountains. Fcp. 8vo. price 5s. 6d.

Martineau. - Church History in England: Being a Sketch of the History of the Church of England from the Earliest Times to the Period of the Reformation. By the Rev. ARTHUR MARTINEAU, M.A. late Fellow of Trinity College, Cambridge. 12mo. price 6s.

Maunder's Biographical Treasury; consisting of Memoirs, Sketches, and brief Notices of above 12,000 Emment Persons of All Ages and Nations, from the Earliest Period of History; forming a new and complete Dictionary of Universal Biography. The Eighth Edition, revised throughout, and brought down to the close of the year 1853. Fcp. 8vo. 10s. cloth; bound in roan, 12s.; calf lettered, 12s. 6d.

Maunder's Historical Treasury; comprising a General Introductory Outline of Universal History, Ancient and Modern, and a Series of separate Histories of every principal Nation that exists; their Rise, Progress, and Present Condition, the Moral and Social Character of their respective inhabitants, their Religion, Manners and Customs, &c. &c. New Edition; revised throughout and brought down to the Present Time. Fcp. 8vo. 10s. cloth; roan, 12s.; calf, 12s. 6d.

Maunder's Scientific and Literary Treasury: A new and popular Encyclopædia of Science and the Belles-Lettres; including all Branches of Science, and every subject connected with Literature and Art. New Edition. Fcp. 8vo. price 10s. cloth; bound in roan, 12s.; calf lettered, 12s. 6d.

Maunder's Treasury of Natural History; Or, a Popular Dictionary of Animated Nature: In which the Zoological Characteristics that distinguish the different Classes, Genera, and Species, are combined with a variety of interesting Information illustrative of the Habits, Instincts, and General Economy of the Animal Kingdom. With 900 Woodcuts. New Edition. Fcp. 8vo. price 10s. cloth; roan, 12s.; calf, 12s. 6d.

Maunder's Treasury of Knowledge, and Library of Reference. Comprising an English Dictionary and Grammar, an Universal Gazetteer, a Classical Dictionary, a Chronology, a Law Dictionary, a Synopsis of the Peerage, numerous useful Tables, &c. The Twentieth Edition, carefully revised and corrected throughout: With some Additions. Fcp. 8vo. price 10s. cloth; bound in roan, 12s.; calf lettered, 12s. 6d.

Merivale. — A History of the Romans under the Empire. By the Rev. CHARLES MERIVALE, B.D., late Fellow of St. John's College, Cambridge. Vols. I. and II. 8vo. price 28s.; and Vol. III. price 14s.

Merivale.—The Fall of the Roman Republic: A Short History of the Last Century of the Commonwealth. By the Rev. CHARLES MERIVALE, B.D., late Fellow of St. John's College, Cambridge. 12mo. price 7s. 6d.

Merivale. — Memoirs of Cicero: A Translation of *Cicero in his Letters*, by Bernard Rudolf Abeken. Edited by the Rev. CHARLES MERIVALE, B.D. 12mo. [*Just ready.*

Milner's History of the Church of Christ. With Additions by the late Rev. ISAAC MILNER, D.D., F.R.S. A New Edition, revised, with additional Notes by the Rev. T. GRANTHAM, B.D. 4 vols. 8vo. price 52s.

James Montgomery's Poetical Works: Collective Edition; with the Author's Autobiographical Prefaces. A New Edition, complete in One Volume; with Portrait and Vignette. Square crown 8vo. price 10s. 6d. cloth; morocco, 21s.—Or, in 4 vols. fcp. 8vo. with Portrait, and Seven other Plates, price 20s. cloth; morocco, 36s.

Montgomery.—Original Hymns for Public, Social, and Private Devotion. By JAS. MONTGOMERY. 18mo. price 5s. 6d.

Moore. — Man and his Motives. By GEORGE MOORE, M.D., Member of the Royal College of Physicians. *Third* and cheaper *Edition.* Fcp. 8vo. price 6s.

Moore.—The Power of the Soul over the Body, considered in relation to Health and Morals. By GEORGE MOORE, M.D., Member of the Royal College of Physicians. *Fifth* and cheaper *Edition.* Fcp. 8vo. price 6s.

Moore.—The Use of the Body in relation to the Mind. By GEORGE MOORE, M.D., Member of the Royal College of Physicians. *Third* and cheaper *Edition.* Fcp. 8vo. 6s.

Moore.—Health, Disease, and Remedy, familiarly and practically considered in a few of their relations to the Blood. By GEORGE MOORE, M.D., Post 8vo. price 7s. 6d.

Moore.—Memoirs, Journal, and Correspondence of Thomas Moore. Edited by the Right Hon. LORD JOHN RUSSELL, M.P. With Portraits and Vignette Illustrations. Vols. I. to IV. post 8vo. price 10s. 6d. each.

The Fifth and Sixth Volnmes of MOORE'S MEMOIRS, JOURNAL, and CORRESPONDENCE, with Portraits of Lord John Russell and Mr. Corry, and Vignettes by T. Creswick, R.A. of Moore's Residence at Paris and at Sloperton. Vols. V. and VI. post 8vo. price 21s.

Thomas Moore's Poetical Works. Containing the Author's recent Introduction and Notes. Complete in One Volume; with a Portrait, and a View of Sloperton Cottage. Medium 8vo. price 21s. cloth; morocco, 42s.

*** Also a New and cheaper Issue of the First collected Edition of the above, in 10 vols. fcp. 8vo. with Portrait, and 19 Plates, price 35s.

Moore. — Songs, Ballads, and Sacred Songs. By THOMAS MOORE, Author of *Lalla Rookh,* &c. First collected Edition, with Vignette by R. Doyle. 16mo. price 5s. cloth; 12s. 6d. bound in morocco.

Moore's Irish Melodies. New Edition with the Autobiographical Preface from th Collective Edition of Mr. Moore's Poetica Works, and a Vignette Title by D. Maclise R.A. 16mo. price 5s. cloth; 12s. 6d. boun in morocco.

Moore's Irish Melodies. Illustrated b D. Maclise, R.A. New and cheaper Edition with 161 Designs, and the whole of th Letterpress engraved on Steel, by F. P Becker. Super-royal 8vo. price 31s. 6d boards; bound in morocco, £2. 12s. 6d.

The Original Edition of the above in imperial 8vo. price 63s. boards; morocc £4. 14s. 6d.; proofs, £6. 6s. boards,—*ma still be had.*

Moore's Lalla Rookh: An Orienta Romance. New Edition, with the Aut biographical Preface from the Collectiv Edition of Mr. Moore's Poetical Works, an a Vignette Title by D. Maclise, R.A. 16m price 5s. cloth; 12s. 6d. bound in morocc

Moore's Lalla Rookh: An Orient Romance. With 13 highly-finished Ste Plates from Designs by Corbould, Meadow and Stephanoff, engraved under the supe intendence of the late Charles Heath. Ne Edition. Square crown 8vo. price 15 cloth; morocco, 28s.

A few copies of the Original Edition, royal 8vo. price One Guinea, *still remain.*

Morton.—A Manual of Pharmacy for t Student of Veterinary Medicine: Contai ing the Substances employed at the Roy Veterinary College, with an attempt at th Classification; and the Pharmacopœia that Institution. By W. J. T. MORTO Professor of Chemistry and Materia Medi in the College. *Fifth Edition* (1854). Fc 8vo. price 10s.

Moseley.—The Mechanical Principles Engineering and Architecture. By the R H. MOSELEY, M.A., F.R.S., Professor Natural Philosophy and Astronomy King's College, London. 8vo. price 24s.

Mure.—A Critical History of the Language and Literature of Ancient Gree By WILLIAM MURE, M.P. of Caldwell. vols. 8vo. price 36s.

Vol. IV. comprising Historical Literature from the Rise of Prose Compositi to the Death of Herodotus. 8vo. wi Map, price 15s.

Murray's Encyclopædia of Geography; Comprising a complete Description of the Earth: Exhibiting its Relation to the Heavenly Bodies, its Physical Structure, the Natural History of each Country, and the Industry, Commerce, Political Institutions, and Civil and Social State of All Nations. Second Edition; with 82 Maps, and upwards of 1,000 other Woodcuts. 8vo. price 60s.

Neale.—"Risen from the Ranks;" or, Conduct *versus* Caste. By the Rev. ERSKINE NEALE, M.A., Rector of Kirton, Suffolk. Fcp. 8vo. price 6s.

Neale.—The Riches that bring no Sorrow. By the Rev. ERSKINE NEALE, M.A., Rector of Kirton, Suffolk. Fcp. 8vo. price 6s.

Neale.—The Earthly Resting Places of the Just. By the Rev. ERSKINE NEALE, M.A. Rector of Kirton, Suffolk. Fcp. 8vo. with Woodcuts, price 7s.

Neale.—The Closing Scene; or, Chri-tianity and Infidelity contrasted in the Last Hours of Remarkable Persons. By the Rev. ERSKINE NEALE, M.A., Rector of Kirton, Suffolk. New Editions of the First and Second Series. 2 vols. fcp. 8vo. price 12s.; or separately, 6s. each.

Newman.—Discourses addressed to Mixed Congregations. By JOHN HENRY NEWMAN, Priest of the Oratory of St. Philip Neri. Second Edition. 8vo. price 12s.

Lieutenant Osborn's Arctic Journal. Stray Leaves from an Arctic Journal; or, Eighteen Months in the Polar Regions in Search of Sir John Franklin's Expedition. By Lieut. SHERARD OSBORN, R.N., Commanding H.M.S.V. *Pioneer*. With Map and Four coloured Plates. Post 8vo. price 12s.

Owen Jones.—Flowers and their Kindred Thoughts: A Series of Stanzas. By MARY ANNE BACON. With beautiful Illustrations of Flowers printed in Colours by Owen Jones. Imperial 8vo price 31s. 6d. elegantly bound in calf.

Owen.—Lectures on the Comparative Anatomy and Physiology of the Invertebrate Animals, delivered at the Royal College of Surgeons in 1843. By RICHARD OWEN, F.R.S., Hunterian Professor to the College. New Edition, corrected. 8vo. with Wood Engravings. [*In the press.*

Professor Owen's Lectures on the Com-parative Anatomy and Physiology of the Vertebrate Animals, delivered at the Royal College of Surgeons in 1844 and 1846. With numerous Woodcuts. Vol. I. 8vo. price 14s.

The Complete Works of Blaise Pascal. Translated from the French, with Memoir, Introductions to the various Works, Editorial Notes, and Appendices, by GEORGE PEARCE, Esq. 3 vols. post 8vo. with Portrait, 25s. 6d.

VOL. 1. PASCAL'S PROVINCIAL LET-ters: with M. Villemain's Essay on Pascal prefixed, and a new Memoir. Post 8vo. Portrait, 8s. 6d.

VOL. 2. PASCAL'S THOUGHTS ON RE-ligion and Evidences of Christianity, with Additions, from Original MSS.: from M. Faugère's Edition. Post 8vo. 8s. 6d

VOL. 3. PASCAL'S MISCELLANEOUS Writings, Correspondence, Detached Thoughts, &c.: from M. Faugère's Edition. Post 8vo. 8s. 6d.

Captain Peel's Travels in Nubia.—A Ride through the Nubian Desert. By Captain W. PEEL, R.N. Post 8vo. with a Route Map, price 5s.

Pereira's Treatise on Food and Diet: With Observations on the Dietetical Regimen suited for Disordered States of the Digestive Organs; and an Account of the Dietaries of some of the principal Metropolitan and other Establishments for Paupers, Lunatics, Criminals, Children, the Sick, &c. 8vo. 16s.

Peschel's Elements of Physics. Trans-lated from the German, with Notes, by E. WEST. With Diagrams and Woodcuts. 3 vols. fcp. 8vo. 21s.

Peterborough.—A Memoir of Charles Mordaunt, Earl of Peterborough and Monmouth: With Selections from his Correspondence. By the Author of *Hochelaga*, &c. 2 vols. post 8vo. price 18s.

Phillips.—A Guide to Geology. By John Phillips, M.A. F.R.S. F.G.S., Deputy Reader in Geology in the University of Oxford; Honorary Member of the Imperial Academy of Sciences of Moscow, &c. Fourth Edition, corrected to the Present Time; with 4 Plates. Fcp. 8vo. price 5s.

Phillips's Elementary Introduction to Mineralogy. A New Edition, with extensive Alterations and Additions, by H. J. BROOKE, F.R.S., F.G.S.; and W. H. MILLER, M.A., F.G.S., Professor of Mineralogy in the University of Cambridge. With numerous Wood Engravings. Post 8vo. price 18s.

Phillips.—Figures and Descriptions of the Palæozoic Fossils of Cornwall, Devon, and West Somerset; observed in the course of the Ordnance Geological Survey of that District. By JOHN PHILLIPS, F.R.S. F.G.S. &c. 8vo. with 60 Plates, price 9s.

Captain Portlock's Report on the Geology of the County of Londonderry, and of Parts of Tyrone and Fermanagh, examined and described under the Authority of the Master-General and Board of Ordnance. 8vo. with 48 Plates, price 24s.

Power's Sketches in New Zealand, with Pen and Pencil. From a Journal kept in that Country, from July 1846 to June 1848. With Plates and Woodcuts. Post 8vo. 12s.

Pulman's Vade-mecum of Fly-Fishing for Trout; being a complete Practical Treatise on that Branch of the Art of Angling; with plain and copious Instructions for the Manufacture of Artificial Flies. Third Edition, with Woodcuts. Fcp. 8vo. price 6s.

Pycroft's Course of English Reading, adapted to every Taste and Capacity: With Literary Anecdotes. New and cheaper Edition. Fcp. 8vo. price 5s.

Dr. Reece's Medical Guide; for the Use of the Clergy, Heads of Families, Schools, and Junior Medical Practitioners: Comprising a complete Modern Dispensatory, and a Practical Treatise on the distinguishing Symptoms, Causes, Prevention, Cure and Palliation of the Diseases incident to the Human Frame. With the latest Discoveries in the different departments of the Healing Art, Materia Medica, &c. Seventeenth Edition, corrected and enlarged by the Author's Son, Dr. H. REECE, M.R.C.S. &c. 8vo. price 12s.

Rich's Illustrated Companion to the Latin Dictionary and Greek Lexicon: Forming a Glossary of all the Words representing Visible Objects connected with the Arts, Manufactures, and Every-day Life of the Ancients. With Woodcut Representations of nearly 2000 Objects from the Antique. Post 8vo. price 21s.

Sir J. Richardson's Journal of a Boat Voyage through Rupert's Land and the Arctic Sea, in Search of the Discovery Ships under Command of Sir John Franklin. With an Appendix on the Physical Geography of North America; a Map, Plates, and Woodcuts. 2 vols. 8vo. price 31s. 6d.

Richardson (Captain).—Horsemanship; or, the Art of Riding and Managing a Horse, adapted to the Guidance of Ladies and Gentlemen on the Road and in the Field: With Instructions for Breaking-in Colts and Young Horses. By Captain RICHARDSON, late of the 4th Light Dragoons. With 5 Line Engravings. Square crown 8vo. price 14s.

"Plain, well-arranged directions to the student in horsemanship, from mounting up to hunting, and to buying or breaking-in a horse. Every page shews the experienced horseman, who handles nothing but what is actually necessary, and to attain that disregards repetition or minuteness."
SPECTATOR.

Riddle's Complete Latin-English and English-Latin Dictionary, for the use of Colleges and Schools. *New* and cheaper *Edition*, revised and corrected. 8vo. 21s.

Separately { The English-Latin Dictionary, 7s.
The Latin-English Dictionary, 15s.

Riddle's Copious and Critical Latin-English Lexicon, founded on the German-Latin Dictionaries of Dr. William Freund. New Edition. Post 4to. price 31s. 6d.

Riddle's Diamond Latin-English Dic-tionary: A Guide to the Meaning, Quality, and right Accentuation of Latin Classical Words. Royal 32mo. price 4s.

Rivers's Rose-Amateur's Guide; contain-ing ample Descriptions of all the fine leading varieties of Roses, regularly classed in their respective Families; their History and mode of Culture. New Edition. Fcp. 8vo. 6s.

Dr. E. Robinson's Greek and English Lexicon to the Greek Testament. A New Edition, revised and in great part re-written. 8vo. price 18s.

"Take it as a whole, for soundness of theology, extent of scholarship, the philosophy of its analysis, and the beauty of its arrangement, this lexicon, while in the modest language of its author 'an unpretending memorial of the state and progress of the interpretation and lexicography of the New Testament at the first half of the nineteenth century,' supplies a model for all future productions of the kind, and in our own day is not likely to be surpassed in value, accuracy, and completeness."
BRIT. AND FOR. EVANGELICAL REVIEW.

Roby.—Remains, Legendary & Poetical, of John Roby, Author of *Traditions of Lancashire*. With a Sketch of his Literary Life and Character by his Widow; and a Portrait. Post 8vo. price 10s. 6d.

Rogers.—Essays selected from Contributions to the Edinburgh Review. By HENRY ROGERS. 2 vols. 8vo. price 24s.

Dr. Roget's Thesaurus of English Words and Phrases Classified and arranged so as to facilitate the Expression of Ideas and assist in Literary Composition. New Edition, revised and enlarged. Medium 8vo. price 14s.

Rowton's Debater: A Series of complete Debates, Outlines of Debates, and Questions for Discussion; with ample References to the best Sources of Information on each particular Topic. New Edition. Fcp. 8vo. price 6s.

Letters of Rachel Lady Russell. A New Edition, including several unpublished Letters, together with those edited by Miss BERRY. With Portraits, Vignettes, and Facsimile. 2 vols. post 8vo. price 15s.

The Life of William Lord Russell. By the Right Hon. Lord JOHN RUSSELL, M.P. The Fourth Edition, complete in One Volume; with a Portrait engraved on Steel by S. Bellin, from the original by Sir Peter Lely at Woburn Abbey. Post 8vo. 10s. 6d.

St. John (the Hon. F.)—Rambles in Search of Sport, in Germany, France, Italy, and Russia. By the Honourable FERDINAND ST. JOHN. With Four coloured Plates. Post 8vo. price 9s. 6d.

"As pretty and pleasant a little volume of sporting adventure as need come from the hand of a devoted son of Nimrod. The book is a very nice book; well got up and tastefully illustrated; and the substance of it is interesting, being a narrative of sport by one who could richly avail himself of unusually favourable opportunities, and who tells his story conversationally and very agreeably" ERA.

St. John (H.)—The Indian Archipelago; Its History and Present State. By HORACE ST. JOHN, Author of *The British Conquests in India*, &c. 2 vols. post 8vo. price 21s.

St. John (J. A.)—There and Back Again in search of Beauty. By JAMES AUGUSTUS ST. JOHN, Author of *Isis, an Egyptian Pilgrimage*, &c. 2 vols. post 8vo. price 21s.

St. John (J. A.)—The Nemesis of Power. By JAMES AUGUSTUS ST. JOHN, Author of *There and Back Again in Search of Beauty*, &c. Fcp. 8vo. [*Just ready.*

Mr. St. John's Work on Egypt. Isis: An Egyptian Pilgrimage. By JAMES AUGUSTUS ST. JOHN. 2 vols. post 8vo. 21s.

The Saints our Example. By the Author of *Letters to My Unknown Friends*, &c. Fcp. 8vo. price 7s.

Schmitz.—History of Greece, from the Earliest Times to the Taking of Corinth by the Romans, B.C. 146, mainly based upon Bishop Thirlwall's History of Greece. By Dr. LEONHARD SCHMITZ, F.R.S.E., Rector of the High School of Edinburgh. New Edition. 12mo. price 7s. 6d.

A Schoolmaster's Difficulties at Home and Abroad:—1. In regard to his Calling; 2. In relation to Himself; 3. As concerning his Charge; 4. About Committees; 5. With Pupil-Teachers; 6. Touching Inspectors; 7. On the matter of Society; 8. In prospect of the Future; and 9. Affecting Personal Relations. Fcp. 8vo. price 4s. 6d.

Sir Edward Seaward's Narrative of his Shipwreck, and consequent Discovery of certain Islands in the Caribbean Sea: With a detail of many extraordinary and highly interesting Events in his Life, from 1733 to 1749, as written in his own Diary. Edited by JANE PORTER. Third Edition; 2 vols. post 8vo. 21s.—An ABRIDGMENT, in 16mo. price 2s. 6d.

The Sermon on the Mount. Printed on Silver; with Picture Subjects, numerous Landscape and Illustrative Vignettes, and Illuminated Borders in Gold and Colours, designed expressly for this work by M. LEPELLE DU BOIS-GALLAIS, formerly employed by the French Government on the great Work of Count Bastard. Square 18mo. price in ornamental boards, One Guinea; or 31s. 6d. bound in morocco.

Self-Denial the Preparation for Easter. By the Author of *Letters to my Unknown Friends*, &c. Fcp. 8vo. price 2s. 6d.

Sharp's New British Gazetteer, or Topo-graphical Dictionary of the British Islands and Narrow Seas: Comprising concise Descriptions of about Sixty Thousand Places, Seats, Natural Features, and Objects of Note, founded on the best Authorities; full Particulars of the Boundaries, Registered Electors, &c. of the Parliamentary Boroughs; with a reference under every name to the Sheet of the Ordnance Survey, as far as completed; and an Appendix, containing a General View of the Resources of the United Kingdom, a Short Chronology, and an Abstract of certain Results of the Census of 1851. 2 vols. 8vo. price £2. 16s.

Sewell. — Amy Herbert. By a Lady. Edited by the Rev. WILLIAM SEWELL, B.D. Fellow and Tutor of Exeter College, Oxford. New Edition. Fcp. 8vo. price 6s.

Sewell.—The Earl's Daughter. By the Author of *Amy Herbert.* Edited by the Rev. W. SEWELL, B.D. 2 vols. fcp. 8vo. 9s.

Sewell. — Gertrude: A Tale. By the Author of *Amy Herbert.* Edited by the Rev. W. SEWELL, B.D. New Edition. Fcp. 8vo. price 6s.

Sewell.—Laneton Parsonage: A Tale for Children, on the Practical Use of a portion of the Church Catechism. By the Author of *Amy Herbert.* Edited by the Rev. W. SEWELL, B.D. New Edition. 3 vols. fcp. 8vo. price 16s.

Sewell. — Margaret Percival. By the Author of *Amy Herbert.* Edited by the Rev. W. SEWELL, B.D. New Edition. 2 vols. fcp. 8vo. price 12s.

By the same Author,

The Experience of Life. New Edition. Fcp. 8vo. price 7s. 6d.

"Those who read for instruction as well as amusement will find in these experiences much moral and pious sentiment gracefully interpreted and practically illustrated." MORNING CHRONICLE.

Readings for a Month preparatory to Confirmation: Compiled from the Works of Writers of the Early and of the English Church. Fcp. 8vo. price 5s. 6d.

"A volume full of devout meditations and holy counsels, which, while it will prove profitable in the hands of candidates for confirmation during the period of preparation for that sacred rite, will be found no less valuable by clergymen as a guide in the instruction of their catechumens." JOHN BULL.

Readings for Every Day in Lent: Com-piled from the Writings of BISHOP JEREMY TAYLOR. Fcp. 8vo. price 5s.

The Family Shakspeare; in which nothing is *added* to the Original Text; but those words and expressions are *omitted* which cannot with propriety be read aloud. By T. BOWDLER, Esq. F.R.S. New Edition, in Volumes for the Pocket. 6 vols. fcp. 8vo. price 30s.

*** Also a LIBRARY EDITION: With 36 Wood Engravings from designs by Smirke, Howard, and other Artists. 8vo. price 21s.

Short Whist; Its Rise, Progress, and Laws: With Observations to make any one a Whist Player. Containing also the Laws of Piquet, Cassino, Ecarté, Cribbage, Back-gammon. By Major A * * * * *. New Edition; to which are added, Precepts for Tyros, by Mrs. B * * * *. Fcp. 8vo. 3s.

Sinclair. — The Journey of Life. By CATHERINE SINCLAIR, Author of *The Business of Life* (2 vols. fcp. 8vo. price 10s.) New Edition, corrected and enlarged. Fcp. 8vo. price 5s.

Sinclair. — Popish Legends or Bible Truths. By CATHERINE SINCLAIR. Dedicated to her Nieces. Fcp. 8vo. price 6s.

"Miss Sinclair has brought to her task a well disciplined mind, and a memory richly stored with the results of extensive and varied reading; and her book not only contains many a clear statement of the truth in opposition to error, backed by solid proof and happy illustration, but it sparkles throughout with many a pertinent anecdote, and many a flash of quiet sarcastic humour." EDINBURGH WITNESS.

Sir Roger de Coverley. From The Spec-tator. With Notes and Illustrations, by W. HENRY WILLS; and Twelve fine Wood Engravings, by John Thompson, from Designs by FREDERICK TAYLER. Crown 8vo. price 15s. boards; or 27s. bound in morocco.—A Cheap Edition, without Wood-cuts, in 16mo. price One Shilling.

Smee's Elements of Electro-Metallurgy. Third Edition, revised, corrected, and considerably enlarged; with Electrotypes and numerous Woodcuts. Post 8vo. price 10s. 6d.

Smith's Sacred Annals.—Sacred Annals: Vol. III. The Gentile Nations; or, The History and Religion of the Egyptians, Assyrians, Babylonians, Medes, Persians, Greeks, and Romans, collected from ancient authors and Holy Scripture, and including the recent discoveries in Egyptian, Persian, and Assyrian Inscriptions: Forming a complete connection of Sacred and Profane History, and shewing the Fulfilment of Sacred Prophecy. By GEORGE SMITH, F.A.S. &c. In Two Parts, crown 8vo. price 12s.

By the same Author,

Sacred Annals: Vol. I. The Patriarchal Age; or, Researches into the History and Religion of Mankind, from the Creation of the World to the Death of Isaac. Crown 8vo. 10s.

Sacred Annals: Vol. II. The Hebrew People; or, The History and Religion of the Israelites, from the Origin of the Nation to the Time of Christ. In two Parts, crown 8vo. price 12s.

The Works of the Rev. Sydney Smith; including his Contributions to The Edinburgh Review. New Edition, complete in One Volume; with Portrait, and Vignette. Square crown 8vo. price 21s.; or 30s. bound in calf.

*** Also a LIBRARY EDITION (the Fourth), in 3 vols. 8vo. with Portrait, price 36s.

The Rev. Sydney Smith's Elementary Sketches of Moral Philosophy, delivered at the Royal Institution in the Years 1804, 1805, and 1806. Second Edition. 8vo. price 12s.

The Life and Correspondence of the late Robert Southey. Edited by his Son, the Rev. C. C. SOUTHEY, M.A., Vicar of Ardleigh. With Portraits, and Landscape Illustrations. 6 vols. post 8vo. price 63s.

Southey's Life of Wesley; and Rise and Progress of Methodism. New Edition, with Notes and Additions by the late Samuel Taylor Coleridge, Esq., and the late Alexander Knox, Esq. Edited by the Rev. C. C. SOUTHEY, M.A. 2 vols. 8vo. with 2 Portraits, price 28s.

Southey's Commonplace Books. Comprising — 1. Choice Passages: With Collections for the History of Manners and Literature in England; 2. Special Collections on various Historical and Theological Subjects; 3. Analytical Readings in various branches of Literature; and 4. Original Memoranda, Literary and Miscellaneous. Edited by the Rev. J. W. WARTER, B.D. 4 vols. square crown 8vo. price £3. 18s.

Each *Commonplace Book*, complete in itself, may be had separately as follows:—

FIRST SERIES—CHOICE PASSAGES, &c. 18s.

SECOND SERIES—SPECIAL COLLECTIONS. 18s.

THIRD SERIES—ANALYTICAL READINGS. 21s.

FOURTH SERIES—ORIGINAL MEMORANDA, &c. 21s.

Robert Southey's Complete Poetical Works; containing all the Author's last Introductions and Notes. Complete in One Volume, with Portrait and Vignette. Medium 8vo. price 21s. cloth; 42s. bound in morocco.

*** Also a New and cheaper Issue of the First collected Edition of the above, in 10 vols. fcp. 8vo. with Portrait and 19 Plates, price 35s.

Select Works of the British Poets; from Chaucer to Lovelace, inclusive. With Biographical Sketches by the late ROBERT SOUTHEY. Medium 8vo. price 30s.

Southey's The Doctor &c. Complete in One Volume. Edited by the Rev. J. W. WARTER, B.D. With Portrait, Vignette, Bust, and coloured Plate. New Edition. Square crown 8vo. price 21s.

Steel's Shipmaster's Assistant, for the use of Merchants, Owners and Masters of Ships, Officers of Customs, and all Persons connected with Shipping or Commerce: Containing the Law and Local Regulations affecting the Ownership, Charge and Management of Ships and their Cargoes; together with Notices of other Matters, and all necessary Information for Mariners. New Edition, rewritten, by G. WILLMORE, Esq. M.A. Barrister-at-Law; G. CLEMENTS, of the Customs, London; and W. TATE, Author of *The Modern Cambist.* 8vo. price 28s.

Stephen.—Lectures on the History of France. By the Right Hon. Sir JAMES STEPHEN, K.C.B. LL.D. Professor of Modern History in the University of Cambridge. Second Edition. 2 vols. 8vo. price 24s

Stephen.—Essays in Ecclesiastical Biography; from The Edinburgh Review. By the Right Hon. Sir JAMES STEPHEN, K.C.B. LL.D. Third Edition. 2 vols. 8vo. 24s.

Stonehenge.—The Greyhound: Being a Treatise on the Art of Breeding, Rearing, and Training Greyhounds for Public Running; their Diseases and Treatment: Containing also, Rules for the Management of Coursing Meetings, and for the Decision of Courses. By STONEHENGE. With numerous Portraits of Greyhounds, &c. engraved on Wood, and a Frontispiece engraved on Steel. Square crown 8vo. price 21s.

"We have not the slightest hesitation in saying that the work under notice is the most copious and complete ever written on the greyhound.....The arrangement of this vast fund of information is lucid, consecutive, and regular, and the style in which it is communicated varied, now technical and scientific, then anecdotal; and, when occasion requires, minutely descriptive, fervent, and often so plain and simple that one might fancy the author was pleasantly speaking to listeners."

BELL'S LIFE.

Stow.—The Training System, the Moral Training School, and the Normal Seminary or College. By DAVID STOW, Esq. Honorary Secretary to the Glasgow Normal Free Seminary. Ninth Edition; with Plates and Woodcuts. Post 8vo. price 6s.

Dr. Sutherland's Journal of a Voyage in Baffin's Bay and Barrow's Straits, in the Years 1850 and 1851, performed by H.M. Ships *Lady Franklin* and *Sophia*, under the command of Mr. William Penny, in search of the missing Crews of H.M. Ships *Erebus* and *Terror*. With Charts and Illustrations. 2 vols. post 8vo. price 27s.

Swain.—English Melodies. By Charles SWAIN. Fcp. 8vo. price 6s. cloth; bound in morocco, 12s.

Swain.—Letters of Laura D'Auverne. By CHARLES SWAIN. Fcp. 8vo. price 3s. 6d.

Tate.—On the Strength of Materials; Containing various original and useful Formulæ, specially applied to Tubular Bridges, Wrought Iron and Cast Iron Beams, &c. By THOMAS TATE, F.R.A.S. 8vo. price 5s. 6d.

Taylor.—Loyola: And Jesuitism in its Rudiments. By ISAAC TAYLOR. Post 8vo. with Medallion, price 10s. 6d.

Taylor.—Wesley and Methodism. By ISAAC TAYLOR. Post 8vo. with a Portrait, price 10s. 6d.

Thirlwall.—The History of Greece. By the Right Rev. the LORD BISHOP of ST. DAVID'S (the Rev. Connop Thirlwall). An improved Library Edition; with Maps. 8 vols. 8vo. price £4. 16s.

Also, an Edition in 8 vols. fcp. 8vo. with Vignette Titles, price 28s.

Thomson (The Rev. W.)—An Outline of the Laws of Thought: Being a Treatise on Pure and Applied Logic. By the Rev. W. THOMSON, M.A. Fellow and Tutor of Queen's College, Oxford. Third Edition, enlarged. Fcp. 8vo. price 7s. 6d.

Thomson's Tables of Interest, at Three, Four, Four-and-a-Half, and Five per Cent., from One Pound to Ten Thousand, and from 1 to 365 Days, in a regular progression of single Days; with Interest at all the above Rates, from One to Twelve Months, and from One to Ten Years. Also, numerous other Tables of Exchanges, Time, and Discounts. New Edition. 12mo. price 8s.

Thomson's Seasons. Edited by Bolton CORNEY, Esq. Illustrated with Seventy-seven fine Wood Engravings from Designs by Members of the Etching Club. Square crown 8vo. price 21s. cloth; or, 36s. bound in morocco.

Thornton.—Zohrab; or, a Midsummer Day's Dream: And other Poems. By WILLIAM THOMAS THORNTON, Author of *An Essay on Over-Population*, &c. Fcp. 8vo price 4s. 6d.

The Thumb Bible; or, Verbum Sempiternum. By J. TAYLOR. Being an Epitome of the Old and New Testaments in English Verse. Reprinted from the Edition of 1693; bound and clasped. 64mo. 1s. 6d

Todd (Charles).—A Series of Tables of the Area and Circumference of Circles; the Solidity and Superficies of Spheres; the Area and Length of the Diagonal of Squares and the Specific Gravity of Bodies, &c. To which is added, an Explanation of the Author's Method of Calculating these Tables Intended as a Facility to Engineers, Surveyors, Architects, Mechanics, and Artisans in general. By CHARLES TODD, Engineer The Second Edition, improved and extended Post 8vo. price 6s.

Townsend.—The Lives of Twelve Eminent Judges of the Last and of the Present Century. By W. C. TOWNSEND, Esq., M.A. Q.C. 2 vols. 8vo. price 28s.

Townsend.—Modern State Trials revised and illustrated with Essays and Notes. By W. C. TOWNSEND, Esq. M.A. Q.C. 2 vols 8vo. price 30s.

Sharon Turner's Sacred History of the World, attempted to be Philosophically considered, in a Series of Letters to a Son New Edition, edited by the Author's Son the Rev. S. TURNER. 3 vols. post 8vo price 31s. 6d.

Sharon Turner's History of England during the Middle Ages: Comprising the Reigns from the Norman Conquest to the Accession of Henry VIII. Fifth Edition revised by the Rev. S. TURNER. 4 vols 8vo. price 50s.

Sharon Turner's History of the Anglo Saxons, from the Earliest Period to the Norman Conquest. The Seventh Edition revised by the Rev. S. TURNER. 3 vols 8vo. price 36s.

THE TRAVELLER'S LIBRARY,

IN COURSE OF PUBLICATION IN PARTS AT ONE SHILLING AND IN VOLUMES PRICE HALF-A-CROWN EACH.

Comprising books of valuable information and acknowledged merit, in a form adapted for reading while Travelling, and also of a character that will render them worthy of preservation.

List of the VOLUMES *already published.*

VOL. I. MACAULAY's ESSAYS on WARREN HASTINGS and LORD CLIVE 2/6

II. ——— ESSAYS on PITT and CHATHAM, RANKE and GLADSTONE.. 2/6

III. LAING's RESIDENCE in NORWAY 2/6

IV. PFEIFFER's VOYAGE ROUND the WORLD 2/6

V. EŌTHEN, TRACES of TRAVEL from the EAST 2/6

VI. MACAULAY's ESSAYS on ADDISON, WALPOLE, and LORD BACON 2/6

VII. HUC's TRAVELS in TARTARY, &c. 2/6

VIII. THOMAS HOLCROFT's MEMOIRS 2/6

IX. WERNE's AFRICAN WANDERINGS 2/6

X. MRS. JAMESON's SKETCHES in CANADA 2/6

XI. JERRMANN's PICTURES from ST. PETERSBURG 2/6

XII. THE REV. G. R. GLEIG's LEIPSIC CAMPAIGN 2/6

XIII. HUGHES's AUSTRALIAN COLONIES 2/6

XIV. SIR EDWARD SEAWARD's NARRATIVE 2/6

XV. ALEXANDRE DUMAS' MEMOIRS of a MAITRE D'ARMES 2/6

XVI. OUR COAL FIELDS and OUR COAL PITS 2/6

XVII. M'CULLOCH's LONDON and GIRONIERE's PHILIPPINES 2/6

XVIII. SIR ROGER DE COVERLEY and SOUTHEY's LOVE STORY 2/6

XIX. JEFFREY's ESSAYS on SWIFT and RICHARDSON and LORD CARLISLE's LECTURES and ADDRESSES 2/6

XX. HOPE's BIBLE in BRITTANY and CHASE in BRITTANY 2/6

XXI. THE ELECTRIC TELEGRAPH and NATURAL HISTORY of CREATION, 2/6

XXII. MEMOIR of DUKE of WELLINGTON and LIFE of MARSHAL TURENNE, 2/6

XXIII. TURKEY and CHRISTENDOM & RANKE's FERDINAND and MAXIMILIAN, 2/6

XXIV. FERGUSON's SWISS MEN and SWISS MOUNTAINS and BARROW's CONTINENTAL TOUR 2/6

XXV. SOUVESTRE's WORKING MAN'S CONFESSIONS and ATTIC PHILOSOPHER in PARIS 2/6

XXVI. MACAULAY's ESSAYS on LORD BYRON and the COMIC DRAMATISTS and his SPEECHES on PARLIAMENTARY REFORM (1831-32) 2/6

XXVII. SHIRLEY BROOKS's RUSSIANS of the SOUTH and DR. KEMP's INDICATIONS of INSTINCT 2/6

XXVIII. LANMAN's ADVENTURES in the WILDS of NORTH AMERICA 2/6

Dr. Turton's Manual of the Land and Fresh-water Shells of the British Islands. A New Edition, with considerable Additions by JOHN EDWARD GRAY: With Woodcuts, and 12 coloured Plates. Post 8vo. price 15s.

Dr. Ure's Dictionary of Arts, Manufac-tures, and Mines: Containing a clear Exposition of their Principles and Practice. The Fourth Edition, much enlarged and corrected throughout; with all the Information comprised in the *Supplement of Recent Improvements* brought down to the Present Time and incorporated in the *Dictionary*: Most of the Articles being entirely re-written, and many new Articles now first added. With nearly 1,600 Woodcuts. 2 vols. 8vo. price 60s.

"Let any well-informed man ask himself how many works he can rely on as authorities upon any given scientific subject; and he will find but very, very few, compared with the entire number of treatises upon it. The fact is, many men have no perception of the beauty, and consequently but little regard for the purity of science; and the publishers print the most inexact and erroneous writing, provided the public will consent to purchase it, which is too generally the case. This remark serves to shew how high an estimate ought to be set upon these volumes of *Dr. Ure's*, which consist chiefly of original and exact treatises, written with so much accuracy and care that they may be universally resorted to as authoritative,—as indeed the former editions have been,—as well by artists and manufacturers as by British and foreign scientific writers. The author has throughout the entire work kept most seriously before his mind the one object of promoting the best and most economical developments of the arts and manufactures; and has produced a work which altogether surpasses every other of its kind with which we are acquainted."
MECHANIC'S MAGAZINE.

Waterton.—Essays on Natural History, chiefly Ornithology. By C. WATERTON, Esq. With an Autobiography of the Author, and Views of Walton Hall. New and cheaper Edition. 2 vols. fcp. 8vo. price 10s.

Separately: Vol. I. (First Series), 5s. 6d. Vol. II. (Second Series), 4s. 6d.

"Mr. Waterton's essays evince throughout the same love of nature, the samefreshness of thought and originality of idea, and the same unartificial mode of treating the subject, as White's Natural History of Selborne; and no one would for a moment hesitate to place side by side in the foremost rank of popular writers on natural history, Gilbert White's *Selborne* and Charles Waterton's *Essays and Autobiography*." WESTMINSTER REVIEW.

Alaric Watts's Lyrics of the Heart, and other Poems. With 41 highly-finished Line Engravings, executed expressly for the work by the most eminent Painters and Engravers. Square crown 8vo. price 31s. 6d. boards, or 45s. bound in morocco; Proof Impressions, 63s. boards.

Webster and Parkes's Encyclopædia of Domestic Economy; Comprising such subjects as are most immediately connected with Housekeeping: As, The Construction of Domestic Edifices, with the modes of Warming, Ventilating, and Lighting them—A description of the various articles of Furniture, with the nature of their Materials—Duties of Servants, &c. New Edition; with nearly 1,000 Woodcuts. 8vo. price 50s.

Willich's Popular Tables for ascertaining the Value of Lifehold, Leasehold, and Church Property, Renewal Fines, &c. Third Edition, with additional Tables of Natural or Hyperbolic Logarithms, Trigonometry, Astronomy, Geography, &c. Post 8vo. price 9s.

Lady Willoughby's Diary (1635 to 1663). Printed, ornamented, and bound in the style of the period to which *The Diary* refers. New Edition; in Two Parts. Square fcp. 8vo. price 8s. each, boards; or, bound in morocco, 18s. each.

Wilmot's Abridgment of Blackstone's Commentaries on the Laws of England, intended for the use of Young Persons, and comprised in a series of Letters from a Father to his Daughter. A New Edition, corrected and brought down to the Present Day, by Sir JOHN E. EARDLEY WILMOT, Bart., Barrister-at-Law, Recorder of Warwick. 12mo. price 6s. 6d.

Youatt.—The Horse. By William Youatt. With a Treatise of Draught. New Edition, with numerous Wood Engravings, from Designs by William Harvey. (Messrs. Longman and Co.'s Edition should be ordered.) 8vo. price 10s.

Youatt.—The Dog. By William Youatt. A New Edition; with numerous Engravings, from Designs by W. Harvey. 8vo. 6s.

Zumpt's Larger Grammar of the Latin Language. Translated and adapted for the use of English Students by Dr. L. SCHMITZ, F.R.S.E., Rector of the High School of Edinburgh: With numerous Additions and Corrections by the Author and Translator. The Third Edition, thoroughly revised; to which is added, an Index (by the Rev. J. T. White, M.A.) of all the Passages of Latin Authors referred to and explained in the Grammar. 8vo. price 14s.

[*March* 1854.

WILSON AND OGILVY, SKINNER STREET, SNOWHILL, LONDON.

BY J. J. GURNEY.

Sabbatical Verses. 8vo. Price 1s. 6d.

Prison Discipline.

Notes on a Visit to some of the Prisons in Scotland and the North of England, in company with Elizabeth Fry, with some general Remarks on the subject of Prison Discipline, 1819. 8vo. Price 3s. 6d.

Tour in Ireland.

Report addressed to the Marquis Wellesley, Lord Lieutenant of Ireland, by Elizabeth Fry and Joseph John Gurney, respecting their late visit to that country, 1828. Price 2s. 6d.

Thoughts on Habit and Discipline.

New Edition, 2s. 6d. cloth; People's Edition, 1s. 6d.

"It is one of those sterling books on self-government which no man can read without receiving both mental and moral benefit. Like all Mr. Gurney's writings, it is strictly orthodox in its views, catholic in its sentiments, apt in its illustrations, clear and forcible in its style."—*Bath Chron.*

"Its tone is decidedly religious; its method is philosophical, its style is popular."—*Athenæum.*

"The work is distinguished by that benevolent and parental mildness which so characterised the life and conversation of the author, and is calculated to win the heart, while it convinces the understanding of the reader."—*Bath Herald.*

"This is one of the most useful works that could be put into the hands of young persons. We have never seen the subject more ably handled."—*Liverpool Courier.*

"We have few books extant containing, in so brief a space, so much sound practical instruction."—*Keene's Bath Journal.*

"Such *thoughts* are the great desideratum of the age, and if carefully read and enforced in daily life, would contribute much to the well-being of society."—*Newcastle Guardian.*

"*Thoughts on Habit and Discipline* should be read by the young man anxious to make his way in the world in an honourable and creditable manner. There is a lovingness about the articles truly refreshing in these times of selfishness and recklessness."—*Lincoln Standard.*

"The younger portion of the community, and all who have influence with the young, whether as parents, or as professional instructors, will find in these papers abundance to repay them for their perusal."—*Baptist Mag.*

"Sound sense and devout feeling are distinguishing characteristics of this useful publication."—*Cheltenham Chronicle.*

"The proper study of such a book will go far to induce many others to tread in the steps of its lamented author, and to perpetuate the race of philanthropists, of which he was, in the true sense of the word, an illustrious example."—*Rochester Gazette.*

BY J. J. GURNEY.

Terms of Union.

Remarks addressed to the Members of the British and Foreign Bible Society. Price 1s.

Strictures on The Truth Vindicated,

with Evidences of the Sound and Christian Views of the Society of Friends on the Subject of the Holy Scriptures. Price 6d.

Address to Mechanics,

On the right Use and Application of Knowledge; delivered to the Mechanics of Manchester, Price 1d.

Essay on Love to God,

considered as a preparation for Heaven. Price 1s. 6d. cloth.

Remarks on the Sabbath;

Its History, Authority, and Use. 18mo. 9d. cloth.

Lock and Key;

Guide to the Instruction of Young Persons in the Holy Scriptures; or Passages in the Old Testament which testify of Jesus Christ, explained by others in the New Testament. Price 2d.

Some Account of John Stratford,

who was Executed in the City of Norwich, for the Crime of Murder. Price 1d.

Winter in the West Indies;

Described in Familiar Letters to Henry Clay, of Kentucky. 18mo. Price 1s. 6d.

Brief Memoirs of T. Fowell Buxton

and Elizabeth Fry. 12mo. Price 9d.

Emilie the Peacemaker;

By Mrs. Thos. Geldart. Price 2s. 6d.; or elegantly boarded, gilt edges, 3s.

"This beautiful story excels almost all the moral and religious tales we know. The best things of Mrs. Sherwood and Mrs. Hofland are in many respects inferior to it; and Miss Edgeworth seldom wrote more vigorously and charmingly; while in purity of sentiment and exquisite illustration of the truth it embodies, it is richer far than are the works of the writers we have named. Seldom has a great lesson been more touchingly taught, or piety of heart and life been rendered more attractive. We cannot omit to speak of, and to praise, the truth to nature, the refinement of mind, the originality of construction, and the delicacy of diction, by which this tale is characterised; and we are sure it will never miss a welcome from young people, nor a cordial appreciation from older readers of pure and simple tastes."—*Nonconformist.*

"We know not when we have read a tale so entirely to our mind as this. It makes us wish we could have our young days over again; for sure we are that with such a monitor as 'Emilie,' we should have been saved from many bitter after feelings of regret. The lesson conveyed in the tale is one of heavenly wisdom, inculcating 'peace upon earth, and good-will towards men, and the heart of every reader must be improved by it."—*Norfolk News.*

"Mrs. Geldart is one of those who think that a soft answer turneth away wrath; and this great truth she wishes to impress on the minds of the young: hence the story of the 'Peacemaker,' which is an account of a family on the eastern coast of England all turned into a happy one by obedience to this truth. Mrs. Geldart is an agreeable writer, and her book is likely to be useful to the class for which it is composed."—*Standard of Freedom.*

Truth is Everything;

By Mrs. Thos. Geldart. Second edition, price 2s. 6d.; or, elegantly boarded, gilt edges, 3s.

"The verdict of a jury of juveniles is that this is 'a dear beautiful book,' and the said verdict is accompanied with a request to the authoress to give us another as soon as may be. We may add that the story is simply and tenderly told; carries unobtrusively in it, not at the end of it, a right lesson; and is the work of a Christian and a lady. Pure, gentle, and devout it therefore is, of course."—*Eclectic Review.*

"This is a charming little book for the young; the matter is very interesting, not over-drawn, while its tenor is to win over youth to the practice and love of truth."—*Patriot.*

"It is written in a plain and simple, yet convincing style; and the incidents are of a most natural description, yet Mrs. Geldart invests them with great interest. The characters of Ellen and Annie Norris, and Mary Marshall, are placed in striking contrast; and although the two former, unfortunately, assimulate the nearest to those we meet with in society, we would urge all our young friends to make the truth-telling Mary Marshall their example."—*Chronicle.*

"'*Truth is Everything*' is a charming tale, attractive from the simplicity and beauty of feeling which pervade it—most useful because it steps not beyond the comprehension of youth. Free from any overstrained odour of sanctity, it yet teaches with earnestness and sincerity the value of religious as well as moral principle, and that no virtue can be exercised—no good principle can be carried out—without strength from above."—*Norwich Mercury.*

Stories of Scotland.

By Mrs. Thos. Geldart. Fcap. 8vo. Price 2s. 6d., or, elegantly boarded, 3s.

"Often as the beauties of Scotland have been delineated, and frequently as its numerous points of interest have been made available for the instruction of the young—from Sir Walter Scott's "Tales of My Grandfather" downwards to the present time—there is scarcely one that will effect greater good than this clever and highly entertaining little volume. The object of its gifted authoress is evidently to blend valuable geographical and historical information in such a manner as to fix the attention of her juvenile readers, and make them imbibe facts which will live in their remembrance as long as they are spared as denizens of the present fleeting world; and whilst she pursues this—the fittest course to make education practical—she never lets an opportunity slip whereby she may influence the heart, and lead it from the contemplation of the things of time and sense to those which are more enduring."—*Bell's Weekly Messenger.*

May Dundas ; or Passages in Young Life.

By Mrs. Thos. Geldart. Price 2s. 6d. cloth, 3s. gilt.

"A book much above the average in the class to which it belongs. The writing is marked by a very considerable degree both of grace and power. The first page bespeaks an author who knows how to describe. The pervading religious tone is satisfactory. Mrs. Geldart possesses the power of natural and refined pathos, especially in connexion with childish feelings. The prettiest thing in the book is the episode of the little girl, with her deep unspoken associations of feeling with her city home, in Finsbury Square, with the stool by the nursery fire, and with the three cornered glazed cupboard, and the china images within, which she remembered her lost mother placing there, and which she herself carried with her when she went away to die."—*Christian Witness.*

Footmarks of Charity.

Containing *The Man in Earnest*—(Sir Thomas Fowell Buxton) *Reminiscences of a Good Man's Life*—(Joseph John Gurney) *The Pathway of Love*—(Mrs. Fry) By Mrs. Thomas Geldart. Price 1s.

"The Sketches are beautiful delineations, of beautiful characters."

"The fame of Buxton filled the world. His praise was on every lip, and respect for his character nestled in every bosom. Those, however, to whom he was only a great man, may, from this pretty 18mo, glean the principal facts of his admirable and philanthropic career."

"This little book, which is a perfect gem of its kind, is from the pen of Mrs. Thos. Geldart. Under the respective titles of "The Man in Earnest," "The Pathway of Love," "Reminiscences of a Good Man's Life." It contains some brief but beautiful sketches of Sir Fowell Buxton, Elizabeth Fry, and Joseph John Gurney. They are written with the simplicity, easy elegance, and truth to nature, which distinguish Mrs. Geldart's style, and will be read with delight in every circle where virtue is reverenced, and active goodness and world-wide philanthropy are admired and appreciated."—*Norfolk News.*

Thoughts for Home; in Prose and Verse.

By Mrs. Thos. Geldart. Elegantly boarded, cloth gilt, 2s. 6d.

Kate Hall; or, One of the Graces.

By Mrs. Thos. Geldart. 18mo. Price 3d.

Brief Memoir of Edward Stanley,

D.D., late Lord Bishop of Norwich. By John Alexander, Minister of Prince's Street Chapel, Norwich. Cloth, 1s.

The Fisherman's Friendly Visitor.

Published quarterly. Price 2d. Copies of Vols. 2 to 6, Price 10d. each.

Fear Not;

(A Selection of Consolatory Texts.) Price 3d.

Heart Discipline.

By James Cooper, of Norwich, with a recommendatory Preface by the Rev. John Angell James, of Birmingham. 12mo. Price 4s. 6d.

"A volume commended in a preface by John Angell James. It is a book of quiet thoughtfulness—a little too introspective, but adapted to check the tendency now prevalent towards the opposite extreme."—*The British Quarterly Review.*

A treatise on "Heart Discipline," by James Cooper of Norwich, a venerable and successful minister of the Gospel, contains practical advice of great value on Spiritual Culture and the Health of the Soul. A recommendatory preface by the Rev. J. A. James, of Birmingham, is prefixed to the volume, which deserves the high eulogies which it receives from that eminent Nonconformist Divine. Scriptural truth and pious counsel are conveyed in simple language and earnest tone, and come with authority from an author who has passed his threescore years and ten, and who, by his pen, now testifies on subjects which he has preached for nearly half a century from the pulpit.—*Literary Gazette.*

"Mr. Cooper, between forty and fifty years ago, was a member of Mr. James's church, as also were his parents. Since his retirement from the pastorate, Mr. Cooper has employed his leisure in the preparation of this volume; "in which," to use Mr. James's words, "he has compressed the spiritual and practical wisdom attained by the reading, reflection, and experience of threescore years and ten." Such a work, so commended, needs no recommendation of ours."—*Patriot.*

www.ingramcontent.com/pod-product-compliance
Lightning Source LLC
LaVergne TN
LVHW021123110826
845150LV00005B/934

* 9 7 8 1 4 2 5 5 5 0 7 3 8 *